NEW TOWN
Pages 68–79
Street Finder maps 9–10

AROUND THE ALSTER
Pages 120–131
Street Finder maps 7–8

*Around
the Alster*

OLD TOWN
Pages 54–67
Street Finder maps 9–10

New Town

Old Town

*Port and
Speicherstadt*

**PORT AND
SPEICHERSTADT**
Pages 80–99
Street Finder maps 5–6

| 0 kilometres | | 2 |
| 0 miles | | 1 |

EYEWITNESS TRAVEL
HAMBURG

EYEWITNESS TRAVEL

HAMBURG

GERHARD BRUSCHKE

LONDON, NEW YORK,
MELBOURNE, MUNICH AND DELHI
www.dk.com

PUBLISHER Douglas Amrine
PRODUCED BY Dorling Kindersley Verlag GmbH, Munich
PUBLISHING DIRECTOR Dr. Jörg Theilacker
PROJECT MANAGER Stefanie Franz
ART DIRECTOR AND DESIGNER Anja Richter
EDITOR Brigitte Maier
PICTURE EDITOR Stefanie Franz
CARTOGRAPHY Anja Richter, Mare e Monte Kartografie
PROOFREADER Philip Anton

CONTRIBUTOR
Gerhard Bruschke

PHOTOGRAPHERS Felix Fiedler, Susanne Gilges, Olaf Kalugin

ILLUSTRATORS Branimir Georgiev, Maria-Magdalena Renker,
Eva Sixt, Dr. Bernhard Springer

ENGLISH TRANSLATION Barbara Hopkinson,
International Book Productions Inc.
EDITOR Helen Townsend
PROOFREADER Susan Thompson

Reproduced in Singapore by Colourscan
Printed and bound in China by L. Rex Printing Company Ltd.

First published in Germany in 2008
by Dorling Kindersley Verlag GmbH, Munich
Published in Great Britain in 2010
by Dorling Kindersley Ltd.,
80 Strand, London WC2R 0RL

. 12 13 14 15 10 9 8 7 6 5 4 3 2 1

Printed with revisions 2010, 2011, 2012

Copyright © 2008, 2012 Dorling Kindersley Verlag GmbH, Munich
© 2009, 2012 Dorling Kindersley Limited, London
A Penguin Company

ISBN 978-1-4053-6875-9

Front cover main image: Speicherstadt, old warehouse district, Hamburg,

MIX
Paper from
responsible sources
FSC
www.fsc.org FSC™ C018179

**The information in this
DK Eyewitness Travel Guide is checked regularly.**
Every effort has been made to ensure that this book is as up-to-date
as possible at the time of going to press. Some details, however,
such as telephone numbers, opening hours, prices, gallery hanging
arrangements and travel information are liable to change. The
publishers cannot accept responsibility for any consequences arising
from the use of this book, nor for any material on third party
websites, and cannot guarantee that any website address in this
book will be a suitable source of travel information. We value the
views and suggestions of our readers very highly. Please write to:
Publisher, DK Eyewitness Travel Guides, Dorling Kindersley,
80 Strand, London, WC2R 0RL, or email: travelguides@dk.com.

◁ **Tugs hauling a vessel in Hamburg Port**

CONTENTS

Bishop Ansgar I. (801–865)

INTRODUCING
HAMBURG

**Vessel in a dry dock
opposite the Landungsbrücken**

The Alster Arcades (Alsterarkaden) – a popular place for ambling

Fountain on the Binnenalster near Neuer Jungfernstieg

Snack bar sign at Hamburg Port ("Sandwiches and a river view")

Hamburg's Rathaus (city hall)

HOW TO USE THIS GUIDE

This guide helps you get the most from your visit to the world-class city of Hamburg. It provides detailed practical information and expert recommendations. *Introducing Hamburg* maps the region and sets modern Hamburg in its historical context. It showcases the city's architectural and cultural attractions, including festivals and events throughout the year. It also provides an overview of the river. *Hamburg Area by Area* describes all the main sights,

using maps, photographs and illustrations. In addition, special attractions outside Hamburg are also covered. Information about hotels, restaurants, shopping, entertainment and children's activities is found in *Travellers' Needs*. The *Survival Guide* offers tips on everything from using Hamburg's medical services, telephones and post offices to the public transport system. Handy *Street Finder* maps on pages 242–257 help you locate everything you need in this fascinating city.

FINDING YOUR WAY AROUND HAMBURG

The city has been divided into six sightseeing areas, each with its own chapter, colour-coded for easy reference. Each chapter begins with a portrait of the area, summing up its character and history. All sights are numbered and plotted on an area map.

1 Area map
For easy reference, the sights in each area are numbered, grouped by category and plotted on the map. The sights are described in detail on the following pages.

Each area has its own unique colour code.

Locator map

2 Street-by-Street map
This gives a view of the heart of each sightseeing area and suggests a walking route. The bird's-eye perspective offers an ideal overview.

The visitors' checklist provides detailed practical information.

A suggested route takes you along the most interesting streets of the area.

3 Star sights
Hamburg's top attractions are given two pages. Historic buildings are dissected to reveal their interiors, while museums are given floorplans.

Stars indicate the most fascinating features that no visitor should miss.

HAMBURG AREA MAP

The colour-coded areas shown on this map *(see inside front cover)* correspond to the six main sightseeing areas of the city. Each is covered by its own full chapter in *Hamburg Area by Area (see pp52–169)*. Throughout this book, the colour codes serve as your guide. The city's most important sights are described in *Hamburg at a Glance (see pp28–43)*. For those who love walking tours, *Three Guided Walks (see pp142–149)* lead you not only to the main attractions but also to some of the city's less-known but no less interesting buildings.

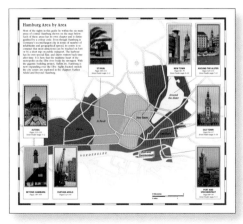

4 Detailed information

All the important sights within each area are described individually. They are listed in order, following the numbering on the area map.

Practical information is provided in an information block. The key to the symbols used is on the back flap.

Colour-coded sections represent collections, helping you to find the important exhibitions.

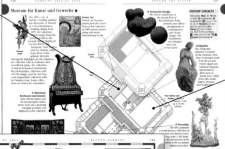

5 Museum floorplans

With the help of these plans you can prepare your museum visits ahead of time. Photos show some of the famous works you will see.

6 Regional map

This provides an overview of the region around Hamburg. The illustration shows the road network and railway lines to help you plan your trip. Interesting travel destinations are numbered and discussed on the following pages.

INTRODUCING
HAMBURG

FOUR GREAT DAYS IN HAMBURG

Hamburg, the "Gateway to the World" and one of Germany's most handsome cities, draws visitors with its special atmosphere and numerous attractions. The itineraries presented here ensure that you experience the sights that make the city so appealing. A day that focuses on

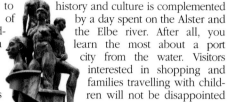

Großneumarkt fountain

history and culture is complemented by a day spent on the Alster and the Elbe river. After all, you learn the most about a port city from the water. Visitors interested in shopping and families travelling with children will not be disappointed either. Prices cover the cost of travel, food and admission.

HISTORY AND CULTURE

- Travel back in time in the hamburgmuseum
- View from "Michel"
- Museum row at the station
- Rathaus

TWO ADULTS allow at least €80

Morning

The **hamburgmuseum** *(see p73)* at Holstenwall (U-Bahn station St Pauli) provides a good overview of the city's history and culture. After this time-travel through Hamburg, head southeast to **St Michaelis** *(see pp74–5)*, a symbol of the city. There is a fabulous view from the tower, nicknamed "Michel". Near the church you can see the **Krameramtswohnungen** *(see p72)*, courtyard apartment dwellings dating from the 17th century. The Krameramtsstuben restaurant offers delicious Hamburg specialities.

Afternoon

The "museum mile" runs to the north and south of the Hauptbahnhof (main train station). Here, the **Hamburger Kunsthalle** *(see pp64–5)* offers famous works ranging from Old Masters to modern art as well as fascinating special exhibitions. In the **Museum für Kunst und Gewerbe** *(see pp130–31)*, the entire world of applied arts is brought together under one roof. Photography and more is on display at the **Deichtorhallen** *(see pp62–3)*.

The dome (1912–24) of Hamburg's Kunsthalle *(see pp64–5)*

Walking through the impressive Kontorhaus district to the west, you will end up at **St Nikolai** *(see p66)*, a tourist attraction and a memorial. In Deichstraße, you can admire the oldest still-intact merchant's houses in the city. Continuing along Rödingsmarkt and Großer Burstah, one of the city's oldest streets, you end up at the **Rathaus** *(see pp60–61)*.

SHOPPING IN STYLE

- Neuer Wall
- Strolling along the Binnenalster
- Dining in the passages
- stilwerk and Hafenbasar

TWO ADULTS allow at least €50 (not including shopping)

Morning

Start your shopping trip at the Stadthausbrücke S-Bahn station, where the **Neue Wall** begins. On both sides of the street, fashion trendsetters have set up shop. Flagship

stores of internationally known labels are located here, offering everything today's well-dressed woman and man cares to wear. At the end of Neue Wall, turn left into **Jungfernstieg**, where the more exclusive boutiques can be found. Here, too, is Alsterhaus, a well-stocked department store. This "luxury mile" continues on into **Große Bleichen**, with its covered passages – an ideal place to stop for lunch.

Bridge leading to stilwerk, a centre for interior design *(see p119)*

◁ *The burning of St Nikolai church during the night of 5–6 May 1842, city view by Peter Suhr (1788–1857)*

Afternoon

From Reeperbahn S-Bahn station, walk south along Pepermölenbek street and turn right into the Fisch-markt. In an old warehouse, **stilwerk** *(see p119)* offers seven floors of gift items and interior design articles for discriminating tastes. A completely different experience is found at **Harry's Hafen-basar** *(see p105)* in the middle of St Pauli. Here you can sift through a curiosity cabinet of wares brought here by sailors from around the world.

A DAY ON THE WATER

- **Along the Alster**
- **Strolling along the Port**
- *Rickmer Rickmers*
- **View from View Point**

TWO ADULTS allow at least €100

Morning

Head to **Binnenalster** (Inner Alster; *see p124*) to enjoy an activity Hamburgers refer to as "Alsterschippern" – boating on the Alster. From April to October, Alster boats docked at the Jungfernstieg leave on round trips that also take in the whole **Außen-alster** (Outer Alster; *see p128*). You can disembark as often as you like, combining your tour of the lake with a walk through Pöseldorf or Winter-hude. The sea air is famous for building an appetite, and the **Alsterpavillon** *(see p124)* can certainly help assuage any hunger pangs.

Afternoon

All roads lead to the **Landungsbrücken** *(see p93)*. As you stroll along these quays, enjoy the sea air and the hustle and bustle. A visit to the almost 100-m (328-ft) long museum ship *Rickmer Rickmers* *(see pp94–5)* provides insight into one of the great eras of sea travel. There are many boat tour companies which offer round trips of the harbour *(see pp48–9)*. These provide an ideal opportunity to see the gigantic project

HafenCity *(see pp90–91)*, a sign of Hamburg's vitality. **View Point** *(see p88)* is the best place from which to see this project in its entirety.

Rickmer Rickmers **museum ship in Hamburg's harbour (see pp94–5)**

A FAMILY DAY

- **Digital Model Railway**
- **Time-trip of horrors**
- **A visit to the zoo**
- **A park and a planetarium**

FAMILY (4 PEOPLE) allow at least €150 (not including the Hamburger Dom)

Morning

Speicherstadt offers attractions for the entire family. Children's eyes open wide in wonder at **Miniatur Wunder-land** *(see p84)*. About six million people have visited the world's largest digitally operated model railway here. **Hamburg Dungeon** *(see p85)* offers visitors a trip back in time through the most gruesome moments in Hamburg's

history – but it is definitely not for the faint of heart. Also of interest to children is the model of the city found in the **HafenCity InfoCenter** *(see pp90–91)*, in Kessel-haus. A multimedia show traces the development of this dynamic section of the city. The bistro there is a good choice for a lunch stop.

Afternoon

Take the U-Bahn to **Tierpark Hagenbeck** *(see pp136–7)*, and enjoy visiting its many outdoor enclosures and its tropical aquarium. One of the high points of a visit to this zoo is watching the giraffes as they are fed. After the zoo, plan a visit to the **Stadtpark** *(see p134)*, which

There is a great deal to discover in Miniatur Wunderland (see p84)

offers every kind of outdoor activity imaginable. The **Planetarium**, in the western part of the park is especially fascinating. Here, you can look into space or attend one of the highly instructive shows. Great fun for young and old alike is to be had at the **Hamburger Dom** *(see pp44–6)*, a festival held three times a year on the Heiligengeistfeld.

The Jugendstil entrance to Tierpark Hagenbeck (see pp136–7)

Putting Hamburg on the Map

Hamburg, with almost 1.8 million inhabitants, is Germany's second-largest city. This city-state, for it is also a German province, covers 755 sq km (290 sq miles), and is bordered by Lower Saxony and Schleswig-Holstein. This metropolis on the Elbe river is one of Europe's most important ports and trading centres. Due to its favourable location near the mouth of the Elbe river, it is known as the "gateway to the world".

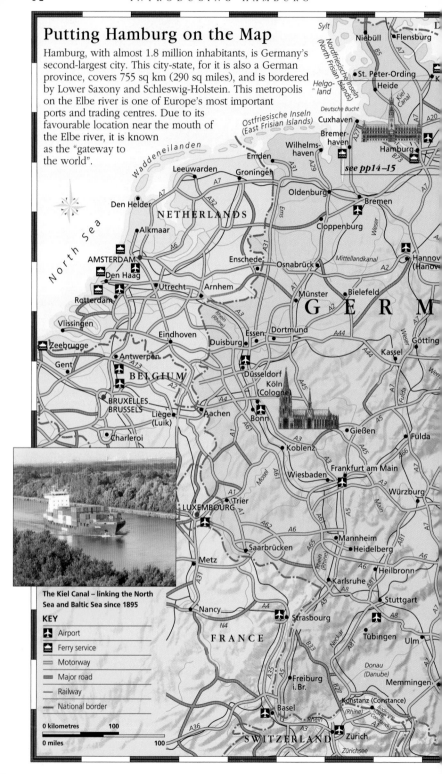

see pp14–15

The Kiel Canal – linking the North Sea and Baltic Sea since 1895

KEY

✈	Airport
⛴	Ferry service
═	Motorway
▬	Major road
—	Railway
—	National border

0 kilometres   100

0 miles   100

The tower of St Michaelis church – the most visible symbol of Hamburg

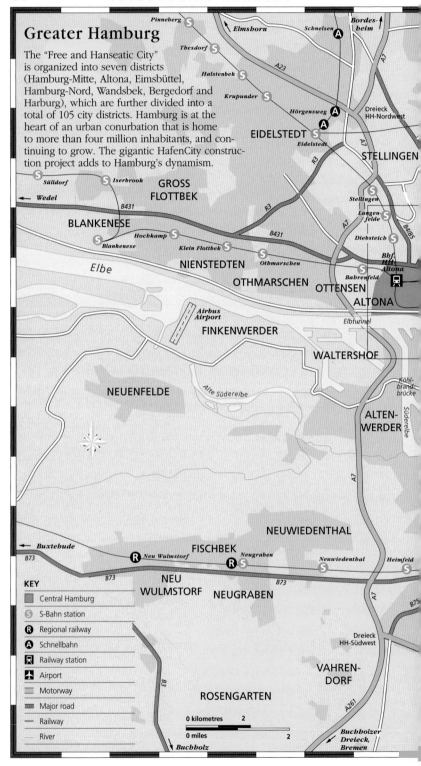

Greater Hamburg

The "Free and Hanseatic City" is organized into seven districts (Hamburg-Mitte, Altona, Eimsbüttel, Hamburg-Nord, Wandsbek, Bergedorf and Harburg), which are further divided into a total of 105 city districts. Hamburg is at the heart of an urban conurbation that is home to more than four million inhabitants, and continuing to grow. The gigantic HafenCity construction project adds to Hamburg's dynamism.

KEY

▩	Central Hamburg
Ⓢ	S-Bahn station
Ⓡ	Regional railway
Ⓐ	Schnellbahn
🚉	Railway station
✈	Airport
▭	Motorway
▬	Major road
—	Railway
—	River

0 kilometres 2
0 miles 2

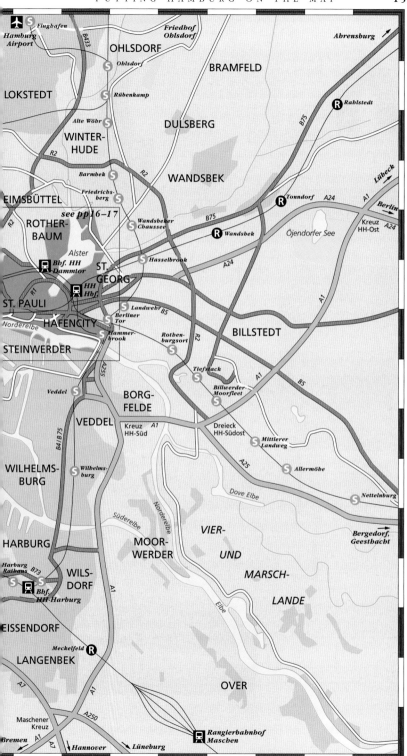

Central Hamburg

Entrance to St Nikolai

The majority of Hamburg's top attractions are located in the city centre, which has been divided into six colour-coded areas. The Old Town (Altstadt) and New Town (Neustadt) are separated by the Alsterfleet. West of the New Town lies the well-known entertainment district of St Pauli, and beyond that Altona, which was an independent town until 1937. South of the Old and New Towns lies the Port and Speicherstadt area. To the north, the area Around the Two Alsters – Binnenalster (Inner Alster) and Außenalster (Outer Alster) – is home to choice residential neighbourhoods, along with the more colourful areas of St Georg and Grindel.

St Michaelis
Lovingly referred to as "Michel" by Hamburgers, this Baroque church has become a symbol of the city (see pp74–5).

Rathaus (Town Hall)
Both the city and the city-state are run from the Rathaus. It is one of Germany's grandest government buildings (see pp60–61).

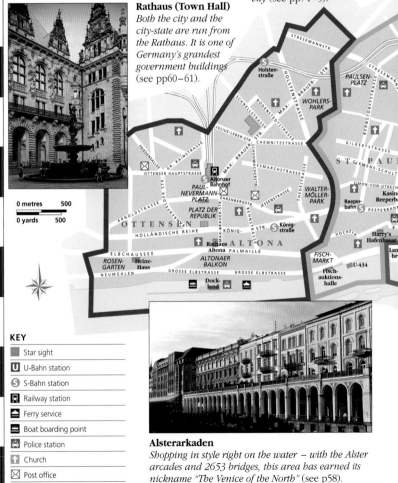

0 metres 500
0 yards 500

KEY

▪	Star sight
U	U-Bahn station
S	S-Bahn station
🚉	Railway station
⛴	Ferry service
🚢	Boat boarding point
🚓	Police station
✝	Church
⊠	Post office

Alsterarkaden
Shopping in style right on the water – with the Alster arcades and 2653 bridges, this area has earned its nickname "The Venice of the North" (see p58).

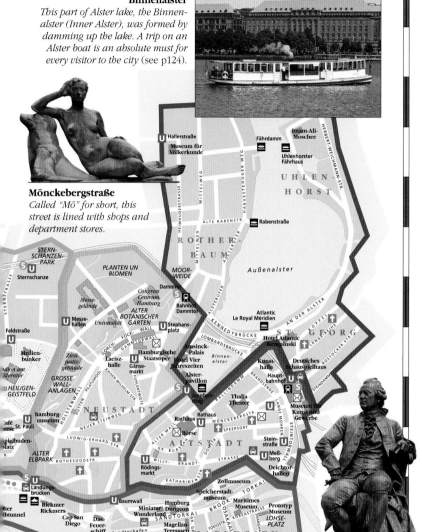

Binnenalster
This part of Alster lake, the Binnen-alster (Inner Alster), was formed by damming up the lake. A trip on an Alster boat is an absolute must for every visitor to the city (see p124).

Mönckebergstraße
Called "Mö" for short, this street is lined with shops and department stores.

Gänsemarkt
A statue of the famous literary figure Gotthold Ephraim Lessing is located in the Gänsemarkt, a lively part of the New Town (see p77).

Kehrwiederspitze
This spit of land is the gateway to Speicherstadt and HafenCity. Many aspects of global trade are steered from the offices located in these two chic complexes (see p84).

THE HISTORY OF HAMBURG

Hamburg's origins date back to the 9th century, when Hammaburg castle was built. Since then, it has evolved to become one of Europe's most important trading centres. The city's prosperity is based largely in its vibrant port and its political independence as a "Free and Hanseatic City". In the 21st century, with the building of HafenCity, Hamburg has begun to expand on the other side of the Elbe river.

EARLY HISTORY

Traces of the earliest settlements in the Hamburg area date back to the Middle Stone Age. Discoveries of tools and weapons north of Hamburg testify to the fact that nomadic hunters camped here as early as 8,000 BC. The first permanent settlements can be traced back to the 4th century AD, at which time Saxon tribes settled in the area of today's Old Town.

THE HAMMABURG

In the beginning of the 9th century, the Saxons were driven out of the area by the Franks under the command of Charlemagne and with the help of their Slavic allies, the Obodrite tribe. After 810, Louis the Pious, who was a son of Charlemagne, built Hammaburg castle, creating the nucleus for modern-day Hamburg. The square fortress, located south of today's church of St Petri, was very imposing with its 130-m (430-ft) high walls. Fifty

The Benedictine monk Ansgar, Hamburg's first bishop

troops were stationed in the fortress. Merchants, fishermen and innkeepers set up shop in front of its gates, and an early marketplace was founded. Hammaburg castle was not only a defensive stronghold, it was also intended to serve as the bishop's residence.

HAMBURG AS A MISSIONARY CENTRE

King Louis the Pious founded the Bishopric of Hamburg in 831, and appointed Ansgar, a Benedictine monk, to be bishop. The terms of the Treaty of Verdun called for the Frankish kingdom to be divided between Louis' two sons. Shortly thereafter, Danish Vikings attacked German settlements on the Elbe river and razed the Hammaburg to the ground. In the 10th century, Archbishop Adaldag built a new fortress. The settlement grew rapidly. In 937 it was awarded market rights, laying the foundation for Hamburg's later prominence as an important centre of trade.

TIMELINE

Prehistoric clay pot in the hamburgmuseum

810 Hammaburg castle is built

845 Vikings raze the Hammaburg

400 BC	0	400 AD	600	800		900

ca. 400 BC
First permanent settlements in the Hamburg area

400
The area known today as Old Town is settled

831 Louis the Pious founds the Bishopric of Hamburg

937 Hamburg is awarded market rights

Louis the Pious

◁ **Doors to the Great Banqueting Hall in the Rathaus** *(see pp60–61)*

Model of the old castle of Hammaburg, which was
built by Louis the Pious in the 9th century

FROM MISSIONARY CENTRE
TO COMMERCIAL CENTRE

The emerging market town recovered
quickly after being attacked by the
Slavic Obodrites in 983. The 11th century was marked by the rivalry
between spiritual and earthly powers.
As a sign of the might of the church,
Archbishop Adalbrand (Alebrand)
built a bishop's tower *(see p59)*. To
create an earthly counterweight to the
bishop's stronghold, Duke Bernhard
II, a member of the Billunger dynasty,
gave orders for the construction of
the Neue Burg (New Castle),
which was later known as
the Alsterburg. The fate of
the church's dominance was
sealed in 1066, when the
Slavs rebelled against the
high tithes they were obliged
to pay to the monasteries.

After the Billunger line died
out in 1106, the Counts of
Schauenburg began to rule
Hamburg in 1111. Under their rule, the
town boomed. Adolf I expanded the

St George, the
dragon-slayer

defence works, dammed up the Alster
to run a corn mill, and built dikes
around several small islands in the
Elbe river so that they could be
settled. His successor, Adolf II, pur-
sued a policy of consolidation with
great success. Under Adolf III, the
town of Neustadt (New Town) was
founded in the territory surrounding
the Neue Berg. It attracted mariners
and merchants who settled there,
especially along the Nikolaifleet.

THE CHARTER
AND ITS AFTERMATH

A milestone for future economic development occurred when Emperor
Frederick Barbarossa conferred a
charter *(Freibrief)* on the town on
7 May 1189. The document, which
recognized the town for the help it
had rendered during the third
Crusade, awarded Hamburg customs
exemption for trade and shipping all
the way from the lower Elbe to the
North Sea. Citizens were also freed
from being conscripted into the army.
Instead they were tasked solely with
the defense of their own town. They
also had the right to fish without
paying the usual obligatory taxes.

The original charter granted by
Emperor Frederick Barbarossa is not
extant; in 1265, a copy, whose
contents were most likely
forged, was created.
Indeed, some historians
maintain that the charter
was a forgery from the
very beginning. Despite
this, Hamburgers throw an
annual party on May 7 to
celebrate their port's birthday
(see p85). Rapid economic
development followed the bestowal
of these trading rights.

TIMELINE

983 The Obodrites
destroy parts of
Hamburg

1040 The bishop
builds a tower as
his residence

1066 A Slavic
rebellion ends
the dominance
of the church

950	1000	1025	1050	1100

Decorative vault element
from the 13th century
found in the Domplatz

1060 The Neue Burg
is built – a sign of
earthly might

1111 The rule of
the Counts of
Schauenburg
begins

Old bell from
the bishop's
tower

A 19th-century painting showing the view of
Hamburg as it would have looked in 1150

SELF-RELIANCE
IN DIFFICULT TIMES

After the Danes conquered Hamburg and the surrounding area in 1201, the city was administered by a Danish governor. Under the occupying power, the Old Town and the New Town grew together politically as well as architecturally. By 1216, Hamburg had one town hall and one court of justice with its own laws. The city began to direct its own external affairs and to determine its own economic policy, entering into trade alliances with other cities such as Lübeck, as well as with dominions both near and far.

In 1227, a coalition of German princes drove out the occupying Danes, and the Schauenburg Count Adolf IV began to rule the city. After this period of political turmoil came to an end, trade flourished once again. The first merchant guilds were established, and foreign trading companies set up their own branches in Hamburg.

Lid of the sarcophagus of
Adolf IV of Schauenburg

The city developed rapidly in the following centuries as the Alster was dammed up to form a lake, and new fortifications consisting of walls, towers and moats were built to protect the city centre. Towards the mid-13th century, these fortifications encircled the entire area of the present-day Old Town. Today, names such as Millerntor, Alstertor and Lange Mühren bear testimony to the locations of those former fortifications. The citizens of Hamburg – demonstrating the self-confidence of true merchants – drew up their own town charter in 1270 and recorded it in their *Ordeelbook*.

The thriving city suffered a terrible setback on 5 August 1284 when a devastating fire roared through it, burning down the houses of the approximately 5,000 inhabitants. Reconstruction, however, started quickly again, and shortly thereafter the city enjoyed a large wave of immigration. There were plenty of jobs to be had, especially in the beer-brewing industry. In fact, at times, there were several hundred Hamburg breweries producing beer, a very important commodity during that time. The city's many and various trading alliances were exceptionally stable, and Hamburg continued to increase in prosperity. The city was also able to acquire a number of properties in the area. At this time, too, many important church buildings were completed and stately homes were built.

1175	1200	1225	1250	1275

1188 New Town is built to the west of Old Town

1189 Emperor Barbarossa awards Hamburg its charter

1227 End of Danish rule

1250 The new fortifications encircle the entire city centre

1284 A huge fire destroys many buildings

1201–27 Hamburg falls under Danish rule

1216 Old Town and New Town are amalgamated

1270 Hamburg is awarded a town charter

*Fragment from the tomb of
Pope Benedict V*

*Hanseatic
seal*

outbreak of the plague, almost half of its entire population – nearly 6,000 inhabitants – perished.

MOORWERDER ISLAND (1395)

Towards the end of the 14th century, Hamburg acquired several towns in the surrounding area. Given this significant growth, the port had to be expanded to sustain the economic might of this Hanseatic city. In 1395, Hamburg acquired an island called Moorwerder. This was a strategically important move and an act of great political prescience. For it was here that the Elbe river divided into two branches. One branch, the more southerly one that carried the largest volume of water, flowed toward Harburg. After acquiring Moorwerder, Hamburg regulated the water flow so that Harburg, its rival to the south, was literally cut off from its water supply. Later, the construction of a number of waterworks ensured that the northern Elbe river around Hamburg became the more important branch of the mighty river. Thus was laid the cornerstone for the city's continued growth.

A miniature decorates the cover of the revised Hamburg Stadtrecht of 1497 (created 1503–1511)

THE HANSEATIC LEAGUE (1321)

In 1321, Hamburg became a member of the Hanseatic League, an alliance of north German cities that had been in existence since the 12th century. Joining the League resulted in an enormous stimulus to the city. Through its membership in this important trade alliance, Hamburg became the leading German trading and warehousing city between the North Sea and the Baltic Sea. Another benefit was that, for several centuries to come, membership in the Hanseatic League secured existing trade routes and promoted the creation of new routes.

Hamburg was dealt a particularly heavy blow in 1350. During an

PIRATES

The prosperity of the city awakened the greed of privateers, among whose ranks Klaus Störtebeker (see p43) could be found. Hamburg sent its own fleet to attack the band of pirates he led, and Störtebeker was beheaded in 1401 in Hamburg in front of a large crowd.

A Kogge was the most common type of ship in the North Sea and the Baltic Sea during the 15th century

(see p43)

TIMELINE

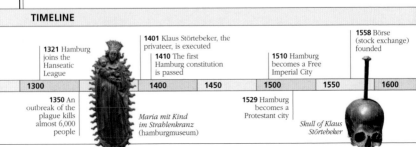

1321 Hamburg joins the Hanseatic League

1401 Klaus Störtebeker, the privateer, is executed

1410 The first Hamburg constitution is passed

1510 Hamburg becomes a Free Imperial City

1558 Börse (stock exchange) founded

1300		1400	1450	1500	1550	1600

1350 An outbreak of the plague kills almost 6,000 people

Maria mit Kind im Strahlenkranz (hamburgmuseum)

1529 Hamburg becomes a Protestant city

Skull of Klaus Störtebeker

A CHANGE OF COURSE

Hamburg's first consti-tution came into effect in 1410. After the death of the last Schauenberg Count in 1459, the city fell under Danish rule. Even so, it became a Free Imperial City in 1510. In 1558, Hamburg merchants founded the stock market (see p66).

It was only in the early 18th century that any significant changes occurred. In 1712, to end the power struggles between the town coun-cil and the town's citizens once and for all, a new constitution was accep-ted. It awarded equal status to both parties. Later, in 1768, the treaty of Gottorp finally put an end to the ancient conflict with Denmark.

Klaus Störtebeker (circa 1360–1401), the most famous pirate

HAMBURG IN THE 19TH CENTURY

Napoleon's troops occupied Hamburg in 1806. At that time it was a city of some 130,000 inhabitants. The Conti-nental System, an embargo on trade with Great Britain dictated by France, proved to be an utter catas-trophe for Hamburg: its economy collapsed almost entirely. Many formerly wealthy merchants had become impoverished by the time the French troops withdrew in 1812.

In 1815, Hamburg joined the German Confederation, and by 1819 it named itself "Freie und Hansestadt" (Free and Hanseatic City). The steady march along the path to prosperity was halted abruptly by the Great Fire of 1842 (see p67). Afterwards, growth seemed to accelerate even more. With the arrival of the steam-ship, trade flourished. In 1847, HAPAG – the Hamburg-American Line – was founded. It quickly grew to become the world's largest shipping com-pany, and ensured Hamburg's trading might throughout the world. After 1850, millions of Europeans emigrated to North America, especially to the United States, on HAPAG ships.

After the German Reich was founded in 1871, Hamburg was at first allowed to store goods in the port area with-out paying excise duties. In 1888, the city was obliged to join the German Customs Union. After the cholera epidemic of 1892, during which more than 860 people lost their lives, Hamburg again demonstrated its self-confidence with the completion of the Rathaus in 1897 (see pp60–61).

Massive damage was inflicted during the Great Fire of 1842

1669 The Hanseatic League, whose influence had been waning in the past decades, collapses

1806–1814 French occupation

Door knocker on the Altes Rathaus

1842 The city centre is heavily damaged by a raging fire

| 1650 | 1750 | 1800 | 1850 | 1900 |

1712 A new constitution ensures equality between citizenry and council

1768 The treaty of Gottorp ends the conflict with Denmark

1819 Free and Hanseatic City of Hamburg

1897 The city hall is completed

Pitcher used by captains of the citizen's militia

The Beatles during one of their legendary shows in the Star-Club in Hamburg

killed in concentration camps during World War II (1939–45). Hamburg was a major target of wartime Allied bombing, due to its large port and industrial centre. Huge sections of the city were destroyed. The heaviest air raid took place in July 1943, claiming some 50,000 lives. On 3 May 1945, Hamburg surrendered to British troops. In 1949, it became an independent German province.

HAMBURG IN THE 20TH CENTURY
In 1910, Hamburg became a city of a million inhabitants; just two years later, its port had become the third-largest in the world after those of London and New York. In 1911, the first tunnel under the Elbe river was built. After World War I (1914–18), under the terms of the Treaty of Versailles, Hamburg was compelled to surrender a large part of its trading fleet. However, the merchant spirit of the city remained intact, and Hamburg acquired new ships. The city's prosperity was reflected architecturally in building projects such as the imposing Kontorhausviertel *(see p63)*.

Under the Nazis, who came to power in 1933, the Greater Hamburg Act was passed, which incorporated Altona, Harburg and Wandsbek into the city. At this time, Hamburg's Jewish population was 19,900. Over the next four years, roughly half that number emigrated or were expelled; almost all the remaining Jews were

THE NORTH SEA FLOOD OF 1962
During the night of 16 to 17 February 1962, Hamburg was devastated by heavy flooding from a severe storm. As gale-force winds caused high volumes of Baltic Sea water to surge forward, the protective dikes were breached, causing water to surge into almost one-sixth of the city. An exemplary rescue action was mounted by Helmut Schmidt, then Police Senator *(see p42)*. In direct contravention of the German Constitution, he ordered the army to be deployed to assist during a civil emergency. His efficient management of the crisis made him a German household name. Despite the amazing efforts of several thousand volunteers, more than 3,000 people perished, and tens of thousands were made homeless. Since the flood, the dike near the mouth of the Elbe has been raised twice. It now stands at 8 m (26 ft). This effectively prevented further flooding, notably during the 1976 and 1990 storms.

Books about the North Sea Flood of 1962

TIMELINE

1910 Hamburg's population reaches 1 million

1943 Heavy air raids reduce large sections of Hamburg to rubble

The Beatles' key to the back-door of the Star-Club

1952 The constitution comes into effect

1900	1915	1930	1950	1960

Albert Ballin (1857–1918)

1937 Greater Hamburg Act is passed; the city grows by incorporating smaller towns

1949 Hamburg becomes a German province

1962 A disastrous flood inundates the city centre with water

HAMBURG BOOMS

In the 1980s, container ship traffic in the port increased substantially and Hamburg became Europe's leading container port. In addition, the opening up of Eastern Europe gave further impetus to the port's development. Hamburg has, in fact, become one of the most important shipping centres in the Baltic Sea area. Hamburg continually strengthened its position as Germany's leading media centre *(see pp40–41)*, and also established itself as the country's musical capital. Each year, the number of tourists visiting this thriving Hanseatic city increases.

The futuristic office building of Dockland, located on the Elbe river near Altona

HAMBURG AFTER 2000

Since the end of World War II, the Social Democratic Party (SPD) customarily received the most votes in the city-state, with few exceptions. Therefore, it always appointed the First Mayor, who is the head of government. The most recent First Mayors were Hans-Ulrich Klose (1974–81), Klaus von Dohnanyi (1981–88), Henning Voscherau (1988–97), and Ortwin Runde (1997–2001). But in 2001, during the Bürgerschaft

Poster showing Helmut Schmidt

election, which determined who would sit in Hamburg's parliament, the Christian Democratic Union (CDU) won an absolute majority and took up the reigns of power under the leadership of Ole von Beust. After the Bürgerschaft elections in February 2008, the first ever coalition between the CDU and Green party at the state level was formed. In July 2010 von Beust retreated. In the following elections the SPD won an absolute majority, and in March 2011 Olaf Scholz became First Mayor.

Hamburg is one of the most ambitious cities in Europe. Renowned architects were hired for numerous projects: futuristic office buildings were built. The Trade Fair was expanded, the airport enlarged, and downtown areas (such as Domplatz) renovated. After HafenCity *(see pp90–91)* is completed, one of the most ambitious urban building projects in Europe will be realised. Given the increase in cruise tourism, a second cruise ship terminal opened in 2010 in Altona. Hamburg won the title of European Green Capital 2011, an award developed by the European Commission.

The Elbphilharmonie, likely to enhance the Hanse city's draw as a cultural destination

1974 The Köhlbrandbrücke is completed	**1975** Opening of the Elbe tunnel for the A7 autobahn		**2000** Building of HafenCity begins	**2006** Some of the football World Cup games are held in Hamburg	**UDO LINDENBERG**
	1987 Town twinning with Dresden				*Udo Lindenberg's star*
1970	**1980**	**1990**	**2000**	**2010**	
	1989 The 800th birthday of the port	**2001** The CDU takes power for the first time. Ole von Beust becomes First Mayor	**2008** A coalition of the CDU and Green party under Ole von Beust	**2011** The SPD wins absolute majority and takes power under Olaf Scholz	
	Uwe Seeler's foot in front of the HSV-Arena				

The south side of Hamburg Dammtor station, built in 1906 *(see p125)* ▷

HAMBURG AT A GLANCE

More than 100 places of interest are described in the *Area by Area* section of this guide. They range from the lively Landungsbrücken *(see p93)* to stately churches, such as St Michaelis *(see pp74–5)*; from the dignified Speicherstadt *(see pp80–99)* to the ultramodern HafenCity *(see pp90–91)*; from the grand Elbchaussee *(see p118)* to the elegant Jungfernstieg *(see pp124–25)*. To help you make the most of your stay in Hamburg, the following pages provide you with a guide to the very best that Hamburg has to offer. Museums and galleries, architectural masterpieces, and beautiful parks and gardens are all featured, as well as an overview of famous Hamburgers and the important role the city plays as a media centre. Below are the top ten attractions to start you off.

HAMBURG'S TOP TEN ATTRACTIONS

Rathaus
See pp60–61

St Michaelis
See pp74–5

Hamburger Kunsthalle
See pp64–5

Speicherstadt
See pp80–99

Planten un Blomen
See pp78–9

Rickmer Rickmers
See pp94–5

Landungsbrücken
See p93

St Pauli Fish Market
See p108

Reeperbahn
See pp102–3

Museum für Kunst und Gewerbe *See pp130–31*

◁ Aerial view of Hamburg's New Town, home to St Michaelis, Speicherstadt and HafenCity

Hamburg's Best: Museums and Galleries

15th-century wood-carving, hamburgmuseum

There are over 80 museums and collections in Hamburg, ranging from the Afghan to the Zoological Museum. Many historically significant works of art can be found here, and some Hamburg museums are among the most renowned in Europe. Collections dedicated to the history of Hamburg are impressive, but enthusiasts of special collections will also find much to enjoy. Unique to the city are the ship museums and those related to seafaring and trade. Once a year on "Lange Nacht der Museen" ("Long Night of the Museums") all the museums stay open overnight.

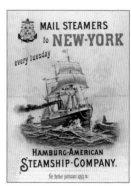

hamburgmuseum
A trip in time from Hamburg's beginnings to the present day. Harbours and ships are central themes in this historical museum (see p73).

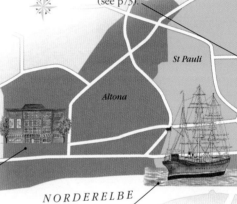

St Pauli

Altona

NORDERELBE

Altonaer Museum
Numerous exhibits on the cultural history of Northern Germany, with an emphasis on Altona, are displayed here (see pp116–17).

Rickmer Rickmers
This three-masted schooner, built in 1896, has been anchored off the Landungsbrücken since 1897 (see pp94–5).

Speicherstadtmuseum
Experience one of Hamburg's greatest traditions in an old warehouse in the middle of Speicherstadt. Tools once used by people living in this part of the city and storage techniques are on show here (see p85).

Museum für Völkerkunde
This museum is far more than just a series of exhibits, it is also dedicated to promoting dialogue between peoples and is a lively meeting place (see p128).

Museum der Arbeit
The changing world of work since the dawn of the Industrial Age is the main focus of this museum housed in a former rubber factory (see p135).

Around the Alster

New Town

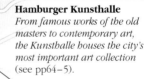

Hamburger Kunsthalle
From famous works of the old masters to contemporary art, the Kunsthalle houses the city's most important art collection (see pp64–5).

Old Town

Port and Speicherstadt

Deichtorhallen
The staging of bold shows has brought these exhibition halls international recognition. Exhibits showcasing the body of work of important artists are combined with interdisciplinary exhibitions (see pp62–3).

Museum für Kunst und Gewerbe
The entire range of applied arts is found here under one roof. This institution is one of the leading museums of its kind in Europe (see pp130–31).

0 kilometres | 1
0 miles | 0.5

Exploring Museums and Galleries

A number of art museums are concentrated along the "museum mile", near the Hauptbahnhof. The themes of museums located in the Speicherstadt range from the history of trade in Hamburg to the city's future development. Some museums cover specialized areas, from trains to wax figures, football (soccer) to fossils, and cinnamon to import duty. The Museumsschiffe (boat museums) are unique.

Das Eismeer (The Polar Sea) (1823–24) by Caspar David Friedrich, Kunsthalle

FINE ART & ARTS AND CRAFTS

Medieval wood-carving in the Museum für Kunst und Gewerbe

Among all the museums, the showpiece is definitely the **Hamburger Kunsthalle**. With its collection of important paintings from the Renaissance onwards, it is one of Hamburg's top attractions. Artists such as Rembrandt, Rubens and Manet are represented here. The adjoining Galerie der Gegenwart displays contemporary art. A visit to this museum complex is a trip through several centuries of art history.

The two **Deichtorhallen** (former market halls) are counted among the largest exhibition spaces in Europe. The halls have a special focus on photography, especially art photography and fashion photography.

In the bright yellow buildings of the **Museum für Kunst und Gewerbe**, everything revolves around applied arts. Highlights include a collection of historic and modern keyboard instruments.

Together, these three important cultural sites are the stars of the so-called "museum mile", which runs north and south of the Hauptbahnhof. They are complemented by smaller collections, including the **Bucerius Kunst Forum** at Rathausmarkt, which mounts four top-quality exhibitions each year.

Two smaller museums are located in Jenischpark. **Jenisch Haus** contains an exhibition of oil paintings and furniture which demonstrates how Hamburg's upper middle class lived. **Ernst Barlach Haus** features the artistic output of this north German artist.

CONTEMPORARY HISTORY

The history of the city from its beginnings around the Hammaburg to the dynamic metropolis it is today is vividly documented in the **hamburgmuseum** (known as the Museum für Hamburgische Geschichte prior to 2006). It houses the largest collection of city history in Germany. A number of model ships and many other exhibits related to shipping round out the collection. The **Krameramtswohnungen** is a

branch of this museum. Here, in this 17th-century apartment building, visitors can tour a period apartment decorated with furniture typical of the time.

Doing double duty as a visitor site and a memorial is **St Nikolai** (Mahnmal St Nikolai) in the Old Town. Significantly damaged during World War II air raids, parts of the church have now been restored, including the tower, which is 147 m (483 ft) high. Exhibits in the adjacent documentation centre provide information about the history of the church.

Cultural history collections from Northern Germany, with an emphasis on fishing and shipping, are found in the **Altonaer Museum**. Photos and documents in the **Speicherstadtmuseum** convey a great deal of knowledge about the history of this unique cluster of warehouses.

The **HafenCity InfoCenter** has been housed in the 100-year-old Kesselhaus (boiler house) of the Speicherstadt, since construction started on this multi-purpose development in 2000. A detailed model introduces and documents the project.

View of the Hanseatic city around 1600, displayed in hamburgmuseum

CULTURAL HISTORY

Ethnological collections from every continent are housed in the **Museum für Völkerkunde**, which is one of the largest of its kind in Europe. The museum hosts a variety of festivals and markets, making it a meeting place for people from around the world throughout the year.

The various changes in the world of work can be traced back to the beginning of the machine age in the **Museum der Arbeit**. Here, visitors learn about work routines in a variety of work places, discovering, for example, what it was like to be employed in a fish factory, or a printing shop.

Much more exotic is the **Afghanisches Museum** (Afghan museum), which presents the rich cultural history of this South Asian country. It exhibits typical Afghani arts and crafts such as colourful carpets and metalwork. In the same building in Speicherstadt, **Spicy's Gewürzmuseum** shows nearly everything that revolves around the precious spices that so delight our taste buds – a festival for the sense of smell.

Old radio telephone in the **Deutsches Zollmuseum**

THE SHIPPING TRADE

A number of museums in Hamburg are dedicated to the shipping trade, which played such a vital role in the city becoming a flourishing port. Some of these museums are located on ships.

A glance behind the scenes of the Cold War can be had by visiting the Russian U-boat **U-434**. Prior to 2002, it belonged to the Russian navy and was employed on espionage missions.

Near the Landungsbrücken, more ship museums lie at anchor. Two very different epochs in shipping history come alive aboard the three-masted schooner **Rickmer Rickmers** and the cargo

freighter **Cap San Diego**. For lovers of old ships, a visit to the **Museumshafen Övelgönne** is a must. Here, you can enjoy seeing many old-timers, among them a high-sea cutter and a fire ship.

Model ships, navigation instruments, globes, maps and many more interesting exhibits illustrating the 3,000-year history of seafaring are found in the **Maritimes Museum**.

Portrait of Johannes Brahms in front of the Musikhalle

And anyone who has always wondered how a completed model ship can find its way into a bottle can learn the answer in the **Buddelschiffmuseum**.

SPECIAL MUSEUMS

Hamburg offers a decent number of unusual museums. The **Deutsches Zollmuseum** (German customs museum) provides an overview of customs history. Of interest are the inventive ways people tried to smuggle goods, only to be caught red-handed. In **Panoptikum**, the largest wax figure exhibition in Germany, more than 120 prominent figures from politicians to entertainers are on display. The racing and sports cars displayed in the **Prototyp Museum**, which opened in 2008, spellbind autosport enthusiasts. The **HSV-Museum** in the Volksparkstadion pays

homage to the successes of this tradition-rich football club. In **Miniatur Wunderland**, a first-class model railway attracts aficionados both old and young. The Earth is the topic of the **RED Gallery**, with its collection of fossils and minerals. The **Johannes-Brahms-Museum** is devoted to the life and works of the famous German composer. In **Beatlemania**, visitors embark on a magical mystery tour. In **Dialog im Dunkeln** (Dialogue in the Dark), the blind lead visitors through pitch-black rooms and let them enjoy a world of sounds and scents. **BallinStadt – Auswandererwelt Hamburg** tells the story of the many emigrants who sought their fortune in far-away countries.

The ship museum **U-434**, once a Russian U-boat

Hamburg's Best: Architecture

Hamburg's architecture varies markedly. Whether the buildings are made of dark red brick, covered with green copper roofs, or are modernistic constructions of steel and glass, the charm of this Hanseatic city is based in part on its traditional as well as its contemporary architecture. The range is broad: stately, solid buildings expressing Hanseatic prosperity vie with architectural expressions of a new light-heartedness. Here and there both these styles are united to create a harmonious whole, as in the Elbphilharmonie, for example. Hamburg's maritime tradition is reflected in many buildings, not just those right on the water.

Statue, Bucerius Kunst Forum

St Michaelis
Hamburg's skyline is dominated by the towers and steeples of its principal churches. Chief among them is the 132-m (433-ft) tall steeple of St Michaelis, known as "Michel" (see pp74–5).

Dockland
Looking a bit like a luxury liner, with its prow jutting out over the water, this futuristic office building was completed in 2005. The five-storey glass-and-steel construction is one of the city's most spectacular (see p149).

St Pauli

Altona

NORDERELBE

Köhlbrandbrücke
With its huge span of over 3,600 m (2.2 miles), this impressive bridge crosses the Köhlbrand to connect the Norderelbe and Süderelbe (see p135).

Landungsbrücken
The central hall of this "floating railway station", built in 1907–09 in Jugendstil (German Art Nouveau style), is 200 m (220 yards) long (see p93).

| 0 kilometres | 1 |
| 0 miles | 0.5 |

Chilehaus
More than five million bricks were used in this world-famous office building designed in the Expressionist style (see p63).

Hauptbahnhof
This Neo-Renaissance building, housing Germany's largest train station, was opened in 1906. It is covered by an enormous roof made of glass and steel (see p62).

Around the Alster

New Town

Rathaus (City Hall)
This august building, adorned with sculptures and crests, is the seat of the Bürgerschaft (parliament) and the Senat (government) of the Freie und Hansestadt (see pp60–61).

Old Town

Port and Speicherstadt

Elbphilharmonie
This ambitious project placed a futuristic concert hall on top of an old warehouse. The tent-like roof is reminiscent of waves and mountains (see pp88–9).

Verlagshaus Gruner + Jahr
With its nautical appearance, this building resembles a steamship. It houses one of the most important media companies in the city (see p146).

Exploring Hamburg's Architecture

Entrance to Palmaille

Hamburg's cityscape is dominated by buildings dating from the 19th and 20th centuries; only a few older buildings still stand today. This is due to the enormous destruction caused by the Great Fire of 1842, and the hail of bombs that rained on the city during World War II. Another factor is that Hamburg's citizens have always had a preference for tearing down old buildings and replacing them with new ones, making their penchant for rebuilding famous even beyond the city's borders. As a merchant town, Hamburg traditionally looks to the future and the current HafenCity project is one of the most ambitious architectural undertakings in Europe.

The Bucerius Kunst Forum, which mounts four exhibitions a year

"OLD" HAMBURG

For many centuries, people in Hamburg used bricks to build apartment buildings, warehouses and factories. A few of these architectural links to "old" Hamburg can still be found in the Old and New Towns – for example on Nikolaifleet in the southwest part of the Old Town. Despite the Great Fire of 1842 breaking out immediately next door, a rare cluster of historic buildings still stands today for all to admire. The warehouses to the back of the brick buildings on **Deichstraße** could be conveniently accessed from the adjacent Fleet canal.

In the New Town, the **Krameramtswohnungen** provide a glimpse into the way

Old Hamburg merchant houses located on Deichstraße

Hamburg's prosperous citizens lived in the 17th century. The half-timbered buildings of the **Beylingstift** in Peterstraße were reconstructed in perfect detail. On **Palmaille**, a lovely street along the bank of the Elbe river, there remain a few apartment buildings that were built for the well-to-do. Built in the Neo-Classical style, these buildings are a testament in stone to Hanseatic wealth and merchant pride.

THE 19TH CENTURY

Buildings constructed during the 19th century borrowed in part from the Italians. The **Alster Arcades**, an elegant colonnade in the Venetian style, was built immediately after the Great Fire. The **Börse** (stock exchange) was also built at this time.

Window in the Fish Auction Hall

This late-Classical building was designed by Carl Ludwig Wimmel and Franz Gustav Forsmann. No sign of Hanseatic restraint can be seen in the Neo-Renaissance **Rathaus** (city hall). The Rathausmarkt (city hall square) was intended to be a kind of Hanseatic Piazza San Marco. All later re-designs of the square remained true to this Venetian theme.

In the late 19th century, the three-halled **Fish Auction Hall**, the **Hotel Vier Jahreszeiten** on Binnenalster and **Rathaus Altona** (Altona city hall) were built. The latter was a centrepiece for the city of Altona, which was independent up to 1937. The **Speicherstadt** (warehouse district) was also built at this time. To erect this ensemble of buildings made of red bricks, the most common construction material in Hamburg, workers' settlements were razed, and some 20,000 people were relocated.

THE CITY'S FIVE PRINCIPAL CHURCHES

Hamburg's skyline is dominated chiefly by the towers and spires of its five main churches. Only a few vestiges remain of the original structure of four of the five: **St Michaelis**, **St Jacobi**, **St Katharinen** and **St Petri**. Surprisingly, some of the interior ornamentation of these places of worship withstood the tests of fire and air raids. **St Nikolai** was erected in 1960–62 to replace the Nikolaikirche that was destroyed in World War II. Its tower is preserved as a memorial, the Mahnmal St Nikolai *(see p66)*. St Michaeliskirche, a massive Baroque church, was rebuilt three times. In 1750, after lightning destroyed the original 17th-century church, a new one arose in its place. This second Michaeliskirche burned to the ground in 1906, but was rebuilt almost immediately. Today St Michaelis' most recent incarnation has become a symbol of the city.

THE 20TH CENTURY

Shortly after 1900, the **Landungsbrücken** quays in St Pauli were built. Some of Hamburg's most important cultural institutions were also built at the beginning of the 20th century. Among them is the **Bucerius Kunst Forum**, located in the former Reichsbank building, and the Neo-Baroque Musikhalle (which was re-named **Laeiszhalle** in 2005). These were designed by Martin Haller *(see p42)*, an architect who oversaw construction of the Rathaus.

In the 1920s, architects rediscovered the city's red-brick building tradition. When the Kontorhausviertel was built in the Old Town, a new generation of red-brick buildings arose – one of daring shapes. A prominent example of this building style is the Expressionist **Chilehaus** by Fritz Höger *(see p42)*. The building's pointed shape is reminiscent of a ship's prow. Around the same time, Fritz Schumacher *(see p42)* built the Museum für Hamburgische Geschichte (called **hamburgmuseum** since 2006) with its imposing roof.

Impressive examples of Industrial architecture from the beginning of the 20th century are **Bahnhof Hamburg Dammtor**, **Hauptbahnhof** and the **Deichtorhallen**. **Heinrich-Hertz-Turm**, which was built by Fritz Trautwein *(see p42)*, stands 279.8 m (918 ft) high – the tallest building in the city.

Transportation routes of note are the **Alter Elbtunnel**, built in 1911, the new tunnel serving the A7 Autobahn, and the **Köhlbrandbrücke**. Notable city centre buildings include **Verlagshaus Gruner + Jahr**, **Kehrwiederspitze** at the entrance to the Speicherstadt, and also the **Passages** located between Rathausmarkt and Gänsemarkt that give a definite flair to the city.

"NEW" HAMBURG

The Elbphilharmonie, HafenCity's star, as it will look on completion

Architects such as Bothe, Richter and Teherani (BRT) and Herzog & de Meuron are responsible for the city's newest architecture. In recent years, futuristic office buildings such as **Dockland**, Berliner Bogen, Deichtor Center, Tanzende Türme as well as ZOB – Bus-Port Hamburg, with its distinctive sickle-shaped roof, have been built. Several buildings of the **HafenCity** complex, due to be completed between 2020 and 2025, are ready. The flagship of this new city district will be the **Elbphilharmonie** (The Hamburg Philharmonic Hall), a glass, roof-top, tent-like structure to be built on top of Kaispeicher A, a warehouse that was built between 1963 and 1966. This spectacular concert hall will be wave-shaped and visible from a great distance.

ARCHITECTURE

132 m (433 ft) tall, completed in 1878

St Petri

124.5 m (408 ft) tall, renovated in 1963

St Jacobi

116.7 m (383 ft) tall, rebuilt in 1957

132 m (433 ft) tall, rebuilt with a steel frame in 1906–12

St Katharinen

St Michaelis

147.3 m (483 ft) tall, completed in 1874

St Nikolai

Hamburg's Best: Parks and Gardens

When Hamburgers want to enjoy nature they do not have to go far. Several lovely recreation areas are located within the city limits – and these are often just a few U-Bahn or S-Bahn stops away from the centre. Hamburg's recreation areas are perfect for taking long, leisurely walks. And, for those who love playing sports or picnicking, the Alstervorland or the Stadtpark are ideal spots. Several museums can be found in the grounds of Jenischpark. Friedhof Ohlsdorf is well suited to contemplation. In Tierpark Hagenbeck, animals from every continent can be admired.

Little hut in Jenischpark

Tierpark Hagenbeck
This world-famous zoo had a revolutionary concept, when it opened in 1907. Its denizens live in spacious outdoor enclosures (see pp136–37)

Volkspark
Despite the presence of the Volksparkstadion (see p134) and the O₂ World Hamburg, Volkspark remains a quiet recreation area. Among its attractions is the oldest dahlia garden in Europe. Joggers appreciate the hilly terrain.

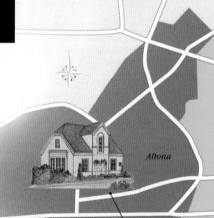

Altona

Heine-Park
This area, with its wonderful old trees, is part of a green belt that runs along the Elbe river. The former home of the banker, Salomon, is today used for exhibitions.

Jenischpark
In this extensive park covering 42 hectares (103 acres) there are two art museums: Jenisch Haus and Ernst Barlach Haus (see p138).

| 0 kilometres | 1 |
| 0 miles | 0.5 |

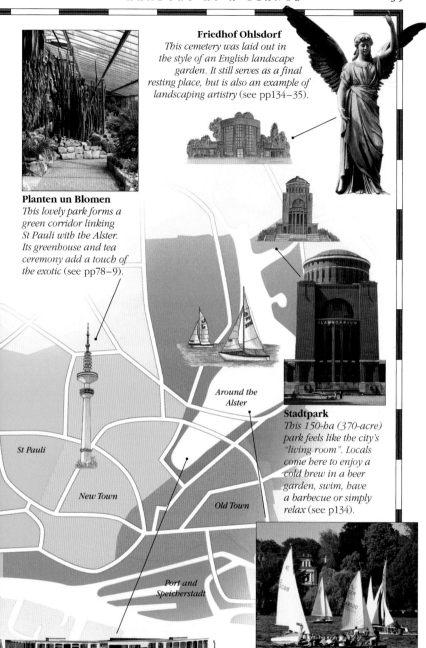

Friedhof Ohlsdorf
This cemetery was laid out in the style of an English landscape garden. It still serves as a final resting place, but is also an example of landscaping artistry (see pp134–35).

Planten un Blomen
This lovely park forms a green corridor linking St Pauli with the Alster. Its greenhouse and tea ceremony add a touch of the exotic (see pp78–9).

Around the Alster

St Pauli

New Town

Old Town

Stadtpark
This 150-ha (370-acre) park feels like the city's "living room". Locals come here to enjoy a cold brew in a beer garden, swim, have a barbecue or simply relax (see p134).

Port and Speicherstadt

Alstervorland
This green space on the western shore of the Außenalster (see p128) is a popular recreation area. Cafés offer patios with a view of the water.

Binnenalster
A trip on an Alster boat provides a beautiful view of the many stately buildings that line the Binnenalster (see pp124).

The Media in Hamburg

Newspaper kiosk in Hamburg

Hamburg is Germany's most important media city. More than 13,000 companies in the industry are headquartered here. Among the prominent firms are some of Europe's most profitable publishing houses, such as Axel-Springer-Verlag (although the editorial departments of *Bild* and *BamS* newspapers moved to Berlin in 2008). Norddeutscher Rundfunk (NDR) is one of the ARD's biggest television stations. It was in Hamburg that the *dpa* rose to become Germany's most important press agency. Many successful movies have used Hamburg as a backdrop.

Ad agency Jung von Matt
In 1991, Holger Jung and Jean-Remy von Matt founded an ad agency that has become highly successful. Now employing some 800 people, this creative think tank has come up with many slogans that have entered the German public consciousness.

ZDF studio in Hamburg
The seventh floor of the Deichtor Center in HafenCity accomodates the offices, where the journalists of the ZDF's regional studio in Hamburg create their reportages.

St Pauli

Altona

NORDERELBE

GEO
GEO, *one of the leading magazines in Germany, has been published monthly since 1976 by Verlagshaus Gruner + Jahr.*

Verlagshaus Gruner + Jahr
The largest magazine and newspaper publisher in Europe publishes about 500 titles in over 30 countries. As early as 1948, even before the German Republic was founded, the first edition of stern *appeared.*

0 kilometres   1

0 miles   0.5

Tagesschau
German television's longest-running news show is produced in Hamburg by the NDR. More than ten million viewers tune in each evening to watch the day's news, shown here with Susanne Daubner.

NDR
This ARD television station produces several of the popular police-drama series Tatort. *Here, Maria Furtwängler is shown in her role as police detective Charlotte Lindholm.*

Around the Alster

New Town

DIE ZEIT

Old Town

ZDF

stern

DER SPIEGEL

Port and Speicherstadt

DIE ZEIT
The editors of the weekly newspaper DIE ZEIT *work from Pressehaus am Speersort, a brick building that forms part of the Kontorhausviertel (warehouse district).*

DER SPIEGEL
With a circulation of almost one million copies, DER SPIEGEL *is the most widely read weekly newsmagazine in Germany. In 2011, the editorial team moved into this building in HafenCity.*

stern
Since 1948 stern *has been giving its readers an overview of the most important themes of the past seven days.* stern *enjoys the highest circulation of any popular magazine in Germany.*

Famous Residents of Hamburg

Among the famous people of Hamburg are the great musicians who have lived and worked here, and the many architects who placed their unmistakable stamp on the city. Forward-looking entrepreneurs have achieved great success here, contributing to the rapid development of the city's economy. Hans Albers, a beloved German actor, expressed the city's soul. Numbered among the many famous personalities intrinsically linked to Hamburg are a former German Chancellor, a boxing world champion, and a legendary pirate who terrorized ships on the Baltic Sea.

**German rock star
Udo Lindenberg (born 1946)**

MUSICIANS

**Composer and pianist
Johannes Brahms (1833–1897)**

Among the musical directors of Hamburg's five principal churches were Georg Philipp Telemann (1681–1767) and his successor, Carl Philipp Emanuel Bach (1714–1788), son of Johann Sebastian Bach. Born in Hamburg, Johannes Brahms (1833–1897) was among the 19th century's most important composers. Felix Mendelssohn Bartholdy (1809–1847), one of the leading musicians in the European Romantic movement, also rose to prominence in Hamburg.

In the field of popular music, Freddy Quinn (born 1931), singer of seamens'

chanties, and rock star Udo Lindenberg (born 1946) – each expressed some of Hamburg's attitude to life in his own way.

ARCHITECTS

One of the proponents of late Classicism is Franz Gustav Forsmann (1795–1879), whose work can be seen in some of the stately villas he built, such as Jenisch Haus (see p138). The Rathaus (city hall) (see pp60–61) was built under the direction of Martin Haller (1835–1925), who also built the Laeiszhalle (see p73). With the Davidwache (see p105) and the hamburgmuseum (see p73), Fritz Schumacher (1869–1947) made his mark on the city's architecture. Fritz Höger (1877–1949) designed several office buildings, among them Chilehaus (see p63), an excellent example of Expressionist architecture.

Fritz Trautwein (1911–1993) was a key figure behind the rebuilding of Hamburg after World War II. In addition to apartment buildings, he designed several U-Bahn stations and the Heinrich-Hertz-Turm (see p77). With projects such as Dockland

(see p34), Berliner Bogen and Tanzende Türme (see p102), Hadi Teherani (born 1954) represents the Hamburg of the future. In 1991, Teherani founded the firm of architects BRT. It is based in the Deichtor Center (see p40), which also has been designed by Teherani.

POLITICIANS

The communist Ernst Thälmann (1886–1944) was elected chair of the KDP (German Communist Party) in 1925. After his arrest in 1933, he spent the rest of his life in concentration camps. Theodor Haubach (1896–1945), also killed by the Nazis, was one of the founders of the democratic protest movement Reichsbanner Schwarz-Rot-Gold. Former German Chancellor Helmut Schmidt (born 1918) earned great respect for his handling of the 1962 Hamburg flood. At the time he was the minister of police.

AUTHORS

Barthold Heinrich Brockes (1680–1747) was an important literary figure of the early Enlightenment. The fame of Friedrich Gottlieb Klopstock (1724–1803) stems largely from his principal work *Der Messias*. Hans Erich Nossack (1901–1977) became famous due to his prose work *Der Untergang* which dealt with the summer 1943 air raids on Hamburg. *Draußen vor der Tür* by Wolfgang Borchert (1921–1947) is one of the most important plays of the early post-war period.

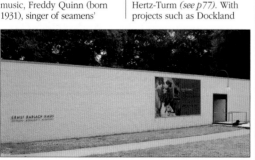

Ernst Barlach Haus, which displays the works of this North German artist

PAINTERS AND SCULPTORS

Meister Bertram (circa 1340–1415), a Gothic painter, enriched Northern German painting by bringing in Italian influences. His chief work, the *Grabower Altar*, can be admired in the Kunsthalle *(see pp64– 5)*. Philipp Otto Runge (1777–1810) is one of the most important representatives of early Romantic art.

Works by Ernst Barlach (1870–1938), a North German Expressionist artist and playwright, are on display in Ernst Barlach Haus *(see p138)*. The animal sculptures of Martin Ruwoldt (1891–1969) grace Alsterpark, Stadtpark and Planten un Blomen.

The Ohnsorg Theater – synonymous for decades with star Heidi Kabel

ENTREPRENEURS

Friedrich Christoph Perthes (1772–1843) is one of the key figures in the German book and publishing trade. In 1796, he founded the first bookstore in Germany here in Hamburg – the cornerstone of today's book trade.

Under the direction of Albert Ballin (1857–1918), HAPAG developed into the world's most important shipping concern. BallinStadt – Auswandererwelt Hamburg *(see p93)*, which opened in 2007, is named after Ballin.

Animal merchant and zoo director Carl Hagenbeck (1844–1930) set a new standard for the treatment of zoo animals when he opened Tierpark Hagenbeck *(see pp136– 37)* in 1907.

Hamburg, the headquarters of so many newspapers and magazine publishing houses *(see pp40– 41)*, owes its position to publishers such as Gerd Bucerius (1906–1995), Axel Springer (1912–1985),

Henri Nannen (1913–1996) and Rudolf Augstein (1923–2002), whose publications dominate the German newspaper and magazine industry.

Albert Darboven (born 1936), owner of a global coffee roasting company, is considered Germany's "coffee king".

ACTORS

Hans Albers (1891–1960) excelled in films such as *Der blaue Engel* (1930), *Große Freiheit Nr.7* (1944), *Auf der Reeperbahn nachts um halb eins* (1954) and *Das Herz von St Pauli* (1957). He was not only the prototypical Hamburg teen, but also a successful singer.

Ida Ehre (1900–1989) opened the Hamburger Kammerspiele in 1945, which evolved to become Germany's leading theatre. The very popular actor Heidi Kabel (1914–2010) was the unchallenged star of the Ohnsorg Theater *(see p129)*.

Raimund Harmstorf (1939–1998) specialized in portraying tough guys. His biggest success was in the role of the brutal Captain Wolf Larsen in a four-part series called *Der Seewolf*.

Evelyn Hamann (1942–2007) was best-known as the partner of Loriot, a beloved German comedian, in many hugely popular comedy sketches.

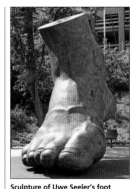

Sculpture of Uwe Seeler's foot in front of the HSV-Arena

SPORTS GREATS

Max Schmeling (1905–2005) was the Heavyweight World Boxing Champion from 1930–32. In 1991, he entered German boxing history as the first German to be named to the International Boxing "Hall of Fame". In 1999 Schmeling was voted Germany's sportsman of the century.

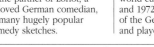

Axel Springer, publisher

Born in Hamburg in 1936, football great Uwe Seeler, affectionately called "our Uwe" by Hamburgers and other Germans, played for Hamburger SV throughout his entire career as well as in four world cups. Between 1954 and 1972, he was a member of the German national team and played in 72 games.

KLAUS STÖRTEBEKER (CA. 1360–1401)

All Hamburg came out to watch his execution. "Our Klaus" was, after all, a hero – someone who stole from the rich and gave to the poor. But did he really deserve such a display of public affection? Wasn't he really just a bloodthirsty pirate? Many legends have grown up around him, including one that says he was born in Hamburg, though others say he was born elsewhere. Störtebeker was the leader of the Vitalienbrüder, a group of pirates who seized numerous ships that plied the Baltic Sea. His goal was to capture Hanse ships, but he was chased off into the North Sea. Klaus Störtebeker was finally caught off the coast of Helgoland and, on 20 October 1401, he was beheaded at Grasbrook, near Hamburg.

The skull of Klaus Störtebeker

HAMBURG THROUGH THE YEAR

Hamburg is an exciting city to visit at any time of the year. The wealth of things to do includes a wide range of cultural events. In summer, there is a lot of activity on the Alster, where a variety of watersports attract young and old. On the Elbe, there is a definite Mediterranean feeling. Three times a year (in spring, summer and winter) a popular festival lasting several weeks is held at the cathedral's Heiligengeistfeld. Among the most-visited attractions are the Fischmarkt, which is held every Sunday morning, as well as the port's annual birthday party at the beginning of May. When it rains, Hamburg's many great museums beckon. Information about current events is available from tourist information offices (see p207).

SPRING

Spring is a particularly good time to travel to Hamburg, because the city turns green extremely early and more events are held outside. As early as May, season begins in the beach clubs on the shores of the Elbe. The plants in Planten un Blomen park bloom in full glory. This is also a good time to amble along Hamburg's luxury shopping streets, admiring the latest fashions.

Hamburg City Beach Club, perfect for relaxing by the water

MARCH

Frühlingsdom *(end Mar–end Apr)*. The season of fairs begins here on the Heiligen-geistfeld. Numerous and varied attractions offer fun and games for young and old.

APRIL

Osterfeuer *(Easter Saturday)*. Easter fires are lit along the banks of the Elbe (Övelgönne to Blankenese) in the evening. **Hamburg Ostertöne** *(Good Friday to Easter Monday)*. This four-day music festival

Crowds at the Port's Birthday Bash, celebrated every May

held at different venues throughout the city is dedicated especially to the works of the composer and pianist Johannes Brahms *(see p42)*, one of the city's most famous citizens.
Lange Nacht der Museen *(one Sat mid-Apr)*. Exhibitions and guided tours until 2am.
Hamburg Marathon *(one Sun in Apr/May)*. More than 20,000 amateur runners compete alongside profes-sionals on the challenging 42-km (26-mile) course which leads them across the entire city.

MAY

The Port's Birthday Bash *(around 7 May)*. A three-day weekend event held at the port between Fish Auction Hall and Kehrwiederspitze. There's action on land, water and in the air. A high point is the Schlepperballet (tug boat ballet; *see p85)*.
Hamburger Surffestival *(a weekend mid-May)*. Surfers and windsurfers meet to party and to see the trends in fashion shows and fascinating films.

Japanese Cherry Blossom Festival *(mid-May)*. To celebrate the cherry blossoms, the Japanese community holds a festival on Außenalster. Around 10:30pm a large fire-works provides a lovely end.
Elbjazz Festival *(a weekend end May)*. Jazz in all varieties around HafenCity.

People enjoying themselves in Tierpark Hagenbeck

Dschungelnächte (Jungle Nights) *(three Sats after the end of May)*. In Tierpark Hagenbeck, Bengal fire, Caribbean rhythms and many more exciting shows captivate visitors until midnight.

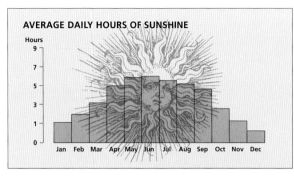

AVERAGE DAILY HOURS OF SUNSHINE

Hours
9
7
5
3
1
0

Jan Feb Mar Apr May Jun Jul Aug Sep Oct Nov Dec

Sunshine Chart
The sun shines the longest in June and July, even when it is warmer in late summer – in August. Spring and early summer are considered the best times to travel to Hamburg. In winter, it is often cloudy and the sun shows itself more rarely.

SUMMER

Summer is *the* outdoor season in Hamburg, when artists and visitors alike are drawn outside to jazz concerts, theatre performances and sporting events. Many of these events take place on or near the water. Films are screened under the starry skies around the city. The many neighbourhood festivals are on a smaller scale, but they offer lots of entertainment and delicious food.

JUNE

Altonale *(first half of Jun).* The largest district festivals, this one draws many visitors with live music, circus acts, theatre, flea markets and much more. At the closing Spaßparade (fun parade), masks, costumes and artistry create a fun-filled atmosphere.
Summer on the Magellan-Terrassen *(Suns early Jun–end Aug).* Performances, lectures, shows and tango-workshops are staged on this open space in HafenCity.

JULY

International German Open Tennis Tournament *(Jul).* Many tennis greats from around the world compete in this 1892 established tournament at Rothenbaum.
Fleetinsel Festival *(Duckstein Festival; ten days end Jul).* Art, culture and culinary delights on Fleetinsel. There is music (from Latin to jazz) on a floating stage, street theatre and outdoor booths.

Planten un Blomen looking lush and attractive in summer

Schleswig-Holstein Music Festival *(mid-Jul–end Aug).* Classical concerts are held in several North German cities. Some of the festival's events are held in Hamburg.
Sommerdom *(end Jul–end Aug).* The second four-week fair is held at the Heiligengeistfeld. Fun for the whole family.
Summer Movies in Sternschanzenpark *(mid-Jul–end Aug).* Open-air screenings in a lovely park located in the heart of the famous Schanzenviertel.

AUGUST

Romantik-Nächte *(three Saturdays in Aug).* Romantic music and classical tones can be heard on every path as visitors stroll around Tierpark Hagenbeck. The musicians are students of Hochschule für Musik und Theater Hamburg.
Hamburg Cruise Days *(a weekend in Aug; every two years).* Maritime event with parades of boats and ships.
International Summer Festival *(two weeks in Aug).* Dance and theatre festival.

Enter the Dragon *(one weekend in Aug/Sep).* A two-day Dragon Boat festival on the Binnenalster with rowing teams from around the world. The boats start in front of Alsterpavillon.
Alstervergnügen *(Thu–Sun end Aug/early Sep).* A fair held on Binnenalster with music, shows, vendors, children's events and a food mile. On the first three days, there is a spectacular fireworks display.

The Sylt fried-fish stand, part of the Alstervergnügen festivities

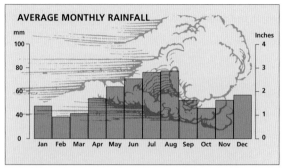

AVERAGE MONTHLY RAINFALL

Rainfall Chart
In Hamburg, rainfall is distributed unevenly throughout the year. This is typical for a city located near a coast. The wettest time of year is summer, the driest time is late winter. Whatever the season, visitors should always be prepared for rain.

Exhibition in the crypt of St Michaelis

AUTUMN

In September, many events still take place outdoors in Hamburg. However, it is becoming a bit too chilly for sports events to be held outside. Still, autumn has its own special mood, especially in the parks, such as in Planten un Blomen. It is also lovely along the Elbe river at this time of year. A stiff breeze often blows off the harbour, but boat trips of the port area are still available. Autumn is also the season for theatre and literature festivals and events dedicated to boats and boating.

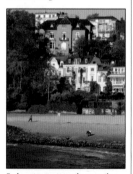

Early autumn atmosphere on the shore of the Elbe river

SEPTEMBER

Stadtpark Revival *(first week-end in Sep)*. Pure nostalgia at the Stadtpark for this Oldtimer Grand Prix, with its 1.7-km (1.05-mile) long racetrack that attracts motor sports lovers.
Harbour Front Literaturfestival *(ten days mid-Sep)*. Authors of all kinds of genres present their books at numerous venues, including the Landungsbrücken, Speicherstadt and HafenCity.
Hamburger Theaternacht *(one Sat mid-Sep)*. At the start of the new season, theatres invite the public to a long night with a full programme.
Reeperbahn Festival *(last weekend in Sep)*. National and international bands perform in clubs on the Reeperbahn, and at open-air venues. One of the best music festivals in Hamburg.
Filmfest Hamburg *(end Sep/early Oct)*. This film festival shows selected films in several cinemas. Classics of the silver screen supplement the premieres being screened.
Hamburger Theater Festival *(end Sep–end Oct)*. Performances by companies from Germany, Austria and Switzerland are staged in various theatres.

OCTOBER

Hanseboot *(end Oct/early Nov)*. International boat show at the trade fair grounds. Over the course of a week, the latest boats and the newest trends in watersports are presented to boating enthusiasts.

Water-Light-Concert in Planten un Blomen *(see pp 78–9)*

NOVEMBER

Hamburger Krimifestival *(one week early Nov)*. Crime writers present their latest murder mysteries. Among the "sites of crime" are the Literaturhaus, several theatres and numerous bookstores.
Winterdom *(early Nov–early Dec)*. This is the third and last of the yearly fairs held at Heiligengeistfeld. Even in late autumn, the view over the city from the giant Ferris wheel is spectacular. A special attraction at the Winterdom are the jugglers dressed in traditional medieval costumes.

AVERAGE MONTHLY TEMPERATURE

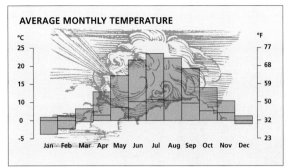

°C / °F chart showing temperatures for Jan Feb Mar Apr May Jun Jul Aug Sep Oct Nov Dec
(°C scale: 25, 20, 15, 10, 0, -5)
(°F scale: 77, 68, 59, 50, 32, 23)

Temperature Chart
The chart shows the average minimum and maximum temperatures for each month. Hamburg is hottest in summer when the thermometer climbs above 30 °C (86 °F). In winter, it can be bitterly cold, with temperatures falling below freezing.

WINTER

A festive atmosphere prevails at the Christmas markets in the centre of town and the adjoining districts. The cold in January and February, which can sometimes be bitter, does not spoil the good mood of Hamburg's citizens. In fact, they embrace the weather and, when the Alster lakes freeze over, have great fun ice skating. In the winter months, bookstores and cultural institutions, such as the Literaturhaus, hold many readings.

DECEMBER

Weihnachtsmärkte (Christmas markets) *(end Nov–24 Dec)*. The whole city gets into the festive mood as Christmas markets spring up here and there around the city. Especially popular and crowded are the markets at Rathausplatz, Gerhart-Hauptmann-Platz, around St Petri church and at the Gänsemarkt. In addition to these larger markets located in Old Town and New Town, the smaller markets held for example in St Pauli, Eimsbüttel or Ottensen also are very fascinating. Each market has its own Christmas tree. Stalls vend various culinary delights.
New Year's Eve *(31 Dec)*. As one year ends and the next begins, Hamburgers are noticeably relaxed. There are large crowds on the

The Hamburger Dom takes place three times a year

waterfront, especially at the Landungsbrücken, where a concert of ships' sirens greets the new year, the heavens above the harbour light up colourfully with spectacular fireworks, thousands of champagne corks pop and complete strangers wish each other a happy New Year. The cheerful celebrations continue long after midnight until the early morning hours.

JANUARY

Ice Fun on the Alster *(when the ice is thick enough)*. When it is bitterly cold outside, and the ice covering the Alster is deemed by the city to be thick enough to be safe, innumerable walkers and ice skaters throng here. It is easy enough to warm up at one of the many mulled wine stands which are set up on the river banks and on the frozen Alster. Sometimes, though, Hamburgers wait expectantly and eagerly for enough of a freeze to create thick ice, only to be disappointed when it does not happen.

FEBRUARY

Reisen Hamburg *(early Feb)*. At this international tourism fair, about 900 exhibitors from around the world showcase their products. Visitors, however, are not only attracted by the informative displays, but also by the opportunity to book their next holiday.

Iced-over ship's prow in Hamburg's wintery harbour

Maskenzauber an der Alster *(weekend before Shrove Tuesday)*. Carnival the Hanseatic way, with style, elegance and "noblesse" held in front of the Venetian-style backdrop of the Alster Arcades. The highlight of the festival is the historic masquerade ball which is held in varying venues. Classes are offered to visitors who wish to learn how to dance historical dances.
LiLaBe *(after Ash Wednesday)*. The largest North German carnival is held at the Fachhochschule Bergedorf. Ten thousand revellers make this two-day festival a giant party.

HOLIDAYS
New Year's Day (1 Jan)
Good Friday (varies)
Easter Monday (varies)
Workers' Day (1 May)
Ascension Day (varies)
Whit Monday (varies)
German Unity Day (3 Oct)
Christmas (25/26 Dec)

A RIVER VIEW OF HAMBURG

A trip to Hamburg's harbour is an absolute must for every visitor to the city. "If you haven't been to the harbour, you haven't been to Hamburg", the locals say. The best way to get to know this area is to take a round trip on one of the boats that depart from all along the Landungsbrücken. The small boats can manoeuvre through even narrow canals as well as the Speicherstadt canals (also known as the Fleete). Large ships offer tours of the container port. Their captains are as witty and knowledgable as they are chatty; they are chock full of maritime lore, which they happily recount. You learn a great deal about the port

Ad for a harbour round trip

and its ships, and you often can see even large freighters from up close.

Ferry routes service practically all corners of the harbour. If you are willing to travel a bit further, you can explore the entire water's edge, from the Landungsbrücken up-river to the newly built Hafen-City (see pp90–91), then further up-river to Museumshafen Övelgönne (see p135) and on to Teufelsbrück. The south shore has its appeal, too. Departing from the Blohm + Voss shipyard, a ferry travels to the Seemannshöft pilot station, on to Finkenwerder and then to the Airbus factory. Flights over the city provide an especially spectacular view of the harbour area.

• **Loudspeaker system that greets all ships**

Hamburg-Finkenwerder

Elbe

Round trip of the Port
No trip to Hamburg is complete without taking one of the harbour or container port round trips on offer.

Ship of the line HADAG No. 62
This harbour ferry offers an interesting trip along the Elbe river from Sandtorhöft to Finkenwerder. It also goes to Landungsbrücken.

Loudspeaker system
All ships entering and leaving Hamburg's busy port are greeted and bid farewell via a loudspeaker system that also plays the national anthems for each ship's home country.

Kreuzfahrtterminal (Hamburg Cruise Center)
*The largest and best-known cruise ships in the world
dock at the Hamburg Cruise Centers – the liner
Clubschiff* AIDAvita *docks here, too.*

**Musical-
Express**
*HADAG ferry
number 73
takes patrons to
the theatre in
the harbour.*

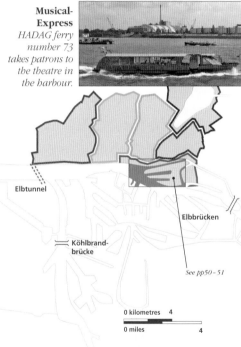

Elbtunnel

Köhlbrand-
brücke

Elbbrücken

See pp50 - 51

0 kilometres 4

0 miles 4

HARBOUR ROUND TRIPS

Barkassen-Centrale
Tel 319 91 61 70.
www.barkassen-centrale.de

Barkassen Meyer
Tel 317 73 70.
www.barkassen-meyer.de

**Bergedorfer
Schifffahrtslinie**
Tel 73 67 56 90.
www.barkassenfahrt.de

Elbe Erlebnistörns
Tel 219 46 27.
www.elbe-erlebnistoerns.de

Hamburg City Tour
Tel 32 31 85 90.
www.hamburg-city-tour.de

Touristik Kontor
Tel 334 42 20.
www.touristik-kontor.de

HARBOUR FERRIES

**HADAG Seetouristik
und Fährdienst AG**
Tel 311 70 70.
www.hadag.de

Max Jens GmbH
Tel 36 66 81.
www.mj-hafenrundfahrt.de

AIR TOURS

Air Hamburg
Tel 70 70 88 90.
www.air-hamburg.de

**CANAIR Luftfahrt-
unternehmen**
Tel 35 51 52 62.
www.canair.de

**Hanseatic Helicopter
Service**
Tel 54 80 29 97.
www.hanseatic-helicopter.de

Köhlbrandbrücke
*The pylons of this steel-and-
cable bridge, designed by Egon
Jux, rise 135 m (443 ft) above
high tide. Since 1974, this
bridge has spanned the 325-m
(105-ft) wide Köhlbrand in
Hamburg's harbour.*

From the Alter Elbtunnel to HafenCity

This section of the Elbe river flows through the heart of Hamburg. There is no other place where the city shows itself to be so confident, so worldly and so dynamic, and nowhere else is it changing so radically. Change is ongoing, with the HafenCity project being an enormous architectural challenge. Most of Hamburg's attractions are found on the north shore of the Elbe.

Alter Elbtunnel
Pedestrians and cyclists reach the south shore of the Elbe river via this tunnel, built in 1911. From the south shore, you can enjoy a fabulous view of the city (see p93).

Landungsbrücken
No visitor to the city should miss the chance to take a walk on the gently moving floating quays and watch the many ships as they glide slowly by (see p93).

Access to the Alter Elbtunnel: Elevators transport cars 23.5 m (77 ft) down into the tunnel's depths *(see p93).*

BEI DEN ST. PAULI LANDUNGSBRÜCKEN

U S Landungs-brücken

Alter Elbtunnel

The Hafen-Hochbahn (elevated port railway) was opened in 1912. A fascinating view of the port can be enjoyed between the stops at Rödingsmarkt and Landungs-brücken *(see p92).*

Blohm + Voss
At the Blohm + Voss GmbH shipyard, ships are still being built and repaired. The shipyard was founded in 1877. Since then, many famous ships have been launched from its docks.

Rickmer Rickmers
Since 1987, this three-masted schooner, built in Bremerhaven in 1896, has been anchored at the Landungsbrücken as a ship museum (see pp94–5).

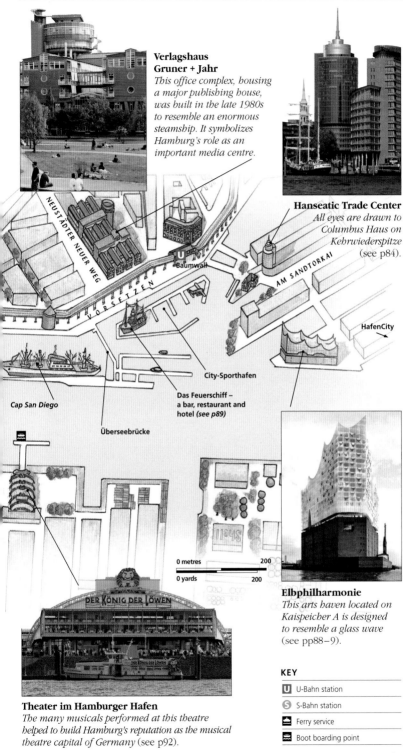

Verlagshaus Gruner + Jahr
This office complex, housing a major publishing house, was built in the late 1980s to resemble an enormous steamship. It symbolizes Hamburg's role as an important media centre.

Hanseatic Trade Center
All eyes are drawn to Columbus Haus on Kehrwiederspitze (see p84).

Neustädter Neuer Weg

Baumwall

Vorsetzen

AM SANDTORKAI

HafenCity

City-Sporthafen

Cap San Diego

Das Feuerschiff – a bar, restaurant and hotel *(see p89)*

Überseebrücke

DER KÖNIG DER LÖWEN

0 metres   200
0 yards   200

Elbphilharmonie
This arts haven located on Kaispeicher A is designed to resemble a glass wave (see pp88–9).

Theater im Hamburger Hafen
The many musicals performed at this theatre helped to build Hamburg's reputation as the musical theatre capital of Germany (see p92).

KEY

U U-Bahn station

S S-Bahn station

Ferry service

Boot boarding point

The Landungsbrücken tower with Columbus Haus behind it on Kehrwiederspitze ▷

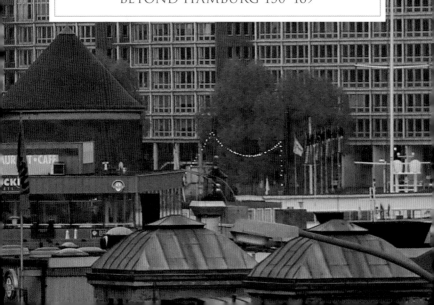

HAMBURG AREA BY AREA

OLD TOWN

Even from afar you can easily recognize the Old Town by the towers and spires of its four main churches. Here, archaeologists still find remnants from Hamburg's past, but unfortunately the visitor won't see many buildings older than 150 years. Large sections of the Old Town were destroyed in the Great Fire of 1842. Only a few old houses in the Deichstraße still stand to bear testimony to the beauty that old Hamburg once possessed.

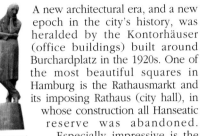

Monument to Heinrich Heine on the Rathausplatz

A new architectural era, and a new epoch in the city's history, was heralded by the Kontorhäuser (office buildings) built around Burchardplatz in the 1920s. One of the most beautiful squares in Hamburg is the Rathausmarkt and its imposing Rathaus (city hall), in whose construction all Hanseatic reserve was abandoned. Especially impressive is the view of the square from the Alster Arcades. With its gleaming white, rounded colonnade, Hamburg expresses its Venetian side.

SIGHTS AT A GLANCE

Churches
St Jacobi **7**
St Katharinen **12**
St Nikolai Memorial **13**
St Petri **4**

Museums and Galleries
Bucerius Kunst Forum **2**
Deichtorhallen **10**
Hamburger Kunsthalle pp64–5 **8**
RED Gallery **16**

Historic Buildings and Monuments
Rathaus pp60–61 **1**

Streets and Places
Alster Arcades **3**
Deichstraße **17**
Domplatz **5**

Theatres
Thalia Theater **6**

Other Attractions
Alsterfleet **15**
Börse **14**
Chilehaus **11**
Hauptbahnhof **9**

0 metres 400
0 yards 400

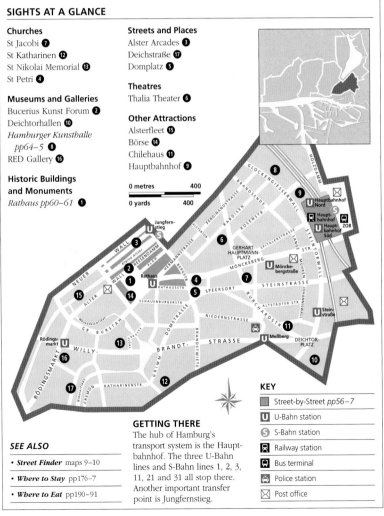

KEY
- ▮ Street-by-Street *pp56–7*
- **U** U-Bahn station
- **S** S-Bahn station
- ▮ Railway station
- ▮ Bus terminal
- ▮ Police station
- ⊠ Post office

GETTING THERE
The hub of Hamburg's transport system is the Hauptbahnhof. The three U-Bahn lines and S-Bahn lines 1, 2, 3, 11, 21 and 31 all stop there. Another important transfer point is Jungfernstieg.

SEE ALSO
- **Street Finder** maps 9–10
- **Where to Stay** pp176–7
- **Where to Eat** pp190–91

◁ Hamburg's Rathaus (city hall), topped by its striking 112-m (370-ft) tall tower *(see pp60–61)*

Street-by-Street: Rathaus and Alster Arcades

Lion at the Rathaus

Built in the Neo-Renaissance style, Hamburg's Rathaus (city hall) is one of its landmark buildings. Both its façade and interior are adorned with lavish ornamentation and opulent decoration. After walking across the extensive Rathausmarkt, you reach the Alster Arcades. Tucked inside the white colonnade are many exclusive shops that entice visitors in for some serious shopping. Take a break and wander into one of the many bistros and cafés here, which offer an excellent view of the Alster.

★ Bucerius Kunst Forum
Since autumn 2002, the former Reichsbank building has been home to the Bucerius Art Forum. Every year four stellar exhibitions are mounted in this imposing Neo-Classical building ❷

★ Hygieia Fountain
After the city had recovered from a cholera epidemic in 1892, this lovely fountain with three basins was built in the interior courtyard of the Rathaus. On top, Hygieia, the Greek goddess of health, watches over the waters.

KEY

– – – Suggested route

0 metres	100
0 yards	100

STAR SIGHTS

★ Alster Arcades

★ Bucerius Kunst Forum

★ Gedenkstein

★ Hygieia Fountain

★ Rathaus

Sculpture
Designed by sculptor Waldemar Otto, this group of figures was installed on the portal of the Börse in 2005.

★ Alster Arcades
After the Great Fire of 1842 that reduced most of the Old Town to rubble and ash, architect Alexis de Chateauneuf designed this colonnade with a Venetian flair ❸

LOCATOR MAP
See Street Finder maps 5–6 & 9–10

★ Gedenkstein
On the back of this monument to those slain during World War I is the reconstruction of a relief by sculptor Ernst Barlach. It depicts a grieving mother with her child.

The Mönckebergstraße
is one of the most popular shopping streets in the city. Extending from the Rathausmarkt to the Hauptbahnhof, it counts among the most visited shopping streets in Germany.

The Rathausmarkt is used year-round for a wide variety of events – from summer concerts and open-air cinema to the Weihnachtsmarkt (Christmas market) in winter.

★ Rathaus
Built in 1886–97 in the Neo-Renaissance style, the Rathaus dazzles visitors with its huge dimensions and its 112-m (367-ft) high tower ❶

Portal
The entrance portal of the Rathaus is adorned with sculptures, paintings and Hamburg's coat of arms. It attests to the pride of the city state.

Façade of the Bucerius Kunst Forum in the former Reichsbank building

Rathaus ❶

See pp60–61.

Bucerius Kunst Forum ❷

Rathausmarkt 2. **Map** 10 D3.
Tel 360 99 60. ⓤ *Jungfernstieg,
Rathaus.* Ⓢ *Jungfernstieg.* 🚌
3, 4, 5, 6, 31, 34, 35, 36, 37.
🕐 *11am–7pm daily (Thu to 9pm).*
⬤ *24 Dec.* 🖼 ♿ 🏠 💻
www.buceriuskunstforum.de

The Bucerius Kunst Forum
(Bucerius Art Forum), established in 2002, is housed in
the former Reichsbank building near the Rathaus. The
Neo-Classical building, which
dates from 1914–17, has a
richly embellished façade.
Depicted on the gables are
workers in various professions
and trades – from Senator to
water carrier – that are typical
for this Hanseatic city.
  Inside the building are
700 sq m (735 sq ft) of gallery
space for the Forum's exhibitions. With its work supported
by the ZEIT foundation, the
institution mounts exhibitions
covering themes from classical times to the present day.
  One of the mandates of the
Bucerius Kunst Forum is to
build bridges between old
art and contemporary art, as
well as between European
and foreign cultures. For
this reason the themes
covered in each exhibition
are broad. The programme
consists of four top exhibitions a year, put together by
renowned guest curators,
supplemented by lectures
and readings.

Alster Arcades ❸

Map 10 D3. ⓤ *Jungfernstieg,
Rathaus.* Ⓢ *Jungfernstieg.* 🚌 *3, 4,
5, 6, 31, 34, 35, 36, 37.*

Alongside the Kleine Alster
run the Alster Arcades (Alsterarkaden), among Hamburg's
most exclusive addresses for
high-quality shopping and
elegant dining. Boutiques and
fashion stores selling designer
goods invite visitors to linger
for a while, as do the wine
bars and bistros. The latter
contribute to the Medi-
terranean flair – especially
in summer.
  The Alster Arcades were
constructed after the Great
Fire of 1842, in which the
majority of the buildings
between Binnenalster and
Rathausmarkt burned down.
Architect Alexis de Chateauneuf designed the colonnade
in Venetian style and also
created the buildings behind
them. Many other architects
and designers took inspiration

from this complex. The
numerous street cafés offer a
lovely view of the water.
  At the south end of the
Alster Arcades is the Schleusenbrücke, a bridge with a
weir that helps regulate the
amount of water flowing into
the Binnenalster.

St Petri ❹

Kreuslerstraße 6. **Map** 10 E3.
Tel 325 74 00. ⓤ *Jungfernstieg,
Rathaus.* Ⓢ *Jungfernstieg.* 🚌 *4, 5,
6, 31, 34, 35, 36, 37.* 🕐 *10am–
6:30pm Mon–Fri (Wed to 7pm),
10am–5pm Sat, 9am–8pm Sun.*
www.sankt-petri.de

Named after the Apostle
Peter, this house of worship is
the oldest of Hamburg's five
parish churches. It is thought
to have been built in the 11th
century and was first mentioned in 1195. Around 1310,
the church began to expand
into a triple-naved Gothic
hall church. Once the second
south nave was added
around 1420, construction
was finally complete.
  In 1842 the church fell
victim to the Great Fire. Very
little was left of the façade.
However, the most important
treasures stored inside were
saved, such as the well-
known bronze door knocker
(1342) in the form of a lion's
head on the west entrance.
  The church was rebuilt on
the old foundations in the
Neo-Gothic style, and was
modelled on the original. It
was consecrated in 1849.

The Gedenkstein, a sober monument to the victims of war

Domplatz with cuboids indicating the layout of the Mariendom

St Petri church survived World War II with relatively little damage. Some of its works of art, among them a Gothic panel (circa 1460) and a wooden statue (circa 1480), depict Bishop Ansgar of Hamburg and Bremen (801–865) who was canonized by Pope Nicolas I. Gracing the façade are sculptures of the Evangelists, among others.

The church spire, which rises 133-m (436-ft) high, was completed in 1878. Visitors can climb 544 steps to the 123-m (402-ft) level, where there is a viewing platform. The view of the inner city from here is fabulous, and the climb is worthwhile.

Domplatz ❺

Map 10 E3–4. Ⓤ *Jungfernstieg, Rathaus.* Ⓢ *Jungfernstieg.* 🚌 *4, 5, 6, 31, 34, 35, 36, 37.* **Showroom** *Kreuslerstraße 4.* **Tel** *32 57 40 27.* 📷 *(due to renovation).*

The Domplatz is considered to be the birthplace of Hamburg. Here, the remains of a building complex were uncovered, which were first thought to be the legendary Hammaburg castle *(see p19)*. The castle was built in 817 by the Franks, and destroyed by the Vikings in 845. Research, however, revealed that the finds were parts of the Mariendom (St Mary's Cathedral), and not the remains of the Hammaburg, from which the city derives its name.

After the excavation, which had been carried out under the direction of the Helms-Museum für Archäologie (Hamburg's archeological museum), was completed, greenery was planted on the Domplatz. The layout of the Mariendom is indicated by 30 white plexiglass cuboids, which can be used as benches. At night, when the cuboids are illuminated, the atmosphere on the Domplatz is particularly enchanting.

At the northern edge of the Domplatz, a stone ring some 19 m (62 feet) in diameter was discovered during excavations carried out in 1962, at a depth of around 3 m (10 ft). These foundations are understood to belong to the Bishop's Castle (Bischofsburg). Dating from the 11th century, it is one of the oldest stone fortresses north of the Elbe. Some excavation finds are on display in the lower level of St Petri's parish house, which, however, is currently closed.

Door knocker, St Petri church

Thalia Theater ❻

Alstertor 1. **Map** 10 E3. **Tel** *32 81 40.* Ⓤ *Mönckebergstraße, Jungfernstieg.* Ⓢ *Jungfernstieg.* 🚌 *4, 5, 6, 31, 34, 35, 36, 37.* 📷 *only groups & per appointment.* **Box office Tel** *32 81 44 44.* 🕐 *10am–7pm Mon–Sat, 4–6pm Sun, hols.* **www**.thalia-theater.de

Named after the Muse of comedy, Thalia Theater is a time-honoured Hamburg institution. It was founded in 1843 by Charles Maurice Schwartzenberger (1805–1896). Since then, the city's oldest theatre company has moved house several times. In 1912, a playhouse was opened in the theatre's current location. That building was destroyed in 1945, but was later rebuilt in 1960, at which time a full programme of plays were staged once again.

Even though today's theatre is not as splendid as others, such as the Deutsches Schauspielhaus *(see p129)*, Thalia Theater definitely numbers among Germany's most famous stages. In 1989, 2003 and 2007 it was voted "Theatre of the Year". Its repertoire includes about 30 productions that change daily. The range of drama covered is broad – from Sophokles over William Shakespeare, Friedrich Schiller and Franz Kafka to contemporary playwrights like Elfriede Jelinek. The tradition-rich Thalia Theater is also well known for its decisive direction: famous directors such as Peter Zadek and Jürgen Flimm have had great successes here.

The Thalia Theater is one of the venues of the Hamburger Theater Festival *(see p46)*, which is held in autumn.

The Muse of comedy on the façade of Thalia Theater

Rathaus ●

Hamburg coat-of-arms on the Rathaus

The Rathaus (city hall) certainly does not reflect that well-known Hamburg characteristic – understatement. Nothing was held back in the construction of this Neo-Renaissance palatial building, erected in 1886–97. Its dimensions are huge (111 m by 70 m/ 365 ft by 230 ft), and its tower is impressive 112 m (365 ft) high. Its façade is richly adorned with sculptures. Among the sculptures are 20 German emperors facing out towards the Rathausmarkt. The seat of the Hamburg City Council and Senate is built atop 4,000 wooden stakes and contains 647 rooms.

★ Parliament Chamber
The seat of parliament is both one of the largest rooms in the Rathaus and also the starkest.

Entrance to the Great Banquet Hall
The interior of this hall was only completed at the beginning of the 20th century.

Four copper figures represent the virtues of a good citizen.

Main entrance

★ Lord Mayor's Chamber
All eyes are drawn to the oil painting by Hugo Vogel in this richly decorated room. It depicts Senators clothed in their official garb during the dedication of the Rathaus in 1897.

★ Great Banquet Hall
This hall is dominated by three enormous chandeliers. The painting in the background is an impression of Hamburg's port at the beginning of the 20th century.

Hygieia Fountain in the courtyard
The bronze figures on the edge of this fountain depict the great significance water holds for many very different professions such as shipping.

The clock face
of the tower clock is 5 m (16 ft) long.

The right wing
of the Rathaus is used exclusively by Hamburg's Senate.

★ Ratsstube
Once a week, the Hamburg Senate goes into session in this chamber. The Lord Mayor takes the place of honour under the canopy, while the Senators and City Council take their seats around the horseshoe-shaped table.

Roof Vault
The arched vault of the Rathaus vestibule is supported by 16 mighty sandstone columns.

STAR SIGHTS

★ Great Banquet Hall

★ Lord Mayor's Chamber

★ Parliament Chamber

★ Ratsstube

St Jacobi

Jakobikirchhof 22. **Map** 10 E3. *Tel 303 73 70.* ① *Mönckebergstraße.* ⑤ *Hauptbahnhof.* 🚍 *4, 5, 6, 31, 34, 35, 36, 37.* ☐ *Apr–Sep: 10am–5pm Mon–Sat; Oct–Mar: 11am–5pm Mon–Sat.* 📞 *call ahead.* **www**.jacobus.de

The Gothic church of St Jacobi, one of the parish churches of Hamburg, was erected in the second half of the 14th century. In the 15th century, the triple-nave hall church was expanded when a second aisle was built on the south side. Of the church's three altars, the St Lucas Altar (circa 1500) is the most valuable. It was originally located in Mariendom (St Mary's Cathedral) in Hamburg. Portraits of the benefactors were depicted on an inside panel, as was usual in the Middle Ages. In the left aisle of the church is a statue of the patron saint, St Jacob, which was carved in the 17th century. Paintings on the ceiling illustrate virtues of good citizens.

A real treasure is the church's organ, built in 1689–93 by Arp Schnitger. Located on the west balcony, this celebrated organ is the largest extant Baroque organ in northern and central Europe. Even Johann Sebastian Bach played on this instrument. It has been restored, and can be heard every Sunday during services and in special organ concerts.

The St Petri Altar (1508), located in the first of St Jacobi's south naves

Hamburger Kunsthalle ⑧

See pp64–5.

Hauptbahnhof ⑨

Kirchenallee. **Map** 10 F2–3. ① *Hauptbahnhof.* ⑤ *Hauptbahnhof.* 🚍 *4, 5, 6, 31, 34, 35, 36, 37, 112.*

Hamburg's Hauptbahnhof, the main train station located on the eastern edge of the Old Town, is northern Germany's most important railway hub. Trains depart from 14 tracks for numerous destinations. Some 450,000 passengers and visitors frequent this station daily, making it one of the busiest in Germany. Several S-Bahn and U-Bahn lines also converge here. Their tracks are located under or beside the station, making it the hub of Hamburg's internal transport system, Hamburger Verkehrsverbund (HVV for short).

Built in the Neo-Renaissance style, the station opened on 6 December 1906. The main hall is 37 m (122 ft) high and covered with a steel and glass roof. The hall itself is 206 m (675 ft) long and 135 m (443 ft) wide – the largest in the country. It was here in 1991 that Wandelhalle opened; this was Germany's first shopping centre to be located in a train station. Along with 70 speciality stores and a wide range of food choices, the Deutsche Bahn (German railway) has its Reisezentrum (travel information centre) here.

A view of Hamburg's Hauptbahnhof

Deichtorhallen ⑩

Deichtorstraße 1–2. **Map** 10 F4. *Tel 32 10 30.* ① *Steinstraße, Meßberg.* ⑤ *Hauptbahnhof.* 🚍 *34.* ☐ *11am–6pm Tue–Sun (first Thu each month 11am–9pm).* 📷 **www**.deichtorhallen.de

These two monumental halls were erected 1911–14 on the grounds of the former Berliner Bahnhof (train station). Measuring 3,800 and 1,800 sq m (50,000 sq ft and 19,000 sq ft) respectively, their steel construction is an example of Jugendstil industrial architecture. At first they were used as market halls, after 1984 they stayed empty for some time.

The Deichtorhallen has been used for art exhibitions since 1989. Over time, it has evolved into one of Europe's largest exhibition centres. The Internationales Haus der Fotografie (International House of Photography) in the south hall focuses on the evolution of photography since its beginnings. In the north hall, exhibitions featuring the works of contemporary painters and sculptors, both famous and not so famous, are mounted. Symposia and discussions with artists round out the programme.

From the grounds of the Deichtorhallen, the **HighFlyer**

Hamburg rises up 150 m (490 ft) into the sky over Hamburg. The view of the city from this ultramodern stationary balloon is breathtaking. The spectacular balloon has a diameter of 23 m (75 ft). The faint of heart will be reassured by the steel cable that permanently anchors the balloon to the ground.

HighFlyer Hamburg
Tel 30 08 69 69. 10am–10pm.
www.highflyer-hamburg.de

Chilehaus ⓫

Burchardplatz/Pumpenstraße.
Map 10 F4. Ⓤ *Steinstraße, Meßberg.* Ⓢ *Hauptbahnhof.*
4, 5, 6, 31, 34, 35, 36, 37.
9am–4pm daily.

The ten-storey Chilehaus (1922–24) is a striking example of the red-brick architecture of the 1920s. Due to its thin, unconventional form, this best-known of all Hamburg office buildings has been nicknamed "Ozeanriese" (ocean giant). With its angular form and a design that emphasizes the vertical, the building is reminiscent of the prow of a ship, especially when viewed from the prow side in the east. In order to create this building, designed by architect Fritz Höger, nearly five million bricks were used.

The name Chilehaus was chosen because the man who commissioned the building, Henry Brarens Sloman, was a Hamburg merchant and shipping magnate who had made his fortune in the saltpetre trade in Chile.

A symbol of Expressionist architecture: the Chilehaus

St Katharinen ⓬

Katharinenkirchhof 1. **Map** 10 D4.
Tel 30 37 47 30. Ⓤ *Meßberg, Rödingsmarkt.* Ⓢ *Jungfernstieg.*
3, 4, 6. ask by phone.
www.katharinen-hamburg.de

Given its proximity to the water, St Katharinen church is also known as the "Mariners' Church". One of the five parish churches in Hamburg, it was first mentioned in 1256. The only remnant of the original building is the base of the tower, which is documented as being the oldest free-standing structure in the city. In 1656-7 the top of the tower of this church was capped by a Baroque-inspired steeple with arches – a significant feature of Hamburg's skyline.

After incurring heavy damage during the air raids of 1943–44, the exterior of the church was rebuilt in its old form. The in former times richly decorated interior is now fairly simple. Among the very few old artworks is a beautiful wooden carving of St Catherine from the 15th century as well as some late Renaissance tombstones dating from the 16th and 17th centuries.

KONTORHAUSVIERTEL

The Kontorhausviertel (warehouse district), with its many impressive office buildings, is located around Burchardplatz between Brandstwiete and Klosterwall, and Steinstraße and Meßberg. Typical architectural elements of these buildings, designed in the Expressionistic style of the 1920s, include using reinforced concrete and red-brick façades, accentuating the vertical by using pillars, installing wide windows and creating imposing entrances. Some of the offices have Paternosters (open-style lifts) that are in use to this day. The most remarkable of all these office buildings is Chilehaus. Other interesting examples are the Sprinkenhof, which is the largest office complex, Montanhof, with its many bay windows, and the Meßberghof, with its elegant spiral staircase that winds its way up eleven storeys.

Façade of the Sprinkenhof, built in 1927–43

Hamburger Kunsthalle ❽

The Hamburger Kunsthalle is the most interesting art gallery in northern Germany. It has a tradition dating back to 1817, when the Kunstverein (friends of the fine arts) was established. The museum opened to the public in 1869. The collection provides a chronological review of European art movements, with an emphasis on 19th-century German Romantics, with works by Caspar David Friedrich and Philipp Otto Runge. A four-storey, cubelike extension, the Galerie der Gegenwart (contemporary gallery), was built in 1996 to a design by the architect O M Ungers. The building is reached by an underground link from the basement of the main gallery.

★ **Morning** *(1808)*
This painting by Philipp Otto Runge was intended to be part of a series called Times of the Day, *but the artist died before completing it.*

Hannah and Simeon in the Temple *(c. 1627)*
Thanks to his mastery of a sense of drama, Rembrandt succeeded in conveying the psychological make-up of his elderly subjects, who have recognized the Saviour in an unspoken message conveyed to the temple by Mary and Joseph.

High Altar of St Petri Church *(1379)*
This painted panel, displaying a wealth of detail, was created by Master Bertram of Minden, the first German artist to be identified by his name. He worked in Hamburg for most of his life.

Cupola Room

Rotunda

Main entrance

Ground floor

Hubertus Wald

★ **The Polar Sea** *(1823–24)*
Caspar David Friedrich's dramatic seascape, with a sinking ship behind the rising ice-floes, is rife with symbolism.

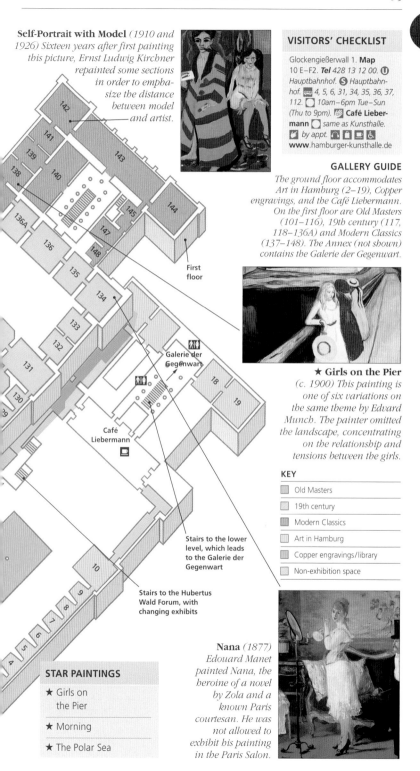

Self-Portrait with Model (1910 and 1926) Sixteen years after first painting this picture, Ernst Ludwig Kirchner repainted some sections in order to emphasize the distance between model and artist.

VISITORS' CHECKLIST

Glockengießerwall 1. **Map** 10 E–F2. **Tel** 428 13 12 00. **Ⓤ** Hauptbahnhof. **Ⓢ** Hauptbahnhof. 🚌 4, 5, 6, 31, 34, 35, 36, 37, 112. ◻ 10am–6pm Tue–Sun (Thu to 9pm). 🍴 **Café Liebermann** ◻ same as Kunsthalle. 📷 by appt. 🎫 🛍 🚻 ♿ **www**.hamburger-kunsthalle.de

GALLERY GUIDE

The ground floor accommodates Art in Hamburg (2–19), Copper engravings, and the Café Liebermann. On the first floor are Old Masters (101–116), 19th century (117, 118–136A) and Modern Classics (137–148). The Annex (not shown) contains the Galerie der Gegenwart.

★ **Girls on the Pier**
(c. 1900) This painting is one of six variations on the same theme by Edvard Munch. The painter omitted the landscape, concentrating on the relationship and tensions between the girls.

First floor

Galerie der Gegenwart

Café Liebermann

Stairs to the lower level, which leads to the Galerie der Gegenwart

Stairs to the Hubertus Wald Forum, with changing exhibits

KEY

◻	Old Masters
◻	19th century
◻	Modern Classics
◻	Art in Hamburg
◻	Copper engravings/library
◻	Non-exhibition space

Nana (1877) *Edouard Manet painted Nana, the heroine of a novel by Zola and a known Paris courtesan. He was not allowed to exhibit his painting in the Paris Salon.*

STAR PAINTINGS

★ Girls on the Pier

★ Morning

★ The Polar Sea

St Nikolai Memorial ⓭

Willy-Brandt-Straße 60. **Map** 10 D4.
Tel 37 11 25. Ⓤ Rödingsmarkt. Ⓢ
Stadthausbrücke. ⮎ 3, 31, 35, 37.
◻ May–Sep: 10am–8pm daily;
Oct–Apr: 10am–5pm daily. ◻ ◻
2pm on Sat and by appointment.
◻ www.mahnmal-st-nikolai.de

The ruins of the church, called Mahnmal St Nikolai, serve both as an attraction and a memorial. The earliest mention of an ecclesiastical building at this location was in 1195. By the middle of the 14th century, the church had been enlarged into a triple-naved hall church; thereafter it remained relatively unchanged for about 500 years. In 1842 it was destroyed during the Great Fire. Afterwards, this house of worship was rebuilt in the Neo-Gothic style from 1846–74. The church's tower, which at 147 m (482 ft) was one of the highest in Germany, was completed in 1874.

During the air raids of 1943, St Nikolai church suffered heavy damage. Due to generous benefactors and public funds, it would have been possible to restore the nearly destroyed tower and the remains of the walls. However, the decision was made not to attempt a complete restoration; instead, in 1960–62, a new St Nikolai church was erected to the northwest of the Außenalster (Harvestehuder Weg No. 114). The ruins of the original church

St Nikolai – a memorial to the victims of war and violence

have become a memorial to the tragic consequences of war and serve as a sober plea for world peace.

The documentation centre adjacent to the church tower has become an international meeting place. Here, exhibits and lectures are held, and visitors learn about the history of the church. A glass elevator, added to the tower in 2005, has become a popular tourist attraction. It takes visitors up 76 m (250 ft) to a viewing platform, which offers a wonderful view of the surrounding area.

St George, the dragon-slayer

The carillon of St Nikolai, which is played every Thursday at noon

Börse ⓮

Adolphsplatz 1. **Map** 10 D3. **Tel** 36 13 83 60. Ⓤ Rathaus. Ⓢ Stadthausbrücke. ⮎ 3, 4, 5, 6, 31, 34, 35, 36, 37. ◻ by appointment.

The Hamburg Börse (stock exchange) was established in 1558 and is considered the oldest institution of its kind in central and northern Europe.

As the trade in goods from the colonies increased, the stock exchange was moved in 1841 from its original location on the Trostbrücke to a new building on Adolphsplatz. Designed by Carl Ludwig Wimmel and Franz Gustav Forsmann in the late-Classical style, this building survived the Great Fire that ravaged the city the following year. The stock exchange is connected to the Rathaus, which was built in 1886–87. Together, these two buildings create an impressive ensemble.

The Börse is run by the Hamburg Chamber of Commerce, which also has its headquarters here. Floor trading of stocks and securities ended in 2003. Only a board hanging on the wall with stock prices testifies to this past activity. Today, traders work in three halls, linked by arcades, using telephones and computers. The Grain Exchange is the only active commodity exchange.

Alsterfleet

Map 9 B5–C3. Ⓤ *Rödingsmarkt.*
Ⓢ *Stadthausbrücke.* 🚌 *31, 35, 37.*

The Alsterfleet is a canal
linking the Binnenalster with
the river Elbe. It runs south
of the Kleine Alster basin
between the Schleusenbrücke
and the Schaartorschleuse,
where it meets the Elbe river
at Baumwall. As early as the
12th century, the water level
of Alster lake was regulated
when the Alsterfleet was
created by straightening out a
previously meandering waterway. Today, the Schaartorschleuse, a lock which was
built in the Alsterfleet in 1967,
serves as a protection against
high tides. It ensures a
constant level of water, which
is about 3 m (10 ft) below
sea-level. In 2003, the city
constructed a pathway
allowing pedestrians to walk
along the Alsterfleet all the
way to the Elbe river.

RED Gallery ⓰

Rödingsmarkt 19. **Map** 9 C4.
Tel 36 90 03 19. Ⓤ *Rödingsmarkt.*
Ⓢ *Stadthausbrücke.* 🚌 *3, 6, 31,
35, 37.* ⏰ *11am–6pm Tue–Sat.*
📷 🎫 📷 **www**.redgallery.de

On the premises once
occupied by the Museum
SteinZeiten, the RED Gallery
was opened in October 2009.
The gallery's name – RED
stands for "Rare Earth Decor"
– is an indication of its unique

Old Hamburg merchant houses on Deichstraße

concept: In fashionable
settings, geological objects
such as fossils, minerals and
gemstones are presented as
"geogenic art". The collection
is truly peerless, and the
pieces of modern art created
from treasures dating back
millions of years can also be
bought. Some exhibits, like
minerals with fascinating
shapes rising some metres
high, have been retained
unchanged. Others have been
given artistic form, and have
been turned into articles of
daily use. Among the latter is
a piece of petrified wood that
functions as a decorative
table top. It has been created
from a trunk of a tree which
is about 220 million years
old. The petrified trunk has
been carved into slabs
and polished.

Deichstraße ⓱

Map 9 C4–5. Ⓤ *Rödingsmarkt.*
Ⓢ *Stadthausbrücke.* 🚌 *3, 4, 6, 31,
35, 37.*

This old merchant street on
Nikolaifleet will be associated
forever with a sad chapter in
the city's history. For it was
here that a fire broke out in
1842, a fire that turned into a
huge conflagration lasting
several days. Starting on 5 May,
in the warehouse of the
house at No. 42, it rapidly
spread to the surrounding
streets and, finally, engulfed
the entire inner city. On
Deichstraße, too, several
houses fell victim to the
raging flames. However, the
majority of these buildings
have since been restored to
their original state.

During a stroll along Deichstraße, you pass by the oldest
extant merchants' houses in
Hamburg. Painted roof beams
still decorate the interior of
No. 25. Bardowicker Speicher
at No. 27, which was built in
1780, is one of the oldest
warehouses in the city. In
spite of the ravages of the
fire, the house at No. 37
survived relatively unscathed;
it is the last merchant house
in Hamburg that has remained
in its original state.

Restaurants have opened up
in several of these old houses;
a few are decorated in traditional Hamburg style. Also
worth seeing are the narrow
channels that run between the
houses and lead to the water.

WASSERTRÄGER HUMMEL

This Hamburg symbol is known far beyond the borders of
the Hanseatic city. A real person stands behind the character
nicknamed "Wasserträger Hummel" (Hummel, the water
carrier): Johann Wilhelm Bentz (1787–1854).
At the time, water carriers supplied clean
drinking water to those who did not live
near the Alster. As Johann went about
his labours, children playing on the
streets taunted the stick-thin water carrier
with cries of "hummel, hummel" ("bee,
bee"). Because he was carrying a heavy
load, Johann could not chase away his
little tormentors. He could only reply,
gruffly, "Mors, Mors" (which in Low
German means "bottom", or in this case,
"little asses"). The slogan of Hamburg's
football fans "Hummel, Hummel! – Mors,
Mors!" derives from this exchange.

**Wasserträger
Hummel**

NEW TOWN

At first glance the name of this part of Hamburg is a bit confusing. After all, this area dates back to the 17th century. An important moment in the development of the New Town occurred when the church of St Michaelis was designated a principal church, considerably enhancing the area's stature. In the 19th century, the old fortifications on the north and west edges of the city

Lessing statue at the Gänsemarkt

were turned into parks and gardens (Alter Botanischer Garten, Große and Kleine Wallanlagen, Elbpark). Locals and visitors alike come here to relax after shopping in the passages between Gänsemarkt and Alsterfleet. Unlike the Old Town, the New Town, which still seems idyllic, has remained a popular place in which to live. Großneumarkt is the area's main square; ringed with restaurants, its weekly market is one of the most colourful in the city.

SIGHTS AT A GLANCE

Historic Streets and Buildings
Bismarck-Denkmal ⑤
Colonnaden ⑩
Gänsemarkt ⑬
Großneumarkt ③
Krameramtswohnungen ②
Passages ⑪

Churches
St Michaelis pp74–5 ①

Museums and Galleries
hamburgmuseum ⑥
Johannes-Brahms-Museum ⑦

Theatres
Hamburgische
  Staatsoper ⑫
Laeiszhalle ⑧

Other Attractions
Fleetinsel ⑨
Heinrich-Hertz-Turm ⑮
Model of Hamburg ④
*Planten un
  Blomen S. 78f* ⑭

SEE ALSO
- **Street Finder** maps 9–10
- **Where to Stay** p178
- **Where to Eat** pp191–2

| 0 metres | 500 |
| 0 yards | 500 |

KEY
▬ Street-by-Street pp70–71
Ⓤ U-Bahn station
Ⓢ S-Bahn station
🚆 Railway station
🚓 Police station
✝ Church
⊠ Post office

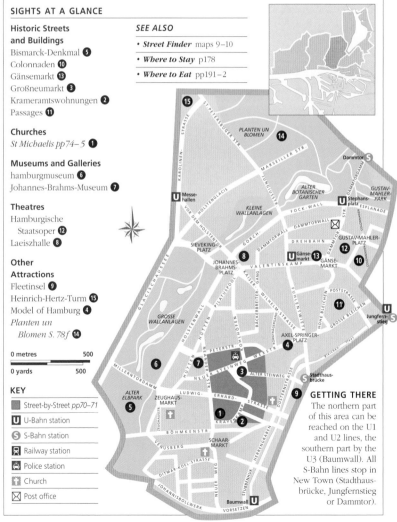

GETTING THERE
The northern part of this area can be reached on the U1 and U2 lines, the southern part by the U3 (Baumwall). All S-Bahn lines stop in New Town (Stadthausbrücke, Jungfernstieg or Dammtor).

◁ The headquarters of Gruner + Jahr with the tower of St Michaelis off to the right *(see pp74–5)*

Street-by-Street: New Town

Statue of Martin Luther

The visual landmark of New Town is the church of St Michaelis, with its 112-m (367-ft) tall steeple. Located close by are the Krameramts-wohnungen. This impressive housing complex was built in the 17th century for widows of small store owners, and it gives an excellent idea of how Hamburg's burghers, the well-off middle class, once lived. After passing by a statue of Zitronenjette, a well-known Hamburg personality, you reach Großneumarkt. This lovely market square was built in the 17th century. With its many restaurants and cafés, it is a favourite with Hamburgers.

Pelikan-Apotheke
This pharmacy has been occupying these rooms since 1651. Its interior is undeniably charming.

NEUER STEINWEG

City Landmark
The sparkling windows of this skyscraper reflect the tower of St Michaelis church.

LUDWIG - ERHARD

★ St Michaelis
The observation platform of this Hamburg landmark offers spectacular views that reach far beyond New Town ❶

★ Krameramts-wohnungen
Widows first dwelled in these two-storey half-timbered houses dating from the 17th century. Today, one of the apartments is open to visitors ❷

| 0 metres | 50 |
| 0 yards | 50 |

KEY

− − − Suggested route

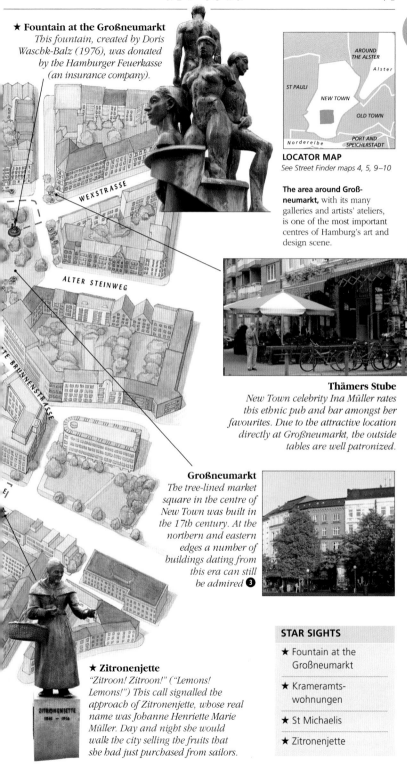

★ **Fountain at the Großneumarkt**
This fountain, created by Doris Waschk-Balz (1976), was donated by the Hamburger Feuerkasse (an insurance company).

LOCATOR MAP
See Street Finder maps 4, 5, 9–10

The area around Groß-neumarkt, with its many galleries and artists' ateliers, is one of the most important centres of Hamburg's art and design scene.

WEXSTRASSE

ALTER STEINWEG

Thämers Stube
New Town celebrity Ina Müller rates this ethnic pub and bar amongst her favourites. Due to the attractive location directly at Großneumarkt, the outside tables are well patronized.

Großneumarkt
The tree-lined market square in the centre of New Town was built in the 17th century. At the northern and eastern edges a number of buildings dating from this era can still be admired ❸

★ **Zitronenjette**
"Zitroon! Zitroon!" ("Lemons! Lemons!") This call signalled the approach of Zitronenjette, whose real name was Johanne Henriette Marie Müller. Day and night she would walk the city selling the fruits that she had just purchased from sailors.

STAR SIGHTS

★ Fountain at the Großneumarkt

★ Krameramts-wohnungen

★ St Michaelis

★ Zitronenjette

St Michaelis ❶

See pp74–5.

Krameramts-wohnungen ❷

Krayenkamp 10. **Map** 9 B4. *Tel 37 50 19 88.* 🚌 *36, 37.* Ⓤ *Baumwall, Rödingsmarkt.* Ⓢ *Stadthausbrücke.* ⬜ *10am–10pm daily (Museum: Apr–Oct: 10am–5pm Tue–Sun; Nov–Mar: 10am–5pm Sat, Sun).* 🎦 *(museum only).*

The Krameramtswohnungen are an ensemble of houses thought to be the last examples of 17th-century Hamburg courtyard apartment dwellings. In 1676 the guild of small shop owners (Kramer-amt) that had existed since the 14th century bought this piece of land across from St Micha-elis and commissioned two-storey half-timbered houses to be built there. The complex was designed for the widows of small shop owners. After the Krameramt was disbanded in 1863, the houses were acquired by the city and con-tinued to be used as homes for the elderly until 1968.

In 1974, the Krameramts-wohnungen were refurbished and some were rented out again. Today you'll find here an art gallery, several shops, a used bookshop, and a restaurant, the Krameramts-stuben, which serves Hamburg specialities. One of the apartments is exhibited by a branch of the hamburg-museum,

Cosy Krameramtsstuben restaurant, part of the Krameramtswohnungen

complete with furnishings that were typical of the age. This is an excellent way to learn how Hamburg's well-off middle class once lived.

Großneumarkt ❸

Map 9 B3. Ⓤ *Rödingsmarkt, Gänsemarkt.* Ⓢ *Stadthausbrücke.* 🚌 *3, 35, 37.*

A popular meeting spot for both Hamburgers and visitors is the Großneumarkt. It was created in the 17th century when the New Town was being built, and was given its name to distinguish it from an older market (called Neumarkt) that was held near the church of St Nikolai. Of the original buildings, there are still a few Neo-Classical houses remaining. The square is especially lively on market days – Wednesdays and Saturday mornings. There are a number of restaurants around the Großneumarkt. Almost all of them offer an opportunity to sit outside and watch the market bustle, when the weather allows. On such days, a beer garden atmosphere springs up on the square. While some restaurants offer inter-national fare, others draw many guests with hearty traditional food. The fountain is an eye catcher.

Fountain on Großneumarkt

Model of Hamburg ❹

Wexstraße 7. **Map** 9 B3. *Tel 428 40 21 94.* Ⓤ *Rödingsmarkt, Gänsemarkt.* Ⓢ *Stadthausbrücke.* 🚌 *3, 35.* ⬜ *10am–5pm Tue–Fri, 1–5pm Sat, Sun.* 🎦

In the exhibition hall of the city's development and environment department (Behörde für Stadtentwicklung und Umwelt), there is a giant 111 sq m (1,200 sq ft) wooden model of Hamburg's inner city on a scale of 1:500. It depicts the area from Övelgönne in the west to Rothenburgsort in the east, and from Harveste-hude in the north to Hafen-City in the south. There is a model of practically every building within this area. Those that already exist are painted white; planned buildings or those under construction are left in plain wood. Streets, greenspaces, and bodies of water are also replicated. This constantly updated model gives a perfect overview of exactly what is being built in the city – and this almost in "real time".

Bismarck-Denkmal ❺

Map 4 E4. Ⓤ *Landungsbrücken, St. Pauli.* Ⓢ *Landungsbrücken.* 🚌 *36, 37, 112.* 📷 *for safety reasons.*

One of the largest monuments in Germany, the statue of Otto von Bismarck (1815–1898) is 34.3 m (113 ft) tall. Standing on a mighty pedestal, the granite figure is 14.8 m (49 ft) high. It depicts the first Chancellor of the German Empire leaning on a sword that itself is 8 m (26 ft) long. Reliefs illustrating scenes from German history embellish the pedestal of the monument. Architect Emil Schaudt and sculptor Hugo Lederer created this impressive memorial between 1903 and 1906. The granite blocks were quarried in the Black Forest (Schwarzwald). Due to its prominent location, this 625-tonne statue can be seen from far away, and especially from the water.

The Johannes-Brahms-Museum in the Peterstraße

hamburg-museum ❻

Holstenwall 24. **Map** 4 E3. **Tel** 42 81 32 23 80. Ⓤ St. Pauli. 🚌 36, 37, 112. ☐ 10am–5pm Tue–Sat, 10am –6pm Sun. 📷 🎫 💻 🛍 ♿ www.hamburgmuseum.de

In 2006, the Museum für Hamburgische Geschichte (Museum of Hamburg History) was renamed the hamburgmuseum. It possesses the largest collection of city history in Germany. As visitors progress through the exhibits, they take a trip back in time through the history of Hamburg – from the construction of Hammaburg castle in the 9th century to the city's development in modern times.

Central themes covered in the hamburgmuseum are the port and shipping as well as industry and trade. Among the many highlights are the ships' models (among them a reproduction of a 14th-century Hanseatic boat) and a model railway.

This red-brick building was designed by the architect Fritz Schumacher in 1922. With its lovely staircase and imposing roofline, the hamburgmuseum is one of Hamburg's most beautiful cultural institutions. The large interior courtyard was

Propeller in front of the hamburgmuseum

covered over with a glass roof in 1989. It is here, in this light-flooded expansive space, that larger exhibits are on display and special events are held.

Johannes-Brahms-Museum ❼

Peterstraße 39. **Map** 9 A3. **Tel** 48 83 27, 41 91 30 86. Ⓤ St. Pauli, Baumwall. 🚌 36, 37, 112. ☐ 10am–5pm Tue–Sun (mid-Oct– mid-Mar: only Tue, Thu, Sat, Sun). 📷 🎫 www.brahms-hamburg.de

Photographs, letters, sheets of music, concert programmes, a piano and a large variety of other mementos documenting the life and work of Johannes Brahms (1833–1897) are presented in this small museum. The Baroque building, which dates from the 18th century and stands under heritage protection, stands not far from the house in which the composer came into the world; it, unfortunately, was destroyed in 1943. The museum contains an interesting small reference library of about 600 volumes and all Brahms' compositions on CD.

Located beside the museum is the Beylingstift, founded in 1751. This picturesque set of half-timbered buildings grouped around an interior courtyard has been painstakingly recreated.

Laeiszhalle ❽

Johannes-Brahms-Platz. **Map** 9 B2. **Tel** 357 66 60. Ⓤ Gänsemarkt, Messehallen. 🚌 3, 5, 34, 35, 36, 112. 💻 www.elbphilharmonie.de/laeiszhalle

At the heart of Hamburg concert life is the Laeiszhalle (pronounced "Leisshalle"), the city's former music hall. Constructed in 1904–08 in magnificent Neo-Baroque style, this concert hall is a wonderful place to enjoy an evening of classical music. Top orchestras, ensembles and soloists can be heard here. The hall is the home of the NDR Symphony Orchestra, the Hamburg Symphony and the Hamburg Philharmonic, among others. Concerts featuring international players are held here, too.

There are two concert halls in the Laeiszhalle: the large hall, with 2019 seats, and the small hall, with 639 seats. On the basement level is the Klingendes Museum (musical museum), where visitors can try their hand at playing one of 100 instruments.

Renaming the museum in 2005 from the Musikhalle to the Laeiszhalle acknowledges the great contribution that was made by a foundation set up by the Laeisz family. This foundation financed the building. The square on which the Laeiszhalle stands was named after famous German composer Johannes Brahms in 1997 on the 100th anniversary of his death.

The hamburgmuseum, where visitors can take a trip through time

St Michaelis ❶

The newest of Hamburg's main churches serves as the city's landmark. Hamburg's skyline would not be the same without the presence of the 132-m (433-ft) high tower, affectionately called "Michel" by Hamburgers. This place of worship has undergone many transformations. The first church, built in 1649–61, was destroyed in 1750 by a strike of lightning; the second (built 1750–62) burned down to the ground in 1906. With the help of numerous donors, the second church was completely rebuilt in 1907–12. The long-standing tradition of the church horn-blowers has endured and can be heard weekdays at 10am and 9pm, and Sundays at noon. The imposing interior of St Michaelis was undergoing an extensive restoration in 2009.

Angel over the pulpit of St Michaelis

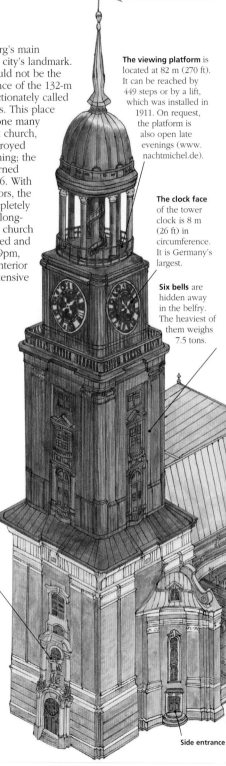

The viewing platform is located at 82 m (270 ft). It can be reached by 449 steps or by a lift, which was installed in 1911. On request, the platform is also open late evenings (www. nachtmichel.de).

The clock face of the tower clock is 8 m (26 ft) in circumference. It is Germany's largest.

Six bells are hidden away in the belfry. The heaviest of them weighs 7.5 tons.

Main Entrance
Above the entrance, Satan writhes at the feet of the Archangel Michael who is shown defeating the Devil with a cross-shaped lance, an allegory for the might of God.

STAR FEATURES

★ Altar

★ Font

★ Pulpit

★ Reliquary

Side entrance

★ Altar
St Michaelis' Neo-Baroque-style altar is an imposing 20 m (65 ft) high. Its centrepiece is a glass mosaic, created in 1911, that shows the risen Saviour with hands raised in blessing.

VISITORS' CHECKLIST

Englische Planke 1a. **Map** 9 B4.
Tel 37 67 80. Ⓤ Baumwall, Rödingsmarkt. Ⓢ Stadthausbrücke.
🚌 36, 37. ☐ **Church and tower** *May–Oct: 9am–7.30 pm daily; Nov–Apr: 10am–5.30 pm daily (entry up to 30 mins. before closing).* 🕆 *10am and 6pm Sun.* 📷 *tower and exhibits.* ♿
www.st-michaelis.de

Organ Detail
On the balcony above the main entrance looms a Steinmeyer organ that was dedicated in 1962. With its 6,665 pipes, it is the largest of the three organs in St Michaelis.

The church balconies are curved and give a sense of movement to the interior of the church.

★ Font
Three angels made of white marble support the font's basin, which is still in use today. The font was made in 1763, in Livorno, and donated to the church by Hamburg merchants who lived there. Along with the reliquary, the font withstood the Great Fire of 1906 unscathed.

★ Pulpit
This elegant pulpit, made of marble, was created after the devastating 1906 fire in the form of a large chalice.

★ Reliquary
Ernst Georg Sonnin, who built the second St Michaelis church, donated this reliquary (1763).

Warehouse façade on Fleetinsel

Fleetinsel 🟒

Map 9 B5–C4. Ⓤ *Rödingsmarkt.*
Ⓢ *Stadthausbrücke.* 🚌 *31, 35, 37.*

More a tongue of land than
an island, Fleetinsel is crossed
by Admiralitätsstraße and lies
between Herrengrabenfleet to
the west and Alsterfleet to the
east. Many of the old warehouses and office buildings
once located here were
destroyed in World War II,
and the area was deserted for
decades. In the 1970s, a few
industrial buildings and office
buildings were constructed.
Then, finally, buildings started
to become more varied.
Today, historic and ultramodern buildings are found
side by side here. Along with
original merchants' offices
and contemporary office
buildings, there are
several galleries, shops, and
cafés as well as the luxurious
Steigenberger Hotel.

Each year, in July, Fleetinsel
changes character entirely
when the Fleetinsel festival
(Duckstein Festival) devoted
to art, culture and the culinary
arts is held here. Over the
course of ten days the area
turns into a bustling piazza
pulsating with energy.
Enthusiastic crowds enjoy
music, street theatre, artists
and comedy. The festival has
become a "must-attend" event
for Hamburgers (see p45).

The Weihnachtsmarkt
(Christmas market) on Fleetinsel is also very popular. The
Fleetinsel can be accessed via
a number of bridges.

Colonnaden 🔟

Map 9 C1–10 D2. Ⓤ *Gänsemarkt,
Stephansplatz, Jungfernstieg.* Ⓢ
Jungfernstieg. 🚌 *4, 5, 34, 36, 112.*

The pedestrianized area
which includes Gustav-Mahler-Platz is one of the most
popular shopping streets in
Hamburg. The Colonnaden
are lined by jeweller's shops,
fashion boutiques, delicatessens and many other
specialist shops with a broad
choice of products that please
every taste. In spite of the
large range of shops and
boutiques, the Colonnaden
offer a more tranquil atmosphere than, for example, the
Mönckebergstraße in Old
Town. The name
Colonnaden stems
from the arcade on
the eastern side of
the street which is
reminiscent of
Italian structures.
On both sides of
the Colonnaden a
number of late 19th
century houses with
Neo-Renaissance
façades remain. On
a shopping expe-
dition, the Colon-
naden are an ideal
addition to areas
like the Jungfern-
stieg or Neuer Wall.
The various res-
taurants and cafés
offering alfresco
dining provide
shoppers with an
opportunity to rest
their feet.

Passages 🕚

Map 9 C1–3, 10 D2. Ⓤ *Gänsemarkt, Jungfernstieg.* Ⓢ *Jungfernstieg.* 🚌 *3, 4, 5, 34, 35, 36.*

The covered arcades and
passages between Rathaus-
markt and Gänsemarkt in the
city centre are a shopping
paradise in any weather.
The variety of shops, which
are mainly small, encompass
a wide range of wares – from
stylish items for the home
to the latest fashions, from
arts-and-crafts to jewellery,
from delicatessens to books.
Cafés and restaurants, found
in every passage, are perfect
places to stop and enjoy a
break from shopping.

Designed as an exclusive
private passage for the
owners of luxury apartments,
the first passage, the
Colonnaden, was built in the
19th century. It is lined with
Neo-Renaissance façades,
lending an Italian flair. One
after the other, new passages
were created, among them
the Gänsemarkt-Passage, the
Galleria and the Bleichenhof.
One of the most spectacular
passages was built in 1980 –
the glass-roofed Hanse-Viertel.
The city now has an extensive
network of covered shopp-
ing streets and they have
become extremely popular
meeting places.

A popular passage in the Hanse-Viertel

The Hamburgische Staatsoper, one of the world's leading stages

Hamburgische Staatsoper ⑫

Große Theaterstraße 25. **Map** 9 C2. **Tel** 35 68 68. Ⓤ Gänsemarkt, Stephansplatz. Ⓢ Dammtor.
🚌 4, 5, 34, 36, 112. **Box office**
🕙 10am–6:30pm Mon–Sat.
www.hamburgische-staatsoper.de

When it was founded in 1678, the Staatsoper (State opera house) was the first opera house in Germany that was open to the public. Previously, only the nobility had been able to enjoy this musical art form. Here was something very new: whoever could pay would be admitted. The location of this opera house changed often; the opera house on Dammtorstraße opened in 1955 with a performance of Mozart's *Magic Flute*. Since then, not only have the "classics" been performed but also more contemporary operas. Today the programme ranges from Handel to Henze.

For many international stars, such as Plácido Domingo, engagements in Hamburg proved to be milestones of their careers. The opera house has also been considered a stronghold of German ballet ever since John Neumeier, a renowned American dancer and choreographer, started a new company here in 1973 along with a ballet centre and integrated ballet school. Most of the operas and ballets are accompanied by the Hamburg Philharmonic State Orchestra.

Pillar on Gorch-Fock-Wall

Gänsemarkt ⑬

Map 9 C2. Ⓤ Gänsemarkt, Stephansplatz. Ⓢ Jungfernstieg.
🚌 4, 5, 34, 36, 112.

The Gänsemarkt is located in the northern part of the New Town, and is one of the liveliest squares in this district. Contrary to its name ("geese market"), geese have never been traded on this almost triangular square. Lined by stores, cafés and restaurants, it is an ideal starting point for a shopping trip. The Jungfernstieg and several passages *(see p76)* converge here.

In 1678, when the Stadttheater (municipal theatre) was built, the square became a focal point of the city's cultural life. After the Stadttheater had been demolished, the Hamburger Nationaltheater was built (1765). Financial problems led to it closing only after a few repertory seasons in 1769. A statue created by Fritz Schaper (1881) commemorates Gotthold Ephraim Lessing, an important literary figure of the Enlightenment who held the post of dramaturge at the Nationaltheater.

The Gänsemarkt boasts interesting architecture from historic red-brick buildings to modern office buildings. The Deutschlandhaus ist a fine example of red-brick architecture. Completed in 1929, it served to house the Ufa-Palast, a cinema equipped with 2600 seats. At this time, the Ufa-Palast was the largest cinema in Europe.

Planten un Blomen ⑭

See pp78–9.

Heinrich-Hertz-Turm ⑮

Lagerstraße 2. **Map** 7 A3.
Ⓤ Sternschanze, Schlump.
Ⓢ Sternschanze. 🚌 35.

Rising up 279.80 m (918 ft), this tower, named after the Hamburg-born physicist Heinrich Hertz (1857–1894), is the city's tallest building. With a nod to the city's landmark church tower, the "Michel" *(see pp74–5)*, the television tower, completed in 1968, is also referred to as "Tele-Michel". At 128 m (420 ft), the observation deck would be the perfect spot from which to enjoy a panoramic view of the city and area, as would the revolving restaurant, 4 m (13 ft) higher up. Unfortunately, since 2001 both the observation deck and the restaurant have been closed indefinitely for repairs.

The Heinrich-Hertz-Turm – Hamburg's tallest building

Planten un Blomen ⑭

Sculpture of a young woman

Located within the former walls of the city, this park, whose Low German dialect name means "plants and flowers", does its name justice. Flower beds delight the eye with their many-coloured blossoms. Idyllic streams and lakes as well as lovingly created theme gardens invite visitors to linger. Those with cultural interests will also find plenty to do here. The multitude of events held in summer include concerts in the music pavilion and water-light-concerts

on the lake. This green girdle on the edge of the New Town continues south into the Wall-anlagen and south-east into the Alter Botanischer Garten.

Rose Garden
More than 300 kinds of roses bloom in this garden. The open-sided pavilion tells visitors all about roses and their care.

① ② ③ ④ ⑤ ⑥

The television tower is Hamburg's tallest building *(see p77).*

ST. PETERSBURGER STRASSE

Waterfalls
Built in 1935, these waterfalls are among the oldest attractions in the park.

★ Water-Light-Concerts
Held on the lake from May to August at 10pm daily (9pm in September), these concerts with colourful fountains and music are a popular attraction.

On the Hamburg-baum, a wooden sculpture carved in 1980, you can discern various figures as well as the Hamburg coat-of-arms.

To Hamburg Trade Fair and U-Bahn Messehallen

KEY

Congress Centrum
  Hamburg ⑫
Greenhouses ⑨
Japanese garden
  with teahouse ⑬
Japanese landscape
  garden ⑪
Medicinal garden ③
Music pavilion ②
Park lake with water-
  light-concerts ⑥
Playground ⑦
Pony riding ⑧
Rose garden ①
Television tower ④
Wallanlagen ⑩
Waterfalls ⑤

★ Japanese Garden with Teahouse
Rocks, waterfalls, plants and ponds are combined into a harmonious ensemble in this tranquil Japanese garden. In the teahouse, the tea ceremony is celebrated.

Japanese Landscape Garden
Yoshikuni Araki designed this garden, which opened in 1988. There seems to be a world of time here to reflect on the elements of nature that have been arranged so artistically.

Greenhouses
Since 1963, plants from many climate zones have thrived in these greenhouses that cover 2,800 sq m (30,000 sq ft).

This monument to Emperor Wilhelm I was unveiled in 1902 on Rathausmarkt and moved to the Wallanlagen in 1930.

0 metres	100
0 yards	100

★ Wallanlagen
Surrounded by greenery, everything you need for outdoor fun is to be found here: there is roller-skating and a mini-golf course. Afternoons from May to August, children can work in a pottery studio.

STAR SIGHTS

★ Japanese Garden with Teahouse

★ Wallanlagen

★ Water-Light-Concerts

ARSEILLER STRASSE

PLANTEN un BLOMEN
ROLLSCHUHBAHN

The Landungsbrücken with a view of the Theater im Hamburger Hafen

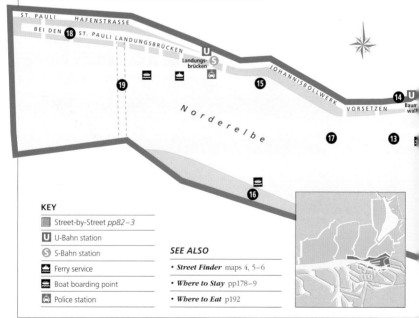

KEY

▪	Street-by-Street *pp82–3*
U	U-Bahn station
S	S-Bahn station
⛴	Ferry service
⛴	Boat boarding point
🚔	Police station

SEE ALSO

- *Street Finder* maps 4, 5–6
- *Where to Stay* pp178–9
- *Where to Eat* p192

PORT AND SPEICHERSTADT

This is the true heart of Hamburg – its port. One of the world's top ten in terms of cargo turnover, it is a universe unto itself, a place where modern technology and painstaking labours complement each other ideally. With the construction of HafenCity, an exciting new area of the city, Hamburg is thrusting into the Elbe river itself. The Elbphilharmonie, a futuristic-looking concert hall, is a symbol of the direction that Hamburg is taking with this project of a century. Speicherstadt, an

Old coffee delivery van

ensemble of red-brick buildings constructed on oak piles, has also seen much change. The area was established at the end of the 19th century, when Hamburg joined the German customs union. It was a place for traders to store their wares duty-free. But since modern container shipping needs less and less warehouse space, media companies, advertising agencies, and several special museums have now found a home in the Speicherstadt among the carpet and spice warehouses.

SIGHTS AT A GLANCE

Museums and Galleries
BallinStadt – Auswandererwelt Hamburg ⑳
Cap San Diego pp98–9 ⑰
Das Feuerschiff ⑬
Maritimes Museum pp86–7 ⑥
Miniatur Wunderland ②

Prototyp Museum ⑫
Rickmer Rickmers pp94–5 ⑮
Speicherstadtmuseum ⑤
Spicy's Gewürzmuseum ③

Historic Buildings
Alter Elbtunnel ⑲
Landungsbrücken ⑱

Theatres
Elbphilharmonie ⑪
Theater im Hamburger Hafen ⑯

Other Attractions
HafenCity pp90–91 ⑦
Hafen-Hochbahn ⑭
Hamburg Cruise Center ⑨
Hamburg Dungeon ④
Kehrwiederspitze ①
View Point ⑩

GETTING THERE
Several S-Bahn lines stop at the Landungsbrücken, as does the U3 underground line, which runs above ground here. To reach HafenCity, take buses Nos. 3, 4 and 6. Once the U4 line is finished (planned for 2012) it will also be accessible via U-Bahn.

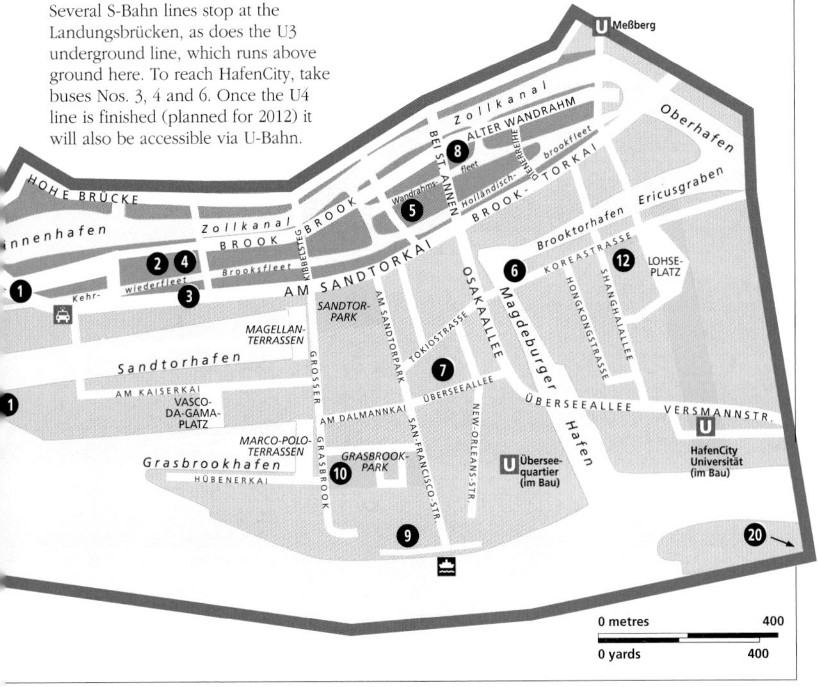

| 0 metres | 400 |
| 0 yards | 400 |

Street-by-Street: Speicherstadt

A typical spice sack

The world's largest warehouse district is located on Brookinsel. Construction began in 1885 as the city prepared for the opening of the freeport of Hamburg in 1888. Dark red brick Neo-Gothic warehouses front the canals which flow here. Inside, precious commodities such as coffee, tea, tobacco, spices and oriental carpets waited to be released from customs. Since the 1980s, Speicherstadt has been undergoing a transformation into an elegant office building and business district.

Miniatur Wunderland has the world's largest model railway **②**

In Hamburg Dungeon dark, dramatic events from the city's past come alive **④**

NIEDER-BAUM-BRÜCKEN

KEHRWIEDER SPITZE

BINNEN-HAFEN

KEHRWIEDER

KEHRWIEDERFLEET

BROOKSFLEE

AM SANDTORKAI

SANDTORHAFEN

Canal Barge Tour
A trip on a barge through the canals is a treat on sunny days and also during evenings, when the warehouses are illuminated.

★ Spicy's Gewürzmuseum
Over 700 exhibits introduce visitors to the world of spices, showing how they are cultivated, processed and packaged. You can also rub many spices between your fingers, smell them, and even taste them **③**

| 0 metres | 400 |
| 0 yards | 400 |

A Typical Warehouse
Warehouses are five to eight storeys tall and equipped with winches. Most are built in the red-brick Neo-Gothic style found in many North German Hanseatic cities.

STAR SIGHTS

★ Kornhausbrücke

★ Speicherstadt-museum

★ Spicy's Gewürzmuseum

HafenCity InfoCenter
A model of HafenCity, Hamburg's newest district, is the heart of this information centre, located in a former boiler house **⑦**

KEY

– – – Suggested route

Deutsches Zollmuseum
This customs museum in Kornhausbrücke, a former customs building, has wonderful exhibits documenting the history of customs over the centuries **8**

LOCATOR MAP
See Street Finder maps 5–6 & 9–10

The Bridges
denote the borders of the port's duty-free zone from which the Speicherstadt has been excluded since 2003.

★ **Kornhausbrücke**
Flanking the entrance to this bridge, named after corn warehouses, are statues of maritime explorers Christopher Columbus and Vasco da Gama by Carl Boerner and Herman Hosaeus (1903).

Dialog im Dunkeln
Blind and seeing-impaired staff guide visitors through pitch-black rooms where recreations of daily occurences, such as street noise, turn into a completely new experience.

★ **Speicherstadtmuseum**
Work equipment and sample wares as well as historic photographs are on display in this museum, which recounts the story of Speicherstadt **5**

Wandrahmsfleet
This canal was named after the Dutch cloth-makers who stretched out their fabric on frames here for it to dry.

Kehrwieder-spitze ❶

Map 9 B5. ⓘ *Baumwall.* 3, 4, 6.

One of the most photographed subjects in the Hanseatic city is this spit of land jutting out from Kehrwieder Island. This is due, above all, to the striking buildings located here, between the Elbe river and the canals, that, when seen together, create a futuristic-looking ensemble. The tower of Columbus Haus is 100 m (328 ft) high, for example.

As the gateway to Speicherstadt and HafenCity, Kehrwiederspitze is an important landmark: everyone who decides to visit the historic warehouses or learn about Europe's biggest construction project will come past here.

The impressive modern architecture on Kehrwiederspitze

Miniatur Wunderland ❷

Kehrwieder 4, Block D. **Map** 9 C5. **Tel** 300 68 00. ⓘ *Baumwall.* 3, 4, 6. ◯ 9:30am–6pm Mon–Fri (Tue to 9pm, Fri to 7pm), 8am–9pm Sat, 8:30am–8pm Sun. 🖼 🚻 📷 www.miniatur-wunderland.de

The eyes of railway fans, both large and small, light up with delight in this extraordinary miniature world. For this is the home of the world's largest computer-controlled model railway, which covers a surface of 1300 sq m (14,500 sq ft). Around 930 trains pull nearly 12,000 wagons along 13 km (8 miles) of tracks through models of real landscapes. Some 3,800 houses, 9,200 cars, 215,000 tiny

people and 230,000 trees are integrated into the model. Push buttons allow visitors to step into the miniature action and make windmills spin or cause spectators to break out into cheers as a goal is scored in the HSV-Arena.

More than six million people have already visited this model railway, which is constantly being expanded and improved upon. With the addition of "Airport", the eighth section was completed in 2011. Other sections depict "Austria", "Switzerland" (both with its gorgeous alpine landscapes), "Hamburg's coast", "Scandinavia" and the "USA" (including natural attractions such as the Grand Canyon and glitzy cities such as Las Vegas). "France" and "Italy" are under construction. The behind-the-scenes tour is highly recommended. Since only a limited number of visitors can be accommodated at any given time, lines can be long. Book your ticket on the Internet in advance.

Miniatur Wunderland – a playground for railway fans

Spicy's Gewürzmuseum ❸

Am Sandtorkai 32, Block L. **Map** 9 C5. **Tel** 36 79 89. ⓘ *Baumwall.* 3, 4, 6. ◯ 10am–5pm Tue–Sun (Jul–Oct: also 10am–5pm Mon). 🖼 www.spicys.de

Fennel and curry powder, cloves, cardamom and saffron, vanilla and cinnamon – in this unusual spice museum, the scent of more than 50 spices perfumes the air. A notice telling visitors to "follow their noses" sends them to the second floor of this warehouse, where the museum has been located since 1993. The museum informs visitors about how to use, properly store, and assess the quality of spices. Photos, maps and displays show where our spices come from and the processes used before they wind up in our food, from cultivation onward. Spicy's is also a hands-on museum in which you are encouraged to touch, smell and even sample the spices on display. Along with the pungent spices themselves, there are a lot of exhibits of tools and other equipment used around the world to gather, process and transport spices.

Hamburg Dungeon ❹

Kehrwieder 2, Block D. **Map** 9 C5.
Tel 36 00 55 20. ⓤ *Baumwall.*
🚌 *3, 4, 6.* ◯ *10am–6pm daily
(Jul, Aug: to 7pm).* 🈳 🈶 🈲
www.the-dungeons.de

Torture, fear and gloom await
visitors to this dark cellar.
Down in these catacombs
the gruesome history of over
2,000 years of Hamburg is
featured, although the city
is not even 1,200 years old.
Even so, this trip through time
offers visitors a great many
horrors, taking them through
the bloodiest periods and
documenting the grisliest
scenes in the city's history.
These include the Inquisition,
the cholera epidemic, the
execution (by beheading) of
the pirate Störtebeker, raging
infernos and a terrible flood –
all of which are experienced
up-close during the 90-minute
interactive tour.

Special effects, eerie background sounds, and clever
lighting increase the ghastly
atmosphere. A visit here is
not recommended for
children under ten years
of age, but older children
and adults will have fun –
as long as their nerves hold
up, of course.

Speicherstadt-museum ❺

St Annenufer 2. **Map** 10 D5.
Tel 32 11 91. ⓤ *Meßberg.* 🚌 *3, 4,
6.* ◯ *Apr–Oct: 10am–5pm Mon–Fri,
10am–6pm Sat, Sun; Nov–Mar:
10am–5pm Tue–Sun.* 🈳 🈶 *11am
Sun (Apr–Oct: also 3pm Sat).* 🖵 🛈
www.speicherstadtmuseum.de

Experience an old as well as
typical part of Hamburg. A
building that is over 100 years
old gives the authentic setting
for this exciting experience. In
this privately operated branch
of the Museum der Arbeit
(Labour Museum; *see p135),*
the history of Speicherstadt
(Dockland) is documented
very lively. Typical work tools
and trade goods – among
them sampling implements
and coffee sacks, tea chests
and balls of rubber – provide

The Brooksbrücke in Speicherstadt, which opened in 1888

a glimpse into the world of
those who worked in this
warehouse district which
once was the largest around
the world. These warehouse
employees appraised the
goods, sorted them and were
responsible for their proper
storage.

This is definitely not your
usual museum collection
where you can look but not
feel. Here, you can also touch
the exhibits and sometimes
even taste them.

The exhibit is accompanied
by historic photographs on
the history of Speicherstadt
and gives an interesting
insight into long-forgotten
occupations that were once
carried out here. Coffee,
cocoa and tea tastings are
held here on a regular basis,
as well as readings by crime
novel authors.

THE PORT'S BIRTHDAY

Hamburgers consider 7 May 1189 to be the birthday of their
port. It was supposedly on this day that Emperor Friedrich
Barbarossa awarded customs-exempt status to ships that
sailed the Elbe river all the way from the city to the North
Sea, guaranteeing the city's merchants the trading privileges
they had long sought. Even when the relevant document
later turned out to be a fake, Hamburgers persist in
believing in its veracity. Every year, on 7 May, thousands
flock to the port to celebrate its birthday. The first gigantic
party was held in 1989 in honour of the port's 800th
anniversary. The highpoints of the three-day festivities are
the parade of tall ships, the dragon boat races and the
tugboat ballet. All along the harbour promenade between
Kehrwiederspitze and the Fish Auction Hall you can listen
to music and see dance, shows and much more.

Hamburg Port's Birthday Bash – the largest port festival in the world

Maritime Museum ❻

International Maritime Museum Hamburg

The International Maritime Museum is the largest seafaring museum in the world. When it was opened in 2008, Prof Peter Tamm's huge private maritime collection found a home fittingly situated at the waterfront in HafenCity. The museum's more than 100,000 exhibits occupy ten storeys or "Decks", as the exhibition spaces are called. Model ships in various scales, navigation instruments, nautical charts, and numerous other items are proof to the important role seafaring plays in the fields of economy, science, history, politics, arts and culture.

Kaispeicher B
The museum in HafenCity.

ROV Cherokee
This remotely operated underwater robot collects data and samples from a depth of up to 1,000 metres.

U-Bahn station Meßberg

★ **Queen Mary 2**
This model of the famous British liner is seven metres long. It took 1200 hours to assemble the around 780,000 LEGO bricks the model ship is made of.

STAR FEATURES

- ★ High-Tech-Globe
- ★ Queen Mary 2
- ★ Wapen von Hamburg III

Lighthouse
The original lighthouse (»Roter Sand«, 1883–85) at the mouth of the Weser river was in operation until 1986.

Sandtorkai ferry

Cruise ships
Visitors are bound to get itchy feet at the sight of these model ships – the luxury liners seem to sail into the blue horizon.

Deck 10 Events and special exhibitions

★ High-Tech-Globe
Geological processes and climate scenarios are projected onto the outer membrane.

Deck 9 The Big World of Little Ships

Deck 8 Art Gallery and Treasure Chamber

Deck 7 Ocean Expeditions

Deck 6 Trade and Travel

Deck 5 Navies of the World

Deck 4 Service on Board

Deck 3 Shipbuilding

Deck 2 Ships under Sail

Deck 1 Explorers of the World (Navigation)

Deck 0 Foyer and Museum Shop

Entrance

★ Wapen von Hamburg III
This convoy ship (1722) protected the citizens of Hamburg against pirate attacks. On a scale of 1:5, the museum's largest model ship represents one historic gem of Hanseatic admiralty.

Astrolabe
Together with other navigation instruments, this goniometer – a copy of a 17th-century original – made orientation on the high seas possible.

HafenCity ●

See pp90–91.

Deutsches Zollmuseum ●

Alter Wandrahm 16. **Map** 10 E4–5.
Tel 428 20 39 11. ● *Meßberg.*
▦ *3, 4, 6.* ○ *Tue–Sun 10am–5pm.*
▨ ▧ www.zoll.de

Is it possible for a subject as dull as customs and excise to be exciting? The Deutsches Zollmuseum (German customs museum) proves it can be: On two floors, the history of customs is traced back into the ancient past in a very lively way. After all, smugglers have shown a great deal of ingenuity in trying to get around customs regulations. Evidence of their creativity is seen in the various objects displayed, which have been used for smuggling: cocaine has been hidden in golf clubs or artificial legs, cigarettes in hats and marijuana woven into wooden baskets.

Other sections of the museum are dedicated to product piracy and customs officers' uniforms. The various customs responsibilities, from the prevention of drug smuggling to environment and consumer protection, are also represented.

Hamburg Cruise Center, where the world's largest cruise ships dock

Hamburg Cruise Center ●

Großer Grasbrook 19. **Map** 5 C5. ▦ *3, 4, 6.* www.hamburgcruisecenter.eu

When luxury liners such as the *Queen Mary II* or the *Freedom of the Sea* pay Hamburg the honour of a visit, they are welcomed by the loudspeakers of Willkommhöft *(see p139)*, followed by crowds of spectators at Hamburg Cruise Center, the city's cruise ship terminal (Kreuzfahrtterminal). In 2010, a total of 104 ocean giants carrying 250,000 passengers steered for the terminal, which had been enlarged in 2006 with a second hall nearby in order to accommodate two large cruise ships at the same time. There is also a smaller terminal in Altona *(see p149)*.

Hamburg Cruise Center is not yet complete, however. Its current setup is temporary until a new section for overseas ships opens in 2012. For this reason, the second hall was designed as a modular construction.

The Cruise Shop located next to the terminal sells travel requisites and souvenirs. The café is frequented by cruise ship passengers and strollers alike.

View Point ●

Map 5 C5. ▦ *3, 4, 6.*

There is a fantastic view of the port from View Point observation platform. When it opened in 2004, it quickly proved to be a magnet for visitors. Up to 25 people at a time are allowed on the observation platform to survey HafenCity. There is often a crowd, since this is also the best vantage point for watching the luxury cruise liners dock at the nearby Hamburg Cruise Center.

When designing View Point, the architects borrowed elements from periscope design. As the HafenCity development grows, the View Point, is constantly moved along its set of rails.

Elbphilharmonie ●

Dalmannkai. **Map** 5 B5.
● *Baumwall.* ▦ *3, 4, 6.*

Once it is completed in 2012, the Elbphilharmonie (Elbe Philharmonic Orchestra) will be one of the architectural attractions in HafenCity. Here, classical music, 21st-century music and other serious music will have a striking new performance space. The Elbphilharmonie has been conceived of as an 110-m (360-ft) high cultural "lighthouse" which will attract many from the surrounding areas. Under a glass tent-like construction that resembles a wavy seascape, two concert halls are being built with approximately 2,150 and 550 seats a piece,

View Point, which offers amazing port views

as well as a high-end hotel and luxury apartments.

The Elbphilharmonie is being built atop Kaispeicher A (the warehouse on quay A), a 37-m (120-ft) tall structure dating from 1963–66. The original façade will remain intact. As conceived by the Swiss architectural firm Herzog & de Meuron, the port's trading past and its new cultural identity will be united in the building's design.

Visitors will travel up an elevator from the parking levels in the warehouse to the roof. Here, a meeting place for all Hamburg is planned: an admission-free plaza with an arching multi-planed roof, from where the public will have great views over the port. The plaza will lead into the foyer of the Elbphilharmonie.

Concert seasons are scheduled to start in 2012. A pavilion on the Magellan-Terrassen (see p91) houses a model of the large concert hall on a scale of 1:10.

On 28 and 29 May 2010 Hamburgers topped out the city's most recent landmark.

Prototyp Museum **⓬**

Shanghaiallee 7. **Map** 6 D4. **Tel** 39 99 69 68. **Ⓤ** Meßberg. **░** 3, 4, 6. **◯** Tue–Sun 10am–6pm. **▨ ✎ ⌂ ▣** www.prototyp-hamburg.de

This museum, which opened in 2008, is dedicated to the fascination of automobiles. The exhibits are displayed on three floors. The emphasis lies on German racing and sports cars dating from the 1940s to the 1960s.

Motorsport aficionados are enthralled by the museum's inventive mode of presentation: The venue exudes the ambience of a meeting place for automobile enthusiasts rather than the atmosphere of a museum; in addition to the 50 or so cars that are on display – from Borgward to Volkswagen and Mercedes to Porsche – interactive displays draw visitors into the world of car racing. The driving simulator in a Porsche 356 Speedster is

The coast guard cutter *Oldenburg* alongside the Deutsches Zollmuseum

fascinating. A soundbox, in which the genuine road noise of historic racing cars can be heard, displays embedded into the floor and a library which contains photographs of racing drivers, are among the further attractions at the Prototyp Museum.

Das Feuerschiff **⓭**

City-Sporthafen. **Map** 9 B5. **Tel** 36 25 53. **Ⓤ** Baumwall. **Ⓢ** Landungsbrücken. **Restaurant ◯** 11am–10pm daily. **Turmbar ◯** 11am–1am daily. www.das-feuerschiff.de

Das Feuerschiff offers a unique kind of maritime ambience. In the middle of the port, this former lightship

(floating lighthouse) welcomes guests who come to enjoy food and drinks in the restaurant and bar (the Turmbar). Another gathering spot is the pub in the machine room, where jazz is played on "Blue Mondays" after 8:30pm and on Sundays after 11am. Cabarets and readings are also staged here.

Built in 1952, this lightship was a navigation aid along the English Channel before being replaced by a larger vessel in 1989. It was sold and rebuilt and has been anchored in front of City-Sporthafen since 1993. Guests can also spend the night in one of several cabins which have been kept in their original state.

DIALOGUE IN THE DARK

"An exhibition to discover the unseen" – this is the motto of Dialog im Dunkeln (Dialogue in the Dark) – a world of experiences located in the Speicherstadt at Alter Wandrahm 4. The idea behind this project, which was established in 2000, sounds simple enough: blind staff members lead visitors in small groups through the pitch-black rooms of an exhibit in which there is literally nothing to see. The tour does, however, open up a world of scents, sounds and textures –

A new level of sensory experience can be reached here

the world of the blind and seeing impaired – as visitors smell, listen and touch. The guides ensure that no one loses their way. During "Dinner in the Dark", visitors' taste buds and table manners are keenly tested. The exhibition is only open for tours (9am–5pm Tue–Fri, 10am–8pm Sat, 11am–7pm Sun), which must be arranged ahead of time by calling 0700 44 33 20 00. Be sure to book an English-speaking guide.

HafenCity ❼

Maritime flair shapes this new city district being built on 155 hectares (380 acres). A "city within a city", it will include apartments for 12,000 people, 40,000 workplaces, cultural institutions and leisure facilities.

Banner, HafenCity

HafenCity will expand the Hamburg inner city by approximately 40 per cent. Nowhere else does the Hanseatic city show its dynamism more than here. Construction began in 2001, and completion is planned for 2020–2025. The rapid progress being made can be seen in HafenCity InfoCenter in the Kesselhaus.

★ Sandtorhafen
Sandtorhafen is the oldest harbour basin in Hamburg. Along Sandtorkai (Sandtor quay), pontoons will be built and traditional Hamburg ships will be docked here.

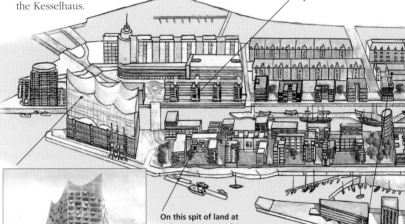

On this spit of land at Dalmannkai, one of the most interesting residential areas in HafenCity is being built. Young and old, families and singles – the range of inhabitants will be diverse.

At Strandkai multi-storey buildings will rise into the sky, offering a fantastic view of the Elbe river, port area, HafenCity and all of Hamburg.

Elbphilharmonie
When the Elbe Philharmonic Orchestra's new home atop the warehouse Kaispeicher A is finished, the city will boast a new concert hall (see pp88–9).

STAR SIGHTS

★ Kaispeicher B

★ Kesselhaus

★ Sandtorhafen

★ Kesselhaus
The HafenCity Info-Center is located in a red brick building built in 1886–87. A detailed scale-model of HafenCity gives visitors a good over-view of the current status of this amazing development.

★ Kaispeicher B
The oldest preserved warehouse in HafenCity has been home to the Maritimes Museum (see pp86–7) since 2008. The exhibition showcases more than 100,000 objects related to shipping. The exhibits are presented on ten levels.

The Science Center will bring an aquarium and a science theatre to the Überseequartier, stimulating attractions for both young and old.

To the east of Magdeburger Hafen are many historic buildings. Here, along with squares and boulevards, a new HafenCity university will be established.

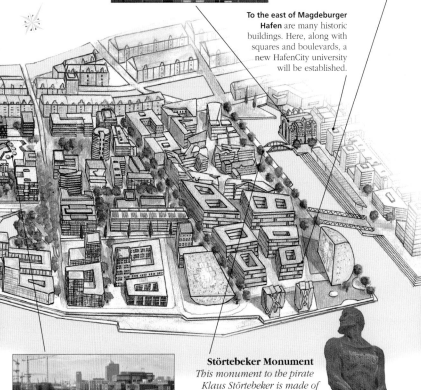

Störtebeker Monument
This monument to the pirate Klaus Störtebeker is made of roughly two tons of bronze and was unveiled in Magdeburger Hafen in 1982. Since 2006, this sculpture by Hansjörg Wagner stood in Großer Gras-brook. After the completion of Maritimes Museum it was re-located back to its former site across from Kaispeicher B.

Traditionsschiffhafen at Sandtorkai
Since 2008, about 20 ancient steamers, motorboats and sailers are anchored in front of the Magellan-Terrassen.

| 0 metres | 100 |
| 0 yards | 100 |

The elevated Hafen-Hochbahn port railway, which provides an impressive view of the port

Hafen-Hochbahn ⑭

Map 4 E–F5, 5 A4–B3.
Ⓤ Rödingsmarkt, Baumwall, Landungsbrücken.

In 1912, after six years of construction, the city's first underground line opened. This meant that Hamburg became the second city in Germany, after Berlin, to have an underground railway. More lines followed. One of the most interesting stretches in the entire Hamburg public transport system is the Hafen-Hochbahn (elevated port railway). This is the section of the U3 line that runs between Rödingsmarkt and Landungsbrücken U-Bahn stations.

A ride on this stretch of the railway offers passengers a wonderful view over Hamburg's bustling port. Starting from Rödingsmarkt station, the train crosses slowly over the bridges along Binnenhafen. Between Baumwall and Landungsbrücken stations, the view opens up to show the harbour. The trip in the opposite direction is just as nice. Just bear in mind that the sightseeing tour ends after three stations, when the U-Bahn goes underground once again.

Rickmer Rickmers ⑮

See pp94–5.

Theater im Hamburger Hafen ⑯

Norderelbstraße 6. **Tel** 42 10 00.
Ⓤ Landungsbrücken. Ⓢ Landungsbrücken. 🚌 www.loewenkoenig.de

Without a doubt, Hamburg is the musical theatre capital of Germany. One of the most popular stages is a theatre built in an old shipyard in 1995, the Theater im Hamburger Hafen. This tent-like building, located on the south side of the port, covers over 5,000 sq m (54,000 sq ft). When the theatre was built, the architects made sure that none of the

1,406 seats on the parquet floor was more than 25 m (80 ft) from the stage. The balcony holds a further 624 seats. Through the glass-fronted façade of the foyer, theatre-goers enjoy a marvellous view of Hamburg's skyline – especially impressive at night when everything is lit up. Bars and the Skyline Restaurant offer a first-class experience. A boat that departs from Landungsbrücken shuttles people to and from the theatre across the Elbe. The shuttle-boat fare is included in the ticket price.

The Lion King has been playing at the Theater im Hamburger Hafen since 2001. This Disney spectacle, with its compelling music, stunning staging, opulent lighting design and inventive costumes, draws young and old alike into its magical African world.

The Theater im Hamburger Hafen, located in an old shipyard

Cap San Diego ⓱

See pp98–9.

Landungs-
brücken ⓲

Between Fischmarkt and Niederhafen.
Map 4D–E5. Ⓤ *Landungsbrücken.*
Ⓢ *Landungsbrücken.* 🚌 *112.*

Hamburg would not be
Hamburg without the
Landungsbrücken (landing
bridges). Every traveller
comes here at least one time
to stroll along the swaying
pontoons, breathe in the sea
air and allow the smells of the
port to linger in their nostrils.
The Landungsbrücken con-
sists of ten floating pontoons,
measuring 700 m (2,300 ft)
altogether. The long passenger hall, which forms part of
the complex, was built in
1907–09. The tower at the
east side of the hall displays
the water level and the time,
with a ship's bell ringing
every half hour.

The first Landungsbrücken
were built in 1839 as a place
for steamships to dock before
heading overseas. During
World War II, the complex
was heavily damaged, so
in 1953–55 new pontoons
were built.

Numerous restau-
rants, bars and food
stalls are found along
the Landungsbrücken,
perfect for a break.
This is the place
where round trips
of the harbour,
offered by various
tour companies,
begin and end.
The passenger
ferries also depart
from here *(see
pp240–41).*
Displays show
the development

**Statue on the
harbour promenade**

of the Port of Hamburg, and
accordion players, souvenir
stands and boat companies
touting their tours add to the
colourful hustle and bustle
here. To cap it all off, a visit
to the museum ship *Rickmer
Rickmers (see pp94–5)*,
moored at Fiete-Schmidt-
Anleger, is an absolute must
for visitors.

The Landungsbrücken with floating pontoons – a symbol of the city

Alter Elbtunnel ⓳

An den Landungsbrücken.
Map 4 D4. Ⓤ *Landungsbrücken.*
Ⓢ *Landungsbrücken.* 🚻 *for
pedestrians and cyclists: 24 hrs daily;
for vehicles: 5:30–8pm Mon–Fri.*
♿ *for vehicles.*

The Alter Elbtunnel (the old
tunnel under the Elbe), which
links the districts of St Pauli
and Steinwerder, is also part
of the Landungsbrücken
complex. When it opened in
1911, the 4.26-km (2.65-
mile) long tunnel was a
sensation. Since the
opening of the new A7
motorway tunnel in 1975,
the old one has become
a nostalgic place. The
tunnel was built as a way
for workers living on the
north side of the Elbe to
get to the shipyards on the
south side, where they
were employed.
Elevators transport
visitors 23.5 m (77 ft)
down into the tunnel's
depths. Drivers also must
take their cars on the
elevators, since there
are no access ramps.
Then, after walking or
driving underneath the
Elbe, they go topside again
by elevator.
The two tunnels are 6 m
(20 ft) in diameter and are
decorated with light-blue
ceramic tiles. Glazed terracotta reliefs depict subjects
associated with the Elbe.
The tunnel is undergoing
an extensive restoration until
2013 but will be in operation.

BallinStadt –
Auswandererwelt
Hamburg ⓴

Veddeler Bogen 2. **Tel** *31 97 91 60.*
Ⓢ *Veddel.* 🚌 *34.* 🚻 🕐 *Apr–Oct:
10am–6pm daily; Nov–Mar: 10am–
4:30pm daily.* ♿ www.ballinstadt.de

BallinStadt opened its doors
in July 2007. The exhibit is
dedicated to the fate of more
than five million people who
emigrated from their homes
in Hamburg to North America
between 1850 and 1934.
Along with the themes of
departure, the sea journey
and arrival in New York, the
exhibition also documents the
reasons why people emigrated
and the initial experiences of
the emigrants in their new
homeland. The complex is
located on the grounds of a
historic emigrant city built
by Albert Ballin, the former
General Director of the
HAPAG shipping company.

A glimpse into the Alter Elbtunnel
under the Elbe river

Rickmer Rickmers ⑮

This three-masted sailing ship *Rickmer Rickmers* is 97 m (318 ft) long, and was built at the Rickmers shipyard in Bremerhaven in 1896. On its first journey it was sent to Hong Kong, where it was loaded with rice and bamboo for the return trip. Later, the freighter was used in the saltpetre trade with Chile. In 1912, the Portuguese Navy commandeered the ship and used it as a school ship until 1962, quartering cadets where freight was once stored. The "Windjammers for Hamburg" association acquired the ship in 1983 and completely restored it. Since 1987, this vessel has been moored as a museum ship at Landungsbrücken.

Rickmer Rickmers as a ship-in-bottle

Washroom
As was the case on most ships, there was not much space here for personal ablutions – even the captain had to make do with the basics.

Deck
In order to protect the wooden deck, the rule on board is "No stiletto heels allowed".

Figurehead
Voyagers on the world's oceans tend to be a bit superstitious, and not without reason. The figurehead was supposed to protect the ship against bad luck and to watch over the ship's course. The model for this figurehead was the four-year-old grandson of the founder of Rickmers shipyards.

★ Cinema
In the cinema, museum visitors can watch films about the history of maritime travel, including some famous ships such as the Gorch Fock.

The heavy anchor chain increases the effective-ness of the anchor.

The keelson (inside keel) runs the length of the ship and strengthens the keel.

★ Map Room
The ship's captain needed precise navigation instruments and nautical charts to find his way on the high seas. A selection of navigational aids are on display in the map room.

VISITORS' CHECKLIST

St Pauli Landungsbrücken (Brücke 1). **Map** 4 E5.
Tel 319 59 59. ⓤ Baumwall.
Ⓢ *Landungsbrücken.*
◯ *10am–6pm daily.* 🌀 🍴
www.rickmer-rickmers.de

Doctor's Office
Rickmer Rickmers *was often at sea for months on end, so a ship's doctor was on board, who was responsible for the crew's health. Great store was set on the quality of the medical equipment and the medicines carried on board.*

The museum has a permanent exhibition that includes nautical instruments and historic pictures.

The life-saver, a key part of a ship's safety equipment, serves here as decoration.

The restaurant on board serves light meals daily from 11am.

STAR FEATURES

★ Cinema

★ Map Room

★ Officer's Mess

★ Officer's Mess
This elegantly decorated officer's mess was a place for the ship's officers to dine and relax.

Cap San Diego ⑰

Frequency dial,
Cap San Diego

The world's largest museum ship, the *Cap San Diego* was built in Hamburg and launched in 1961. Her seaworthiness is demonstrated when she makes excursions to Cuxhaven and Kiel or takes part in great parades. During the rest of the year, this general cargo vessel, which once sailed between Europe and the east coast of South America, lies anchored at its dock at the Überseebrücke. You can get a good idea of what it was like to live on board from the museum's displays, or by having a meal in the restaurant. Rooms can be rented for parties, concerts, exhibitions and overnight stays. Not only young guests are regularly invited to "Klabauternacht" (goblin night). During these spooky evenings, maritime history comes alive.

★ **Permanent Exhibits**
The exhibition "A Suitcase Packed With Hope" documents the fate of emigrants who left Europe from Hamburg's port.

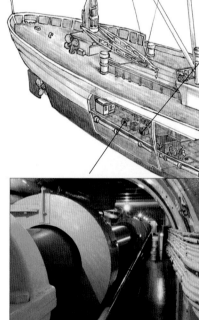

★ **Shaft Tunnel**
The shaft tunnel is a very narrow room that houses the shaft drive. Visitors can walk through the 40-m (130-ft) long tunnel, which links the machine room with the ship's propeller.

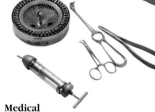

Medical Instruments
The Cap San Diego *had its own sick bay so that those who fell ill on the high seas could be properly treated.*

◁ The tanker *Loch Rannoch* in dry dock

★ Radio Room
The radio room in the Cap San Diego is in its original condition. Thanks to the help of former marine radio operators, the equipment – such as the receiver or the USW – is kept in top condition.

VISITORS' CHECKLIST

Museum ship *Cap San Diego*, Überseebrücke. **Map** 9 A5. *Tel* 36 42 09. Ⓤ *Baumwall*. Ⓢ *Landungsbrücken*. ⬜ 10am–6pm daily. ⬜ ⬜ ⬜ ⬜ ⬜ www.capsandiego.de

The Bridge
The bridge is the most important place on a ship. The radar equipment and the steering column, with its compass and automatic pilot, are found here, as is the speaking-tube linking the bridge with the captain's cabin and the machine room.

★ Salon
A library and bar are located in this elegant salon, as well as the dining room. It was designed by Hamburg architect Cäsar Pinnau.

On-board cranes meant that the *Cap San Diego* was not dependent on the infrastructure of the ports where it docked.

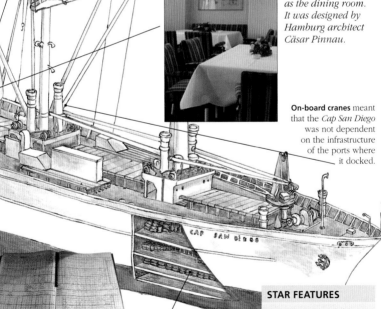

Ship's Log
The ship's log, which documented the ship's journeys, is stored in the chart room along with the maritime charts.

The *Cap San Diego*
has five cargo hatches. Two rooms below deck are used for cold storage.

STAR FEATURES

★ Permanent Exhibits

★ Radio Room

★ Salon

★ Shaft Tunnel

ST PAULI

Once an unloved suburb, today St Pauli probably is Hamburg's best-known district. In the 18th century, booths for an annual fair were set up on Spielbudenplatz. Soon after, workers in the "world's oldest profession" moved in, and seamen recovered from their journeys in the arms of attractive women, leaving part of their wages behind on the bedside table. Even today, the erotic dominates the scene. And yet, the red light is beginning to fade – St Pauli is undergoing a transformation. The Reeperbahn (the red-light district) of the future will become more mainstream and less the exclusive province of a subculture. The first step was the rebuilding of Spielbudenplatz. Popular attractions such as the Schmidt Theater will be preserved by the developers of the "new" St Pauli, and the local football club, FC St. Pauli, will certainly survive.

Sculpture of a fisherwoman

SIGHTS AT A GLANCE

Museums and Galleries
Beatlemania 10
Harry's Hafenbasar 5
Panoptikum 1
U-434 6

Streets and Parks
Hafenstraße 8
Sternschanzenpark
  and Water Tower 11

Theatres
Schmidt Theater
  and Schmidts Tivoli 2
TUI Operettenhaus 3

Other
Attractions
Davidwache 4
FC St. Pauli pp110–11 9
St Pauli Fish Market 7

SEE ALSO

• *Street Finder* maps 3–4
• *Where to Stay* pp179–80
• *Where to Eat* p193

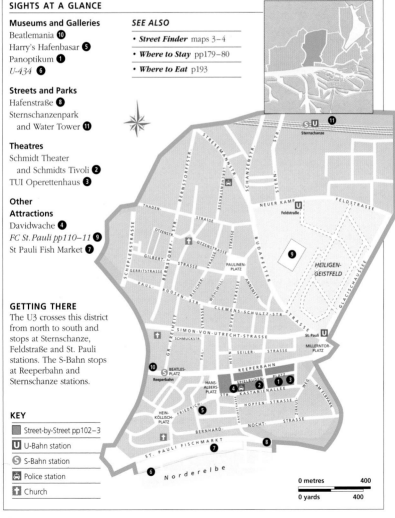

GETTING THERE
The U3 crosses this district from north to south and stops at Sternschanze, Feldstraße and St. Pauli stations. The S-Bahn stops at Reeperbahn and Sternschanze stations.

KEY

▨	Street-by-Street pp102–3
U	U-Bahn station
S	S-Bahn station
▥	Police station
✚	Church

0 metres	400
0 yards	400

◁ **A Caribbean feeling at the beach of the Elbe river on warm, sunny days**

Street-by-Street: The Reeperbahn

Star in front of Café Keese

This district of Hamburg is one of the most famous in Germany, thanks to the Reeperbahn (red-light district), the fish market, the actor Hans Albers and FC St. Pauli football club. Here, the alternative culture scene has space to unfold. Bizarre stores, noisy pubs, curious museums and ribald theatres all contribute to St Pauli's appeal. The St. Pauli Museum (Davidstraße 17; www.st-pauli-museum.com) recounts the district's illustrious history. Many events are held on the renovated Spielbudenplatz, among them concerts, theatrical performances and markets.

★ Panoptikum
In this wax museum, more than 120 well-known figures are on display: politicians, actors, pop stars, scientists, and athletes **1**

★ TUI Operettenhaus
This venue is one of the largest musical theatres in Hamburg. Shows like Cats *or* Mamma Mia *have attracted millions of visitors for years.*

KASTANIENALLEE

BEIM TRICHTER

TAUBENSTRASSE

REEPERBAHN

SPIELBUDEN-PLATZ

Spiel-budenplatz
The two moveable stages at both ends of the square can be illuminated spectacularly at night.

Tanzende Türme
The two towers – striking architectural landmarks designed by Hadi Teherani – are reminiscent of a dancing couple.

Note:
North is the **bottom** side of this map.

N

Café Keese
Café Keese is a hub of Hamburg's nightlife and music scene. The Hotel Café Keese resides above this popular gathering place.

0 metres 50

0 yards 50

★ Schmidt Theater
With vaudeville, comedy and live music, the Schmidt Theater is synonymous with St Pauli's colourful culture ❷

Schmidts Tivoli
This intimate musical theatre has long gained recognition for hosting fancy shows ❷

LOCATOR MAP
See Street Finder maps 3–4

KEY

– – – Suggested route

KASTANIENALLEE

FRIEDRICHSTR.

DAVIDSTRASSE

HANS-ALBERS-PLATZ

REEPERBAHN

REEPERBAHN

Hans-Albers-Statue
Hans Albers was a beloved Hamburg actor and singer. His bronze likeness was created in 1986 by Jörg Immendorff.

Herzblut St. Pauli is one of the most ethnic bars/restaurants in the Reeperbahn. Maritime, St Pauli and football paraphernalia adorn its interiors.

Davidwache
The most famous police station in Germany was built in 1913–14 and now stands under heritage protection ❹

St. Pauli Theater
Following a repositioning, the performances of classical and modern plays staged in this theatre wittingly take their cue from New York City Broadway shows.

STAR SIGHTS

★ Panoptikum

★ Schmidt Theater

★ TUI Operettenhaus

Panoptikum ❶

Spielbudenplatz 3. **Map** 4 D4. **Tel**
31 03 17. ⓤ St. Pauli. Ⓢ Reeperbahn.
🚌 36, 37, 112. ⬜ 11am–9pm Mon–
Fri, 11am–noon Sat, 10am–9pm Sun.
🔲 🔲 🔲 **www**.panoptikum.de

The raucous and highly original Schmidt Theater

Hamburg's Panoptikum is the oldest and largest wax figure museum in Germany. Over 120 personalities from the worlds of politics, culture, science, showbusiness and sport are on display, each dressed in the appropriate garb. Anyone who is anyone can be seen here, from Napoleon to Madonna, Lady Di to Albert Einstein, Cleopatra to Elvis Presley, or from Michael Schumacher to Romy Schneider playing the role of Sisi. Of course unique Hamburgers such as Uwe Seeler and Hans Albers are not forgotten either. Two new figures are added each year. Among the most recent is Daniel Radcliffe as Harry Potter. An audio tour provides etailed information about each figure.

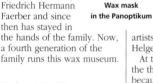

Wax mask in the Panoptikum

Even when the face of St Pauli is constantly changing, the Panoptikum is an institution that remains the same. It was opened in 1879 by Friedrich Hermann Faerber and since then has stayed in the hands of the family. Now, a fourth generation of the family runs this wax museum.

Schmidt Theater and Schmidts Tivoli ❷

Spielbudenplatz 24–25 and 27–28.
Map 4 D4. **Tel** 31 77 88 99.
ⓤ St. Pauli. Ⓢ Reeperbahn. 🚌 36,
37, 112. 🔲 🔲 **www**.tivoli.de

Raucous entertainment, comedy and musical theatre are the calling cards of the Schmidt Theater. Its mission to be different showed on its very first performance starting on 8/8/1988 at 8:08pm. The cornerstone of the terrific success of this stage is the owner and actor Corny Littmann (alias Herr Schmidt) along with Ernie Reinhard (alias Lilo Wanders).

The "Schmidt" became well-known throughout the country due to monthly television broadcasts of the Schmidt Show, which started in the early 1990s. The theatre gained a reputation as a crucible for talent, and it proved to be a springboard for the careers of artists such as Rosenstolz and Helge Schneider.

At the beginning of 2004, the theatre had to close because the building was in such disrepair it had to be torn down. In summer 2005 (on 8 August, naturally), the theatre reopened and celebrated with a colourful gala. Some of the funds for the new building were raised by finding seat sponsors, and many prominent Hamburgers purchased seats. Now there are 400 seats serving a very mixed audience in the restored theatre.

Schmidts Tivoli opened next door in 1991. It is known for its musicals, which are created in-house from the first spark of an idea to the premiere. A long-running hit was the 1950s revue *Fifty-Fifty*; the St Pauli musical *Heiße Ecke* is legendary with more than one million spectators.

The Reeperbahn – once thought to be "the world's most sinful mile"

TUI Operetten-haus ❸

Spielbudenplatz 1. **Map** 4 D4.
Tel 31 11 70. Ⓤ *St. Pauli.* Ⓢ *Reeper-bahn.* 🚌 *36, 37, 112.* 📠
www.tuioperettenhaus.de

Up until World War II, a theatre once stood here where this operetta house now stands. Here, in 1912, the hit song well-known to most Germans *Auf der Reeperbahn nachts um halb eins* (On the Reeper-bahn at Twelve-thirty at Night) was first played at the stage. Music is of course an important feature of the Ope-rettenhaus – after all, it is one of Hamburg's most important music stages.

Starting in 1986, one of the world's most successful musicals – *Cats* – was staged here for a total of 15 years. Following in the footsteps of this huge success was a German version of *Mamma Mia*. This musical brought the top hits of the Swedish group ABBA to the big stage, and was an enormous box-office success since its premiere in November 2002. This production was the first non-English version of the musical, although the songs themselves were sung in English.

However, in September 2007, *Mamma Mia* was performed for the last time. It was replaced by a musical by German rock star Udo Jürgens called *Ich war noch niemals in New York* (I Have Never Been to New York), which had its world premiere in December 2007. Since Decem-ber 2010, *Sister Act* has enter-tained audiences with the tumultuous story about a lounge singer who is chased by gangsters and goes into hiding at a Roman convent.

Davidwache ❹

Ecke Spielbudenplatz / Davidstraße.
Map 4 D4. Ⓤ *St. Pauli.* Ⓢ *Reeper-bahn.* 🚌 *36, 37, 112.*

The Davidwache is home to Hamburg's police station No. 15. The building was constructed in 1913–14 by Fritz Schumacher in the style

The TUI Operettenhaus, with its eye-catching façade

of a middle-class Hamburg home. About 120 police officers are stationed here, working in four shifts. They patrol a district that is only 0.85 sq km (0.33 sq miles) in size; it is the smallest police beat in the city. Given its location in the heart of the red-light district, it is also the "hottest" beat.

Davidwache became well-known mainly through numerous film and TV pro-ductions such as the movie *Polizeirevier Davidwache* (Davidwache police station), which opened in 1964. The Davidwache served as model for the popular TV series *Großstadtrevier* (metropolitan police district), although it was filmed in other buildings. Protected as a heritage build-ing, the red brick Davidwache was expanded in 2005 when a modern annex was added.

The Davidwache police station, in the heart of the red-light district

Harry's Hafenbasar ❺

Erichstraße 56. **Map** 3 C4. *Tel 31 24 82.* Ⓢ *Reeperbahn.* 🚌 *36, 37, 112.* 🕐 *12am–6pm Tue–Sun.* 📷
📠 www.hafenbasar.de

This store full of curiosities is a museum and bazaar all in one. Here, there is nothing that cannot be found! When sailor Harry Rosenberg had to retire from the sea for health reasons, he opened a bazaar on the harbour in 1954. Along with all the things he had collected, he soon also added items brought to him by sailors hoping to supplement their basic wages.

In the store's 20 rooms, visitors can browse and discover curiosities to their heart's content. Items for sale include masks from Africa, shrunken heads from South America, Buddhas from Thailand, musical instruments from the Caribbean, old books and nautical charts, stuffed animals and much more. Hardly anyone who comes in here fails to feel the call of faraway places. And quite a few collectors have found rare things here.

Harry Rosenberg, the sailor and entrepreneur, died in 2000 at the age of 75 years. Since then, his daughter Karin has run the Hafenbasar. Still today, sailors come from faroff lands into the store, wanting to sell the odd treasures.

U-434 ⑥

St. Pauli Fischmarkt 10. **Map** 2 F4
Tel 32 00 49 34. ⓘ *Landungs-brücken.* Ⓢ *Reeperbahn, König-straße.* 🚌 *112.* ⏱ *10am–6pm Mon–Sat, 11am–6pm Sun.* 📷 📹
www.u-434.de

This submarine was built in 1976 at a shipyard in the Russian city of Gorki (today Nishnij Nowgorod), and served as a spy submarine in the Russian North Sea flotilla until 2002. The U-434 was also used for secret operations in US territories like the Atlantic seaboard. Today, the submarine functions as a museum.

During a visit to the U-boat, which is 90 m (295 ft) long and barely 9 m (30 ft) wide, visitors learn all about life on board. The crew consisted of 84 people (16 officers and 52 men), and there were provisions to last them up to 80 days. Also on board were about 32,000 litres (7,000 gallons) of fresh water.

Statue of a fisherman

The largest space in the U-434 is the torpedo room, with its six torpedo tubes. Up to 24 torpedoes could be carried on board. Some sections of the U-boat – for example the command centre – can only be seen on a guided tour. Tours last approximately 45 minutes.

St Pauli Fish Market ⑦

Between Hafenstraße and Große Elbstraße. **Map** 3 B5. ⓘ *Landungs-brücken.* Ⓢ *Reeperbahn, Königstraße.* 🚌 *112.* ⏱ *mid-Mar–mid-Nov: 5–9:30am Sun; mid-Nov–mid-Mar: 7–9:30pm Sun.*

A stroll through the St Pauli Fish Market (Fischmarkt) is an absolute must for every visitor to the city. Probably no other weekly market in Germany attracts such a crowd. The mix is unique: night owls and early-risers, bargain-hunters and shoppers looking for a unique experience, business people and punks flock to the fish market starting in the wee hours of the morning. And it's worth getting up early. The best bet is to skip breakfast and indulge in the delicacies offered here at every turn. More than just fish is for sale. Along with trout, eel, flounder and other fish, market-criers, screaming at the top of their voices, hawk many other kinds of wares. These include potted plants, fruit, small animals, jewellery, bric-à-brac, souvenirs and much more. And when "cheese Tommi", "eel Dieter", or "banana Fred" praise their wares, large crowds gather around their stands to listen. Haggling is part of the fun, and many of the sellers, who are known as "rappos", have

Graffiti art on a building located in Hafenstraße

a rapier-quick repartee – this is also part of the charm of the St Pauli fish market.

But all those who can't or won't get up at such an early hour might still find a bargain when they do arrive. As the market draws to a close, the unsold wares are often hawked at cut-rate prices. At 9:30am, a gong is struck, and the vibrant market is over.

The market's party centre is the Fish Auction Hall (Fisch-auktionshalle; *see pp118–19*). No fish have been auctioned off here for a long time. Instead, the hall is now a place where people meet for an early drink. With free admission and live music, people enjoy jazz and rock well into the afternoon.

Hafenstraße ⑧

Map 4 D–E4. ⓘ *Landungsbrücken.* Ⓢ *Landungsbrücken.* 🚌 *112.*

For many years, a dispute centred around the Hafenstra-ße kept the city in a state of high alert. A mayor resigned, protests and demonstrations were watched anxiously throughout Germany, and the situation was even described as being akin to a civil war. It all began, when empty houses on the Hafenstraße (Nos. 116–126) – as well as some buildings in the Bern-hard-Nocht-Straße nearby (Nos. 16–24) – were slated to be torn down to make way for a modern building on the harbour's edge. Alternative types occupied the houses, and there were repeated

Lively crowds at the Sunday morning St Pauli Fish Market

◁ Brew kettles on the former grounds of the Bavaria-Brauerei in St Pauli violent encounters between the squatters, their sympathizers and the police. It was only during the mid 1990s that the conflict was defused, after the houses were sold to a cooperative. Hamburgers are reminded of those turbulent times by graffiti and protest paroles in front of the houses.

House No. 89 – which, however, is located a bit further down the Hafenstraße directly on the Elbe river – is home to the Beachclub StrandPauli (end Apr–end Sep: noon–11pm Mon–Thu, noon–midnight Fri and Sat, 10am–11pm Sun).

The water tower in Sternschanzenpark has housed a hotel since 2007

FC St.Pauli ❾

See pp110–11.

Beatlemania ❿

Nobistor 10. **Map** 3 C4. ☎ 31 17 18 18. Ⓢ *Reeperbahn.* 🚌 *36, 37, 112.* ◷ *10am–7pm Mon–Sun.* 🖼️ 🎫 🚻 🖥️ www.beatlemania-hamburg.com

Hamburg was a milestone in The Beatles' career, gigs in the legendary Star-Club in St Pauli triggered the band's international breakthrough. Beatlemania – an absolute must for fans – presents a first hand portrayal of the Liverpudlian band.

The time journey proceeds from top to bottom. A lift transports visitors to the fifth floor which documents the arrival of The Beatles in Hamburg. Stairs lead to the subjacent floors. Visitors are invited to explore a backstage area, a Yellow Submarine, a recording studio and other areas. Live performances and videos with John, Paul, George and Ringo are shown on displays. In every room of the museum, a different song by The Beatles is played; the oversized record sleeves on the walls and on boards provide a suitable setting. There is also a reconstruction of the room of a female fan overindulging in Beatlemania. The room is stuffed with all kinds of devotional objects (including a giant poster from the German magazine BRAVO).

Beatlemania is a hands-on museum: Visitors can make photos of themselves with the typical bowl cut – a popular souvenir among fans of the Fab Four. And it requires only one click in the photo booth to make yourself appear on Sgt. Pepper's, one of the most famous record sleeves in music history.

Sternschanzenpark and Water Tower ⓫

Ⓤ *Sternschanze, Schlump.* Ⓢ *Sternschanze.* 🚌 *4.*

The lively Schanzenviertel is known for its alternative scene, its multicultural atmosphere, its quaint shops and many bars and cafés. Named after Sternschanzenpark, it is located in the north of the St Pauli district. All through the year, people who live in this densely developed area enjoy coming to the park for walks, to play sports or to attend cultural events like the Summer Movies *(see p45).*

The water tower is the main landmark of the district, and it can be seen from a great distance. Built in 1909, it rises 57.5 m (189 ft) above the park. After it was decommissioned in 1961, the city considered various ways to use the water tower, which had fallen into a state of disrepair. However, none of the proposals could be carried out.

It was only in 2003, some 13 years after being sold to an investor, that a decision about the fate of this industrial monument was finally made. By allowing a hotel *(see p180)* to be built inside the tower (which is under heritage protection), it became feasible to renovate it. Since 2007 the tower has been in use once again – after a 45-year break.

Sgt. Pepper's Lonely Hearts Club Band (1967) record sleeve in Beatlemania

FC St. Pauli ❾

FC St. Pauli club logo

An essential element of St Pauli is its football (soccer) club, which was founded in 1910. While it cannot boast the world-renowned players or championship titles of the more successful (and wealthier) clubs like rival HSV *(see p 134)*, FC St. Pauli is loved by local residents. The fans do not seem to mind which of the three professional German leagues the team plays in. A great time is guaranteed at every home game on the Heiligengeistfeld. Up to 23,000 spectators fill the seats of the Millerntor stadium, which is undergoing renovation through 2014. The football season runs from August to May.

Pirate Flag
FC St. Pauli's flag with skull and crossbones harks back to Hamburg's history of piracy embodied by Klaus Störtebeker; the team itself is considered to be a "league raider".

Offices
Distances within the club are short: The new office building is also located at the stadium.

FC St. Pauli returned to the first German league for the 2010 season. Fans were key to this success; at home games, the stadium becomes a cauldron seething with emotion.

Since its founding in 1910, FC St. Pauli's home field has been the Heiligengeistfeld. During its eventful history it has been the subject of many newspaper headlines.

The emblem on the club's premises testifies to the self-confidence and creativity of the team and its fans.

This club symbol, carved from stone, is located at the south entrance of the stadium at Millerntor.

The League's Pirates
The pirate flag was first hoisted in the stadium in the mid-1980s and has become a symbol of the rebellious and combative nature of the club and its fans.

Former Clubhouse
This FC St. Pauli clubhouse, where cups and pictures documenting club history were displayed, was torn down in 2007. In the course of refurbishing the stadium grounds, a new clubhouse was built; it is integrated into the grandstand.

VISITORS' CHECKLIST

Headquarters of FC St. Pauli since 1910 e.V., Auf dem Heiligengeistfeld. **Map** 4 D–E2.
Tel 31 78 74 51. Ⓤ St. Pauli, Feldstraße. 🚌 3, 36, 37.
🕐 10am–5pm Mon, Wed, Fri, 2pm–5pm Tue, 10am–7pm Thu.
@ info@fcstpauli.com
www.fcstpauli.de

Retter (Saviour) T-shirt
FC St. Pauli is strapped for cash and only survives thanks to a range of large-scale "Retter" (saviour) campaigns.

The Hamburg city gate is at the heart of the club's logo.

THE STADIUM
Millerntor-Stadion (Millerntor Stadium) was called Wilhelm-Koch-Stadion from 1970–98. By 2014, if all goes according to plan, it will have been completely rebuilt. It has been the site of many memorable football games. Fans still rave about the game on 6 February 2002 when the club, which was ranked at the bottom of the Bundesliga listings, bested FC Bayern München 2 to 1. Since the famous Munich club had won the World Cup a few days earlier, FC St. Pauli fans celebrated their "World Cup champion beaters" in a big way. In 2007, FC St. Pauli was promoted from the amateur league to the second Bundesliga, in 2010 it once again joined the first Bundesliga for one season. But, no matter what the league, the club can rely on the support of its fans. Depending on the score, the fans chant or the team is spurred on to even greater effort with cries of "St. Pauli! St. Pauli!"

The Heart of St Pauli
The club enjoys many different kinds of support. Along with PSD Bank Nord and Do You Football, Astra beer is another major sponsor of FC St. Pauli.

ALTONA

Prior to 1937, Altona was an independent city belonging to Schleswig-Holstein. With the formation of Greater Hamburg, the city became part of its larger neighbour, a neighbour of which it had always been critical. Even today, Altona's residents think of themselves as Altonaers and not as Hamburgers. But even for many Hamburgers, Altona was too close. Their rivalry stretches back into the distant past. A sore point was always the question of

Sign for the path from Altona to Blankenese

who had jurisdiction over the lucrative fish market, Altona, or Hamburg and St Pauli? Altona is an excellent starting point for a stroll along Hamburg's port lands. The best view of this area is from the Altonaer Balkon. Most of the area's other attractions are also located south of the railway station (Altonaer Bahnhof), around the Platz der Republik. Both the lovely street of Elbchaussee and the Elbuferweg, an attractive path along the Elbe, start in Altona.

SIGHTS AT A GLANCE

Museums
Altonaer Museum ❸

Historic Buildings
Fish Auction Hall ❿
Rathaus Altona ❺

Streets and Squares
Elbchaussee ❼
Palmaille ❽
Platz der Republik ❶

Other Attractions
Altonaer Balkon ❻
Köhlbrandtreppe ❾
Monument by Sol LeWitt ❹
Neue Flora ⓬
stilwerk ⓫
Stuhlmannbrunnen ❷

KEY

▨	Street-by-Street pp114–15
Ⓢ	S-Bahn station
🚉	Railway station
🚢	Boat boarding point
👮	Police station
✝	Church
✉	Post office

SEE ALSO

• *Street Finder* maps 1–2

• *Where to Stay* p180

• *Where to Eat* pp193–5

GETTING THERE
The Altonaer Bahnhof is one of the most important transport hubs in the city. S-Bahn lines 1, 3, 11 and 31 take you there, as do many buses. The S1 and S3 lines also stop at Königstraße.

0 metres	500
0 yards	500

◁ **The old Fish Auction Hall (1886) on the border with St Pauli** *(see pp118–19)*

Street-by-Street: Altona

One of the major highlights of a walk through Altona, a district of Hamburg, is the white Rathaus (city hall), which is located in a former railway station. Across from the Rathaus is the Platz der Republik, an oasis of tranquillity richly adorned with sculptures. Benches on the Altonaer Balkon beckon you to stop and rest.

Sculpture on the Altonaer Balkon

From here, there is a wonderful view of the port and the Elbe with the Cruise Center, which opened in 2010. With a bit of luck you can watch an ocean giant steering the terminal. Also worth seeing is the Palmaille, a boulevard laid out in the 17th century.

★ **Palmaille**
The tree-lined boulevard dates from the 17th century. It ends in the Elbchaussee.

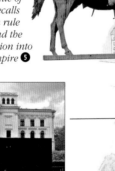

★ **Rathaus Altona**
In front of the grand Rathaus (city hall) of Altona, this equestrian statue of Emperor Wilhelm I recalls the time of Prussian rule (1867–71) and the ensuing integration into the German Empire ❺

KÖNIGSTR.

PALMAILLE

MAX-BRAUER-ALLEE

MAX-BRAUER-ALLEE

★ **Monument by Sol LeWitt**
This black cube in front of the Rathaus is entitled Black Form – Dedicated to the Missing Jews *(1987). It is a memorial to the Altona Jews who were murdered by the Nazis* ❹

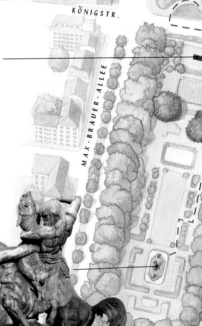

Stuhlmannbrunnen
Two giant centaurs fighting over a fish are the focus of this fountain, which was erected in 1900. They symbolize the age-old rivalry between the two fishing ports of Altona and Hamburg ❷

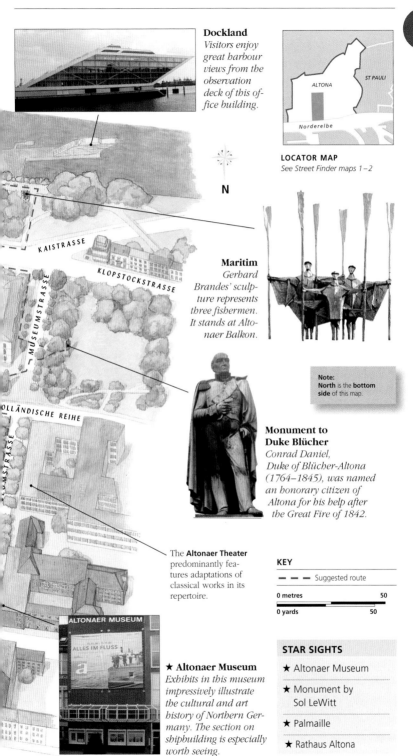

Dockland
Visitors enjoy great harbour views from the observation deck of this office building.

LOCATOR MAP
See Street Finder maps 1–2

ALTONA   ST PAULI
Norderelbe

Maritim
Gerhard Brandes' sculpture represents three fishermen. It stands at Altonaer Balkon.

KAISTRASSE

KLOPSTOCKSTRASSE

MUSEUMSTRASSE

OLLÄNDISCHE REIHE

Note:
North is the **bottom side** of this map.

Monument to Duke Blücher
Conrad Daniel, Duke of Blücher-Altona (1764–1845), was named an honorary citizen of Altona for his help after the Great Fire of 1842.

The **Altonaer Theater** predominantly features adaptations of classical works in its repertoire.

ALTONAER MUSEUM
ALLES IM FLUSS

★ Altonaer Museum
Exhibits in this museum impressively illustrate the cultural and art history of Northern Germany. The section on shipbuilding is especially worth seeing.

KEY

– – – Suggested route

0 metres	50
0 yards	50

STAR SIGHTS

★ Altonaer Museum

★ Monument by Sol LeWitt

★ Palmaille

★ Rathaus Altona

The green expanse of the Platz der Republik

Platz der Republik ❶

Map 1 C3–4. Ⓢ *Altona, Königstraße.* 🚌 *1, 2, 15, 20, 25, 36, 37, 112.*

This green park-like square between the Rathaus (city hall) and the railway station is 250 m (820 ft) long. Built in 1895, it was intended by the city fathers to be an oasis of tranquillity in the middle of a bustling district. Around the square are several imposing buildings in the Historical style. These include the railway station and the Rathaus (city hall) as well as the Altonaer Museum and the Königliche Eisenbahndirektion (royal railway administration), among others. Here, city administration, culture and economy are grouped together.

This square with its monuments – Stuhlmannbrunnen at the north end and the Monument by Sol LeWitt at the south end – is popular with Altona's residents as a place for walks. Visitors to the Altonaer Museum also enjoy the green expanse.

Stuhlmann-brunnen ❷

Platz der Republik. **Map** 1 C3. Ⓢ *Altona, Königstraße.* 🚌 *1, 2, 15, 20, 25, 36, 37, 112.*

Berlin sculptor Paul Türpe chose a highly dramatic scene for this fountain, created in 1900. It presents two mighty centaurs – creatures from Greek mythology with the upper bodies of humans and the lower bodies of horses – in the throes of fighting over the prize, an enormous fish. The fountain's main water jet shoots up high out of the fish's mouth. Surrounding the combatants are other bronze mythological figures – Triton, the son of the ocean god Poseidon, and a Nereid, a sea nymph – as well as four lizards spouting extra jets of water; they are seemingly upset by the fact that a fish has been caught.

This striking fountain tableau symbolizes the long-standing rivalry between the fishing ports of former neighbours Altona and Hamburg that dates

Stuhlmannbrunnen: two mighty centaurs battling over a giant fish

back to the 16th century. At the time, Altona was considered to be the centre of the German fishing industry. However, the more Hamburg rose in prominence, the more bitterly it fought Altona over fishing rights.

The fountain, which is 7.5 m (25 ft) high, was named after its benefactor, Günther Ludwig Stuhlmann, a wealthy citizen of Altona.

In the 1970s, extensive restoration work was carried out since parts of the bronze figures had begun to show signs of severe corrosion. Repairs were financed primarily through donations given by Altona residents.

In the year 2000, a hundred years after its creation, the Stuhlmannbrunnen once again regained its former lustre and was re-dedicated on the Platz der Republik.

Sign for the Altonaer Museum of Northern German cultural history

Altonaer Museum ❸

Museumstraße 23. **Map** 1 C3. **Tel** *42 81 35 35 82.* Ⓢ *Altona, Königstraße.* 🚌 *1, 2, 15, 20, 25, 36, 37, 112.* ◻ *10am–5pm Tue–Sun.* 🈲 🗹 *call ahead.* ▢ ▢ ♿ **www.**altonaermuseum.de

The daily life and history of Northern Germany are the primary themes explored in the Altonaer Museum's collection. The typical ways in which country people lived is shown in reconstructed living quarters and mills.

In 2008, the shipbuilding exhibition was expanded; it documents the maritime side with ships' figureheads, nautical instruments and model

The blinding white Rathaus Altona (city hall), built in 1896–98

ships. There is also a gallery with landscape paintings and arts and crafts (including porcelain, glassware and pottery). Folk costumes and other garb trace the history of peasant and middle-class fashions through the 18th and 19th centuries.

Monument by Sol LeWitt ④

Platz der Republik. **Map** 1 C4. Ⓢ *Altona, Königstraße.* 🚌 *1, 2, 15, 20, 25, 36, 37, 112.*

At the south end of the Platz der Republik is a cuboid stone monument to Altona's decimated Jewish community. Titled *Black Form – Dedicated to the Missing Jews*, it is a memorial to the deportation and murder of Altona's Jews during the Nazi period, and also to their unborn children.

Altona's Jewish community originated in the 16th century. In 1691, the Jewish communities of Hamburg, Altona and Wandsbek joined together to form a "triple community"; the seat of the Chief Rabbi was located in Altona. The community thrived and grew steadily, especially during the 19th century, due to immigration by Jews from Eastern Europe.

The deportation of Altona's Jewish citizens began in 1941; barely two years later, there were no Jews left in the city. The synagogues were destroyed in 1943 during bombing-raids.

Sol LeWitt (1928–2007), an American artist and a proponent of minimalist art, finished this sculpture in 1989. Concrete blocks were cemented together to form a cuboid structure covering an area of 5.5 m (18 ft) by 2 m (6.5 ft) and rising up 2 m (6.5 ft) high. Once formed, the monument was finished in dark black. In keeping with the artist's minimalist style, the memorial has no inscription.

Rathaus Altona ⑤

Platz der Republik 1. **Map** 1 C4. **Tel** 428 11 01. Ⓢ *Altona, Königstraße.* 🚌 *1, 2, 15, 20, 25, 36, 37, 112.*

Altona's architectural showpiece is its Rathaus (city hall). It was built in 1896–98 on the grounds of the first Altona railway station, which was in use from 1844–1895, after which a new station opened.

Lizard, Stuhlmannbrunnen

The Rathaus, which has four wings, was designed by Joseph Brix and Emil Brandt in the Neo-Renaissance style. The relief of a ship sailing into stormy waters, which decorates the gable above the entrance, was carved by sculptors Karl Garbers and Ernst Barlach. It is entitled *Ein Genius geleitet das Stadtschiff* (a genius steers the city ship).

The Rathaus was severely damaged during World War II and there was not much left of the interior.

In front of the city hall is an equestrian statue of Emperor Wilhelm I, which was created in 1898 by Gustav Eberlein. Grouped around his feet are smaller monuments to Prussian heroes.

Altonaer Balkon ⑥

Map 2 D4. Ⓢ *Altona, Königstraße.* 🚌 *1, 2, 15, 20, 25, 36, 37, 112.*

Stretching to the south of the Rathaus and running parallel to the Elbe river is this park, the Altona "Balcony". Tourists and locals alike come here to enjoy one of the very best views of the city. From here, there is a fantastic view of the Elbe river, the Köhlbrandbrücke (*see p135*) that crosses it, and of the port area, whose true extent can only truly be appreciated from this vantage point. On New Year's Eve, residents of Altona and the nearby district of Ottensen flock to the Altonaer Balkon to enjoy the fireworks.

The park is home to the bronze sculpture *Maritim* (1965) by Gerhard Brandes, which depicts three fishermen holding aloft their six oars.

There is plenty of activity in the park, especially in good weather. Then, the benches are full, people play boules and visitors enjoy the view on the docks and the passing ships through binoculars.

The Elbuferweg, a path running along the shore, begins here. You can walk or cycle along it towards Blankenese and Övelgönne, with its historical ships, or stroll along the path to the centre of town.

View from the Altonaer Balkon – one of the best in the city

A villa entrance on the Palmaille

Elbchaussee ❼

Map 1 A4–C4. 📷 36.

The Elbchaussee is definitely the most famous street in the city after the infamous red-light Reeperbahn. Its fame is due in part to its wonderful location high above the Elbe, and partly to the large number of elegant villas that were built here.

The Elbchaussee is about 9 km (6 miles) long, runs parallel to the Elbe and links Altona with Blankenese. Among wealthy Hanseatics this street is considered to be the best address in the city. A small difference plays a big role here, however: houses with an uneven number face the Elbe and are considered to be on the "right" side of the street.

Visitors do not have to worry about such distinctions, but may encounter another problem. Today, there is a lot of traffic on the Elbchaussee. But as long as you stay on the Elbe side, you'll enjoy walking past impressive villas, surrounded by beautifully manicured gardens. Many of the villas were built in the 18th and 19th centuries, when Blankenese was located outside the gates of Hamburg and rich merchants wanted to live at a dignified distance from their city offices. Some of these dwellings were used only on weekends or exclusively as summer homes.

The atmosphere along the Elbchaussee was an

Decoration on the Palmaille

inspiration for many artists. In 1902, during a stay in Hotel Louis C. Jacob (see p183), Max Liebermann painted *Die Terrasse im Restaurant Jacob in Nienstedten*, which today hangs in the Hamburger Kunsthalle (see pp64–5).

Palmaille ❽

Map 2 D4. 📷 Königstraße. 📷 36, 37.

This magnificent boulevard runs east parallel to the Elbe river above the Altonaer Balkon. The street's name is derived from *palla a maglio*, a ball game imported from Italy that is a cross between croquet and golf. Duke Otto V of Holstein-Schaumburg had three lanes built here in 1638–39 for playing this game. After suffering extensive damage in a fire in 1713, the area was planted with four rows of linden trees at the beginning of the 18th century.

Starting in 1786, the regional architect for Holstein, Christian Frederik Hansen, built several Neo-Classical homes here for the well-to-do. Those living here at the time included noblemen, magistrates and wealthy merchants.

During World War II, most of these buildings were destroyed and only a few remained unscathed. The trio of homes at Nos. 116, 118 and 120 are a perfect ensemble of Neo-Classical buildings.

Köhlbrand-treppe ❾

Between Carsten-Rehder-Straße and Breite Straße. **Map** 2 E4. 📷 Königstraße. 📷 36, 37.

The massive Neo-Gothic Köhlbrandtreppe, built in 1887, looks especially monumental when seen from the edge of the Elbe. This stairway enabled workers to move easily from their homes in the densely populated upper part of town down to their shifts on the port. The construction of the staircase was financed by Prussians; Altona once belonged to Prussia. Still today, a small figure of Roland guards the coats-of-arms of Prussia and Altona that are carved above the small fountain. Ornamental ovals depict Neptune and Mercury as symbols of seafaring and trade. From the staircase, there is a view of the shipyard Blohm + Voss on the opposite shore.

Fish Auction Hall ❿

Große Elbstraße 9. **Map** 2 E4. **Tel** 32 31 04 20. 📷 Königstraße, Reeperbahn. 📷 36, 37, 112 www.fischauktionshalle.de

It can be very quiet here on weekdays, but when the "Fischmarkt" (fish market) opens in St Pauli on Sunday mornings, hordes of people flock to Altona's Fish Auction Hall (Fischauktionshalle). Live music (mainly jazz, rock and oldies) entertains the crowds,

A splendid villa with well-tended gardens on the Elbchaussee

and breakfast is available between 6am and noon. On the gallery, you can choose between the captain's brunch or a classic Altona fish market buffet. Downstairs, there are food stalls selling *Fischbröt-chen* (fish in a bun), crabs or *Matjeshering* (salted herring). Beer, champagne, coffee and tea are also available.

The triple-naved hall was built in 1896. Two years later, Hamburg – ever the competitor – built its own Fish Auction Hall in St Pauli. In 1933, the two fish markets were combined, but Altona's auction hall had a big advantage: it had a direct link to the railway, which meant that more fish were sold here.

The Hamburg Fish Auction Hall was torn down in 1971. Altona's hall has been completely reconstructed after sustaining severe bomb damage in World War II. It is now an event centre. The solid construction of the building ensures its survival in case of flooding during storm tides. Yet, with its domes and gables, it is very appealing.

Entrance to the Fish Auction Hall in Altona

stilwerk ⓫

Große Elbstraße 68. **Map** 2 E4.
Tel 288 09 40. Ⓢ *Königstraße,
Reeperbahn.* **Building** ◻ *7:30am –
9pm Mon–Fri, 8am–8pm Sat,
9:30am–8pm Sun.* **Stores** ◻
*10am–7pm Mon–Fri, 10am–6pm
Sat, 1–6pm Sun.* ▢
www.stilwerk.de

It's all about style in stilwerk. The centre for interior design has branches in Berlin, Düsseldorf, and Vienna. The Hamburg subsidiary spreads over 11,000 sq m (118,000 sq ft) of space. The vendors sell upmarket household and garden furniture, beds, home accessories, consumer electronics, carpets, lamps, fabrics, and gift items. But stilwerk is not just another shopping mall; the architecture of this building is interesting in itself. Stilwerk is located in a red-brick building (1910), which once housed a malt factory. The building's history transfers visitors back into Hamburg's Hanseatic past. Within the centre, more than 30 shops on seven floors are grouped around a covered interior courtyard. Glass elevators transport visitors between floors. A popular way of experiencing the centre, is to go to the top floor

Fountain below the Köhlbrandtreppe

by elevator, and then walk downstairs, getting an overview of the select choice of commodities presented on the individual floors, and a thorough impression of the building's interior design.

Exhibitions form an integral part of stilwerk's concept. In the lobby, displays present the latest trends from internationally renowned designers.

Neue Flora ⓬

Stresemannstraße 159a. **Map** 2 E1.
Tel 43 16 50. Ⓢ *Holstenstraße.* 🚌 *3.
See also Entertainment p213.*
www.neueflora.de

Since it opened with *Phantom of the Opera*, the Neue Flora theatre (built in 1989–90) has become famous throughout Germany. From *Titanic* to *Dance of the Vampires* to *Dirty Dancing*, big musicals continue to be staged here. In November 2008, Phil Collins' musical *Tarzan* premiered at the Neue Flora.

The theatre has almost 2,000 seats arranged in amphitheatre style. There is a live music club here, too, as well as facilities for banquets and conferences.

AROUND THE ALSTER

Two lakes, the smaller southern Binnenalster (Inner Alster) and the larger northern Außenalster (Outer Alster), form a delightful part of the cityscape. They were created by the damming of the Alster river; they were separated when the Wallanlagen fortifications were built in the 17th century.

Detail on the Alsterarkaden

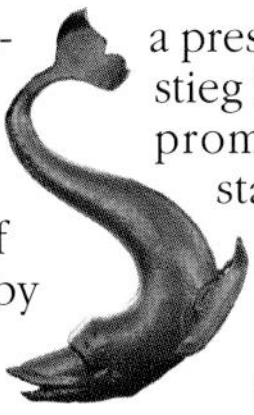

Crossing the lakes today are two major bridges: the Lombardsbrücke and the Kennedybrücke. The district Around the Alster is considered to be a prestigious address. The Jungfernstieg is one of Europe's best-known promenades, and world-famous stars and celebrities stay in the Atlantic Kempinski and Vier Jahreszeiten hotels. Both Pöseldorf, an elegant residential district second only to Blankenese, and Grindel, with its university and student quarter, are located on the Außenalster. Cultural attractions are well represented here by several museums and the Deutsches Schauspielhaus.

SIGHTS AT A GLANCE

Museums and Galleries
Museum für Kunst und Gewerbe pp130–31 12
Museum für Völkerkunde 8

Historic Buildings
Bahnhof Hamburg Dammtor 5
Hotel Atlantic Kempinski 9
Hotel Vier Jahreszeiten 4

Districts and Streets
Jungfernstieg 3
Pöseldorf 6
St Georg 10

Other Attractions
Alsterpavillon 2
Außenalster 7
Binnenalster 1
Deutsches Schauspielhaus 11
Imam Ali Mosque 15
Literaturhaus 14
Ohnsorg-Theater 13

GETTING THERE

All ICE and IC trains arriving in and departing from Hamburg stop at Bahnhof Hamburg Dammtor, as do S-Bahn lines 11, 21 and 31. The U1 travels through the southern and western part of this area. Bus No 6 travels closely along the Eastern shore of the Außenalster.

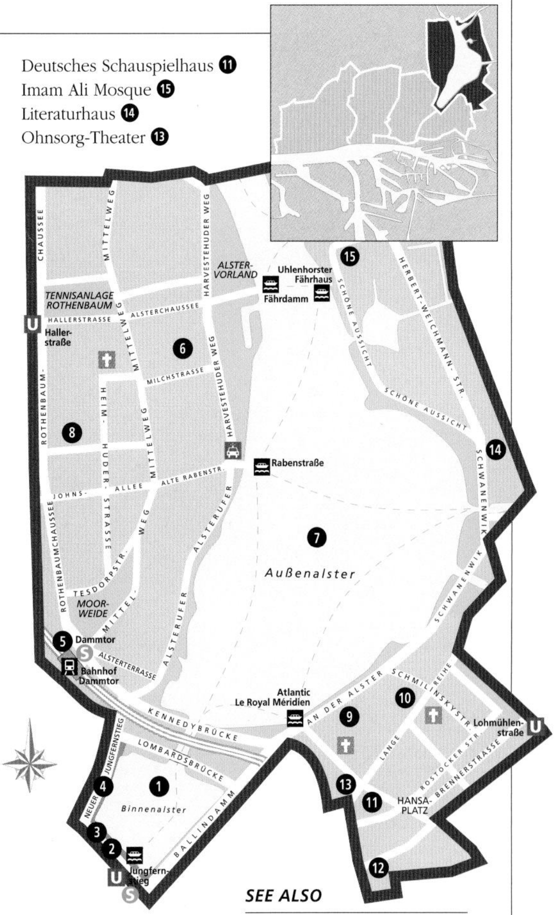

KEY
Street-by-Street *pp122–23*
U-Bahn station
S-Bahn station
Railway station
Boat boarding point
Church

0 metres 300
0 yards 300

SEE ALSO

• ***Street Finder*** maps 7–8, 9–10
• ***Where to Stay*** pp180–82
• ***Where to Eat*** pp195–7

◁ **An Alster excursion boat *(see pp240–41)* on the Binnenalster at Jungfernstieg**

Street-by-Street: Around the Alster

Some districts that border the Alster, including Rotherbaum and Harvestehude, are counted among the most prestigious addresses in Hamburg. Visitors will also feel welcome here, since the Binnenalster is lined with acclaimed hotels, and the Jungfernstieg is one of Europe's most attractive shopping streets. Cafés, such as the Alsterpavillon, are a delightful place to stop and relax and enjoy a view of the water. It is a matter of debate among Hamburgers as to which spot along the shore of the Alster offers the best view of the almost 40-m (131-ft) high Alster fountain.

Windsbraut on the Alster

★ Heine-Haus
Ricardo Bahre designed this beautiful Jugendstil building in 1903. It is named for the residence of Salomon Heine that once stood here.

★ Alsterpavillon
The terrace of this popular café offers an unforgettable view of the Binnenalster ❷

JUNGFERNSTIEG

BINNEN-ALSTER

★ Jungfernstieg
The Jungfernstieg is an ideal place for shopping, strolling and relaxing ❸

STAR SIGHTS

★ Alsterpavillon

★ Heine-Haus

★ Jungfernstieg

Swans live on the Außenalster (Outer Alster) from spring to autumn. An officially appointed "Father of Swans" takes care of them and ensures their wellbeing.

| 0 metres | | 50 |
| 0 yards | | 50 |

Nivea Haus
An oasis of wellness in the city centre; visitors to the Nivea Haus are pampered with relaxing massages.

Alsterkunst
(Art along the Alster). Numerous statues adorn the embankment of the Alster.

LOCATOR MAP
See Street Finder maps 7–8, 9–10

Amsinck-Palais
This palace was built in 1831 by Franz Gustav Forsmann and was sold to the merchant Gustav Amsinck in 1899. It is well-known for its guilded railings.

NEUER JUNGFERNSTIEG

Hotel Vier Jahreszeiten
For over 100 years, the Hotel Vier Jahreszeiten (Hotel Four Seasons) has been welcoming international guests to the Binnenalster. When it first opened in 1897, there were only 11 rooms, but under the direction of its first owner Friedrich Haerlin, it developed into a luxury hotel ❹

Binnenalster
The Binnenalster covers some 18 hectares (44 acres). One of the best ways to view its wonderful fountain and the imposing buildings lining its shores is by excursion boat ❶

Alster Boats
Numerous tour boats cruise the Alster. A trip on board provides a perfect vantage point for viewing the stately buildings along the Alster, with many points for disembarking.

KEY

 – – – Suggested route

The terrace at the Alsterpavillon – Hamburg's best-known café

Binnenalster ❶

Map 10 D–E2. Ⓤ *Jungfernstieg.*
Ⓢ *Jungfernstieg.* 🚌 *4, 5, 34, 36.*

Hamburg's inner city owes much of its charm to the Binnenalster (Inner Alster). When the city was reconstructed after the Great Fire (1842), the lake shore was reconfigured to make it accessible from all sides. The lake covers 18 ha (44 acres) and is separated from the larger Außenalster (Outer Alster) by the Kennedybrücke and the Lombardsbrücke.

In the middle of the lake, shooting water nearly 60 m (197 ft) into the air, is the Alster fountain. It operates between 9am and 11pm from spring to autumn. Alster excursion boats dock at the southwest side of the lake. An impressive backdrop is provided by stately buildings (such as the Hotel Vier Jahreszeiten), office buildings, including HAPAG-Lloyd's headquarters, and the shopping oases Alsterhaus and Nivea Haus.

Alsterpavillon ❷

Jungfernstieg 54. **Map** 10 D2.
Tel *350 18 70.* Ⓤ *Jungfernstieg.*
Ⓢ *Jungfernstieg.* 🚌 *4, 5, 34, 36.*
⭘ *8am–1pm Mon–Thu, 8am–3am
Fri–Sat, 9am–1am Sun.*

From this café, directly on the Binnenalster, you can enjoy one of the loveliest views in Hamburg. The wide steps offer a perfect place to relax, and are also used for events.

The Alsterpavillon (Alster Pavilion) survived the extensive rebuilding which took place at the start of the 21st century and changed the southern shore of the lake.

Hamburg's best-known café has enjoyed a long history. The first pavilion to be located here was built in 1799. Patrons of the fifth pavilion (built in 1914), came to enjoy swing music at tea dances in the Roaring Twenties. During the National Socialist period, this dance café was frowned upon; it was given the nickname "Jew aquarium" and was set on fire in 1943.

The current Alsterpavillon – a half-circle with a flat roof – was built in 1953, but has failed to regain the glamour of former days. Many different operators have tried to make a go of it here using various concepts. Since 2001, the café

**Windsbraut on
the Binnenalster**

has been named "Alex im Alsterpavillon". In summer, the terraces are very popular, and the all-you-can-eat buffet (served 8am–noon Mon–Sat) and the Sunday brunch (9am–2:30pm Sun) also attract the hordes.

Jungfernstieg ❸

Map 9 C2, 10 D2–3.
Ⓤ *Jungfernstieg.* Ⓢ *Jungfernstieg.*
🚌 *4, 5, 34, 36.*

The Jungfernstieg is one of Hamburg's oldest streets. It acquired its name in the 17th century after it had become the most popular promenade for well-to-do Hamburgers – especially among young women ("Jungfern").

In this sense, it hasn't changed to this day, although its look is different. The first change was in 1838, when Jungfernstieg became the first street in Germany to be asphalted. Then after the Great Fire of 1842, the south side was completely rebuilt. In 2004–2006 the pavements were widened and, with the exception of the Alster-pavillon, all the buildings along the water's edge were demolished. With the addition of new grandstand-like steps along the edge of the shore, Hamburg can now claim to have one of Europe's most attractive promenades.

A good part of this is due to the presence of Alsterhaus (*see p202*), a department store with a long tradition. Flagship stores of major fashion houses are also located here, alongside exclusive jewellery and interior design shops.

**The 40-m (131-ft) high fountain
in the Binnenalster**

Together with two other streets, Große Bleichen and Neuer Wall which lead off to the southwest, Jungfernstieg is today a luxury shopping mile made even more attractive by the white arches of the Alster Arcades *(see p58)*.

Neuer Jungfernstieg is a street running along the west side of the Binnenalster. Its appeal lies less in shopping opportunities than in the impressive buildings which line it.

Hotel Vier Jahreszeiten ❹

Neuer Jungfernstieg 9–14. **Map** 7 C5. *Tel* 34 94 31 51. Ⓤ *Jungfernstieg, Gänsemarkt, Stephansplatz.* Ⓢ *Jungfernstieg.* 🚌 *4, 5, 34, 36.* **www**.hvj.de

Ever since the Swabian Friedrich Haerlin acquired houses along the Binnenalster's western shore and opened up a luxury hotel in 1897, the Vier Jahreszeiten (Four Seasons) has welcomed guests from around the world. A who's-who of the German Empire and the Roaring Twenties frequented this grand hotel. Under the direction of Haerlin's son, Fritz, who took over the hotel in 1932, and his descendants, the hotel has remained a favourite with the rich and

Hotel porter

famous. Film stars such as Sophia Loren, opera singers such as Plácido Domingo, business czars including Aristotle Onassis, and rock musicians such as the Rolling Stones have stayed in this magnificent white building. The hotel has been part of the luxury hotel group Fairmont Hotels & Resorts since 2007. Hanseatic understatement has always been a hotel trademark; you won't find glitter and opulent furniture here. But the ambience is splendid – not least due to the Gobelins (tapestries) and oak in the salon off the entrance.

Bahnhof Hamburg Dammtor ❺

Theodor-Heuss-Platz. **Map** 7 B4. Ⓤ *Stephansplatz.* Ⓢ *Dammtor.* 🚌 *4, 5, 34, 112.*

Without a doubt, this glass-and-steel Art Nouveau building is Hamburg's most beautiful train station. At the time it was built, in 1903, state guests were greeted here; it was therefore also known as the "Kaiserbahnhof" (the Emperor's train station). Due to its proximity to the Messezentrum (trade fair) and Kongresszentrum (conference centre), Dammtor is now also called the "Messebahnhof" (trade fair

station). Each day, about 200 long-distance trains (including ICE and IC trains), 100 local trains and 500 S-Bahns serving three lines stop here.

The station's hall is 23 m (75 ft) high, 112 m (367 ft) long and 35 m (115 ft) wide. Around 100 years after it was first built, the hall and train platforms were extensively renovated. Its appeal comes from its ceiling, which resembles a vaulted roof.

Pöseldorf ❻

Map 7 C1–2, 8 D1–2. Ⓤ *Hallerstraße.* 🚌 *34.*

Between the Außenalster and Mittelweg and between Harvestehuder Weg and Badestraße lies Pöseldorf, the Alster's finest area. Its character is best expressed by the antique dealers, galleries and exclusive fashion boutiques here. German fashion designer Jil Sander opened her first store here in the Milchstraße in 1967. The most fashionable villas outside of Blankenese are located in Pöseldorf. Among the large companies headquartered in this area is the publisher Milchstraße am Mittelweg. Despite the elite ambience, a lively bar scene has sprung up here. The Hochschule für Musik und Theater (Music and Theatre School) is also here, on Harvestehuder Weg No. 12.

The railway station Hamburg Dammtor – an Art Nouveau building dating from 1903

The Hotel Atlantic Kempinski, located directly on the Alster

Außenalster ❼

Map 8 D1–E4. 🚌 6, 25, 34, 37.

This lake, measuring some 3 km (1.8 miles) in length, was formed by damming up the river Alster. It is a perfect place to sail or paddle a boat. A large number of restaurants line its shore; these are often hopelessly crowded during good weather. Excursion boats ply the Alster on a zig-zag course, and passengers can embark and disembark at the dock of their choice. Along the lake's western shore stretches an expansive green space, the Alstervorland, which is used for leisure activities. Joggers in particular love the 7.6-km (4.7-mile) loop through the park.

Sculpture, Hotel Atlantic Kempinski

Museum für Völkerkunde ❽

Rothenbaumchaussee 64. **Map** 7 B2. **Tel** 428 87 90. 🚇 Hallerstraße. 🚌 34. ◯ 10am–6pm Tue–Sun (Thu to 9pm). 📷 🖥 🖩 www.voelkerkundemuseum.com

A cross-section of the world's cultures is on display in this anthropological museum, which was founded in 1879. Since 1912, it has been housed in its current stately building. About 350,000 items and almost as many documentary photographs are on display here. The exhibits have been gathered from areas as disparate as Africa, Oceania, the Americas and the Far East. Unique in Germany is the archive dedicated to exploring the modern-day belief in witchcraft.

Each autumn, a "Peoples' Market" is held in the museum's rooms, with exhibitors from around the world showing and selling their works.

Hotel Atlantic Kempinski ❾

An der Alster 72–79. **Map** 8 D4. **Tel** 288 80. 🚇 Hauptbahnhof. 🚊 Hauptbahnhof. 🚌 4, 5, 6, 31, 34, 35, 36, 37. www.atlantic.de

Hamburgers fondly call this hotel, which was built in 1909, "the white palace on the Alster". In its 252 spacious rooms and suites, travellers from around the world are provided with every comfort to make their stay in Hamburg perfect. The guest book contains names of such luminaries as Herbert von Karajan, Charles de Gaulle and Michael Jackson. Politicians meet in the Atlantic Kempinski to exchange opinions at the highest level.

The hotel's façade, as well as its multifaceted interior, has often served as a location for films and television shows. In 2004 the Hotel Atlantic Kempinski created a splash by being the first to open a private cinema in a German hotel. Up to eight people can watch films in this deluxe cinema.

The Außenalster – popular for sailing, rowing and canoeing

◁ Southwest view of the Binnenalster, with the towers of the Rathaus and St Nikolai Memorial in the distance

St Georg 🔟

Map 8 D4–F5. Ⓤ *Hauptbahnhof, Lohmühlenstraße.* Ⓢ *Hauptbahnhof.* 🚌 *4, 5, 6, 31, 34, 35, 36, 37.*

From the splendid buildings along the Alster to student digs, from pricey restaurants to local eateries, from boutiques to corner shops – this district can hardly be beaten in terms of diversity. The street Lange Reihe exudes multicultural flair. Snack bars and shops selling arts and crafts can be found here. German actor Hans Albers was born on this street (No. 71). "Koppel 66" (No. 75) is home to ateliers for jewellery-making, book design and writing instrument design, as well as a vegetarian café.

Deutsches Schauspielhaus 11️⃣

Kirchenallee 39. **Map** 8 E5. *Tel 24 87 13.* Ⓤ *Hauptbahnhof.* Ⓢ *Hauptbahnhof.* 🚌 *4, 5, 6, 31, 34, 35, 36, 37.* **Box office** 🕙 *10am–7pm Mon–Sat.* 🖥 *www.schauspielhaus.de*

Germany's largest traditional theatre was built at the end of the 19th century in the Neo-Classical style. In 1900, it opened with a performance of Goethe's *Iphigenie auf Tauris (Iphigenia in Taurus).* It became world-renowned under the direction of Gustaf Gründgens (1955–63), when plays such as Goethe's *Faust* were staged. The Peter Zadek era (1985–89) ruffled feathers due to its provocative, socially engaged productions. The stage has kept up this experimental tradition. It was voted "Theatre of the Year" in 1996, 1997, 2000 and 2005.

The building's façade is decorated with busts of the most famous German literati, among them Goethe, Schiller, Lessing and Kleist. The theatre accommodates 1,200 people and features two balconies, loges, gilded ornamentation and classic red seats.

Museum für Kunst und Gewerbe 12️⃣

See pp130–31.

Entrance to the turquoise-coloured Imam Ali Mosque

Ohnsorg-Theater 13️⃣

Ernst-Merck-Str. 9. **Map** 10 F2. *Tel 350 80 30.* Ⓤ *Hauptbahnhof.* Ⓢ *Hauptbahnhof.* 🚌 *4, 5, 6, 31, 34, 35, 36, 37.* **Box office** 🕙 *10am–7pm Mon–Sat, 2–6pm Sun.* 🖥 *www.ohnsorg.de*

The theatre is an integral part of Hamburg. It has become famous throughout Germany due to televised broadcasts featuring Heidi Kabel & Co. Based in new premises since 2011, the stage still premieres several comedies in a repertory season. Sometimes the programme includes more serious drama such as Bertolt Brecht's *Mudder Courage.*

Germany's largest traditional theatre, Deutsches Schauspielhaus

Literaturhaus 14️⃣

Schwanenwik 38. **Map** 8 F2. *Tel 22 70 20 11.* 🚌 *6, 37.* 🖥 *www.literaturhaus-hamburg.de*

Hamburg has a lively literary scene and many well-known authors live here. An important centre for the German

literary world is located in a former merchant's villa built in 1868 and under heritage protection since 1989.

The Literaturhaus does not just see itself as a platform for readings by authors like at the Hamburg Krimifestival *(see p46),* but also as a forum for public discussion. You can browse to your heart's content in the large bookstore of this literary meeting place.

The café is considered to be one of the most beautiful cafés in Hamburg, in part due to its lovely plaster work and ceiling paintings. Guests can take their time reading national and international newspapers here over a cup of tea or coffee.

Imam Ali Mosque 15️⃣

Schöne Aussicht 36. **Map** 8 E1. *Tel 22 12 20.* 🚌 *6, 25.* 🕙 *9am–6pm daily.* 🖥 *www.izhamburg.com*

Muslims from around the world meet in the Imam Ali Mosque (Imam-Ali-Moschee), which is also the seat of the Hamburg Islamic Centre. Two minarets flank the mosque's turquoise-coloured exterior, which is crowned by a dome. Displayed in the prayer room is the largest hand-knotted round carpet in the world. Twenty-two carpet-makers laboured for three years to create this amazing 200-sq m (2,200-sq ft) carpet, which weighs one ton; the rug alone makes a visit to the Iman Ali Mosque worthwhile.

Museum für Kunst und Gewerbe ⑫

Baroque angel

The MKG, one of Europe's leading applied arts museums, is housed in a Neo-Renaissance building dating from 1876. Its collection, which ranges from the ancient world to the present day, is displayed on four floors. The European, Near Eastern and Far Eastern collections show extraordinary diversity. Among the highlights are the Japanese art collection with its teahouse and woodblock prints, the collection of historical musical instruments, the photography collection with 100,000 images and the Art Nouveau (Jugendstil) collection with its Parisian room. Some collections are closed for restoration.

Poster Art
French Art Nouveau posters form the cornerstone of this collection of 20th-century posters, along with many international works.

Second floor

First floor

★ **Historical Keyboard Instruments**
Some 400 European and 30 non-European instruments, each one a stunning example of artistry, are displayed in this collection.

★ **Middle Ages**
The European collection (Byzantium to Historicism) includes a large number of excellent works from the Middle Ages.

STAR EXHIBITS

★ Forum for Design

★ Historical Keyboard Instruments

★ Middle Ages

★ Porcelain

Entrance to the museum

In Hubertus Wald Kinderreich children can try their hands at being designers, architects or artists.

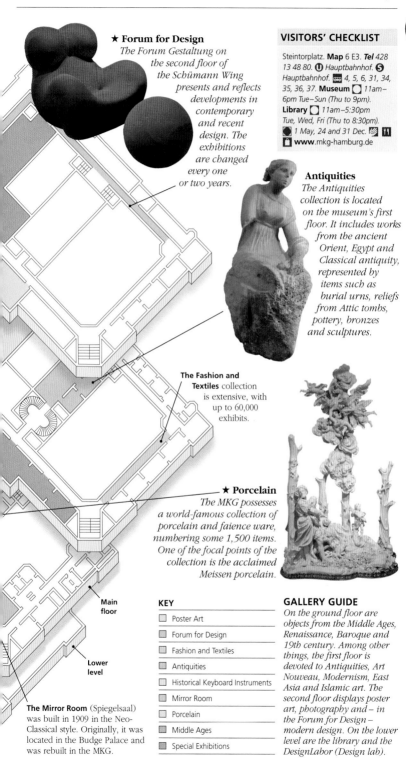

★ Forum for Design
The Forum Gestaltung on the second floor of the Schümann Wing presents and reflects developments in contemporary and recent design. The exhibitions are changed every one or two years.

Antiquities
The Antiquities collection is located on the museum's first floor. It includes works from the ancient Orient, Egypt and Classical antiquity, represented by items such as burial urns, reliefs from Attic tombs, pottery, bronzes and sculptures.

The Fashion and Textiles collection is extensive, with up to 60,000 exhibits.

★ Porcelain
The MKG possesses a world-famous collection of porcelain and faience ware, numbering some 1,500 items. One of the focal points of the collection is the acclaimed Meissen porcelain.

Main floor

Lower level

The Mirror Room (Spiegelsaal) was built in 1909 in the Neo-Classical style. Originally, it was located in the Budge Palace and was rebuilt in the MKG.

KEY
- Poster Art
- Forum for Design
- Fashion and Textiles
- Antiquities
- Historical Keyboard Instruments
- Mirror Room
- Porcelain
- Middle Ages
- Special Exhibitions

GALLERY GUIDE
On the ground floor are objects from the Middle Ages, Renaissance, Baroque and 19th century. Among other things, the first floor is devoted to Antiquities, Art Nouveau, Modernism, East Asia and Islamic art. The second floor displays poster art, photography and – in the Forum for Design – modern design. On the lower level are the library and the DesignLabor (Design lab).

FURTHER AFIELD

Along with the many attractions found in its centre, the nearby districts and outlying areas of this Hanseatic city also have much to offer. Sights include modern architecture, interesting museums and, above all, extensive parks, which provide Hamburgers with a place to retreat from the stresses of daily life. These varied destinations outside the city gates make for ideal excursions, whether your interest lies in greeting or bidding

Bear on the gate of Tierpark Hagenbeck

farewell to ships in Willkommhöft, admiring the gorgeous floral displays in Altes Land or watching the birds and seals on the North Sea and in the tidal mud flats of the Wattenmeer (Wadden Sea). Trips inland offer an agreeable change of pace from the bustling city centre. Most excursions can be made using public transport, but there is one special experience that is exclusive to automobile drivers: a drive over the Köhlbrandbrücke with its magnificent view of Hamburg's skyline.

SIGHTS AT A GLANCE

Museums and Galleries
Museum der Arbeit ❺
Museumshafen Övelgönne ❼

Parks and Green Spaces
Friedhof Ohlsdorf ❹
Jenischpark ❽
Stadtpark ❸
Tierpark Hagenbeck pp136–7 ❷

Modern Architecture
HSV-Arena and HSV-Museum ❶
Köhlbrandbrücke ❻

Other Attractions
Altes Land ❾
Blankenese ❿
Hamburg Wadden Sea National Park pp140–41 ⓬
Insel Neuwerk ⓭
Willkommhöft ⓫

KEY

▨	Hamburg city centre
✈	International airport
▣	Railway station
▭	Motorway
▬	Major road
—	Railway

GETTING THERE
Most sightseeing attractions can be reached by public transport (HVV). There are passenger boats to access the coast, while private vehicles can cross the Elbe river by ferry at Glückstadt.

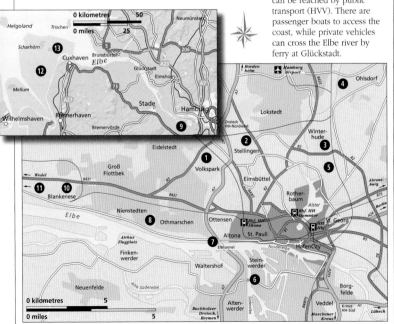

◁ The Museum der Arbeit, in a former boiler house, demonstrating change in an industrialized world *(see p135)*

The HSV-Arena, the home stadium of the Hamburg football club

HSV-Arena and HSV-Museum ❶

Sylvesterallee 7. *Tel 41 55 15 50.*
Ⓢ *Stellingen.* 🚌 *22.* 🚋 *1pm, 3pm, 5pm Mon–Fri, 11am, 1pm, 3pm, 5pm Sat, Sun (except on game days).* **Museum** ⬜ *10am–7pm daily.*
🅿️ ♿ **www**.*imtech-arena.de*; **www**.*hsv-museum.de*

The home stadium of HSV, the Hamburg football (soccer) club, has had many names. Originally it was called Volksparkstadion, since 2001 AOL Arena, since 2007 HSH Nordbank Arena, and since July 2010 its official name is Imtech Arena. The stadium was the site of five games during the FIFA World Cup in 2006, including a quarter-final game. 2010 it hosted the UEFA Europa League Final. Not only is it one of Europe's most modern football stadiums, but it also has an interesting construction history.

Unlike the other FIFA World Cup stadiums, the arena wasn't built from scratch, but on the grounds of the Volksparkstadion, which was torn down in several stages starting in June 1998. The playing field was "rotated" and new stands were built. In August 2000, the last roof membrane was attached. All 57,000 seats (including a 10,000 person standing room section and 4,200 business-seats) are covered.

A 90-minute tour gives visitors a look inside the world of professional football. The HSV often plays to a full stadium, so book early for tickets to home games. From time to time the stadium also holds open-air concerts, featuring rock and pop stars, such as the Rolling Stones or Bruce Springsteen.

In 2004, the HSV-Museum opened here. Visitors can learn everything there is to know about the HSV, which was founded in 1887. Along with trophies, there are original shirts belonging to legendary HSV players.

Tierpark Hagenbeck ❷

See pp136–7.

Stadtpark ❸

Winterhude. ⓤ *Saarlandstraße, Borgweg, Sierichstraße, Hudtwalckerstraße.* Ⓢ *Alte Wöhr.* 🚌 *6, 20, 23, 25, 26.*

With its large number of leisure activities, this is one of Hamburg's most beloved and largest parks. The city acquired the grounds of this former hunting preserve in 1902, and created the Stadtpark on an area of 150 ha (371 acres). There are sun-bathing meadows, a lake with boats for hire, an outdoor public pool, an open-air stage, a festival meadow, a beer garden, barbecues, restaurants, trails and football fields.

An architectural highlight within the park is the water tower (1912–15), which has been home to the **Planetarium** since 1930. The massive dome measures 21 m (69 ft) in diameter. Thanks to state-of-the-art computer software and simulation technology, this planetarium presents stunning 3-D shows. On the reclining seats, visitors can relax as they turn their attention from Earth to the stars. Special shows also take viewers deep inside the universe, focus on the Big Bang and the Earth's creation, or investigate cosmic collisions, making the science of astronomy a true adventure.

🏛 **Planetarium**
Hindenburgstr. 1b. *Tel 42 88 65 20.*
⬜ *9am–5pm Mon, Tue, 9am–9pm Wed, Thu, 9am–10pm, Fri, noon–10pm Sat, 10am–8pm Sun.* 🅿️ ♿
📷 **www**.*planetarium-hamburg.de*

Friedhof Ohlsdorf ❹

Fuhlsbüttler Straße 756.
Tel 59 38 80. ⓤ *Ohlsdorf.*
Ⓢ *Ohlsdorf.* 🚌 *39.* ⬜ *Apr–Oct: 8am–9pm; Nov–Mar: 8am–6pm.*
www.*friedhof-hamburg.de*

Friedhof Ohlsdorf is one of the largest cemeteries in the world. With its impressive garden design and countless artfully sculpted graves, it is a place of international importance. Since it opened in 1877, some 1.4 million burials have taken place in the cemetery.

Many well-known people have been laid to rest in Friedhof Ohlsdorf, such as actors Hans Albers and Gustaf Gründgens, zoo founder Carl Hagenbeck,

The planetarium with its impressive dome in the Stadtpark

The Köhlbrandbrücke spanning the Elbe

shipbuilder Hermann Blohm and shipping magnate Albert Ballin. A stroll through this burial ground takes you back in time through Hamburg's history.

Museum der Arbeit ❺

Wiesendamm 3. *Tel* 428 13 30.
Ⓤ Barmbek. Ⓢ Barmbek.
☐ 1pm–9am Mon, 10am–5pm Tue–Sat, 10am–6pm Sun.
www.museum-der-arbeit.de

Industrial history is featured in this excellent museum of work, which opened in 1997 in a former rubber factory. The central themes of the museum are the changes to the way people have lived and worked since the mid-19th-century. Whether printing plant, office, harbour or fish factory – you can learn about traditional Hamburg professions here. Great store is laid on lively presentation: visitors can set machines in motion and create things in various workshops.

A large collection on the history of tobacco, the Tabakhistorische Sammlung Reemtsma, displays everything to do with smoking. The exhibition covers four centuries of tobacco history, with displays that include tobacco pouches, pipes, advertising posters and cigarette packaging from around the world.

The Museum der Arbeit has two branches: the Speicherstadtmuseum *(see p85)*, and the Hafenmuseum Hamburg (harbour museum), located at Australiastr., Kopfbau Schuppen 50A.

Köhlbrand-brücke ❻

5 km (3 miles) southwest of the city centre.

Serving both as a landmark and a major traffic route, the 3.6-km (2.25-mile) long Köhlbrandbrücke was opened in 1974 after four years of construction. The bridge arches gracefully over the Köhlbrand channel, linking two parts of the Elbe – the Norderelbe and the Süderelbe. The four-lane highway on-ramps, supported by 75 pillars, lead to the cable-stayed bridge, with its two 135-m (443-ft)-high pylons.

The Köhlbrandbrücke is for use by motor vehicles exclusively; bicyclists and pedestrians are not allowed to cross it. Even at high tide, large ships can easily pass under this bridge, with its clearance of 53 m (174 ft).

Museumshafen Övelgönne ❼

Övelgönne, Anleger Neumühlen.
Map 1 A5. *Tel* 41 91 27 61.
🚌 36, 112. 🚌 62. ☐ daily.
🎫 by appointment. **www**.
museumshafen-oevelgoenne.de

Ferries sailing for Landungsbrücken or Finkenwerder stop at the Neumühlen ferry docks, where the Museumshafen Övelgönne (Övelgönne museum harbour) is located. Founded in 1977 by the "Vereinigung zur Erhaltung historischer Wasserfahrzeuge", an association dedicated to preserving historic ships and boats, the museum harbour survives without state subsidies; its work is supported only by membership fees and donations.

It is a magical draw for old-ship enthusiasts, with many to be admired from the dock here. There are German and Dutch flat-bottomed boats, the former lightship *Elbe 3* (built in 1888), the lighter *Elfriede* (1904), the tugboats *Tiger* (1910) and *Claus D.* (1913), and even an icebreaker, the *Stettin* (1933). All these "old-timers" are still seaworthy. Some still make excursions – mainly on weekends – so it is best to view the boats during the week. When the owner or crew is present, you can often go on board for a peek below deck.

HADAG FERRY NO. 62

If you want to see the Elbe shore from the water, the best way is to ride the HADAG ferry No. 62. The ferry departs every 15 minutes from Sandtorhöft and, after a 33-minute journey, arrives at Finkenwerder on the south shore of the Elbe. There are several places where you can break up your journey and re-embark later: the Landungsbrücken (at pier 3) the ferry docks of Altona (below the Altonaer Balkon), Dockland (near the futuristic-looking office building of the same name) or Neumühlen (where the Museumshafen Övelgönne is located). Finally, the ferry crosses over to the opposite Elbe shore and lands at Finkenwerder. With luck, you will be able to see the Airbus planes that are built there taking off or landing. (www.hadag.de)

HADAG Ferry No. 62 – an ideal form of transport for visitors

Tierpark Hagenbeck ❷

Opened by Carl Hagenbeck in 1907, the world's first cageless menagerie revolutionized the way animals were kept in zoos. Today, it is owned by the sixth generation of Hagenbecks. Some 1,850 animals representing 210 species live in free outdoor enclosures spread across 25 ha (62 acres) of land. Especially notable is the zoo's elephant breeding programme. In 2007, the Tropical Aquarium was built; it contains more than 14,000 exotic animals from 300 species. The on-site Lindner Park-Hotel *(see p183),* the world's first zoo-themed hotel, opened in 2009.

Statue of Hagenbeck with a lion

Japanese Island
Bronze statues, fountains and three ginkgo trees beautify this island. Flamingos live on the water here, too.

KEY

African Panorama ⑰

Bird House ⑪

Elephant House ③

Elephants' Outdoor Enclosure ④

Hagenbeck's Old Training School ⑫

Himalayan Tahr Cliffs ⑮

Historic Jugendstil Entrance ⑳

Humboldt Penguins ⑬

Japanese Island ⑩

Kamtschatka Bears ⑲

Leopards ⑧

Lion Ravine ⑯

Nepalese Temple ①

Orangutan House ⑤

Pavilion ⑱

Pink Pelicans ⑨

Polar Bears ⑭

Siberian Tigers ⑦

Thailand Pavilion ⑥

Tropical Aquarium ②

```
0 metres        100
0 yards         100
```

STAR SIGHTS

★ Kamtschatka Bears

★ Orangutan House

★ Tropical Aquarium

Flamingo Lodge, open during the summer

Himalayan Tahr Cliffs
Himalayan tahrs, which are related to wild goats, live on an artificial cliff that has been under heritage protection since 1997.

African Panorama
Mainly Chilean and Cuban flamingos live on the large pond here. The lion ravine is an outdoor enclosure without any bars, surrounded by a wide moat.

Siberian Tigers
These tigers, who have produced several sets of offspring, are an example of the great success of the zoo's breeding programmes. In the wild, they are threatened with extinction.

VISITORS' CHECKLIST

Lokstedter Grenzstraße 2. **Tel** 530 03 30. ① *Hagenbecks Tierpark.* 🚌 22, 39. ⏰ Mar–Oct: 9am–6pm daily (July, Aug: to 7pm); Nov–Feb: 9am–4:30pm daily (box office closes one hour before). 📷 **Tropical Aquarium** ⏰ 9am–6pm daily. 📷 www.hagenbeck.de

Year-round restaurant at the playground

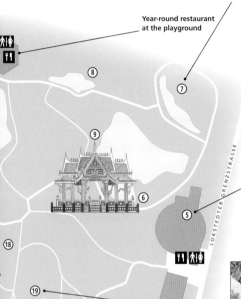

★ **Orangutan House**
Visitors love watching these large simians play and climb here. The house is covered by a glass dome that can be partly opened.

LOKSTEDTER GRENZSTRASSE

★ **Kamtschatka Bears**
Four of these brown bears have lived in Tierpark Hagenbeck since 2007. When they stand upright, they can loom as tall as 3.20 m (10.5 ft).

Location of the Lindner Park-Hotel Hagenbeck

Main entrance

Pink Pelicans
On land, these birds appear to be clumsy and slow. But when they take wing, they are elegant fliers. Since they are used to a warm climate, they winter in heated quarters.

★ **Tropical Aquarium**
Experience sharks here as well as land animals from the tropics and sub-tropics.

Jenischpark ❽

Othmarschen. Ⓢ *Klein Flottbek.*
🚌 *15, 21, 36, 39.*

North of the Elbchaussee, in the Othmarschen quarter of Altona, is the Jenischpark, which stretches over 42 ha (104 acres) of land. It is considered to be one of the most outstanding examples of an English landscape garden in Northern Germany. This beautiful park, with its giant old maples, oaks and chestnut trees, was designed in 1797 for the merchant Johann Caspar Voght. Afterwards, it became the property of the merchant and, later, Senator, Martin Johann von Jenisch.

Jenisch commissioned architect Karl Friedrich Schinkel to draw up plans for a Neo-Classical villa to be built on the highest spot in the park. Completed in 1831–34, it is today known as Jenisch Haus. As a branch museum of the Altonaer Museum, it displays artworks and applied arts. The various periods are displayed in an interesting fashion: the Neo-Classical rooms on the ground floor are decorated with furniture and paintings made during the time the house was created. The rooms on the first floor are decorated with Baroque, Rococo and Biedermeier furnishings. The second floor is reserved for an exhibit on painting, drawing, garden design and architecture.

Nearby is Ernst Barlach Haus, which opened in 1962 as the first private museum in the Hanseatic city, thanks to the financial support of the tobacco company's Hermann F. Reemtsma Foundation. The museum displays a collection of lithographs, bronzes and ceramics by the North German artist Ernst Barlach (1870–1938).

🏛 **Jenisch Haus**
Baron-Voght-Straße 50. *Tel 82 87 90.* ◻ *11am–6pm Tue–Sun.* 🖼 ◻ 🚻 limited. **www**.altonaermuseum. de/jenisch.haus.de

🏛 **Ernst Barlach Haus**
Baron-Voght-Straße 50a. *Tel 82 60 85.* ◻ *11am–6pm Tue–Sun.* 🖼 📷 **www**.barlach-haus.de

Ernst Barlach Haus in Jenischpark

Altes Land ❾

Southwest of Hamburg. *Tel 04142 81 38 38.* Ⓢ *Neugraben, then bus.* 🚢 **www**.tourismusverband-stade.de or **www**.tourismus-altesland.de

The Altes Land (old country) is the largest continuous fruit-growing district in central Europe, with over 4,000 ha (3,500 acres) of orchards. This fertile marshland is located on the south side of the Elbe, just outside the gates of Hamburg, and stretches between Stade and Buxtehude. About three quarters of the Altes Land is planted with apple trees; especially high yields are given by the Gravenstein, Jonagold, Holstein Cox and Elstar varieties. Cherry and pear trees are also cultivated.

The area was settled as early as the 12th and 13th centuries by the Dutch, who made it arable and erected dikes to protect the cultivated areas. The Altes Land is a popular destination, especially in spring, when the entire region is a sea of blossoms. But also in summer this is an ideal area for enjoying long hikes and cycling trips. During the autumn harvest, the area bustles with activity.

Jenisch Haus, standing at the highest point in the park

The Museum Altes Land in Jork shows how the region developed. On summer weekends, HADAG boats *(see p240)* bring sightseers here from the Landungsbrücken (at pier 2). The Lühe-Schulau ferries sail year-round between Willkommhöft and Lühe-Anleger, a gateway to the Altes Land.

🏛 **Museum Altes Land**
Jork, Westerjork 49. *Tel 04162 5715.* ◻ *Apr–Oct: 11am–5pm Tue–Sun; Nov–Mar: 1–4pm Wed, Sat, Sun.* 🖼

Blankenese ❿

Ⓢ *Blankenese.* 🚌 *1, 22, 36, 48, 49.*

Hamburg's most elegant suburb started off as a small fishing village and was once considered a great distance from the gates of the city. For a long time, it was an important stop for ferries. Well into the 18th century, residents of Blankenese lived mainly from seafaring and fishing. Then, wealthy Hamburg merchants discovered this idyllic village and built imposing country houses here. Not much has changed in this respect: Blankenese is still an affluent area to this day.

A walk through the Treppenviertel (stair district) is especially interesting. This district is a chaotic mix of stairways and alleyways located between Strandweg along the Elbe shore and Am Kiekeberg, a road that runs along the cliffside. Your efforts at climbing the stairs are rewarded by a superb view over the Elbe river and the opposite shore. Carefully tended parks such as Goßlers Park, Hessepark and Baurs Park are also lovely places for a stroll.

Willkommhöft ⓫

Wedel, Parnaßstraße 29, Schulauer
Fährhaus. *Tel* 04103 920 00. Ⓢ
Wedel. 🚌 *189.* ◯ *8am to sunset
daily (at the latest 8pm).* **Museum**
◯ *Mar–Oct: 10am–6:30pm daily;
Nov–Feb: 10am–6pm Sat, Sun.*
🖼 ⏸ 🖥 *9:30am–10pm daily.*
www.schulauer-faehrhaus.de

Every ship that sails into the
port of Hamburg or leaves
the Hanseatic city via the
Elbe river has to pass by Willkommhöft (Welcome Point),
a battery of loudspeakers
belonging to the city of Wedel
in Holstein. The system began
operation in 1952. It is located
on the shore of the Elbe on
the grounds of the Schulauer
Fährhaus, a popular sightseeing destination with a
café and restaurant.
    Loudspeakers greet or bid
farewell to every passing ship
that registers over 500 gross
tons. They're greeted in the
ship's national language,
followed by a rendition of
their national anthem. More
than 150 anthems are stored
on the hard drive of the
computer-controlled system.
    Visitors to the Schulauer
Fährhaus are also provided
with a wide range of details
about the route and cargo of
the ship that has just been
hailed, courtesy of the shipping
news (Schiffsmeldedienst).
    In the basement of Schulauer
Fährhaus is the Buddelschiffmuseum (ship-in-bottle museum). This is a real treasure; be
sure to treat yourself to a visit.
The collection contains over
200 ships-in-bottles – from a
model of the legendary sailing
ship *Gorch Fock* to
Viking ships to
minuscule ships in
light bulbs which
you almost need a
magnifying glass to
see. Also, the mys-
tery of how a ship
actually gets into a
bottle is revealed.
    The Muschel-
museum (shell
museum), also
located in the base-
ment of Schulauer
Fährhaus, displays
a collection of
about 1000 ocean
shells and sea-snail
shells from around
the world. Antique
items related to the
ocean and sea
travel are also
exhibited here.

A house in the elegant Blankenese district

Hamburg Wadden Sea National Park ⓬

See pp140–41.

Neuwerk ⓭

110 km (68 miles) northwest of
Hamburg. **www**.neuwerk-insel.de

This small North Sea island
(about 40 inhabitants) is part
of the Freie und Hansestadt
Hamburg (Free and Hanseatic
City of Hamburg). At low tide
it can be reached from Cuxhaven by walking over the
mud flats; you can also get
there on horseback or in a
horse-drawn carriage. Just be
sure to keep an eye on the
tides! At high tide, it is accessible by boat. The island's
landmark is its substantial
lighthouse. It dates back to
the early 14th century, when
it was a fortified tower protecting the mouth of the Elbe
from North Sea pirates.
    A walk around Neuwerk
takes about an hour. A
section of Neuwerk is a
designated bird refuge. If you
would like to stay overnight
and wait for the next low
tide, there are a variety of
guest rooms available.

Reederei Cassen Eils
Cuxhaven, Bei der Alten Liebe 12.
Tel 0180 522 86 61.
www.neuwerkreisen.de

**Wattwagenfahrten
Volker Griebel**
Tel 04721 290 76.

Willkommhöft with its battery of loudspeakers to greet huge vessels from around the world

Hamburg Wadden Sea National Park ⑫

In 1990, this park (the Nationalpark Hamburgisches Wattenmeer) was created to protect the Wadden Sea west of the mouth of the Elbe. The area, which covers 137 sq km (53 sq miles), encompasses several islands and vast tidal mud flats; 97 per cent of it is under water. Many animals call this park home: seabirds find ideal breeding grounds, and countless migratory birds pause here on their journey. Harbour seals and grey seals feel right at home, too. Favourite activities in this area are walking on the tide flats, bird-watching and viewing seals from the banks. The national park was declared a World Heritage Site by UNESCO in 2011. There is one bathing beach and several boat docks.

NIGEHÖR

SCHARHÖRNLOCH

NORDERTILL

WITTSANDLOCH

HAMBURG
WADDEN SEA
NATIONAL PARK

★ Wagon Ride
Riding in a horse-drawn wagon on the islands in the national park is both an ideal method of transport and a wonderful experience. Riding is possible when the tide goes out and the mud flats start to dry.

Oystercatchers
One of the common birds on the North Sea Coast is the oystercatcher. Adults have long, bright-red beaks.

Salt Marshes
The Wadden Sea is a unique environment. In the marshes between the mainland and the sea, the soil's salt content is high, and salt-tolerant plants have rooted here. These salt marshes are an important breeding ground for many types of birds.

★ Scharhörn

This 20-ha (49-acre) island is a resting place and breeding ground for myriad seabirds. The island's only human resident is a ranger, who watches over the birds and teaches visitors about the island's history and its winged inhabitants.

VISITORS' CHECKLIST

100 km (62 miles) northwest of Hamburg. **Regional map** p133. **Nationalpark-Station Neuwerk Tel** 04721 692 71. **Authority for Urban Development & the Environment (NP-Verwaltung) Tel** 040 428 40 33 92. ☐ *call ahead (depends on the tides).* **www**.nationalpark-hamburgisches-wattenmeer.de

ELBE

SCHARHÖRN

KLEINER

VOGELSAND

NEUWERK

EITZENBALJE

ELBE-NEUWERK-FAHRWASSER

★ Neuwerk

The largest of the three islands in this park is Neuwerk, which covers 300 ha (740 acres). Its lighthouse can be seen from afar (see p139).

KLOCH

MUSCHELLOCH

BAKENLOCH

ELBE-WESER-FAHRWASSER

Haus Bernstein
Amber is the theme of Haus Bernstein on Neuwerk. It was once deemed the "gold of the North", and this museum displays beautiful examples. Tours are offered to the north side of the island where amber has been found.

STAR SIGHTS

★ Neuwerk

★ Scharhörn

★ Wagon Ride

0 kilometres 2

0 miles 2

THREE GUIDED WALKS

Hamburg is an excellent city for walking, since most of its attractions lie close to one another. Several city passages and shopping streets, as well as the harbour promenade, are reserved for pedestrians. Hamburg's many parks and green spaces offer a welcome respite from the bustle of the city centre, and many stretches along the Elbe shore are pedestrianized. The walks suggested in this chapter take you on routes of discovery through very different parts of the city.

Paving stone memorial to a victim of the Nazis

The first walking route runs through the Old Town, which is criss-crossed by many canals, taking you from the Hamburg Rathaus through the Kontorhausviertel to Deichstraße. The distinctive buildings that are found here chronicle the various eras of the city's history – from its origins right up until the 21st century.

The second walk takes you east along the harbour promenade, starting at the Landungsbrücken and on past the Speicherstadt to Hafen-City. The contrast between dark red-brick buildings and ultra-contemporary architecture is fascinating. In HafenCity, you can see clearly how dynamically the Hanseatic city is evolving.

The third walking route takes you from the Landungsbrücken on the Elbe's shore west to Altona. Many spots along the way offer an intriguing view over the portlands. All the walk routes start and end within easy reach of public transport. For each walk, suggestions are made for perfect places to take a break.

CHOOSING A WALK

The Three Walks
The map shows the location and routes of the three guided walks in relation to the main sightseeing areas in Hamburg.

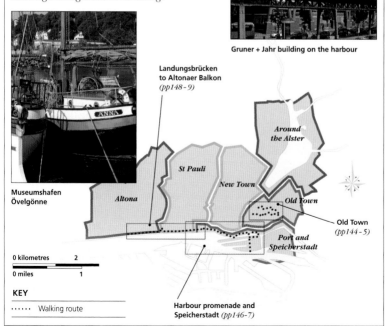

Gruner + Jahr building on the harbour

Landungsbrücken to Altonaer Balkon *(pp148–9)*

Around the Alster

St Pauli

New Town

Old Town

Old Town *(pp144–5)*

Port and Speicherstadt

Museumshafen Övelgönne

Altona

0 kilometres   2

0 miles   1

KEY

······ Walking route

Harbour promenade and Speicherstadt *(pp146–7)*

◁ Small fountain on the Neo-Gothic Köhlbrandtreppe *(see p149)* from 1887

A Two-Hour Walk in the Old Town

Although many of its buildings were razed in the Great Fire of 1842 or destroyed in World War II, a walk through the Old Town allows you to trace the history of Hamburg back to its beginnings. A more recent chapter in the city's history is evidenced by the Kontorhausviertel, out of which Hamburg grew to become an economic centre from the 1920s onward. The Old Town gets its ambience from many of the city's most striking ecclesiastical buildings, as well as several publishing houses, and the remaining canals and modern commercial streets which are partly pedestrianized.

Sprinkenhof ⑥

Rathaus to Kontorhausviertel

Dating from 1897, the Hamburg Rathaus (city hall) ①, with its 112-m (367-ft) high tower, impresses not only with its sheer size but also with its opulently decorated façade, which includes several statues of emperors. At first glance, this splendour might not seem typical of the utilitarian architecture more usually found in Hamburg. However, due to its important role as the seat of parliament and Senate, Hamburg's citizens loosened their purse-strings. Rathausmarkt ② is an imposing square; its builders took inspiration from St Mark's Square in Venice.

Leave the Rathausmarkt via Mönckebergstraße, Hamburg's main shopping street, which leads east. After about 200 m (660 ft), turn right into Kreuslerstraße, where the entrance to the church of St Petri ③ is located. In the basement of the parish house, there is a showroom displaying foundations of the nearly

Door knocker on St Petri ③

1,000-year-old Bischofsburg (Bishop's Castle). After crossing Speersort, you reach Domplatz ④, which is flanked by the headquarters of the weekly newspaper *DIE ZEIT*. After the excavation on Domplatz was completed, greenery was planted on the place.

Follow Speersort east, where it turns into the Steinstraße. Soon you will reach a courtyard, Jacobikirchhof, which surrounds the church of St Jacobi ⑤.

Across from the church, leading off from Steinstraße, is Mohlenhofstraße. Walk south along it and you will come to Burchardplatz. This square is at the heart of the Kontorhausviertel, an architecturally impressive office building quarter from the 1920s. The largest of these office buildings, with their red-brick façades, is Sprinkenhof ⑥ on the east side of Burchardplatz.

The headquarters of *DIE ZEIT* ④

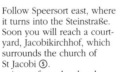

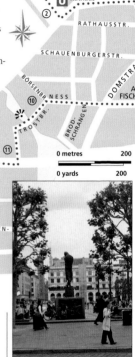

Rathausmarkt with the Alster Arcades in the background ②

Terracotta ornaments decorated with symbols of trade and industry embellish its façade. A bit more conspicuous due to its angular shape is Chilehaus ⑦, opposite Sprinkenhof. It was built in 1922–24 by Fritz Höger and is considered to be a groundbreaking example of red-brick Expressionism.

Kontorhausviertel to Rödingsmarkt

Walk east around the "prow" side of Chilehaus and follow Pumpen street west. As it continues, the street changes its name several times. Just before it meets Domstraße – at this point it is called Große Reichenstraße – you will see Afrikahaus ⑧ at No. 27 on the left side of the street. This building was commissioned by the shipping company Woermann and built in 1899. It marries utilitarianism with a

Entrance to Afrikahaus ⑧

showy façade. Among the striking African-themed decorations is the figure of a warrior at the entrance, as well as two cast-iron elephants and a palm mosaic in the inner courtyard.

The contrast between old and new architecture can be seen most clearly when you turn left into Domstraße and pass by Zürichhaus ⑨. This building, erected in 1989–92, continues the Hamburg office-building tradition but, with its red-brick, steel and glass exterior, also represents a style that began in the early 1990s, and is typical for newer office building design.

Cross Domstraße and return to Große Reichenstraße. After a short walk, turn left onto the bridge, the Trostbrücke ⑩. The first bridge to be built here was mentioned in 1266. It linked the town of the bishopric around Hammaburg castle with the new merchant town. Statues of the founders – Bishop Ansgar of Hamburg and Bremen as well as Duke Adolf III of Schauenburg – flank the bridge. Follow the short street Neue Burg, then turn right into Willy-Brandt-Straße. Here, the ruins of St Nikolai church ⑪, destroyed in World War II, have been preserved as a memorial – the Mahnmal St. Nikolai.

After continuing for about 150 m (492 ft), turn left onto the Holzbrücke, a bridge, and cross over Nikolaifleet. Then turn right into Cremon, a street lined with several old warehouses. At the end of this street, keep to the right and cross over the Nikolaifleet again and turn right into Deichstraße ⑫, which provides a very good idea of how old Hamburg once looked. Plaques on the exteriors of the buildings provide information about the rich history of some of the houses here.

Deichstraße leads into Willy-Brandt-Straße, which takes you west towards Rödingsmarkt street. From here, you can return back to your starting-point on U-Bahn line No. 3.

View from the Trostbrücke ⑩

TIPS FOR WALKERS

Starting point: Rathaus.
Length: 3 km (2 miles).
Duration: 2 hours.
Getting there: U-Bahn line 3.
St Petri: ⬛ 10am–6:30pm Mon–Fri (to 7pm Wed), 10am–5pm Sat, 9am–9pm Sun (see p58).
St Jacobi: ⬛ Apr–Sep: 10am–5pm Mon–Sat; Oct–Mar: 11am–5pm Mon–Sat (see p62).
St Nikolai: ⬛ May–Sep: 10am–8pm daily; Oct–Apr: 10am–5pm daily (see p66).
Stopping-off points: There are a large number of restaurants in the Old Town. Some of the most popular ones are located in the Deichstraße, including the Kartoffelkeller (No. 21), Deichgraf (No. 23), and Alt Hamburger Aalspeicher (No. 43).

STEINSTRASSE

SPEERSORT

BURCHARDSTR.

PENSTEHL NIEDERNSTR.

EICHENSTR. HOPFENSACK

Ⓤ Meßberg

Statue on Mönckebergstraße

KEY

• • • Walking route

🔆 Viewpoint

Ⓤ U-Bahn station

St Nikolai Memorial ⑪

A Three-Hour Harbour and Speicherstadt Walk

Each visitor to this Hanseatic city comes to the Landungsbrücken at least once. It is not only the unique atmosphere and the wonderful water views that draw people
here, but also the many museum ships. Speicherstadt,
a giant warehouse complex, embodies more than 100
years of port and trading history. Carpets, coffee, tea,
and cocoa and other trading goods are still stored
behind the red-brick exteriors. Recently, however,
Speicherstadt has been undergoing a huge change due
to the reduced demand for storage space. Museums,
and even a theatre, have moved into former warehouses.
South of Speicherstadt a whole new city district –
HafenCity – is being built.

**Accordion player at
the Landungsbrücken ①**

**Landungsbrücken
to Kehrwiederspitze**
Starting at the Landungs-
brücken ①, walk east along
the broad promenade at the
water's edge. As you stroll by
the accordion players singing
chanties, and captains touting
round-trip excursions on their
boats, you experience the
typical harbour flair. The 97-m
(318-ft) long, three-master
Rickmer Rickmers ②, built in
1896, has been
anchored here as a
museum ship since 1987.
A tide-marker on the shore
shows how high the Elbe
reached during the devastating flood of 1962. A bit further east, you can visit the
160-m (525-ft) long freighter
Cap San Diego ③, which was
brought back to Hamburg's
port in 1986. A little further
still and you reach a lightship ④, anchored since 1993
in Hamburg's City-Sporthafen.
On the other side of the street
is the headquarters of
publisher Gruner + Jahr ⑤,
with its four main sections
facing the Elbe, looking like
a gigantic steamship. Behind
Baumwall U-Bahn station you
will see Slomanhaus ⑥ on
the left. This office building,

TIPS FOR WALKERS

Starting point: S- and U-Bahn
station Landungsbrücken.
Length: 5 km (3 miles).
Duration: 3 hours.
Getting there: S-Bahn 1, 3,
U-Bahn 3.
Rickmer Rickmers: ☐ 10am–
6pm daily (see pp94–5).
Cap San Diego: ☐ 10am–6pm
daily (see pp98–9).
Hamburg Dungeon: ☐
10am–6pm daily (Jul–Aug:
10am–7pm) (see p85).
Miniatur Wunderland: ☐
9:30am–6pm Mon–Fri (to 9pm
Tue, to 7pm Fri), 8am–9pm Sat,
8:30am–8pm Sun (see p84).
Stopping-off points: Cafés at
the Landungsbrücken, one in the
coffee roasting house and a
bistro in HafenCity InfoCenter.

| 0 metres | 250 |
| 0 yards | 250 |

The Landungsbrücken, seen from the floating quays ①

View Point ⑱, offering the best view of the port

place to buy Persian goods. On the opposite side of the street is the most northerly row of buildings in HafenCity *(see pp90–91)*. Walk back a short way along Sandtorkai, turn right, and cross over the canal, Kehrwiederfleet, via Kehrwiedersteg. Keep right and you will reach Theater Kehrwieder ⑨, where musical entertainment, variety theatre, and plays are part of the regular programme. A few steps further along is a coffee roasting house, where coffee from around the world, from Costa Rica to Ethiopia to Indonesia, is wrapped up in sacks. Attached to the roasting house is a museum featuring everything to do with coffee. This warehouse also is home to Miniatur Wunderland ⑩ and Hamburg Dungeon ⑪; long lines often form in front of these two attractions. At the end of the building, turn left and cross the canal Brooksfleet on the bridge Auf dem Sande. On the corner of Am Sandtorkai is an old boiler house which houses the HafenCity InfoCenter ⑫; the entrance is in the back. Here you'll find a scale model of the city and all sorts of information about the HafenCity project.

Walk a short distance west. On the first floor of Am Sandtorkai 32 is the Afghanisches Museum (Afghan museum) ⑬ and on the second floor Spicy's Gewürzmuseum ⑭ –

the spice museum. Now walk east along Sandtorkai. After about 0.5 km (0.3 miles) keep to the left, walk over the Neuerwegsbrücke, and then turn right. Here you pass by the Speicherstadtmuseum ⑮, located at St. Annenufer. Behind this museum, first turn left into the street Bei St. Annen and then right into Alter Wandrahm. The Deutsches Zollmuseum (German customs museum) ⑯ is located at No. 16. At No. 4 you can experience "Dialog im Dunkeln" ("Dialogue in the Dark") ⑰.

Speicherstadt to HafenCity

Continue walking south along Poggenmühle street, then turn right into Brooktorkai and keep going along this street – past more warehouses – until you come to Große Grasbrook. Turn left here and walk to View Point ⑱. Along the way, you will get an impression of the tremendous upheaval this section of Hamburg is undergoing. From the View Point observation platform there is a fantastic view over the HafenCity construction site, the Kreuzfahrtterminal (Cruise Center) ⑲, the Speicherstadt and the Elbe.

You can return by first taking MetroBusses No. 3, 4 or 6 from the Marco-Polo-Terrassen stop to the Rathaus and then taking the U-Bahn line 3 back to the Landungsbrücken.

constructed in 1908–09, is the headquarters of Reederei Sloman, a shipping company. Now turn right and cross over a bridge, the Niederbaumbrücke. You are nearing Kehrwiederspitze ⑦ at the entrance to Speicherstadt.

Speicherstadt

Once you have passed Kehrwiederspitze, keep walking south. Turn left into the street called Am Sandtorkai, which is at first lined with buildings that belong to the Hanseatic Trade Center complex. Awaiting you behind Kehrwiedersteg, in Persienhaus ⑧ on Sandtorkai, is something exotic: along with a carpet warehouse, whose treasures can be viewed, there is a

KEY

··· Walking route

🔆 Viewpoint

🇺 U-Bahn station

🇸 S-Bahn station

The frequently updated scale model in HafenCity InfoCenter ⑫

A Two-Hour Walk to Altonaer Balkon

This walking route ambles west along the Elbe river. It starts at the Landungsbrücken and continues on to the Fischmarkt (fish market) – a magnet for night owls and tourists – then on to Altona and the Altonaer Balkon. Along the way are many vantage points offering some of Hamburg's most beautiful and panoramic views. You also will discover the latest changes to the area, as construction along the Elbe shore is proceeding apace. Here – and at HafenCity further east – you will see at first hand the impressive architectural growth of the city.

Fish Auction Hall (Fischauktionshalle) ④

the south shore of the river. Once you have passed the tunnel entrance, continue along the Hafenstraße to the St Pauli Fischmarkt ③. On Sunday mornings the crowds are huge, but at other times of the week you can enjoy the view of the water in peace and quiet. Here, Pepermölenbek street leads off to the north; it once marked the boundary between Altona and Hamburg. On the left side of Große Elbstraße is the Fish

Auction Hall (Fischauktions-halle) ④ built in 1896. The U-boat *U-434* moored in front of it is now a museum.

Recently, Große Elbstraße has been undergoing massive reconstruction. In accordance with the city fathers' wishes, city planners are designing a promenade with a nautical flair here. To this end, old industrial buildings and ware-houses are being turned into exclusive apartment buildings, shopping centres and

Stadtlagerhaus ⑤ – a warehouse topped by a modern glass cube

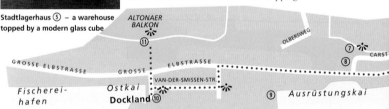

Landungsbrücken to Köhlbrandtreppe

Starting from the S-Bahn and U-Bahn station Landungs-brücken, walk west past the striking domed passenger halls serving the Landungs-brücken ① and past the entrance to the Alter Elb-tunnel ② (old Elbe tunnel), a walking and cycling tunnel to

KEY

··· Walking route

🔆 Viewpoint

U U-Bahn station

S S-Bahn station

The once embattled Hafenstraße in St Pauli, declaring "No man is illegal"

company headquarters. Ware-houses are being expanded and modernized, or com-pletely rebuilt in the process. The rebuilding of the quays of this former lumber port began with Stadtlagerhaus (No. 27) ⑤, an old store-house. A multi-storey glass cube was set on top of this building between 1998 and 2001. It is one of the archi-tectural pearls along the Elbe shore, receiving design praise.

The seven-storey stilwerk ⑥ suits the newly conceived Große Elbstraße. Opened in 1996, this shopping centre is known for stocking home furnishings and home decor in a red-brick building dating from 1910. In stilwerk's lobby there are occasional exhibitions presenting the latest home-decorating trends.

After walking a bit further along, it is worth looking to your right to admire the Neo-Gothic stairway – the Köhlbrandtreppe ⑦ with its small fountains, constructed in 1887. Here, too, is the famous Haifischbar ⑧ *(see p193)*, a bar steeped in tradition, whose decorations still include ships-in-bottles, dusty ships' models and old photographs of Hamburg entertainment greats such as Hans Albers, Heidi Kabel and Freddy Quinn. In recent years, the pub has faced increasing competition from modern bars and restaurants.

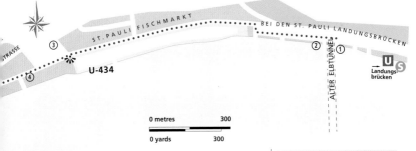

Figure on a fountain at Fischmarkt ③

terminal supports the Hamburg Cruise Center in HafenCity. West of here is Dockland ⑩, an office building in the shape of a parallelogram with its bow jutting out over the water. From the observation deck of this building visitors enjoy great harbour view. The cruise terminal and Dockland are important links in the "pearl necklace", as the city-planners like to call the row of modern buildings that are continually being constructed along the Elbe shore.

Turn right into Elbberg street which leads up to the Altonaer Balkon ⑪ (Altona balcony) located above the Große Elbstraße and parallel to the Elbe river. This terrace offers the loveliest view in Hamburg of

Relaxing at the Haifischbar ⑧

Övelgönne and further west to Blankenese, without being disturbed by cars.

To return to your starting point on the Elbe shore, take the S-Bahn (lines 1, 3, 11 or 31) from Bahnhof Altona (Altona station). To get to the station, turn north, cross over Klopstockstraße, walk past the Rathaus Altona (city hall), the Platz der Republik and continue straight ahead to the station.

Köhlbrandtreppe to Altonaer Balkon

Continuing along the shore of the Elbe river to the west, you reach the cruise terminal (Kreuzfahrtterminal) Altona ⑨, that opened in 2010. Occasionally, luxury liners call at this terminal. This new

much of the portlands and the Köhlbrandbrücke. Spend some time here to enjoy it. The Elbuferweg, a path along the Elbe, starts here on this green space with its wonderful panoramic view. You can walk or cycle along the water all the way to Museumshafen

Dockland office building, shaped like a ship's prow ⑪

TIPS FOR WALKERS

Starting point: S-Bahn and U-Bahn station Landungsbrücken.
Length: 3 km (2 mile).
Duration: 2 hours.
Getting there: S-Bahn 1 or 3, U-Bahn 3.
Stopping-off points: There are a lot of restaurants along the route, some with terraces directly on the Elbe shore. Among the best-known restaurants are Lutter & Wegner (Große Elbstraße 49), Au Quai (Große Elbstraße 145b–d) and the Riverkasematten (Fischmarkt 28–32). Hearty Hanseatic fare is served in the restaurant Haifischbar (Große Elbstraße 128).

Pavilion on the beach promenade in Borkum *(see p160)* ▷

BEYOND HAMBURG

BEYOND HAMBURG

or those wanting to venture beyond the city, there are plenty of enticing getaways. The Free and Hanseatic City of Hamburg is bordered by Lower Saxony and Schleswig-Holstein; both provinces offer a host of attractions for day trips or excursions lasting several days. Among the most fascinating destinations are the North and East Frisian Islands. The city-state of Bremen also has much to offer.

Nature-lovers and water-sports fans are drawn to the North Sea coast. Unique flora and fauna can be found in the two parks that line it – the Wadden Sea National Park of Lower Saxony and the Wadden Sea National Park of Schleswig-Holstein. Both are parts of the region Wadden Sea that was declared a World Heritage Site by UNESCO in 2009. The Frisian Islands are known for their beaches and sand dunes. Watersports fans love it here, and on sunny days wicker beach chairs stretch as far as the eye can see. Some of the islands are car-free, allowing visitors to enjoy nature at its best on foot, by bicycle, or in a horse-drawn carriage.

One of the special attractions of this land-within-the-sea is walking on the Watt, as the tidal flats of the Wadden Sea are known locally. Walks are best undertaken with a guide, who will

Bacchus at the Bremen Rathaus

explain the unique and fascinating Wadden Sea environment.

Those who yearn for a more action-filled getaway can journey to the island of Sylt, which is known for its parties and visiting celebrities. In the evenings you can plunge into the nightlife scene, while days can be spent relaxing or embarking on some upscale shopping.

The architecture of the Old Town of Bremen with its Weser Renaissance buildings, is fascinating. Its Rathaus and Roland statue were declared a World Heritage Site in 2004.

Alternatively, you can visit Museumsdorf Cloppenburg and learn about the hard lives of farmers. Or to keep with a nautical theme, visit the Kiel Canal. Every year some 40,000 large ships sail by on it, almost close enough to touch. The canal links the North Sea with the Baltic Sea.

The East Frisian Islands with their sand dunes under an endless sky *(see p160–61)*

◁ Lighthouse and thatched house on Sylt *(see pp 156–7)*

Exploring Beyond Hamburg

With so many attractions in the surrounding area, Hamburg is a perfect jumping-off point for excursions to places such as the North Sea islands or Bremen. The bucolic charms of the North and East Frisian Islands are a pleasing contrast to urban Hamburg. Along with tidal flats, beaches and water sports, the islands also offer a wide range of spas and wellness resorts – just the right thing for a relaxing getaway. Bremen's city centre is of interest for its lovely Renaissance buildings; the port of Bremerhaven on the Weser river has a completely different character to the port of Hamburg. Museumsdorf Cloppenburg, a museum village, documents the hard existence of farmers in earlier times.

**The Bremer Town Musicians –
a symbol of this Hanseatic city**

**Sunset above the Wadden Sea
(Wattenmeer)**

SIGHTS AT A GLANCE

The northern beach on the East Frisian Island of Borkum

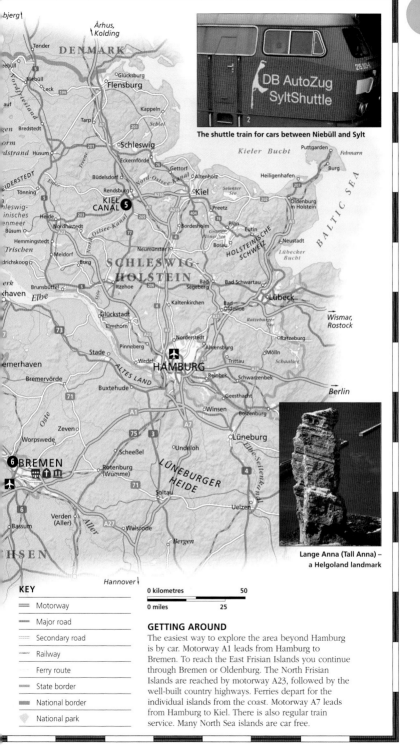

bjerg\

Århus,
\Kolding

DENMARK

Tønder

ebüll
Niebüll
Leck

Glücksburg

Flensburg

Kappeln

auf

gen Bredstedt

Tarp

Schlei

orm
rdstrand Husum

Schleswig

Eckernförde

Kieler Bucht

Puttgarden

Fehmarn

The shuttle train for cars between Niebüll and Sylt

IDERSTEDT

Tönning

Büdelsdorf

Gettorf

Altenholz

Burg

Heiligenhafen

hleswig-
inisches
enmeer

Heide

Rendsburg

KIEL 5
CANAL

Kiel

Selenter
See

Oldenburg
in Holstein

Nordhastedt

Preetz

Büsum

Hemmingstedt

Meldorf

Trischen

drichskoog

Burg

Bordesholm

Neumünster

Plön

Großer
Plöner See

Bosau

Eutin

HOLSTEINISCHE
SCHWEIZ

Neustadt

Lübecker
Bucht

BALTIC SEA

**SCHLESWIG-
HOLSTEIN**

erk

Brunsbüttel

khaven *Elbe*

Itzehoe

Bad
Segeberg

Bad Schwartau

Bad
Oldesloe

Lübeck

Kaltenkirchen

Ratzeburger
See

Wismar,
Rostock

Glückstadt

7

73

Elmshorn

Norderstedt

Ratzeburg

Pinneberg

Ahrensburg

Mölln

Schaalsee

Stade

ALTES LAND

Wedel

Trittau

emerhaven

Bremervörde

HAMBURG

Reinbek

Schwarzenbek

Berlin

Buxtehude

Geesthacht

Oste

Winsen

Boizenburg

Zeven

A1

Lüneburg

Worpswede

75 3

Scheeßel

Undeloh

Elbe-Seitenkanal

6 **BREMEN**

Rotenburg
(Wümme)

**LÜNEBURGER
HEIDE**

71

Soltau

4

Lange Anna (Tall Anna) –
a Helgoland landmark

Verden
(Aller)

A27

Walsrode

Uelzen

6

Bassum

Aller

Bergen

HSEN

Hannover

KEY

===	Motorway
—	Major road
===	Secondary road
---	Railway
	Ferry route
	State border
===	National border
◆	National park

0 kilometres   50

0 miles   25

GETTING AROUND

The easiest way to explore the area beyond Hamburg
is by car. Motorway A1 leads from Hamburg to
Bremen. To reach the East Frisian Islands you continue
through Bremen or Oldenburg. The North Frisian
Islands are reached by motorway A23, followed by the
well-built country highways. Ferries depart for the
individual islands from the coast. Motorway A7 leads
from Hamburg to Kiel. There is also regular train
service. Many North Sea islands are car free.

For additional key symbols *see back flap*

Sylt ●

Sylt is the largest of the North Frisian Islands *(see p158)*, covering an area of 99 sq km (38 sq miles). Since 1927, it has been linked with the mainland by the Hindenburgdamm, a causeway reserved solely for train traffic. The fine sand beaches of Sylt are renowned, and on lovely summer days more than 12,000 wicker beach chairs are set up for visitors. The island's main town,

Silhouette of Sylt Westerland, offers a wide range of activities year-round. There's dining and shopping, spas and nightlife, beach saunas and art previews, beach parties and New Year's Eve galas. Westerland's motto is "see and be seen", but the island's other towns also have their charms. Sylt is a paradise for watersport lovers.

★ Red Cliffs

These 30-m (100-ft) high cliffs (Rotes Kliff) between Wenningstedt and Kampen owe their red colour to oxidized iron particles. The cliffs are an island landmark and a navigation aid for sailors.

★ Westerland

A lively town encircled by beautiful nature, Westerland is the heart and soul of Sylt. Those who holiday here combine nights of parties with relaxation in the Syltness-Center.

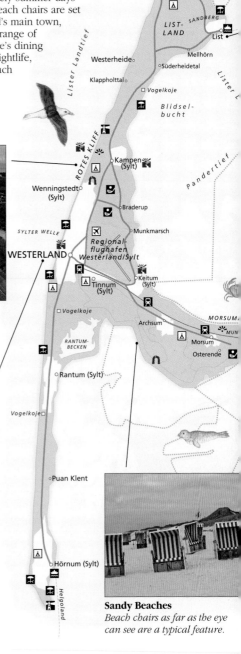

Sandy Beaches
Beach chairs as far as the eye can see are a typical feature.

Leuchtturm Westerellenbogen
ELLENBOGEN
Leuchttu Osterellen
MÖVENBERG
LIST-LAND
SANDBERG
List
Mellhörn
Lister Landtief
Westerheide
Süderheidetal
Lister L
Klappholttal
Vogelkoje
Blidsel-bucht
ROTES KLIFF
Kampen (Sylt)
Wenningstedt (Sylt)
Pandertief
Braderup
Munkmarsch
SYLTER WELLE
Regional-flughafen
WESTERLAND
Westerland/Sylt
Keitum (Sylt)
Tinnum (Sylt)
Vogelkoje
MORSUM
Archsum
MUN
RANTUM-BECKEN
Morsum
Osterende
Rantum (Sylt)
Vogelkoje
Puan Klent
Hörnum (Sylt)
Helgoland

★ Dune Landscape
Long stretches of dunes are typical of the Sylt landscape. Some of these "hills of sand" are overgrown with plants, including protected species.

VISITORS' CHECKLIST

200 km (124 miles) northwest of Hamburg. **i** *Tourist-Information Westerland (Straßraße 35).* **Tel** 0180 500 99 80. **www**.westerland.de **www**.wattenmeer-national park.de

The Wadden Sea (Wattenmeer) – UNESCO World Heritage Site since 2009 – is ruled by the rhythm of the tides. Walks along the flats at low tide are popular.

Holiday Paradise
Sylt attracts many visitors with more than 1,700 hours of sunlight a year, pleasant temperatures, a healthy North Sea island climate, attractive coastal villages and easy access via car shuttle train.

Højer○

MARGRETHE-
KOOG

DENMARK

RICKELS-
BÜLLER
KOOG

HINDENBURGDAMM

GERMANY

FRIEDRICH-
WILHELM-
LÜBKE-
KOOG

Niebüll

Sylt Shuttle
(car transport Niebüll–Westerland, 40 min)

Oster Ley

Hörsbüllsteert

ALTER
KOOG

*Wadden Sea
National Park of
Schleswig-Holstein*

KEY

▬	National border
····	National park border
▬	Road
—	Railway
🚉	Railway station
⛴	Ferry service
✈	Domestic airport
🏖	Beach
🗼	Lighthouse
⛺	Camping
⛳	Golf course
🎇	Scenic area
⌂	Archeological site, ruins
☀	Viewpoint

STAR SIGHTS

★ Dune Landscape

★ Red Cliffs

★ Westerland

0 kilometres   5
0 miles   3

North Frisian Islands ❷

This group of islands (the Nordfriesische Inseln) lies off the western shores of Schleswig-Holstein. Between the larger islands of Föhr, Amrum, Pellworm and Nordstrand lie the smaller Halligen islands. Storm tides have repeatedly left their mark here; in 1634, a storm tide forever separated the islands of Pellworm and Nordstrand. Among the most popular seaside resorts are Westerland and Kampen, on the largest island of Sylt *(see pp156–7)*, and Wyk on Föhr. Although the islands are surrounded by the Wadden Sea National Park of Schleswig-Holstein, they do not belong to this nature reserve.

Sand dunes in a nature reserve in the north of Sylt, the largest of the North Frisian Islands *(see pp156–7)*

Föhr

160 km (100 miles) northwest of Hamburg. 🚶 8,600. 🚢 *from Dagebüll.* **www**.foehr.de

The largest town on this 82-sq km (32-sq mile) island is the seaside resort of Wyk, located in the southeast. It is known for its year-round health and wellness facilities. One of Föhr's special attractions is AQUAFÖHR, the popular waterwaves pool. For something different, a visit to the Bronze Age burial mounds in the southwest is rewarding.

Nowhere on the island is more than a 15-minute walk from a beach. Every year on 21 February "Biikebrennen" time is celebrated. This time-honoured ritual is also observed on other North Sea islands, when island residents light bonfires to chase away the long, dark winter.

One of many seals that can be seen on the Wadden Sea sandbanks

Amrum

150 km (95 miles) northwest of Hamburg. 🚶 2,300. 🚢 *from Dagebüll.* **www**.amrum.de

Amrum's biggest dunes reach 32 m (105 ft) in height. In the centre of the island, drifting dunes meet wooded areas and heath. In the harbour of Wittdün, the main town, ferries and fishing boats vie for space. Among the interesting sites to visit are Viking graves. Ornithologists treasure the rich birdlife. In the 19th century, before tourism became the main source of income, this 20-sq km (8-sq mile) island lived from whaling.

Pellworm

140 km (87 miles) northwest of Hamburg. 🚶 1,100. 🚢 *from Strucklahnungshörn to Nordstrand.* **www**.pellworm.de

A large part of Pellworm (36 sq km/14 sq miles) lies under sea level. It is protected from the sea by a dike measuring 8 m (26 ft) high and 28 km (17 miles) long. There are no sand beaches, but it is possible to swim. The island's landmark is the 12th-century church of St Salvator in the west, whose organ, dating from 1711, is still used to give concerts.

Nordstrand

120 km (75 miles) northwest of Hamburg. 🚶 2,000. **www**.nordstrand.de

In contrast to the other North Frisian Islands, Nordstrand (50 sq km/19 sq miles) can be reached by car over a causeway linking the island to the mainland. Many tourists come here between May and July to enjoy the North Frisian Lammtagen (lamb days), when they can learn all about herding sheep. An entertaining time for all is guaranteed, thanks to the exhibits, music and markets. The rose garden at Osterdeich is worth a visit.

Halligen

🚶 300. **www**.halligen.de

These ten marsh islands around Pellworm cover a total area of 23 sq km (9 sq miles); some were once parts of larger islands that were divided by storm tides. Several of the Halligen islands are not protected by dikes, so are constantly eroded as storm tides wash over them. Buildings on the inhabited islands are erected on artificial mounds of earth to protect them from the tides. Walking tours of the tidal flats, salt marsh explorations and bird-watching expeditions are popular activities. It is lovely here in late summer, when lavender transforms the islands into a blanket of violet blossoms.

Helgoland ❸

In 1890, Germany received Helgoland from Britain in exchange for Zanzibar. Lying well out in open seas, 70 km (44 miles) from the mainland, the island always held great strategic importance. After 1945, Britain used Helgoland as a bombing target before returning it to Germany in 1952. The main island covers about 1 sq km (0.39 sq mile). The nearby dune, a popular spot for swimming and sunbathing, is a stretch of land measuring 0.7 sq km (0.27 sq miles).

VISITORS' CHECKLIST

About 70 km (44 miles) from the mainland. 🚶 1,400. 🚢 Hamburg, Bremerhaven, Cuxhaven, Wilhelmshaven. 🛈 Lung Wai 28 (04725 20 67 99). www.helgoland.de

Lange Anna ③
Tall Anna, measuring 48 m (157ft) high, is the best known red sand-stone cliff. Nearby is the Lummenfelsen, the smallest nature reserve in Germany.

Harbour ①
On the flat part of the island is Unterland, a small post-war town with a harbour. Fishermen store their nets in the characteristic colourful little houses known as Hummerbuden (lobster huts).

0 metres 100
0 yards 100

③ Lange Anna

Oberland ②

① Harbour

Oberland ②
In the upper part of the island stands the St Nikolai church, dating from 1959. Nearby, and worth a visit, are 16th-century tombs.

KEY

– – – Suggested route

TIPS FOR WALKERS

Starting point: Harbour
Length: 1.7 km (1.1 miles).
Stopping-off points: Restaurants all over the island.
Tip: Go bird-watching at the Lummenfelsen.

East Frisian Islands ●

German name of the Kiel Canal

The islands of Borkum, Juist, Norderney, Baltrum, Langeoog, Spiekeroog and Wangerooge form a chain extending from west to east along the coast of Lower Saxony. The western shores of these East Frisian Islands (Ostfriesische Inseln) are slowly being eroded by constant winds, but protective structures save them from heavy damage. These islands, together with the Watt tidal mud-flats, belong to the Wadden Sea National Park of Lower Saxony. All the East Frisian Islands are car-free, except for Borkum and Norderney.

The Große Kaap (1872) on Borkum, a historic navigation aid

Borkum

220 km (137 miles) west of Hamburg.
🏘 *5,400.* ⛴ *from Emden.*
www.borkum.de

The most westerly of the East Frisian Islands, and the largest in the group, Borkum covers 31 sq km (12 sq miles). It is a North Sea therapeutic spa, offering a wide range of spa facilities. Interesting buildings include the old and new light-houses – the Alter Leuchtturm (1576) and the Neuer Leucht-turm (1879). Family fun is guaranteed at the wellness and adventure pool complex, Gezeitenland. It offers treats such as a sauna with a North Sea view. Every year, in December, a Blues festival is held on the island.

Juist

210 km (137 miles) west of Hamburg.
🏘 *1,800.* ⛴ *from Norddeich.*
www.juist.de

The charming island of Juist, with its lovely 17-km (11-mile) sandy beach, is appropriately named "magic land" by its

tourist board. The 16.4-sq km (6.3-sq mile) island has several bird sanctuaries and the largest freshwater lake in the group, the Hammersee. In 2008, the Seebrücke Juist (Juist pier) opened. You can stroll along it as far as the harbour entrance. Each year, at the end of May, the Juister Musikfestival (Juist Music Festival) is held, featuring bands from across Europe.

Norderney

190 km (118 miles) west of Hamburg.
🏘 *6,000.* ⛴ *from Norddeich.*
www.norderney.de

Sandy beaches stretching 14 km (9 miles) offer pure relaxation on this 26-sq km (10-sq mile) island, which also has an extensive hiking-trail network. Other popular attractions are the Kurtheater (spa theatre), dating from 1894, and the observatory.

In 1797, Norderney became the first North Sea therapeutic spa in Germany. The Bade-museum (bath museum) features the history of the island's spa culture.

Baltrum

190 km (118 miles) west of Hamburg.
🏘 *500.* ⛴ *from Neßmersiel.*
www.baltrum.de

Wellness spas and fabulous bathing fun in SindBad make Baltrum a popular destination for all those seeking relaxation. The island is only 6.5 sq km (2.5 sq miles) in size, so small that everything can be reached easily on foot.

Langeoog

170 km (106 miles) west of Hamburg.
🏘 *2,000.* ⛴ *from Bensersiel.*
www.langeoog.de

Dunes and sandy beaches are the hallmarks of this 20-sq km (7.7-sq-mile) island. The spa and wellness centre offer many kinds of therapies. You can

A car ferry plying the Kiel Canal at Brunsbüttel

also visit the maritime distress observation station, the Schifffahrtsmuseum (seafaring museum), the Heimatmuseum (local history museum) and the water tower. Lale Andersen ("Lili Marleen") is buried in the cemetery, Dünenfriedhof.

Spiekeroog

160 km (99 miles) west of Hamburg.
🚶 *800.* 🚢 *from Neuharlingersiel.*
www.spiekeroog.de

Unusual for a North Sea island are the relatively large tree populations to which Spiekeroog owes its nickname, "the green island". The first forests were planted in the mid-19th century. Spiekeroog is 18 sq km (7 sq miles) in size. Its church (1696) is the oldest house of worship on the East Frisian Islands. The Spiekerooger Muschelmuseum (Spiekeroog shell museum) has a collection of over 3,000 shells. A lovely thing to do is to take a trip on the Museumspferdebahn, a horse-drawn railway, which operates from April to September. Sporty people can participate in the game of Bosseln, a popular ball-game played throughout the East Frisian Islands.

Wangerooge

150 km (93 miles) west of Hamburg.
🚶 *1,000.* 🚢 *from Harlesiel.*
www.wangerooge.de

The most easterly of the East Frisian Islands is tiny Wangerooge, measuring only 5 sq km (2 sq miles). Since 1884, it has been accredited as having sea-water therapeutic baths. A lighthouse, the Alter Leuchtturm (1856), houses the Inselmuseum, a museum of local history. The Nationalpark-Haus, open year-round, displays exhibits related to the Watt tidal mud-flats.

Kiel Canal ❺

Herring Gull

Known in Germany as the Nord-Ostsee-Kanal but internationally as the Kiel Canal, this man-made waterway is the most travelled in the world. Each year, more than 40,000 ships traverse this canal between the mouth of the Elbe and the Kiel fjords as a short-cut, saving themselves roughly 320 km (200 miles) that it would otherwise take to go around Denmark. The canal links the North Sea at Brunsbüttel with the Baltic Sea at Kiel. It is 98 km (61 miles) long and 11 m (36 ft) deep, with a maximum width of 162 m (531 ft) at the water line and 90 m (295 ft) at the bottom. After eight years of construction, the canal (originally named Kaiser-Wilhelm-Kanal) opened on 21 June 1895. It was re-named Nord-Ostsee-Kanal in 1948.

Eight roads and four railway lines cross over the canal on ten bridges. Ferries ply the waters between the north and south shores. There are locks at both ends of the canal to control the differences in water levels caused by the tides.

The Kiel Canal – important in international freight shipping

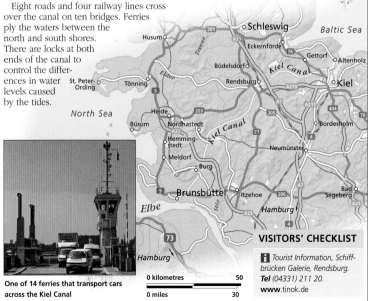

One of 14 ferries that transport cars across the Kiel Canal

0 kilometres   50
0 miles   30

VISITORS' CHECKLIST

ℹ️ *Tourist Information, Schiffbrücken Galerie, Rendsburg.*
Tel *(04431) 211 20.*
www.tinok.de

Bremen 6

Bremen, together with its deep-water port Bremerhaven, constitutes a separate city-state. The townscape is dominated by what the citizens call "the parlour", the area around the statue of Roland, the magnificent cathedral and the town hall. In 787 Bremen became a diocesan town, in 965 it was granted market rights and in 1358 it joined the Hanseatic League. The harbour of Bremen was developed in 1827, and during the 19th century the city's wealth was based on the tobacco, coffee and cotton trades. Today, Bremerhaven is Europe's biggest port-of-loading for the fishing and automobile industries.

Statue of the Bremen Town Musicians by Gerhard Marcks

🏛 Rathaus
See pp 164–5.

🏛 Schütting
Marktplatz.
Opposite the town hall stands this mansion used by the Merchants' Guild for their conventions. It was built in 1537–39 by the Antwerp architect, Johann der Buschener, in the Dutch Mannerist style. Its eastern gable is by local builder, Carsten Husmann (1565).

⛪ Pfarrkirche Unser Lieben Frauen
Unser-Lieben-Frauen-Kirchhof 27.
⏰ *11am–4pm Mon–Sat, 11:30am–1pm Sun.*
Work on this three-aisled early Gothic hall-church started in 1229. The Romanesque tower of a previous church on the site was integrated as the building's northern spire. At the end of the 14th century, the choir was extended, and a southern aisle was added. The church's colonnade dates from the 19th century. Striking 14th-century frescos adorn the crypt.

Gabled houses and the statue of Roland on the Marktplatz

Exploring Bremen

Most of Bremen's sights are located in the Old Town, on the east bank of the Weser river. The area is surrounded by a green belt – the Wallanlagen, the site of the city's former fortifications. The Überseemuseum (ethnography museum) is close to the Hauptbahnhof (central train station). A 10-minute tram ride takes you from here to the Marktplatz, and in 15 minutes you reach Schwachhausen, where the Focke-Museum is based.

🏛 Marktplatz
On the main square of medieval Bremen are the town hall, cathedral and the Schütting (guildhall); gabled houses are on the west side.

In front of the town hall stands the largest statue of Roland in Germany, measuring 10 m (32 ft). Together with the town hall, it was named a UNESCO World Heritage Site in 2004. Roland was a peer in Charlemagne's court. Over time, he has come to symbolize market rights and freedom in Germany. Roland's gaze is directed towards the cathedral, the residence of the bishop, who often sought to restrict the city's autonomy. The sword of justice symbolizes the judiciary's independence; the inscription cites the emperor's edict, conferring town rights on Bremen.

Also here is a monument dedicated to the **Bremen Town Musicians** (1953) – a donkey, dog, cat and cockerel, characters from a Grimms fairy tale.

The late Renaissance façade of Bremen's Rathaus (town hall)

St-Petri-Dom

Sandstraße 10–12. 10am–5pm Mon–Fri, 10am–2pm Sat, 2–5pm Sun (June–Sep: until 6pm Mon–Fri, Sun). **Tower** Apr–Oct: 10am–4:30pm Mon–Fri, 10am–1:30pm Sat, 2–4:30pm Sun (June–Sep: until 5:30pm Fri, Sun). **Bleikeller** Apr–Oct: 10am–4:45pm Mon–Fri, 10am–1:45pm Sat, noon–4:45pm Sun (June–Sep: until 5:45pm Fri–Sun). **Museum** 10am–4:45pm Mon–Fri, 10am–1:30pm Sat, 2–4:45pm Sun. www.stpetridom.de

This magnificent cathedral, with its vast twin-towered façade, dates from the 11th century. Enlarged in the 16th century, the church contains elements of different styles – from Romanesque to late Gothic. From 1532 to 1638, during the Protestant Reformation, the cathedral was

The Mannerist Schütting (guildhall), a meeting place for merchants

mostly closed. Extensive rebuilding took place at the end of the 19th century.

Inside you can view the old chancel (1518), which now functions as the organ parapet, fragments of Gothic stalls and the pulpit (1638), with its wood carvings. There are also memorials, including one to Provost Segebade Clüver (1547). The eastern crypt has

Bas-reliefs on the western choir stalls in the St-Petri-Dom

interesting cubiform capitals, while in the western crypt visitors can admire the sculpture of Christ the Omnipotent (1050) and the baptismal font with its 38 bas-reliefs and bowl, supported by four lions with riders.

In the **Bleikeller** (lead cellar), six preserved mummies are on show. The **Museum** records the history of the cathedral and archbishopric, and stores treasures retrieved from the tombs of Bremen's archbishops. Opened in 1998, the cathedral's garden (Bibelgarten) is a peaceful retreat from the bustle of the city.

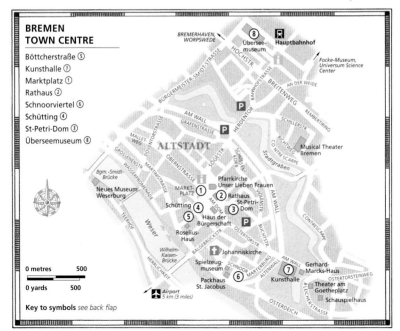

BREMEN TOWN CENTRE

Böttcherstraße ⑤
Kunsthalle ⑦
Marktplatz ①
Rathaus ②
Schnoorviertel ⑥
Schütting ④
St-Petri-Dom ③
Überseemuseum ⑧

0 metres 500
0 yards 500

Key to symbols see back flap

Bremen Rathaus

Bremen's town hall was built in 1405–10. The late Gothic red-brick building is decorated with medieval statuary, including lifesize sandstone sculptures of the Emperor Charlemagne and the seven Electors. The façade, having been completely reworked by the architect Lüder von Bentheim in 1608–12, is considered to be an outstanding example of Weser Renaissance architecture. The frieze above the arcade represents an allegory of human history. The town hall and the statue of Roland were named as World Heritage Sites by UNESCO in 2004.

Façade
The original Gothic building was clad with an outstanding Weser Renaissance façade designed by Lüder von Bentheim in 1608–12.

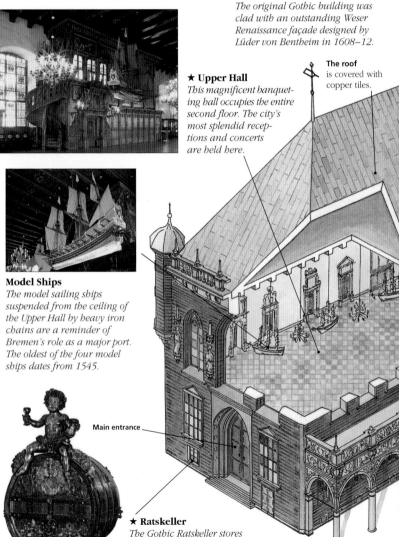

The roof
is covered with copper tiles.

★ **Upper Hall**
This magnificent banqueting hall occupies the entire second floor. The city's most splendid receptions and concerts are held here.

Model Ships
The model sailing ships suspended from the ceiling of the Upper Hall by heavy iron chains are a reminder of Bremen's role as a major port. The oldest of the four model ships dates from 1545.

Main entrance

★ **Ratskeller**
The Gothic Ratskeller stores hundreds of wine barrels adorned with figures such as Bacchus.

★ **Ornamental Gable**
*The architect Lüder
von Bentheim
embellished the
town hall façade by
adding a Flemish-style
stepped gable that is
five storeys high.*

VISITORS' CHECKLIST

Am Markt 21. **Town Center**
see p163. **Tel** *(0421) 36 10.*
 *ask by phone.*
www.rathaus-bremen.de
Bremen central tourism
Findorffstr. 105.
Tel (0180) 510 10 30.
www.bremen-tourismus.de

**The middle
projection**
with the striking
pediment was
added in the
17th century.

**The Judgment
of Solomon**
*The mural (1532)
of Solomon's court
in the Upper Hall is a
reference to the room's
former dual function
as a council-chamber
and courtroom.*

Arcades
*Above
every arcade
there are figures
representing the
history of Bremen and
the virtues of the state.*

STAR FEATURES

★ Ornamental Gable

★ Ratskeller

★ Upper Hall

Art Nouveau Room
*The lower room of the
two-storey Gülden-
kammer owes its 1905
Art Nouveau (Jugendstil)
makeover to the artist
Heinrich Vogeler. The
gilded leather wallpaper
dates from the early
17th century.*

⊞ Böttcherstraße

Paula-Modersohn-Becker-Museum, Museum im Roselius-Haus Böttcherstraße 6–10. **Tel** (0421) 338 82 22. ◻ 11am–6pm Tue–Sun. 🅰 ⬜ www.pmbm.de

From 1924–31, this street was transformed into an Expressionist-style lane by Ludwig Roselius, a wealthy coffee merchant. Later the Nazis preserved the Böttcherstraße as an example of degenerate art. On the entrance gate is Bernhard Hoetger's bas-relief, *Der Lichtbringer* (1920), which represents the Archangel Michael fighting a dragon.

Today the lane is lined by museums and shops. The **Paula-Modersohn-Becker-Museum** displays paintings and graphic art by the artist as well as Bernhard Hoetgers' oeuvre. In the 16th century **Roselius-Haus** you can admire the original period interiors as well as low German art from the 14th to the 19th centuries.

⊞ Schnoorviertel

Spielzeugmuseum im Schnoor Schnoor 24. **Tel** (0421) 32 03 82. ◻ 11am–6pm daily. 🅰

The Schnoor is part of Bremen's oldest district. One of the city's poorest and most densely populated areas before World War II, it miraculously escaped wartime destruction. It has been restored gradually since 1958 and now teems with restaurants, cafés and

Der Lichtbringer bas-relief at Böttcherstraße

galleries. In the centre of the district is the Gothic **Johannis-kirche** (14th century). The red-brick church once belonged to the Franciscans. In accordance with the order's rules it has no tower, although this is compensated for by a decorative gable with blind arcades on the western façade. The **Spielzeugmuseum** (toy museum) is also worth a visit.

⚏ Kunsthalle Bremen

Am Wall 207. **Tel** (0421) 32 90 80. ◻ 10am–9pm Tue, 10am–6pm Wed–Sun. 🅰 www.kunsthalle-bremen.de

The gallery showcases masterpieces from the 14th century to contemporary art. The Old Masters wing features works by Dürer, Altdorfer, Rubens and Rembrandt. The French and the German 19th and 20th century artists such as Beckmann and Kirchner are striking. After renovation the museum re-opened in 2011.

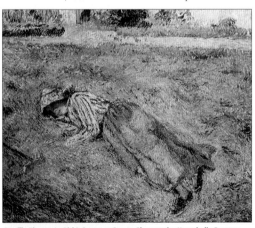

Camille Pissarro's *Girl Lying on a Grassy Slope* at the Kunsthalle Bremen

⚏ Überseemuseum

Bahnhofsplatz 13. **Tel** (0421) 16 03 81 01. ◻ 9am–6pm Tue–Fri, 10am–6pm Sat & Sun. 🅰 ⬜ ⊞ www.uebersee-museum.de

Opened in 1896, this museum was originally devoted to German colonialism. Today, it is still a museum of overseas countries, transporting visitors to faraway lands and explaining their cultural history, ecology and current situation. While largely dedicated to the culture of non-European nations, there is also an exhibition entitled "Bremen – Hanseatic City by the River". The spacious halls are filled with palm trees, models of South Pacific houses and boats, temples and a Japanese garden. Innumerable plants and stuffed animals are placed next to ethnological exhibits.

⚏ Focke-Museum

Schwachhauser Heerstraße 240. **Tel** (0421) 699 60 00. ◻ 10am–9pm Tue, 10am–5pm Wed–Sun. 🅰 ⬜ ⊞ ⬜ www.focke-museum.de

This excellent museum presents Bremen's art and culture from the Middle Ages to the present day. Exhibits from patrician houses and original sculptures from the façade of the town hall testify to the wealth of this Hanseatic city. Other sections are devoted to the archeology of the region and to whaling.

The nearby **Rhododendron-Park**, part of the Bürgerpark, offers a pleasant respite from the museums. Covering 46 ha (114 acres), it includes 2,000 varieties of rhododendron and azalea, which turn the park into a sea of blossoms from late April to June.

⚏ Universum Science Center

Wiener Straße 1a. **Tel** (0421) 334 60. ◻ 9am–6pm Mon–Fri 10am–7pm Sat & Sun. 🅰 ⬜ ⊞ www.universum-bremen.de

In this centre, the wonders of the world are spectacularly presented. The fantastic journey across the "continents" (Humankind, Earth and Cosmos) features experimental areas and large-scale projections. It is fun for adults and children alike.

PAULA MODERSOHN-BECKER (1876–1907)

A pupil of Fritz Mackensen and the wife of Otto Modersohn, Paula Modersohn-Becker was the most significant artistic figure in Worpswede. She learned about the Impressionist use of colour during visits to Paris, and her own unique style was a precursor to Expressionism. She became famous

for naturalistic paintings of poor, starving, and even dying country folk, as well as self portraits and still lifes. Her watercolours and prints were also acclaimed. She died in childbirth at the age of 31. This is how she was commemorated on her tombstone, in the village cemetery in Worpswede, by the sculptor Bernhard Hoetger.

Girl playing a flute in birch woods (1905)

Exhibits in the Große Kunstschau in Worpswede near Bremen

Environs: 50 km (31 miles) to the north lies **Bremerhaven**, with the **Deutsches Schifffahrtsmuseum**. This superb marine museum, designed by Hans Scharoun, displays originals and models of a wide range of ships, dating from the beginnings of seafaring to the present day. One of the highlights is the *Hansekogge* (1380), an oak wood merchant ship retrieved from the Weser river in 1962. In the open-air section of the museum are the last great German sailing boat *Seute Deern*, the polar ship *Grönland* and *Wilhelm Bauer*, a U-boat from World War II.

The Klimahaus Bremerhaven 8° Ost, the city's most recent attraction, opened in 2009. The exhibition revolves around climate and climate change. Visitors embark on a journey following the 8th degree of longitude, crossing different climate zones.

From 1884 to World War II, the small village of **Worpswede**, 28 km (17 miles) northeast of Bremen near the Teufelsmoor, was a famous artists' colony. Apart from poets such as Rainer Maria Rilke, and architects including Bernhard Hoetger, the village's fame rested principally on the painters Fritz Mackensen, Otto Modersohn, Hans am Ende, Fritz Overbeck and Heinrich Vogeler. The greatest artist here was Paula Modersohn-Becker. Work by the founding members is on display in the **Große Kunstschau** and the **Worpsweder Kunsthalle**.

Verden an der Aller, the quaint bishop's residence and once a free town of the Reich, is known to sports enthusiasts thanks to its horse-breeding centres and the **Deutsches Pferdemuseum** (horse

museum). In the city centre, the early 13th-century Andreaskirche contains the brass tomb of Bischof Yso, and the Johanniskirche (12th–15th century) features Gothic murals and ceiling frescos. Above the town rises the Dom (1290–1490) with a copper saddle roof. The tower, cloister and the eastern section of the three-aisled hall-church are Romanesque. North of the cathedral, the Domherrenhaus (1708) houses the **Historisches Museum**, with exhibits on cultural history and ethnology.

🏛 **Deutsches Schifffahrtsmuseum**
Bremerhaven, Hans-Scharoun-Platz 1. *Tel (0471) 48 20 70.* ◻ Nov–Mar: 10am–6pm Tue–Sun; Apr–Oct: 10am–6pm daily. 📷

🏛 **Klimahaus Bremerhaven 8° Ost**
Am Längengrad 8. *Tel (0471) 902 03 00.* ◻ Apr–Oct: 9am–7pm Mon–Fri, 10am–7pm Sat, Sun; Nov–Mar: 10am–6pm daily. 📷 🚻

🏛 **Große Kunstschau Worpswede**
Lindenallee 5. *Tel (04792) 13 02.* ◻ 10am–6pm daily. 📷 🚻

🏛 **Worpsweder Kunsthalle**
Bergstraße 17. *Tel (04792) 12 77.* ◻ 10am–6pm daily. 📷 🚻
www.worpsweder-kunsthalle.de

🏛 **Deutsches Pferdemuseum**
Verden, Holzmarkt 9. *Tel (04231) 80 71 40.* ◻ 10am–5pm Tue–Sun. 🚻 www.dpm-verden.de

🏛 **Historisches Museum**
Verden, Untere Straße 13. *Tel (04231) 21 69 .* ◻ 10am–1pm, 3–5pm Tue–Sun. 📷 www.domherrenhaus.de

The Dom in Verden an der Aller, with its unusually high-pitched roof

Museumsdorf Cloppenburg ❼

Over 50 structures built in Lower Saxony between the 16th and 19th centuries can be viewed in this 20-ha (49-acre) open-air museum. Moved from their original locations and reassembled here, these buildings document the development and variety of rural architecture, Lower Saxon artisanry and the way rural people lived. The region's main building styles are the half-timbered, thatch-roofed, Lower German Hallenhaus and the East Frisian Gulfhaus, a type of farmhouse in which people and animals lived together under one roof. Special themed exhibitions expand and complement the collections.

Dutch Mill
Just the timber cap of the windmill needs to be turned in this type of windmill (1764) from Bokel in Cappeln.

★ Haake Farmstead
The Haake farmstead from Cappeln (1793) is supported by four rows of posts and is therefore known as a Vierständerhaus (four-posted house).

Storage building
This type of multi-purpose building (before 1792, from Norddöllen) served as carriage house and workshop. The attic was used for storage.

Zaunscheune, a type of stable, from Varenesch

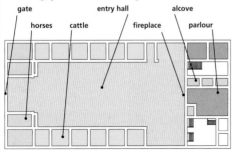

PLAN OF A FARMSTEAD

The entry hall is also the heart of the farmstead. It is a covered courtyard with farmhouse gate and stable doors. The living quarters surround the parlour.

gate   horses   cattle   entry hall   fireplace   alcove   parlour

STAR SIGHTS

★ Fireplace

★ Haake Farmstead

★ Parlour

★ Fireplace
Close to the wall of the living quarters was an open fireplace that warmed the entire house. The fire also was used for food preparation.

VISITORS' CHECKLIST

150 km (93 miles) southwest of Hamburg. (04471) 948 40.
Mar–Oct: 9am–6pm; Nov–Feb: 9am–4:30pm.
(04471) 94 84 23.
www.museumsdorf.de

Alcoves
Alcoves off the living room served as tiny bedchambers. They were locked during the day.

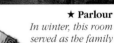

★ Parlour
In winter, this room served as the family living room. On Sundays and holidays, it was the dining and sitting room. It contained the best furniture.

Brewing outbuilding from Visbek

Entry hall
This type of farmstead is known as a Hallenhaus. The entry was the farmstead's principal room and inner courtyard. From here, there was access to the stables, attic and living quarters.

Pig stable
This 18th-century small pig stable from Klein Mimmelage features a thatched roof with deep eaves, which protected the feeding troughs lined up along the wall from the elements.

TRAVELLERS' NEEDS

WHERE TO STAY

Whether you are on holiday, a business trip or a short jaunt – the Hanseatic city of Hamburg is a great place to stay. With its around 300 hotels, there is something to suit every taste and budget. The accommodations range from the luxurious to the inexpensive, from impeccably appointed five-star hotels to avant-garde designer hotels, from low-cost chains to classic pensions providing excellent value for money. Some hotels have their own spas where guests can relax and be thoroughly pampered after a busy day. If you're looking for something out of the ordinary, you won't be disappointed either: what could be more fitting in this maritime city than spending a night on a ship? The list of hotels provided on pages 176–183 helps you choose a place to stay. The list is organized by area and price category, and includes every type of hotel.

Hotel porter

Entrance to the luxurious Hotel Atlantic Kempinski (see p182)

FINDING A HOTEL

Most of Hamburg's attractions are located in the city centre area and can be reached easily on foot or with the excellent public transit system. If your visit is primarily intended to see the sights, then it is best to select a hotel close to the centre of town. Business travellers might prefer a hotel near the airport or the trade fair, depending on their needs.

Several of the finest hotels in Hamburg are found in the elegant city districts located around the Binnenalster and the Außenalster. But even in the district of Blankenese, which is just a few kilometres west of Hamburg, there are a number of exclusive hotels in tranquil settings that are ready to welcome guests. If you are looking for a place to relax, then this might well be the right area for you.

In the Old Town and in St Pauli, there are a great many places to stay for budget-conscious visitors who are not bothered by noise. The entertainment district of St Pauli, in particular, never seems to quiet down completely.

Irrespective of the price category, a hotel room with a view of Hamburg's harbour is always a good choice.

HOTEL CATEGORIES AND AMENITIES

Hamburg has a wide range of hotels in all price categories. Five-star hotels offer every comfort a traveller could expect. Hotel rooms in these luxury accommodations are spacious and decorated with top-quality furniture. They are usually bright and come equipped with the latest technology, such as sound-proof windows, ingenious bathrooms with upscale fixtures and amenities, as well as the most up-to-date communications gadgets. Along with exquisite and elegant restaurants, luxury hotels usually also offer fitness centres, and wellness areas with saunas, massage and often swimming pools.

An interesting alternative for guests who take a special delight in extravagance are the so-called boutique hotels, which are also known as designer hotels. In recent years, several boldly designed hotels have opened in Hamburg. They captivate with their unique design and colour-schemes as well as their sophisticated use of light. As soon as you enter a boutique hotel, you almost enter another world. Some of these unusual hotels have been constructed in buildings that were originally designed with other purposes in mind. They include a former post office, an old coal storage warehouse and a former high-class brothel. Fortunately, design does not always have to come at a price. The cost of staying in some boutique

Hotel Vier Jahreszeiten *(see p182)* – a fantastic location on the Binnenalster

◁ **Terrace of the café and restaurant Alex in Alsterpavillon *(see p124)***

Lobby of the Maritim Hotel Reichshof *(see p177)*

hotels is certainly in the mid price-range. This is also true for hotels that are located in historic buildings, such as in magnificent Art Nouveau (Jugendstil) villas. Even these hotels with their magical ambience do not have to be expensive.

At the other end of the price spectrum are the simple, sparse rooms that usually are furnished with a television and telephone but the bathroom might be down the hall. This kind of accommodation is popular with tourists who spend their time sightseeing and taking in the town, returning just to sleep.

HOTEL CHAINS

When you stay in a chain hotel such as **Best Western**, **Dorint**, **Mercure** or **Ramada** you always can rely on a high degree of comfort and cleanliness. Guests here always know what to expect. The majority of these hotels cater to the needs of business travellers, and offer conference rooms with the necessary equipment. Chain hotels often have attractive weekend deals to fill up their rooms; it can pay to look into these offers. Also check to see if the hotel has a bonus programme if you travel to Hamburg with an airline or in a rental car. Many chain hotels have agreements with airlines and car rental companies, and you might be eligible for a reward such as a discount or bonus air miles.

The popular agency **einfach Hamburg** is not a hotel chain in the usual sense, but rather a very loose association of hotels. It consists of several hotels located in different districts. Each is distinguished by its intimate atmosphere, and each can be counted among the city's most attractive hotels. This small hotel group considers itself an alternative to international hotel chains.

SHIP HOTELS

You can also stay overnight in the very place where Hamburg is at its most quintessential – in the harbour. The passenger cabins of the museum ship *Cap San Diego (see pp98–9)*, which has been anchored in the harbour since 1986, were renovated in the style of the 1950s; they still exude the charms of the glory days of sea travel. A former lightship, **Das Feuerschiff** *(see p89)*, is also enjoying a second career in tourism just a few ships

Pure modern style at the boutique hotel East *(see p179)*

away. Here guests are gently rocked to sleep in the former captain's cabin and the cabins where the crew slept. The space in these "floating hotels" is a bit snug, but it is also very cosy.

HOW TO BOOK

As in other countries, you can book your Hanseatic accommodation at your convenience directly by telephone, by fax or online. A good way of learning about the features of a hotel – and what it will cost – is to visit the website of the hotel you are considering. In the hotel listings on pages 176–183, contact information (including websites, phone and fax numbers) has been provided for every hotel that appears. You can also book rooms in practically every hotel in Hamburg through the Hamburg tourist office, **Hamburg Tourismus GmbH**.

It is a very good idea to book ahead, especially in summer, when important trade fairs are being held, and during the Port's Birthday at the beginning of May *(see p85)*. At such times it may be difficult to find a room at short notice.

Of course, many hotels may also offer last-minute discounts for rooms that have not been reserved. A number of hotels catering to business travellers offer special discounts at weekends, making staying in these hotels from Friday to Sunday cheaper than on weekdays.

HOTEL RATES AND DISCOUNTS

Several hotels offer interesting discounts, often combined with the purchase of tickets for musicals or other events. These discounts also often include the much sought-after – and therefore quickly sold-out – tickets for boat tours during the Port's Birthday Bash. All-round packages that include transportation, shuttle from the airport to the hotel, an overnight stay and one or two events are increasingly popular.

The bright colours of the bar in Le Royal Méridien *(see p182)*

HIDDEN EXTRAS

At some hotels, the cost of the room does not include breakfast. There is often an additional cost for parking. Charges may be incurred for using fitness centres and spa facilities.

Telephone calls made from your hotel or hotel room can be very expensive. You may well pay a steep price for drinks and snacks from the mini-bar. Tipping is usually expected only in the largest and most expensive hotels.

DISABLED TRAVELLERS

Many of the larger hotels offer rooms with wheelchair access and services tailored to disabled visitors' needs. Often this is not the case in smaller hotels, pensions, and bed-and-breakfasts, which may not even have a lift. Before you book, if you or a travelling companion has special needs, contact the hotel and discuss your requirements, such as lifts or doors that are wide enough for wheelchairs.

The **Senatskoordinator für die Gleichstellung behinderter Menschen der Freien und Hansestadt Hamburg** produces a brochure with information for the disabled. You can also find out more information on the Internet at **www.behinderten-ratgeber. de**, a comprehensive gateway to people with special needs.

TRAVELLING WITH CHILDREN

In many hotels, young children can stay in their parents' room for free or for a small extra charge. Children's cots are usually available and can be placed in your room as needed. Hotels that are especially well-equipped for children are given a special symbol in the hotel listings. Standard equipment in these hotel restaurants or breakfast rooms includes high chairs, while menus always include the option of children's portions. Some hotels offer special family packages such as two connecting rooms or one large room with a separate sleeping area. Of course, self-catering flats offer more room for the entire family.

Sign at the Nippon Hotel *(see 181)*

The package tour operator Happy Hamburg Reisen, which belongs to **Hamburg Tourismus GmbH**, offers special deals for families who travel to Hamburg by train. The package includes train travel and accommodation at a reasonable price.

Another family-friendly and budget-conscious option is the **A&O Hostel Hamburg**. Just 400 m (0.25 miles) from the Hauptbahnhof, this hostel offers single, double and multi-bed rooms (all with bath), and an option for groups and school classes, as well as for families.

PRIVATE HOMES AND SELF-CATERING FLATS

A good yet relatively inexpensive alternative to hotel rooms are rooms in private homes; they often include breakfast. Aside from the price, their attraction for cost-conscious travellers is the chance to stay with local families who usually provide valuable tips and information on sightseeing.

The agency **bed & breakfast** specialises in renting simply furnished rooms in private homes. Their package deals are interesting, such as the one offering a two-night stay, breakfast, and a one-hour introductory sailing course. The agency tailors its offers to your needs and also helps you plan your stay in Hamburg. The **Hamburger Privatzimmervermittlung** helps individual travellers as well as tour groups of up to 15 people find a place to stay. **Bedroomforyou** rents elegantly decorated rooms in the homes of well-off middle-class Hamburgers.

Ideal for families or for longer stays are self-catering flats. Completely furnished, and well-located near transit routes, they provide accommodation for up to six people. They can be booked through agencies such as **Ferienwohnungen in Hamburg**. Private rooms (some with private baths), suites and self-catering flats also are available for rent in several Hamburg districts by **Zimmer Frei Hamburg**.

Breakfast room in the Hotel Schwanenwik *(see p181)*

BUDGET ACCOMMODATION

An inexpensive way of spending time in Hamburg is to stay at one of the city's many youth hostels (Jugendherberge). To be eligible, you must be a member of the German Youth Hostel Association or of any other national youth hostel association. All you need is a membership card. You can get a German card by applying online (www.jugendherberge.de).

The **Jugendherberge auf dem Stintfang** is a very popular hostel located just above the Landungsbrücken. All the two- to six-bed rooms have a shower and toilet. There is a fantastic view of the harbour through the huge lobby windows. Other popular youth hostels are the Jugendherberge Horner Rennbahn near the Horn racetrack and the **Hamburger Jugendpark Langenhorn** (no youth hostel pass needed) in the north.

Hotel Am Holstenwall Novum *(see p178)*, which houses Bar 509

CAMPING

For a city, Hamburg and its environs offer an astonishing number of camping sites. Directly on the shores of the Elbe at Blankenese – in the extreme west of Hamburg – stretches the campground **Elbe Camp**.

Approximately 25 km (16 miles) southeast of the city centre (about 30 minutes by car) is the well-equipped campground on the Elbe **Campingplatz Stover Strand**, which has a flat sandy beach and a marina with 100 berths for sailboats and motorboats. Almost just as far to the northeast of the city centre (about 35 minutes by car) is the idyllic campground **Campingplatz ABC am Großensee**. Here visitors can enjoy the charms of this landscape with its many lakes formed by glaciers during the Ice Age.

DIRECTORY

HOTEL CHAINS

Best Western
Tel 0800 212 58 88.
www.bestwestern.de

Dorint
Tel 0180 226 25 24.
www.dorint.com

Mercure
Tel (069) 95 30 75 92.
www.mercure.com

Ramada
Tel (00800) 87 33 37 37.
www.ramada.de

einfach Hamburg
Ifflandstr. 85.
Tel 279 29 50.
www.einfach-hamburg.de

SHIP HOTELS

Cap San Diego
Überseebrücke.
Tel 36 42 09.
www.capsandiego.de

Das Feuerschiff
City-Sporthafen.
Tel 36 25 53.
www.das-feuerschiff.de

RESERVATIONS

Hamburg Tourismus GmbH
Steinstr. 7.
Map 10 E3.
Tel 30 05 13 00.
www.hamburgtourismus.de

DISABLED TRAVELLERS

Senatskoordinator für die Gleichstellung behinderter Menschen
Osterbekstr. 96.
Tel 428 63 57 24.

TRAVELLING WITH CHILDREN

A&O Hostel Hamburg
Amsinckstr. 6–10.
Tel 644 21 04-56 00.
Hammer Landstr. 170.
Tel 644 21 04-55 00.
www.aohostels.com/de/hamburg

PRIVATE HOMES AND SELF-CATERING FLATS

bed & breakfast
Markusstr. 9.
Tel 491 56 66.
www.bed-and-breakfast.de

Bedroomforyou
Tornquiststr. 1.
Tel 40 18 61 37.
www.bedroomforyou.de

Ferienwohnungen in Hamburg
Tel 643 14 34.
www.hamburg ferienwohnungen.de

Hamburger Privatzimmervermittlung
Bramfelder Str. 46.
Tel 22 69 00 89.
www.hamburger-privatzimmer.de

Zimmer Frei Hamburg
Steilshooper Str. 186.
Tel 27 87 77 77.
www.zimmerfrei hamburg.de

BUDGET ACCOMMODATION

Hamburger Jugendpark Langenhorn
Jugendparkweg 60.
Tel 531 30 50.
www.hamburger-jugendpark.de

Jugendherberge auf dem Stintfang
Alfred-Wegener-Weg 5.
Tel 31 34 88.
www.jugendherberge.de/jh/hamburg-stintfang

CAMPING

Campingplatz ABC am Großensee
Trittauer Str. 11.
22946 Großensee.
Tel (04154) 606 42.
www.campingplatz-abc.de

Campingplatz Stover Strand
Stover Strand 10.
21423 Drage.
Tel (04177) 430.
www.camping-stover-strand.de

Elbe Camp
Falkensteiner Ufer 101.
Tel 81 29 49.
www.elbecamp.de

Choosing a Hotel

The hotels on the following pages have been
selected because they offer good value, a wide range
of amenities and an attractive location. Entries are
listed by area and, within each area, alphabetically
by price category. All hotel rooms have a private
bathroom unless otherwise noted.

PRICE CATEGORIES
Price categories for a standard double
room per night, including breakfast,
service charges and tax:

€ under €80
€€ €80–120
€€€ €120–160
€€€€ €160–200
€€€€€ over €200

OLD TOWN

Annenhof
W   €

Lange Reihe 23, 20099 **Tel** *24 34 26* **Fax** *24 55 69* **Rooms** *13*   **Map** *6 E2*

The colourful rooms in this lovingly restored Jugendstil building (1870) have names such as "blue", "red", "lilac",
"green" or "orange". Along with the colour-saturated tones, wooden floors and plaster ceilings help to create an
intimate, friendly atmosphere. Coffee and tea are free, shower and WC are off the hall. **www.hotelannenhof.de**

Galerie Hotel Petersen
⑪ W   €€

Lange Reihe 50, 20099 **Tel** *24 98 26* **Fax** *24 98 26* **Rooms** *5*   **Map** *6 E2*

Whether in Biedermeier, Art Deco or contemporary – the five hotel rooms in this classic town house built in 1790 are
lovingly decorated with choice furnishings and art. Individualists, above all, will delight in the creative atmosphere of
this charming hotel. **www.ghsp.eu**

Hotel Alte Wache
P ⑪ 🖥 🐾 🛏 W   €€

Adenauerallee 25, 20097 **Tel** *284 06 60* **Fax** *280 17 54* **Rooms** *100*   **Map** *6 E2*

An oasis of tranquillity in the middle of Hamburg. All rooms have a desk, TV, radio and mini-bar. Conference rooms
for up to 150 participants are located on site. The breakfast buffet offers many choices, providing a perfect start to
a day in the Hanseatic city. **www.hotel-alte-wache.de**

Hotel Continental
P 🖥 🛏 W   €€

Kirchenallee 37, 20099 **Tel** *18 88 11 50* **Fax** *18 88 11 51 11* **Rooms** *35*   **Map** *6 E2*

Hanseatic flair with up-to-date comfort – the Hotel Continental, an upmarket hotel, has a friendly atmosphere that
guarantees to make its guests feel right at home. All the rooms are equipped with a TV, telephone and mini-bar; the
breakfast buffet has everything you could wish for. **www.hotel-continental.de**

Hotel Mercedes
P 🖥 🛏 W   €€

Steindamm 51, 20099 **Tel** *280 12 18/19* **Fax** *230 23 67* **Rooms** *19*   **Map** *6 E2*

The Hotel Mercedes is small and very fine, with an almost family-like atmosphere. It's just the right place for those
who value personalized service. The clientele is international, and there is always a world traveller or two among the
guests. All rooms have a TV and telephone. **www.hotel-mercedes.de**

Hotel Village
W   €€

Steindamm 4, 20099 **Tel** *480 64 90* **Fax** *48 06 49 49* **Rooms** *20*   **Map** *6 E2*

A hotel for all those who love the unusual. Only the plushy ambience serves to remind patrons of the Hotel Village's
colourful past as a high-class brothel. The rooms are extravagantly furnished with silk carpets, canopies, and mirrors
over the beds (some rooms have four-poster beds). Coffee is free. **www.hotel-village.de**

Junges Hotel
P ⑪ 🖥 🐾 🛏 W   €€

Kurt-Schumacher-Allee 14, 20097 **Tel** *41 92 30* **Fax** *41 92 35 55* **Rooms** *128*   **Map** *6 F2*

Just like the name says, this hotel is young ("Junges") and different. Its atmosphere has profited greatly from the
judicious use of warm, rich colour-tones in the indoor and outdoor areas. Children up to the age of 12 can stay at
no extra charge in their parents' room. There is a Finnish sauna and a bio-sauna. **www.junges-hotel.de**

Suitehotel Hamburg City
P 📺 🖥 🗐 🛗 🛏 W   €€

Lübeckertordamm 2, 20099 **Tel** *27 14 00* **Fax** *27 14 01 40* **Rooms** *186*   **Map** *6 F1*

Guests at this all-suite hotel can enjoy the fitness centre, as well as a 10-minute massage, which is included in the
price. The 4elements bar is open around the clock. Children up to the age of 12 can stay at no extra charge in their
parents' room. If you stay longer than three days a rental car is for free. **www.suitehotel.com**

Eleazar Novum City Center Hamburg
P 🖥 W   €€€

Bremer Reihe 12–14, 20099 **Tel** *878 87 70* **Fax** *878 87 71 11* **Rooms** *103*   **Map** *6 E2*

This well-run hotel was completely renovated in 2007. The rooms are modern in brown with stylish furniture. Each
room has a balcony, TV and Internet access. In the lobby, free daily newspapers are available. The spa area also has
a sauna. **www.eleazar-novum.de**

Key to Symbols *see back cover flap*

Hotel City House
P ⚡ W   €€€

Pulverteich 25, 20099 **Tel** *280 08 10* **Fax** *280 18 38* **Rooms** *30*   **Map** 6 F2

This hotel is located in a villa built in 1905 and is perfect for a short holiday as well as a longer stay. Each of the hotel's rooms has a different decor, but all have features like stucco ceiling, wooden furniture and light fabrics. **www.raphaelhotels.de/hotel-city-house**

Hotel Graf Moltke
P ⚡ ⚡ ⚡ W   €€€

Steindamm 1, 20099 **Tel** *24 42 41 10* **Fax** *24 42 41 16 11* **Rooms** *97*   **Map** 6 E2

Completely renovated in 2008, this hotel is ideally situated for exploring the city centre. The generously sized rooms in this five-storey building are decorated in contemporary style and are tastefully done. There is no price mark-up during trade fairs. **www.hotel-hamburg-graf-moltke.de**

Hotel Königshof Novum
P ⚡ W   €€€

Pulverteich 18, 20099 **Tel** *284 07 40* **Fax** *28 40 74 74* **Rooms** *21*   **Map** 6 E2

Much store is set on the modern in the elegant interior design of this hotel. The generous use of wood, and a Mediterranean colour-palette, underscore the nature of this hotel. The restaurant Hofgarten is popular with the public, as well as with hotel guests. **www.koenigshof-hamburg.de**

Hotel Senator
P ⚡ ⚡ ⚡ W   €€€

Lange Reihe 18–20, 20099 **Tel** *24 19 30* **Fax** *24 19 31 09* **Rooms** *56*   **Map** 6 E2

The hotel rooms are decorated in a welcoming style and have modern communication gadgets. Business travellers stay here, too. Features of the hotel are the winter garden and "wellness rooms", which feature a waterbed and/or a steam shower. **www.hotel-senator-hamburg.de**

InterCityHotel Hamburg Hauptbahnhof
P ⚡ ⚡ ⚡ ⚡ ⚡ ⚡ W   €€€

Glockengießerwall 14/15, 20095 **Tel** *24 87 00* **Fax** *24 87 01 11* **Rooms** *155*   **Map** 6 D2

Typical for the chain, this hotel is located right next to the main train station. Rooms are sound-proof and decorated in greens and yellows. There are five conference rooms. The restaurant specializes in regional cuisine. Free use of public transit (HVV) for hotel guests. **www.hamburg-hauptbahnhof.intercityhotel.de**

Maritim Hotel Reichshof
P ⚡ ⚡ ⚡ ⚡ ⚡ W   €€€

Kirchenallee 34–36, 20099 **Tel** *24 83 30* **Fax** *24 83 38 88* **Rooms** *303*   **Map** 6 E2

This hotel, with its Classicist atmosphere, is steeped in tradition. It was opened in 1910, and its restaurant, Restaurant ClassiC, is decorated in the style of a luxury cruise-liner of the period. Conference rooms are available for up to 180 people. Relaxation is mandatory in the pool area with its steambath and sauna. **www.maritim.de**

Quality Hotel Ambassador
P ⚡ ⚡ ⚡ ⚡ ⚡ ⚡ W   €€€

Heidenkampsweg 34, 20097 **Tel** *238 82 30* **Fax** *23 00 09* **Rooms** *124*

Business travellers and tourists alike thoroughly enjoy staying here. The decor of the technically perfectly appointed rooms is based around clean shapes and light fabrics. There is a pool, sauna and steam bath. The hotel bar LUX entertains with live piano music in winter. **www.ambassador-hamburg.de**

Best Western Hotel St. Raphael
P ⚡ ⚡ ⚡ ⚡ W   €€€€

Adenauerallee 41, 20097 **Tel** *24 82 00* **Fax** *24 82 03 33* **Rooms** *110*   **Map** 6 F2

This hotel is much loved by business travellers. Every room (among them 12 designer rooms) is up-to-date and individually decorated. Le Jardin, the hotel restaurant, prepares culinary delights. In the wellness area, with its sauna and whirlpool, guests relax above the roofs of the city. **www.straphael-hamburg.bestwestern.de**

Europäischer Hof
P ⚡ ⚡ ⚡ ⚡ ⚡ ⚡ W   €€€€

Kirchenallee 45, 20099 **Tel** *24 82 48* **Fax** *24 82 47 99* **Rooms** *275*   **Map** 6 E2

Along with generously sized rooms and five conference rooms, this hotel also offers a wide programme of fitness and wellness activities. A special feature is the EURO-Therme, which has a 150-m (492-ft) long water slide. Your room pass also serves as a free three-day long public transit (HVV) pass. **www.europaeischer-hof.de**

Park Hyatt Hamburg
P ⚡ ⚡ ⚡ ⚡ ⚡ ⚡ ⚡ W   €€€€€

Bugenhagenstr. 8, 20095 **Tel** *33 32 12 34* **Fax** *33 32 12 35* **Rooms** *252*   **Map** 10 F3

Maritime flair and contemporary furnishings are combined beautifully in this top hotel located in a former office building. The rooms are spacious and come equipped with the latest gadgets. The wellness area Club Olympus Spa & Fitness offers everything mere mortals need to help turn themselves into gods. **www.hamburg.park.hyatt.de**

Sofitel Hamburg Alter Wall
P ⚡ ⚡ ⚡ ⚡ ⚡ ⚡ ⚡ ⚡ W   €€€€€

Alter Wall 40, 20457 **Tel** *36 95 00* **Fax** *369 50 10 00* **Rooms** *241*   **Map** 9 C3

Hanseatic elegance meets French *savoir vivre*. From its business services to its beauty salon – the Sofitel Hamburg Alter Wall location in the city centre is a truly stellar five-star-hotel catering to both business travellers and tourists. Luxury decor and clean lines are hallmarks of the interior. **www.sofitel.com**

Steigenberger Hotel Hamburg
P ⚡ ⚡ ⚡ ⚡ ⚡ W   €€€€€

Heiligengeistbrücke 4, 20459 **Tel** *36 80 60* **Fax** *36 80 67 77* **Rooms** *233*   **Map** 9 C3

This red-brick building on Alsterfleet looks like a giant ship. The hotel lobby is bright due to its many windows. Whether you stay in a superior room or a comfort suite – every room is perfectly equipped. Events can be booked here for up to 300 people, such as literary dinners in the winter garden. **www.steigenberger.com/hamburg**

NEW TOWN

Hotel am Holstenwall Novum

🅿 🍴 🛗 ⛱ 🐾 📶   €€€

Holstenwall 19, 20355 **Tel** *31 80 80* **Fax** *31 80 82 22* **Rooms** *67*   **Map** *9 A3*

Comfortable rooms are tucked away behind the 19th-century exterior of this hotel. The new owners (since 2003) have breathed fresh air into the hotel. There is a conference room, the "Meisterzimmer", for meetings. Bar 509 attracts guests and locals with speciality coffees and cocktails. **www.novum-hotels.de**

Baseler Hof

🍴 ⛱ 🐾 📶   €€€

Esplanade 11, 20354 **Tel** *35 90 60* **Fax** *35 90 69 18* **Rooms** *167*   **Map** *10 D1*

The staff of this hotel will help you plan your stay in Hamburg. Included in the room price is a three-day public transit (HVV) pass. The Kaffee- and Weinhaus Kleinhuis has an excellent kitchen with regional dishes and also serves excellent coffees and more than 50 wines by the glass. **www.baselerhof.de**

Mercure Hotel Hamburg an der Messe

🅿 🍴 🛗 📺 ⛱ 🐾 📶   €€€

Schröderstiftstr. 3, 20146 **Tel** *45 06 90* **Fax** *450 69 10 00* **Rooms** *180*   **Map** *7 A3*

This hotel, directly opposite the Hamburger Fernsehturm (TV tower) and trade fair grounds, was built in 2002. It offers good value; the rooms are pleasant and comfortable, with conference rooms for up to 170 people. The Olive Tree restaurant indulges guests with Mediterranean dishes, the Lemon bar with colourful cocktails. **www.mercure.com**

Madison Hotel

🅿 🍴 🏊 📺 ⛱ 🛗 ♿ 🐾 📶   €€€€

Schaarsteinweg 4, 20459 **Tel** *37 66 60* **Fax** *37 66 61 37* **Rooms** *166*   **Map** *9 B4*

The luxurious interior of the Madison Hotel combines exclusivity with functionality. Features of the hotel are its spacious, colour-coordinated rooms with their wide windows and the large fitness- and wellness-oasis, the Meridian Spa. **www.madisonhotel.de**

Radisson Blu Hotel

🅿 🍴 🏊 📺 ⛱ 🛗 🐾 📶   €€€€

Marseiller Straße 2, 20355 **Tel** *350 20* **Fax** *35 02 35 30* **Rooms** *556*   **Map** *5 B1*

This 27-floor hotel is Hamburg's tallest. The rooms are decorated in a timeless style and provide all the amenities you come to expect in a first-class hotel. Trader Vic's Restaurant and the Mai Tai Bar exude Pacific charm. Hamburg's highest club offers a first-class panoramic view of the city. **www.radissonblu.com/hotel-hamburg**

Renaissance Hotel Hamburg

🅿 🍴 📺 ⛱ 🛗 ♿ 📶   €€€€

Große Bleichen, 20354 **Tel** *34 91 80* **Fax** *34 91 89 69* **Rooms** *184*   **Map** *9 C3*

The Renaissance is located in a grand red-brick building. Rooms are decorated in appealing tones, and the conference rooms are equipped with the latest technology. Esprit restaurant serves German cuisine. The hotel's location close to the passages is ideal for those who love to shop. **www.renaissance-hamburg.com**

SIDE

🅿 🍴 🏊 📺 ⛱ 🛗 ♿ 🐾 📶   €€€€€

Drehbahn 49, 20354 **Tel** *30 99 90* **Fax** *30 99 93 99* **Rooms** *178*   **Map** *9 C2*

Luxury meets lifestyle. The postmodern architecture of this 12-storey designer hotel attracts many famous patrons, especially from the world of show business. The atrium-style lobby soars up to the eighth floor; a computer runs the ingenious ever-changing light installation. **www.side-hamburg.de**

PORT AND SPEICHERSTADT

Stella Maris

⛱ 🐾 📶   €€

Reimarusstr. 12, 20459 **Tel** *319 20 23* **Fax** *317 43 13* **Rooms** *49*   **Map** *9 A4*

A hotel just like Hamburg: nautical and modern. The rooms in the Stella Maris are decorated in light colours and furnished in contemporary style. Guests can play billiards in the clubroom. At cooler times of the year, the fireplace in the Kaminzimmer makes the room especially cosy. **www.raphaelhotels.de/hotel-stella-maris**

Arcadia Hotel Belmondo Hamburg

🅿 🍴 📺 ⛱ 🛗 ♿ 🐾 📶   €€€

Spaldingstr. 70, 20097 **Tel** *23 65 04 00* **Fax** *23 65 06 29* **Rooms** *100*   **Map** *6 F3*

Tasteful and cosy rooms, with every kind of comfort that tourists and business travellers expect. Guests can unwind at the end of the day in the stylish restaurant. Very good value. There is no charge for the daily newspaper or the use of a bicycle. The spa area has a sauna. Every room has a desk. **www.azimuthotels.de**

Gresham Carat Hotel Hamburg

🅿 🍴 ⛱ 📶   €€€

Sieldeich 5–6, 20539 **Tel** *78 96 60* **Fax** *78 61 96* **Rooms** *90*   **Map** *6 ?*

For those who want to experience HafenCity up close, Carat, renovated in 2008, is a perfect place to stay. It is just a few minutes away from the Hamburg Cruise Center. Rooms are decorated in an Irish style. The all-day restaurant, Limerick, serves German and international cuisine, the Shannon Bar tends towards Irish food. **www.carat-hotel-hamburg.de**

Holiday Inn Hamburg

🅿 🍴 🏨 🎬 📋 🛗 ♿ 🚼 🐾 Ⓦ   €€€

Billwerder Neuer Deich 14, 20539 **Tel** *788 40* **Fax** *78 84 10 00* **Rooms** *385*

Holiday Inn is one of the largest and best-equipped hotels in Hamburg; many rooms offer a fascinating view of the Elbe and the port. The service is superb. The interiors of the rooms, from their furnishings to colour schemes, are perfectly decorated. **www.holidayinn.de**

Hotel am Elbufer

🅿 🍴 🚼 Ⓦ   €€€

Focksweg 40a, 21129 Hamburg **Tel** *742 19 10* **Fax** *74 21 91 40* **Rooms** *14*

Many regular guests relish the familiar atmosphere of this small hotel. The rooms are well appointed, and every detail has been thought through. For those whose rooms look out on the Elbe, giant ocean-going vessels seem close enough to touch. The ferry brings you quickly into the city. Extensive breakfast buffet. **www.hotel-am-elbufer.de**

The Rilano Hotel Hamburg

🅿 🍴 🎬 📋 ♿ 🚼 Ⓦ   €€€

Hein-Sass-Weg 40, 21129 **Tel** *300 84 90* **Fax** *300 84 96 90* **Rooms** *170*

Opened in 2006, this hotel is located in Finkenwerder, not too far from the Airbus factory. The hotel has its own ferry dock, and Hamburg city centre can be easily reached by water. The rooms are all decorated in contemporary style. **www.rilano-hamburg.de**

Mercure Hotel Hamburg City

🅿 🍴 🎬 📋 ♿ 🚼 🐾 Ⓦ   €€€€

Amsinckstr. 53, 20097 **Tel** *23 63 80* **Fax** *23 42 30* **Rooms** *187*

Whether you are travelling on business or for pleasure, you will feel very comfortable in this hotel. The rooms are appointed with contemporary furniture; the sauna and whirlpool offer relaxation. The Dialogue restaurant pampers with international specialities, while Studio M bar serves long drinks from around the world. **www.mercure.com**

ST PAULI

A & O Hotel Hamburg Reeperbahn

🅿 🎬 Ⓦ   €

Reeperbahn 154, 20359 **Tel** *317 69 99 46 00* **Fax** *317 69 99 46 90* **Rooms** *308*   **Map** *3 C4*

Why not choose a lodging located on Hamburg's best-known street? This budget-conscious option belongs to the A&O Hostel Hamburg chain *(see p174–5).* With rooms that are functionally furnished, the house provides the amenities to be expected in a budget hotel. **www.aohostels.com**

Fritzhotel

🚼 Ⓦ   €€

Schanzenstr. 101–103, 20357 **Tel** *82 22 28 30* **Fax** *822 22 83 22* **Rooms** *17*

Unconventional and inventive are two words that well describe this hotel – making it the appropriate place to stay for those guests who know full well how to enjoy the lively Schanzenviertel. The rooms are bright and friendly, the colour scheme is restrained. The design is almost minimalistic, but stylish. **www.fritzhotel.com**

Hotel St. Annen

🅿 🎬 🚼 Ⓦ   €€

Annenstr. 5, 20359 **Tel** *317 71 30* **Fax** *31 77 13 13* **Rooms** *36*   **Map** *4 D3*

This hotel is close to the Reeperbahn and yet very quiet. All the rooms are different, but the colour-scheme of each is dominated by warm tones, and each is furnished with high-quality cherry wood furniture. The Weinbar is a perfect place for sampling wines, especially those from South Africa. Cosy garden terrace. **www.hotelstannen.de**

YoHo

🍴 ♿ 🚼 Ⓦ   €€

Moorkamp 5, 20357 **Tel** *284 19 10* **Fax** *28 41 91 41* **Rooms** *30*

The name is short for "Young Hotel", and this defines its clientele – which not only includes world travellers. The ambience in this white Jugendstil villa is refreshingly young, and guests under the age of 26 even get a discounted rate. Breakfast at friendly communal tables is an ideal way of making contacts. **www.yoho-hamburg.de**

East

🅿 🍴 🎬 📋 ♿ Ⓦ   €€€€

Simon-von-Utrecht-Str. 31, 20359 **Tel** *30 99 30* **Fax** *30 99 32 00* **Rooms** *70*   **Map** *4 E2*

Not too far from the Reeperbahn, an old iron foundry was turned into a boutique hotel of the first order by star architect Jordan Mozer. This luxurious temple to good living has an international reputation. It combines style, trendiness and ambience. The rooms, lofts and suites are very spacious. **www.east-hamburg.de**

Empire Riverside Hotel

🅿 🍴 🎬 📋 📋 ♿ Ⓦ   €€€€

Bernhard-Nocht-Str. 97, 20359 **Tel** *31 11 90* **Fax** *31 11 97 06 01* **Rooms** *327*   **Map** *4 D4*

Above the Landungsbrücken, on the grounds of a former brewery, rises this modern bronze hotel. Clean, modern lines characterize the rooms, which are located between the fourth and the 20th floors; each has a panorama window covering an entire wall. Wonderful views from the 20up Skybar on the 20th floor. **www.empire-riverside.de**

Hafen Hamburg

🅿 🍴 🎬 🚼 Ⓦ   €€€€

Seewartenstr. 9, 20459 **Tel** *31 11 30* **Fax** *31 11 37 06 01* **Rooms** *353*   **Map** *4 E4*

This privately run, traditional hotel above the Landungsbrücken is considered the most Hanseatic and most nautically styled of all Hamburg hotels. Ships' models and ships' clocks hang on the walls. The view of the port from the Tower Bar on the twelfth floor could not be better. **www.hotel-hafen-hamburg.de**

Mövenpick Hotel Hamburg
Sternschanze 6, 20357 **Tel** *334 41 10* **Fax** *33 44 11 33 33* **Rooms** *226*

This hotel, located in the 57.5-m (189-ft) high water tower in Sternschanzenpark, opened in 2007. The rooms are distributed across all 20 floors. The restaurant's delights include Swiss dishes. The Cave bar is housed in the historic red-brick cellar. Conference rooms for up to 180 people are available. **www.moevenpick-hotels.com**

ALTONA

ETAP Hotel Hamburg Altona
Holstenkamp 3, 22525 **Tel** *85 37 98 20* **Fax** *85 37 98 24* **Rooms** *180*

Those who like to save on hotel costs will definitely not be in for a shock when they get the bill here. All rooms in this chain hotel are identically furnished and equipped with a colour TV. The breakfast buffet is extensive. Hamburg city centre can be reached in just a few minutes on the U-Bahn. **www.etaphotel.com**

Schanzenstern Altona
Kleine Rainstr. 24–26, 22765 **Tel** *39 91 91 91* **Fax** *39 91 91 92* **Rooms** *33*   **Map** *1 C3*

Although backpackers stay in the Schanzenstern, this hotel is much more than just a backpackers' hostel. The apartments on the top floor also have enough room for families. The breakfast buffet offers a great deal of choice and mainly serves organic products. **www.schanzenstern-altona.de**

25 Hours Hotel Hamburg No. 1
Paul-Dessau-Str. 2, 22761 **Tel** *85 50 70* **Fax** *85 50 71 00* **Rooms** *128*   **Map** *1 A1*

In late 2003, Hamburg's first "low-cost designer hotel" opened. All those who check in here beam themselves into another world – there are eye-popping colours and odd forms wherever you look. Trendy design characterizes communal spaces such as the Open-Air Lounge on the roof. **www.25hours-hotels.com/hamburg**

InterCity Hotel Hamburg Altona
Paul-Nevermann-Platz 17, 22765 **Tel** *38 03 40* **Fax** *38 03 49 99* **Rooms** *133*   **Map** *1 C3*

The rooms are tastefully and comfortably furnished, and the conference rooms are equipped with the latest presentation technology. Your room pass lets you travel for free on local public transit. Guests over 65 years of age are eligible for discounts. **www.intercityhotel.com/hamburg_altona**

Best Western Raphael Hotel Altona
Präsident-Krahn-Str. 13, 22765 **Tel** *38 02 49 11* **Fax** *38 02 44 44* **Rooms** *40*   **Map** *2 D3*

Despite its modern decor, this chain hotel has a cosy atmosphere. It is well located right near Bahnhof Altona, the railway station of Altona. Children up to the age of 12 can stay at no extra charge in their parents' room. Another feature of this hotel is its sauna. **www.raphaelhotels.de/best-western-raphael-hotel-altona**

Boston Hamburg
Missundestr. 2, 22769 **Tel** *589 66 67 00* **Fax** *589 66 67 77* **Rooms** *46*   **Map** *2 E1*

This is a modern and soberly decorated designer hotel directly beside the Neue Flora – the ideal location for a weekend of musicals. The rooms have either a bath with a rain showerhead or corner bathtubs. The bar and lounge area is open until late in the night. **www.boston-hamburg.de**

Gastwerk Hotel Hamburg
Beim Alten Gaswerk 3, 22761 **Tel** *89 06 20* **Fax** *890 62 20* **Rooms** *141*   **Map** *1 A1*

A successful mix of industrial romantic and modern design. The designers turned the coal warehouse of a former gasworks into a hotel. In some rooms, the old red-brick walls have been left exposed. Regional and international specialities are featured in the hotel restaurant, Mangold. **www.gastwerk.com**

AROUND THE ALSTER

Hotel am Rothenbaum
Rothenbaumchaussee 107, 20148 **Tel** *44 60 06* **Fax** *44 93 74* **Rooms** *28*   **Map** *7 B2*

This extremely cosy hotel is conveniently close to the well-known international tennis court complex. Modern design paired with a well-coordinated colour scheme makes it easy to feel right at home here. All rooms have a telephone and cable TV, some also have a balcony or a roof terrace. **www.hotel-am-rothenbaum.com/about.html**

Hotel Amsterdam im Dammtorpalais
Moorweidenstr. 34, 20146 **Tel** *441 11 00* **Fax** *45 68 20* **Rooms** *34*   **Map** *7 B3*

This former residence of well-to-do Hamburgers is located in one of the most beautiful areas of town, guaranteeing its patrons a peaceful stay with a very special atmosphere. Each room is unique down to the last detail, and the styles range from flowery traditional to contemporary. **www.hotelamsterdam.de**

Key to Price Guide *see p176* **Key to Symbols** *see back cover flap*

Hotel Brennerhof Garten

`P` `☆` `🛗` `W`   €€

Brennerstr. 70–72, 20099 **Tel** *280 88 80* **Fax** *28 08 88 88* **Rooms** *45*   **Map** *8 F4*

Located in two buildings that are 150 m (500 ft) apart, the Brennerhof has often served as a location for movie and television productions, and many famous artists have stayed here. It is fitting that film posters and prints decorate the walls. The breakfast room is decorated in the style of an artists' café. **www.hotel-garten.de**

Hotel Fresena im Dammtorpalais

`☆` `🛗` `☆` `W`   €€

Moorweidenstr. 34, 20146 **Tel** *410 48 92* **Fax** *45 66 89* **Rooms** *23*   **Map** *7 B3*

This hotel is located on the third floor in the architecturally appealing Dammtorpalais. Bahnhof Dammtor and the trade fair grounds are just a few minutes away by foot. The hotel rents bikes, and you can have the hotel book tickets for you for some cultural events. **www.hotelfresena.de**

Hotel-Pension Fink

`P` `☆` `🛗` `W`   €€

Rothenbaumchaussee 73, 20148 **Tel** *44 05 71* **Fax** *45 71 62* **Rooms** *8*   **Map** *7 B2*

Guests who are price-conscious and yet demanding will experience great service in this hotel, which was refurbished. Rooms in this Jugendstil villa, which is under heritage protection, are tastefully decorated. The hotel is well situated for public transport. **www.hotel-fink.de**

Hotel Vorbach

`P` `☆` `🛗` `☆` `W`   €€

Johnsallee 63–67, 20146 **Tel** *44 18 20* **Fax** *44 18 28 88* **Rooms** *120*   **Map** *7 B3*

This unusual hotel in Harvestehude stretches over an assemblage of three buildings built during the Hamburg Gründerzeit. High ceilings, plaster ornamentation and Art Deco elements give the spacious rooms a unique charm. This hotel is also well suited for longer stays. **www.hotel-vorbach.de**

Schwanenwik

`P` `W`   €€

Schwanenwik 29, 22087 **Tel** *220 09 18* **Fax** *229 04 46* **Rooms** *18*   **Map** *8 F3*

This white villa in the Uhlenhorst district is a peaceful place in which to stay. Patrons enjoy either a view of the Alster or the park-like garden. All rooms are equipped with a TV, Internet access and telephone. The Literaturhaus is only a few steps away. The Alster shore beckons guests for a walk. **www.hotel-schwanenwik.de**

Aussen Alster

`P` `🍴` `☆` `☆` `🛗` `W`   €€€

Schmilinskystr. 11, 20099 **Tel** *284 07 85 70* **Fax** *28 40 78 57 77* **Rooms** *27*   **Map** *8 E4*

Hidden behind a white façade is a hotel that appeals due to its airy design and clean lines. It is only a very short walk from the Aussen Alster to the Außenalster, where a sailboat owned by the hotel awaits hotel patrons. The kitchen of the hotel's Italian restaurant offers creative cuisine. **www.aussen-alster.de**

Crowne Plaza

`P` `🍴` `♨` `TV` `☆` `目` `♿` `☆` `🛗` `W`   €€€

Graumannsweg 10, 22087 **Tel** *22 80 60* **Fax** *220 87 04* **Rooms** *285*   **Map** *8 F3*

Hanseatic flair and dignified elegance are the hallmarks of the Crowne Plaza, whose rooms come equipped with the latest technology. Architecturally, the spacious atrium dominates. For relaxation, guests head to the comfortable wellness area or the King George Bar. **www.ichotelsgroup.com**

Hotel All Seasons Hamburg City Nord

`P` `🍴` `♨` `☆` `目` `♿` `☆` `🛗` `W`   €€€

Holsteinischer Kamp 59, 22081 **Tel** *239 09 50* **Fax** *239 09 53 90* **Rooms** *67*

The comfortable rooms are designed to create a sense of well-being. A visit to the swimming pool or the sauna ensures relaxation. In the hotel's cosy bar, you can sample delicious snacks or artfully mixed cocktails and unwind as the day draws to a close. **www.accorhotels.com**

Hotel Smolka

`P` `☆` `☆` `🛗` `W`   €€€

Isestr. 98, 20149 **Tel** *48 09 80* **Fax** *480 98 11* **Rooms** *37*

The Smolka is located in the district of Harvestehude. This is a choice district in which to live, and has many green spaces. Each room is furnished differently. The hotel lobby, restaurant and bar are very elegant. The biggest weekly market in Hamburg is held right around the corner. **www.raphaelhotels.de/das_smolka**

Hotel Wagner im Dammtorpalais

`P` `☆` `☆` `🛗` `W`   €€€

Moorweidenstr. 34, 20146 **Tel** *450 13 10* **Fax** *45 01 31 69* **Rooms** *44*   **Map** *7 B3*

Several very different hotels are located in this Jugendstil palace, which is under heritage protection. Rooms in the Hotel Wagner are decorated in contemporary style and equipped with modern technology. The breakfast room has the feeling of a coffee house. **www.hotel-wagner-hamburg.de**

InterContinental Hamburg

`P` `🍴` `♨` `TV` `☆` `目` `☆` `🛗` `W`   €€€

Fontenay 10, 20354 **Tel** *414 20* **Fax** *41 42 22 99* **Rooms** *281*   **Map** *7 C3*

Located in a park on the Außenalster, this hotel could not be better situated. Diners in the roof-top restaurant enjoy a sensational view. The rooms provide every convenience for business travellers and holiday makers alike. The fitness and wellness facilities are of the finest quality. **www.intercontinental.com**

Nippon Hotel

`P` `🍴` `☆` `W`   €€€

Hofweg 75, 22085 **Tel** *227 11 40* **Fax** *22 71 14 90* **Rooms** *42*   **Map** *8 E1*

Paper-covered sliding walls, futons and Japanese tatami mats – this hotel reflects Japanese aesthetics down to the last detail. Traditional Far Eastern living is enhanced by Wa-Yo restaurant, which serves more than just sushi. Free daily newspapers are available. **www.nippon-hotel-hh.de**

Novotel Hamburg Alster
Lübecker Str. 3, 22087 **Tel** *39 19 00* **Fax** *31 19 01 90* **Rooms** *210*   **Map** *8 F4*

The five-storey Novotel offers every comfort for both tourists and business travellers. The rooms are decorated in a light colour scheme and are furnished with coffee tables, desks and art prints. Mediterranean specialities are featured in Thyme restaurant, and the Alster Lounge also spoils hotel guests. **www.novotel.com**

Wedina
Gurlittstr. 23, 20099 **Tel** *280 89 00* **Fax** *280 38 94* **Rooms** *59*   **Map** *8 E4*

This hotel is housed in four buildings whose exteriors are painted in deep rich colours. The "red" building exudes the charm of the 1980s, the "yellow" has a Mediterranean ambience, the "blue" features rooms dedicated to authors and the "green" is just the thing for lovers of the avant garde. All in all, an original place to stay. **www.wedina.de**

Garden Hotels Hamburg
Magdalenenstr. 60, 20148 **Tel** *41 40 40* **Fax** *41 40 420* **Rooms** *58*   **Map** *7 C2*

Family-run luxury hotel with that certain something in the heart of Pöseldorf. The three splendid Jugendstil villas radiate Hanseatic flair. Tastefully chosen artworks, such as lithographs and marble sculptures, and valuable furnishings create a harmonious ambience. **www.garden-hotels.de**

The George Hotel
Barcastraße 3, 20087 **Tel** *280 03 00* **Fax** *28 00 30 30* **Rooms** *125*   **Map** *8 F4*

Opened in 2008, this hotel is decorated in British style. The rooms are decorated in a brown colour-scheme, and have elegant wallpapers. The Italian bar DaCaio and the Spa Center, which sports an African theme, provide a fascinating contrast to the hotel's restrained elegance. **www.thegeorge-hotel.de**

Grand Élysée
Rothenbaumchaussee 10, 20148 **Tel** *41 41 20* **Fax** *41 41 27 33* **Rooms** *511*   **Map** *7 B3*

Comfortable rooms, exclusive suites and first-class cuisine – the Élysée is definitely one of Hamburg's top places to stay. The reception hall, with its restaurants, bars and shops, is actually large enough to saunter through on a stroll, and is appropriately named the Boulevard. The wellness and spa area is a world unto itself. **www.grand-elysee.com**

Boulevard Hotel
Hofweg 73, 22085 **Tel** *227 02 20* **Fax** *227 67 72* **Rooms** *12*   **Map** *8 E1*

This splendid Jugendstil villa was completely refurbished in 1995 and now combines modern style with romantic charm. Light colours, soft carpets and high-quality materials give the rooms a pleasing atmosphere. Romantic rooms underneath the sloped roof are available for couples. **www.boulevardhotel.de**

Hotel Abtei
Abteistr. 14, 20149 **Tel** *44 29 05* **Fax** *44 98 20* **Rooms** *11*

The Abtei, located in the well-to-do district of Harvestehude, is considered the loveliest small hotel in the city. That's no surprise, given that each room in this mansion, which was built in 1897, has been individually decorated with antiques. The hotel restaurant, Prinz Frederik, is a Hamburg gourmet destination. **www.abtei-hotel.de**

Hotel Atlantic Kempinski
An der Alster 72–79, 20099 **Tel** *288 80* **Fax** *24 71 29* **Rooms** *252*   **Map** *8 D4*

Here you can live just like a celebrity *(see p128)*. Since it opened in 1909, this grand hotel has been the first choice of world-famous celebrities and inseparable from the history of Hamburg and its social life. Both the exterior and interior of this bright white palace have served as settings for film classics. **www.atlantic.de**

Hotel Vier Jahreszeiten
Neuer Jungfernstieg 9–14, 20354 **Tel** *34 94 31 51* **Fax** *34 94 26 06* **Rooms** *156*   **Map** *7 C5*

A hotel with a long tradition in a wonderful city-centre location *(see p125)*. When you enter this hotel on the Binnenalster, you enter another world: wood-panelled walls, Art Deco accents and elevators which conjure up a sense of nostalgia. In contrast, the rooms are very modern, and the restaurants are gourmet temples. **www.hvj.de**

Le Royal Méridien
An der Alster 52–56, 20099 **Tel** *210 00* **Fax** *21 00 11 11* **Rooms** *284*   **Map** *8 E4*

This hotel is a consummate example of a successful marriage between modern luxury and timeless elegance. The high-tech rooms include things as power showers and plasma TVs. The conference rooms are unmatched. Earthlings get a taste of heavenly delights in Le Ciel restaurant on the ninth floor. **www.leroyalmeridienhamburg.com**

FURTHER AFIELD

Best Western Queens Hotel
Mexikoring 1, 22297 **Tel** *63 29 40* **Fax** *63 29 44 00* **Rooms** *182*

This hotel is located directly on Stadtpark, which serves as the green lungs of the city. Snacks and drinks can be enjoyed at the Bierstube Störtebeker. The facilities of the leisure-time oasis Vitalis include a sauna and steam bath. Business travellers appreciate the excellent business facilities. **www.best-western-queens-hotel-hamburg.de**

Hotel Helgoland
Kieler Str. 173–177, 22525 **Tel** 85 70 01 **Fax** 851 14 45 **Rooms** 110

Whether you are visiting Hamburg to take in a musical, see the city or do business, the Hotel Helgoland in Eimsbüttel is a sound choice at a reasonable rate. The hotel offers special package deals that include tickets to musicals or trips to Helgoland. Well located for public transport. **www.hotel-helgoland.de**

Hotel Schümann
Langenhorner Chaussee 157, 22415 **Tel** 531 00 20 **Fax** 53 10 02 10 **Rooms** 34

The Schümann is handily located near the airport and offers good value for money along with the atmosphere of a privately run family hotel. Each room is individually decorated, cosy and has cable TV. The breakfast buffet offers a wide choice. **www.hotel-schuemann.de**

Landhaus Flottbek
Baron-Voght-Str. 179, 22607 **Tel** 822 74 10 **Fax** 82 27 41 51 **Rooms** 25

An old farmhouse from the 18th century has been lovingly restored with an eye to detail, combining the nostalgic charm of a country house with modern comforts. All rooms have telephone. The restaurant features the cuisine of Holstein. **www.landhaus-flottbek.de**

NH Hamburg-Horn
Rennbahnstr. 90, 22111 **Tel** 65 59 70 **Fax** 65 59 71 00 **Rooms** 172

This hotel is located east of Hamburg at the Horn racetrack, where each year in July the Deutsches Derby (German Derby) is held. The rooms, some with a view of the racetrack, are attractively furnished with up-to-date technology. **www.nh-hotels.com**

Nige Hus
Insel Neuwerk, 27499 **Tel** (047 21) 295 61 **Fax** (047 21) 288 25 **Rooms** 9

Relaxation between clouds, the tide flats and the ocean is the promise made by this hotel on Neuwerk island (see p139). It is an ideal starting-off point for tours of the tidal mudflats (the Watt), or walks to the lighthouse. The rooms are spacious. Use of wicker beach chairs and bicycles is free. **www.inselneuwerk.de**

Reiterhof Ohlenhoff
Ohlenhoff 18, 22848 Norderstedt **Tel** 528 73 20 **Fax** 52 87 32 10 **Rooms** 26

It is not far from here to the city, the airport or the countryside. This privately run hotel is located on the grounds of a horse stables that is still in use, not far from the gates of Hamburg. It appeals to those who appreciate the typical, idyllic North German surroundings after a day in the city. **www.hotel-reiterhof-ohlenhoff.de**

Eggers
Rahlstedter Str. 78, 22149 **Tel** 67 57 80 **Fax** 67 57 84 44 **Rooms** 102

The unique quality of this hotel in Rahlstedt can be sensed as soon as you step inside: stylish architecture, tasteful design, luxury materials, harmonizing colours and innovative technology. The opulently furnished rooms provide every comfort needed and are decorated in contemporary style. Top-notch restaurant with terrace. **www.eggers.de**

Hotel Böttcherhof
Wöhlerstr. 2, 22113 **Tel** 73 18 70 **Fax** 73 18 78 99 **Rooms** 155

No matter whether you opt for a room, studio, junior suite or an apartment – this hotel in Billbrook beguiles its patrons with its many comforts. As soon as you enter the stylish, spacious reception hall you know a pleasant stay is guaranteed. The spa area offers a lot of treatments. **www.boettcherhof.de**

Steigenberger Hotel Treudelberg
Lemsahler Landstr. 45, 22397 **Tel** 60 82 20 **Fax** 608 22 88 88 **Rooms** 225

Here in the Alster Valley on the northern edge of the city tourists find utter relaxation and business travellers everything they need for a successful stay. The Treudelberg has its own 18-hole golf course and a beauty salon. Sunday brunch in the Szenario restaurant is very popular. **www.treudelberg.com**

Strandhotel Blankenese
Strandweg 13, 22587 **Tel** 86 13 44 **Fax** 86 49 36 **Rooms** 14

Maritime lightness and Hanseatic tradition merge seamlessly in this old Jugendstil hotel with its towers and bay windows. It is located in the Treppenviertel in Blankenese. Each room has its own character. Hotel patrons have a view of the Elbe as they dine in the restaurant. **www.strandhotel-blankenese.de**

Lindner Park-Hotel Hagenbeck
Hagenbeckstraße 150, 22527 **Tel** 800 80 81 00 **Fax** 800 80 81 88 **Rooms** 158

The exotic combined with friendly service are the hallmarks of the world's first zoo-themed hotel, located at Tierpark Hagenbeck (see pp136–37). The rooms are decorated either in an African or Asian style. Tourists and business travellers alike come to this hotel, opened in 2009, and embark on a journey to far-off continents. **www.lindner.de**

Louis C. Jacob
Elbchaussee 401–403, 22609 **Tel** 82 25 50 **Fax** 82 25 54 44 **Rooms** 85

Pampering guests to the utmost is a matter of honour for the staff of this luxury hotel in Nienstedten on the Elbe. Its antiques and art collection are a delight for art lovers. The Elbe view from the terrace, with its old linden trees, was a source of inspiration for Max Liebermann, an Impressionist who sojourned here. **www.hotel-jacob.de**

WHERE TO EAT

Hamburg's gastronomic scene is diverse and, especially in districts such as Pöseldorf, St Georg or HafenCity, constantly changing. Trends come and go, and new establishments are continually opening, some-times with inventive themes. Hamburg is a true gourmet para-dise; few other cities in Germany can pride themselves on having so many restaurants with first-class cuisine. However, the city also offers a vast range of reasonably priced restaurants serving very good food. Appropriately,

The sign of Café Paris on Rathausplatz

the culinary emphasis in this port city is on fish. Since Hamburg is a cosmopolitan city, you can find specialities from every country in the world here. You can dine on won-derful Portuguese, Greek, Vietnamese or Arab food here, as well as a range of other national cuisines. Many of the finest establishments in the city are described in the list of selected restaurants on pages 190–97, which covers a wide variety of price catego-ries. A selection of cafés and snack bars is provided on pages 198–201.

The Fischerhaus (see p193) is known for its classic fish dishes

TYPES OF RESTAURANTS

Since many Hamburgers relish good food, it is an excellent sign when a restaurant counts many locals among its patrons. During your stay, you will quickly be able to identify which restaurants cater to tourists and which offer a truly genuine Hansea-tic experience. The harbour, of course, gives the city a very special atmosphere. There's nothing quite like dining with a view of the port as you watch the boats or a large ocean-going vessel slowly pass by.

Several upmarket restau-rants have opened in the gaps between the newly built office buildings shimmering in the sun, especially in the

stretch along the harbour nicknamed the "pearl necklace" by Hamburgers – between the Fischmarkt and Övelgönne. Most restaurants on the harbour promenade have terraces that sometimes are so close to the water that you are in danger of getting wet from a wake. Diners also have a lovely water view from many restaurants around the Alster, especially those with terraces on wooden jetties.

Restaurants located inside former warehouses, such as in the Deichstraße (see p67) or in other old buildings including the Krameramts-wohnungen (see p72) have a very special atmosphere.

One of the city's most active ethnic communities are the Portuguese. In the Portuguese district, which is located around the Ditmar-Koel-Straße to the north of the

Landungsbrücken, there are many establishments serving Portuguese cuisine of excellent quality.

One original Hamburg gastronomic idea turned out to be a huge hit – a restaurant chain specializing in steaks called Block House. It was founded in 1968 in the Hanseatic city and now has 14 establishments in Hamburg, as well as subsidiaries throughout Germany and in some other European countries.

RESERVATIONS AND DRESS CODE

It is always a good idea to make a reservation for fancy or gourmet restaurants. For the most popular establish-ments, especially those with a view of the harbour, it is necessary to book several

The trendy bar in the lobby of stilwerk (see p119)

**Die Bank brasserie *(see p192)* in
what was really once a bank**

days in advance. For most
other restaurants, there is
only need to book ahead for
Friday and Saturday dining.

Even though there is no
dress code, it is a good idea
to dress up a bit if you go to
a fancy restaurant. Although
Hamburgers are quite tolerant, they do set store by the
way people dress and act.

PRICES AND TIPS

The range of restaurants
covers all price categories.
Most establishments post a
menu with prices beside the
entrance. To avoid surprises,
look it over before you go in.

One of the key factors that
determines the prices a restaurant charges is its location.
Prices are usually higher at
establishments that are closer
to the Elbe, as well as those
on elegant boulevards, such
as the Jungfernstieg or the
Neue Wall. In the most inexpensive restaurants, you can
expect to pay about 15 Euros
for a three-course meal not
including alcoholic beverages.
In the top restaurants, or those
in a choice location, you can
end up paying much more
than 50 Euros. Of course,
ordering the better wines will
usually inflate the size of your
bill significantly.

All prices include taxes and
service, but it is usual to add
about a 10 per cent tip. It's
appropriate to tip more for
especially good service. While
many of the better restaurants
accept credit cards, smaller
pubs or cafés usually do not.

VEGETARIANS

Since many restaurants in
Hamburg specialize in fish
dishes, fish lovers will find
a great deal of choice here.
Although strict vegetarian
restaurants are still rather rare,
most dining establishments
include dishes without meat
or fish on their menus. You
can also get good salads just
about anywhere.

If you have special dietary
requirements, do not hesitate
to ask the staff; they will
usually make every effort to
accommodate your wishes.
Sometimes you might even be
offered a specially prepared
meal. More and more chefs
are using healthy, nutritious
and fresh ingredients.

CHILDREN

Some Hamburg restaurants –
especially those in the higher
price brackets – are not
geared to the needs of
children. However, most of
them do have high-chairs
on hand and offer children's
meals. If you have a push-
chair with you, ask the staff
where you should leave it.

While you are out and
about with children during
the day, the city's fast-food
restaurants or snack bars are
a convenient choice for a
bite to eat *(see pp198–201)*.
They do not just offer food
that kids like, but some also
have a children's section
where the little ones can
run about and play.

SMOKERS

Smoking is not permitted in
Hamburg's restaurants, cafés
or bars. You can only smoke
in establishments with separate, well-ventilated rooms.

**Max & Consorten *(see p195)*, a
restaurant on the edge of St Georg**

DISABLED TRAVELLERS

Many Hamburg restaurants
have limited wheelchair
access, and in many establishments tables are often placed
close together, making it difficult for those in wheelchairs
to get around. And, quite
often, the toilets are located
in the basement, and can only
be reached by stairs since
there is no elevator. Sometimes the hallway leading to
the toilets – even if they are
on the ground floor – is very
narrow, making it difficult to
navigate. To be sure of a
comfortable experience, it is
best to check ahead when
you make your reservation.

Canal-side dining in style at the Rialto *(see p192)*

The Flavours of Hamburg

The gates of the Elbe metropolis have always stood wide open to welcome the world, and this is reflected in its cuisine. Many ingredients and spices commonly used in Europe today were once unknown or rare, and started their conquest of the Continent from Hamburg's port and warehouses. The cuisine of the Hanseatic city is dominated by a wide variety of fish dishes. Hearty stews and a wide range of vegetables and fruits enrich the gastronomic offerings. The hamburger, famous the world over, actually has nothing at all to do with the city.

Crisp, freshly picked apples from the Altes Land

Baltic Sea; some gourmet restaurants order fish caught in the Mediterranean and Atlantic directly from the Paris market halls. Fish is prepared in every conceivable way in Hamburg. The most popular kinds are eel *(Aal)*, plaice *(Scholle)*, pike *(Hecht)*, herring *(Hering)* and pike-perch *(Zander)*. The fish may be fried or steamed; baked, smoked or marinated; or made into tasty fish soups and stews.

Potatoes usually accompany traditional North German dishes. They are served either boiled, in their jackets, pan-fried, or as delicious potato salad. Green beans or a green salad are also often served with fish dishes. Fish sauces usually have a cream

The daily menu displayed in front of a Hamburg restaurant

FISH DISHES

To get an idea of the many kinds of fish used in Hamburg cuisine, you must stroll through the St Pauli Fish Market *(see p108)* just once. The catch comes in fresh each day from the Elbe river as well as the North Sea or

Franzbrötchen with chocolate
Franzbrötchen with raisins
Whole wheat bread
Kopenhagener
Rye bun
Croissant

Different kinds of bread, buns and baked goods

TYPICAL NORTH GERMAN DISHES

Hamburg cuisine is dominated by a mixture of fish dishes and hearty home-style fare. Some dishes are inextricably linked with the city of Hamburg, such as *Labskaus*, *Finkenwerder Scholle* (a plaice dish) and *Matjes* (salt herring) dishes. *Hamburger Aal-suppe* (Hamburg eel soup) once had everything in it except eel. If the soup does contain eel, then this is a concession to tourists. This soup gets its sweet-sour taste from dried fruit (mainly apples). An odd-sounding yet beloved dish is *Birnen, Bohnen und Speck* (pears, green beans and bacon). The flavour contrast between the smoked bacon, the slightly bitter beans and the sweetness of the pears makes for a delicious combination. If speed is of the essence, then many Hamburgers will choose a *Frikadelle* (kind of hamburger) or a *Fischbrötchen* (fish in a bun) from a *Fischbude*, a booth that sells fish.

Cabbage rolls on cooked carrots

Labskaus is a traditional seaman's dish that gets its characteristic red colouring from red beetroots *(see box on p187)*.

Prawns, shrimp, crayfish, rollmops, mussels and other fish delicacies

or mustard base. Overall, Hamburg is an ideal city in which to enjoy tasty simple fare as well as creative modern variations.

SOUPS AND STEWS

In the countryside surrounding Hamburg there is a lot of farming activity. Livestock graze and crops are cultivated in the fields. There are all sorts of vegetables, potatoes and fruit – important ingredients for hearty soups and stews that Hamburgers love. The Altes Land *(see p138)*, just outside the city gates, is the largest continuous fruit-growing district in Central Europe. Among the better-known soups and stews are *Birnen, Bohnen und Speck* (pears, green

beans and bacon) and *Grünkohltopf mit Kassler und Kochwurst*, (kale with ham and sausage), and Labskaus (seaman's stew).

Dat Backhus outlet located on the Binnenalster

BAKED GOODS AND DESSERTS

In Hamburg, you can choose from a cornucopia of baked goods. There are many different kinds of bread and pastries such as *Franzbrötchen* (a raised pastry with a sweet filling) and *Hanseat* (pastry fingers with a red-white glaze). *Kopenhagener*, puff-pastry delicacies, are filled with marzipan or jam, *braune Kuchen* are cookies baked until crisp and are a bit like *Lebkuchen* (spice cookies). Mouth-watering desserts include *Rote Grütze*, made of cooked red berries, and *Hamburger Sandkuchen*, a kind of Madeira cake.

LABSKAUS

This classic Hamburg dish is a traditional seaman's stew that is very popular along the entire North German coast, even though it might look a bit unpromising at first glance. This stew is made of finely chopped salted beef, potatoes, red beetroots and other kinds of vegetables, such as celery and leek, as well as salted herring. A fried egg is placed on top, and dill pickles are served on the side. It is accompanied by flavourful farmer's bread. Nothing tastes better with Labskaus than a cool beer.

Finkenwerder Scholle (Finkenwerd plaice) is a common way of preparing plaice. It generally features a bacon-and-onion stuffing.

Matjes (salt herring) with beans is one of the most popular herring dishes. In spring, when "young" herring are available, it is a real delicacy.

Rote Grütze is a mixture of cooked red berries and a bit of red wine. This tasty dessert is often served with vanilla sauce or cream.

What to Drink

Just as in most other regions of Germany, beer is the most popular alcoholic drink in Hamburg, too. The city has a beer-brewing tradition going back centuries. Many Hamburgers are especially proud of the Astra label. The many kinds of schnapps – strong distilled spirits (not all of which are clear) – are typical of Northern Germany, as is tea. Among the alcohol-free refreshments, fritz-kola and Bionade have greatly increased their market shares in the past few years.

Advertising for Duckstein beer

Coasters and bottle caps of popular beers

BEER

Beer has a long tradition in the Hanseatic city; in fact, during the Middle Ages Hamburg's reputation stood or fell on the quality of its beer. The Holsten brewery, founded in 1879, is the largest brewery. Located on the Holstenstraße in Altona, it has been part of the Carlsberg-Deutschland Group since 2004. The premium label, Duckstein, is brewed there. The Holsten logo showing a knight on a galloping horse is known around the world. Offerings from other North German breweries are also plentiful in Hamburg; these include Wicküler, Jever, Beck's and Flensburger.

Wicküler beer   **Holsten beer**   **Jever beer**

ASTRA

Astra is more than "just" a Hamburg beer label. Several different types of beer are sold in the greater Hamburg area under this name: Urtyp, Exclusiv, Pilsener and the slightly stronger Rotlicht. Until 2003, Astra beer (as well as Astra Alsterwasser) was made in the Bavaria-St.-Pauli brewery located between the Reeperbahn and Landungsbrück-en. The buildings have since been torn down, and Astra brewery was taken over by Holsten brewery, but this original Hamburg product still remains a Reeperbahn icon.

Bright red Astra advertising, an integral part of St Pauli

ALSTERWASSER

This beverage mix – known in southern Germany as a Radler and in England as a shandy – consists of one-half lemon-flavoured soda and one-half lager. It was once always freshly mixed in restaurants, bars and private homes. Since the German beer tax law was altered in 1993, Alsterwasser and its cousins have been sold in bottles by beverage companies. A tip: if you want to make your own Alsterwasser, first pour in the lemon soda, then the beer, otherwise the beer will not be able to develop a creamy head.

Rotlicht and Urtyp – two beers from Astra brewery

Alsterwasser, a mix of beer and lemon-flavoured soda

SPIRITS AND LIQUEURS

There is a wide choice of spirits in shops, restaurants and bars. A schnapps rounds off a meal or provides a bit of welcome warmth on a damp day. Among the classics are herbal liqueurs, such as Wattenläufer, aniseed schnapps such as Küstennebel, or the distilled Aquavit, flavoured with caraway seeds. While sailors once drank straight rum, today, when the weather is miserable in Hamburg, people enjoy a Grog (a shot of rum with hot water).

Wattenläufer   Egg liqueur   Aquavit   Küstennebel

fritz-limo and fritz-kola – non-alcoholic beverages originating in Hamburg

NON-ALCOHOLIC DRINKS

It is safe to drink Hamburg tap water – and it has been safe since before the days of Wasserträger Hummel *(see p67)*. But most people order a bottle of mineral water in a restaurant – sparkling or still. Apart from the usual soft drinks found everywhere, there are a few new speciality beverages originating in Hamburg that have become well-known throughout Germany and even beyond its borders.

A cola drink by the name of fritz-kola originated in the Hanseatic city and has been on the market since 2003. It has a higher caffeine content than the market leader and was at first only sold in Hamburg bars before moving beyond the city boundaries. Along with fritz-kola, the company created a soft-drink series called fritz-limo.

Bionade is a fermented herbal fruit drink made with natural products. It comes in various flavours – Elderberry, Lychee, Herbs, Ginger & Orange, Quince and Active (with more minerals). In 1997, Bionade began to conquer Hamburg's beverage market – first in fitness-centres, then in trendy bars and finally as a drink for the masses.

Bionade, a herbal, fruit soft drink

Mineral water and "Apfelsaftschorle"

Mineral water

HOT DRINKS

Although the American coffee shop, with its bewildering number of flavoured coffee varieties, has become well-established in Hamburg there is still nothing like a good cup of unadulterated coffee – meaning no added flavours. Apart from the commonly available filter coffee, espresso and cappuccino are also popular drinks. There are also some tea salons in Hamburg, where tea preparation is still treated as a real ritual, attracting tea aficionados.

A cup of coffee – espresso or cappuccino

East Frisian black tea

Choosing a Restaurant

The restaurants in this guide have been selected because of their good food, interesting location or special atmosphere. They are listed by area and, within each area, alphabetically by price category. Information about cafés and snack bars is provided on pages 198–201.

PRICE CATEGORIES
Price for a three-course meal per person with a half bottle of wine, including taxes and service:

€ under €25
€€ €25–35
€€€ €35–45
€€€€ €45–55
€€€€€ over €55

OLD TOWN

Daniel Wischer €
Spitalerstr. 12, 20095 **Tel** 32 52 58 15   **Map** 10 E3

Hamburg's oldest fish fryer opened in 1924. Since then, its motto has been "there's always fish, and fish always sells". The food on offer ranges from Matjes (salted herring) to pollack. The homemade potato salad tastes very good on the side. This is a reasonably priced option when you're in a hurry. ● Sun.

Ti Breizh €
Deichstr. 39, 20459 **Tel** 37 51 78 15   **Map** 9 C4

This restaurant brings the spirit of Brittany to the Alster. Delicious galettes and crêpes, filled with either a savoury or sweet filling (from goat's cheese, poultry or Dijon mustard sauce to chestnut ice-cream), delight all lovers of hearty French cuisine.

Café Paris €€
Rathausstr. 4, 20095 **Tel** 32 52 77 77   **Map** 10 D3

Authentic French food served in a lovely Jugendstil atmosphere in a high-ceilinged room at the foot of the Rathaus. A downtown mix of stock brokers, shoppers and visitors to the city dine under ceiling mosaics on delicious dishes such as coq au vin, tripe capped with puff-pasty or steak tartar with capers and mustard. Food just like chez maman.

Fillet of Soul €€
Deichtorstr. 2, 20095 **Tel** 70 70 58 00   **Map** 10 F4

Art meets gastronomy at this restaurant in the Deichtorhallen, which considers itself equal in its own way to the art displayed in the museum. Carrot and apple soup with hazelnut pesto, ocean perch fillet poached in a Thai curry stock or beef simmered in stock (Tafelspitz) with asparagus make a very good base for enjoying the artists' works.

Golden Cut €€
Holzdamm 61, 20099 **Tel** 85 10 35 32   **Map** 10 F2

Dine and chill out under one roof in this restaurant and club. Curried-carrot soup with sautéed prawns, fillet of pike-perch on cabbage cooked with champagne or five-spice breast of duck are pure culinary delights. After dining, you can dance away the night in the lounge. The trendy Golden Cut is one Hamburg's places to see and be seen.

Le Plat du Jour €€
Dornbusch 4, 20095 **Tel** 32 14 14   **Map** 9 C3

French bistro food at its finest – charming and seductive. Guests can choose from a set menu or create their own. Dishes such as scampi provençal or rack of lamb with a rosemary-infused sauce almost guarantee a holiday mood. The homemade patés are available in various degrees of richness.

Mama €€
Schauenburgerstr. 44, 20095 **Tel** 36 09 99 93   **Map** 10 D3

The owners of Mama have created a modern version of a trattoria. There are flawless Italian dishes including pizza, pasta, antipasti and great desserts. The decor is remarkable. You sit either on low stools with huge cushions, on traditional wooden benches, or at a 6-m (20-ft) long table.

Turnhalle St. Georg €€
Lange Reihe 107, 20099 **Tel** 28 00 84 80   **Map** 6 E1

This is a very chic establishment in which guests feel right at home. Located in a school gymnasium with huge arched windows, built in 1889, this is a restaurant, café, bar and lounge all in one. The owners succeed in managing a gastronomic balancing act between pizza and pasta on the one hand and entrecôte and bouillabaisse on the other.

Cox €€€
Lange Reihe 68, 20099 **Tel** 24 94 22   **Map** 6 E1

This hip restaurant with a bistro feel offers a choice of dishes from many European cuisines. Guests sit on red leather banquettes at small tables and enjoy stewed duck served with apple-horseradish sauce, lamb stew with olives and sun-dried tomatoes or simple gnocchi with rosemary.

Key to Symbols see back cover flap

Le PaqueBot 🍴📷 €€€€
Gerhart-Hauptmann-Platz 70, 20095 **Tel** *32 65 19* **Map** *10 E3*

This Art Deco restaurant in the Thalia Theater is ideal if you are going to the theatre. Some people come before and after the show. After performances, actors from the Thalia Theater arrive. Bœuf bourguignon with bacon and mushrooms is hearty fare, the salads are much lighter. You simply must try the mango sorbet.

Alt Hamburger Aalspeicher 📷 €€€
Deichstr. 43, 20459 **Tel** *36 29 90* **Map** *9 C4*

Eel is one of the specialities of this restaurant, located in a warehouse built in the 16th century. Guests select "their" eel and later peel off the skin of the freshly smoked eel. Then it is time for a Kornbrannt (corn schnapps) – to clean your fingers. If this does not appeal, then you can choose Matjeshering (salted herring) with pan-fried potatoes.

Deichgraf 🍴📷🍷 €€€€
Deichstr. 23, 20459 **Tel** *36 42 08* **Map** *9 C4*

Would you like to dine in a traditional restaurant that serves authentic Hanseatic cuisine? The Deichgraf is just the place. Among the classic dishes are fillet of sturgeon on beetroot salad and mullet in a mussel-saffron stock served on pearl barley risotto. A dessert favourite is caramelised pineapple with chocolate froth.

Saliba Alsterarkaden 🌱🍴📷🍷 €€€€
Neuer Wall 13, 20354 **Tel** *34 50 21* **Map** *10 D3*

This Syrian restaurant brings a touch of the Orient to the Old Town. Hardly anyone who comes here can resist lamb cooked with dates and pomegranates. A strong cup of mocha rounds out the meal. An international crowd gathers here under the white arches of the arcade along Alsterfleet.

Tschebull 📷 €€€€
Mönckebergstr. 7, 20095 **Tel** *32 96 47 96* **Map** *10 D3*

In the heart of Hamburg's Old Town, Tschebull offers authentic Austrian fare such as Viennese Schnitzel and Kärntner Käsenudeln (pasta au gratin with cheese) as well as fish dishes and seafood. The desserts are delightful. Try Salzburger Nockerln (sweet soufflé) oder Kaiserschmarrn (sugared pancakes with raisins). Separate bar and lounge. ⬤ *Sun.*

NEW TOWN

Marinehof 🌱📷 €€
Admiralitätstr. 77, 20459 **Tel** *374 25 79* **Map** *9 B4*

Located on Fleetinsel, this light-filled restaurant has become a meeting-place for people working in media, especially those in production companies, who meet here after work for a snack. Potato gnocchi and lentil-and-spinach soup are especially popular. The Italian almond cake is to die for. ⬤ *Sun.*

Marblau 🍴 €€€
Poolstr. 21, 20355 **Tel** *35 01 65 55* **Map** *9 B2*

Southern Europe meets the Orient. This restaurant serves specialities from all the Mediterranean countries. Classic Spanish and Italian dishes are prepared with Oriental spices and herbs. The ambience is perfect: the ceilings are as azure blue as the summer sky. The walls are cleverly decorated with photographs printed on canvas.

Matsumi 🍴 €€€
Colonnaden 96, 20354 **Tel** *34 31 25* **Map** *9 C1*

Delicacies for those in the know are served in the oldest Japanese restaurant in Hamburg. The cold green-tea noodles with a sour dip are bold but popular with regulars. No less exotic are the fried eel and prawn dumplings with lotus root. There is a huge choice of sakes, and Japanese beer flows from the taps.

Shalimar 🌱🍴📷 €€€
ABC-Straße 46–47, 20354 **Tel** *44 24 84* **Map** *9 C2*

Here, traditional Indian cuisine, from mild to devilishly hot, is served between golden columns. There is a wide range of dishes, such as vegetable curry with rice, chicken fillet in yoghurt sauce and fillet of lamb in ginger sauce. Children's portions are available for the little Maharajahs. And all this takes place under the watchful eyes of a giant Buddha.

Old Commercial Room 🍴🍷 €€€€
Englische Planke 10, 20459 **Tel** *36 63 19* **Map** *9 A4*

Most patrons of this traditional Hamburg restaurant come from outside the city. Plaice Büsum style with saltwater shrimp, beef roulade with red cabbage and potato dumplings and, of course, *Labskaus* (seaman's stew) are the menu's hits. Overseas guests in particular love the polished setting.

Rialto 🌱🍴📷🍷🎵 €€€€
Michaelisbrücke 3, 20459 **Tel** *36 43 42* **Map** *9 C4*

Fans of light Mediterranean cuisine are in the right place in the Rialto. Red snapper wrapped in a banana leaf with spinach salad, or goat's cheese on beetroot carpaccio are typical dishes. Pictures of landscapes hang on the walls, elegant tables and subdued lighting create a cosy atmosphere. On warm days, the terrace is busy.

Zu den alten Krameramtsstuben am Michel
🎵 🖼 €€€€

Krayenkamp 10, 20459 **Tel** *36 58 00* **Map** 9 B4

In a narrow cul-de-sac at the foot of St Michaelis church is this unique 17th-century building complex *(see p72)*. Traditional Hamburg fare is served here beneath wooden ceilings. Freshly caught fish is prepared in the traditional way. There is no better or more original atmosphere in which to enjoy *Labskaus* (seaman's stew) than right here.

Die Bank
🏠 🍴 €€€€€

Hohe Bleichen 17, 20354 **Tel** *238 00 30* **Map** 9 C2

The maxim of this brasserie in a former bank building is "transition". Chef Fritz Schilling understands this to mean a culinary mix of the traditional and the modern. The menu opens to reveal "bank secrets" such as the gold hamburger with goose liver and truffle sauce. A chickpea stew with wild shrimp is another classic.

[m]eatery
🏠 €€€€€

Drehbahn 49, 20354 **Tel** *30 99 95 95* **Map** 9 C2

The restaurant in the designer hotel SIDE *(see p178)* opened in 2009 with a truly innovative concept. Steaks figure centrally on the menu. The meat is derived from Argentina, the U.S.A and Schleswig-Holstein. The restaurant is one of the best steak houses in Hamburg. Burgers and steak tartare are available as well.

PORT AND SPEICHERSTADT

Oberhafen Kantine
€

Stockmeyerstr. 39, 20457 **Tel** *32 80 99 84* **Map** 6 E4

This traditional Hamburg restaurant originated in a Kaffeeklappe (coffee flap), where workers picked up their snacks. After thorough renovation it was reopened in 2006. The restaurant serves Hanseatic classics such as *Labskaus*, meatballs, beef goulash or fried eggs with bacon.

Schönes Leben
🖼 🖼 €€

Alter Wandrahm 15, 20457 **Tel** *180 48 26 80* **Map** 6 D4

Café and restaurant all in one, this establishment serves breakfast from 10am; at lunchtime, patrons enjoy a reasonably priced main course with side dishes from a buffet. Cakes and coffee are available in the afternoons, meat, fish and vegetable dishes and pasta for dinner. The brunch on Sundays and holidays (10am–2:30pm) is very popular.

Weinrestaurant Schoppenhauer
🏠 🖼 €€

Reimerstwiete 20–22, 20457 **Tel** *37 15 10* **Map** 5 C4

Oak beams and an ethnic bar contribute to the rustic atmosphere of this wine restaurant located in a 17th-century half-timbered house. The menu features traditional dishes like roast beef, rump steak or soured meat in jelly. The Schoppenhauer is also an ideal place to simply enjoy a glass of wine. ⚫ *Sun.*

Die Fischküche
🏠 €€€

Kajen 12, 20459 **Tel** *36 56 31* **Map** 9 C5

The fish here is so freshly prepared that they seem to have leapt straight from fish-hook to plate. For a snack, the herring on black bread is a good choice. A typical menu starts with lobster soup, followed by a fillet of pike-perch in a sauerkraut crust. A cosy restaurant, where the green plants grow like the algae in the ocean. ⚫ *Sun.*

Brook
🏠 🖼 €€€€

Bei den Mühren 91, 20457 **Tel** *37 50 31 28* **Map** 10 D5

Brook, which has a very cosy atmosphere, is the ideal place for a romantic candlelight dinner. The kitchen's creations are really extraordinary: flounder fillet on lime-infused mashed potatoes or tuna with artichokes and pesto – and all this with a view of the Speicherstadt. ⚫ *Sun.*

CARLS
🏠 €€€€

Am Kaiserkai 69, 20457 **Tel** *300 32 24 00* **Map** 5 B5

Brasserie, bistro and bar in one. This gastronomic outpost of the Louis C. Jacob hotel *(see p183)* is located directly beside Hamburg's newest landmark, the Elbphilharmonie. The French-Hanseatic cuisine pleases even the most demanding palates. Rooms are stylish, with dark wooden floors and giant chandeliers.

VLET
🏠 €€€€€

Am Sandtorkai 23/24, 20457 **Tel** *334 75 37 50* **Map** 5 C4

Soon after it opened in 2008, this gourmet restaurant located in a stylishly renovated warehouse developed into one of the most popular restaurants in the Speicherstadt. The pike-perch fillet or veal tenderloin, eel soup or steak tartare please even the most demanding palates. The cheese platters are sensational. ⚫ *Sun.*

Wandrahm
🖼 €€€€€

Am Kaiserkai 13, 20457 **Tel** *31 81 22 00* **Map** 5 C5

Elegant and chic, but not too understated, is the atmosphere of Wandrahm restaurant, which offers everything. Mornings it is a coffee- and tea-shop, at lunch it is a place for a quick repast, the afternoon is sweetened with homemade cakes, and evenings, it serves unusual dishes. The ingenious lighting system adjusts to the changing rhythm of the music.

Key to Price Guide *see p190* **Key to Symbols** *see back cover flap*

ST PAULI

Hamborger Veermaster
V   €

Reeperbahn 162, 20359 **Tel** *31 65 44*   **Map** *3 C4*

This long-established restaurant on the Reeperbahn offers traditional Hamburg cuisine – from *Labskaus* (seaman's stew) to shrimp soup and *Pannfisch* (braised fish with home fries) – in a cosy, maritime atmosphere. Choose *Rote Grütt* as dessert. Lively music completes this authentic St. Pauli experience. *Jan–Easter: Sun–Thu.*

Bullerei
€€

Lagerstr. 34b, 20357 **Tel** *33 44 21 10*

Celebrity chef Tim Mälzer established this restaurant in the renovated halls of the old Hamburg abattoir. Aficionados of hearty fare cherish the lamb shoulder cooked in milk, fillet steak, gnocchi, mushroom stew, Burger Magnifico (with minced meat and mozzarella) and cod rissoles. The Bullerei offers good value for money.

Fischerhaus
V &   €€€

St. Pauli Fischmarkt 14, 20359 **Tel** *31 40 53*   **Map** *2 E4*

North German cuisine and a rustic atmosphere harmonize perfectly here. Along with classics such as eel soup and *Labskaus*, guests relish fillet of ocean perch, white halibut and giant prawns. The Neptune fish platter is enough to satisfy three people. Many Fish Market visitors end their shopping trip here.

La Vela
€€€

Große Elbstr. 27, 22767 **Tel** *38 69 93 93*   **Map** *2 E4*

La Vela is an Italian restaurant in a top location at the start of "gastronomy mile" between the Fischmarkt and Övelgönne. A very popular appetizer is cream of sugar pea soup flavoured with vanilla. Lasagne or tagliatelle with asparagus tips are among the choices for mains. Sunday is family day.

Nil
€€€€

Neuer Pferdemarkt 5/6, 20359 **Tel** *439 78 23*   **Map** *4 D2*

The 1950s decor creates a unique atmosphere. Guests dine on three levels and, in summer, in the courtyard too. Many organic ingredients are used here, and Ayurvedic ideas flow into the preparation of some of the dishes. Chicory stuffed with spinach or asparagus with ham and mushrooms are especially popular. *Jan–Nov: Tue.*

Schauermann
€€€€

St. Pauli Hafenstr. 136–138, 20359 **Tel** *31 79 46 60*   **Map** *3 C4*

An oasis of minimalist style with turquoise and black leather seats. The dishes seem even more opulent in contrast. Scallops on fennel and blood-orange salad, or sautéed fillet of ocean perch delight all those who love to feast on the bounty of the sea. There is a lovely view of the Elbe river from the terrace. *Sun.*

Artisan
€€€€€

Kampstr. 27, 20357 **Tel** *42 10 29 15*   **Map** *4 D1*

This small restaurant offers creative cuisine in a living-room atmosphere. The set menus (three to seven courses) change every week. After sampling an appetizer, such as chicken with squid and apple, you know you are in for variety. One surprise follows another all the way to dessert. A wine is paired with each course. *Sun, Mon.*

ALTONA

Altamira
€

Bahrenfelder Str. 331, 22761 **Tel** *85 37 16 00*   **Map** *1 C1*

Supposedly this is where the best tapas north of Barcelona are to be had. But this Spanish restaurant is also well-known for its spicy dishes such as *pimientos de padrón* or tiger shrimp in a garlic and white-wine sauce. Not only the food but also the cacti create a Mediterranean feeling. Later in the evening, recorded salsa music is played.

Bolero
€

Bahrenfelder Str. 53, 22765 **Tel** *390 78 00*   **Map** *1 C3*

Fajitas, enchiladas, nachos and more – in brief, typical Mexican food that fills you up. The tortillas, which guests can load up with vegetables and meat as they choose, are extremely popular. And the brunch buffet fulfils every wish. The pasta dishes vary daily. There are 120 entries on the cocktail menu.

Haifischbar
€

Große Elbstr. 128, 22767 **Tel** *380 93 42*   **Map** *2 E4*

The furniture is a bit dusty and you should not expect any culinary highlights here – just *Matjes*, plaice and *Labskaus*. But even so, the Haifischbar, open around the clock, is imbued with the romance of seafaring and is well loved by its guests. German stars such as Hans Albers, Freddy Quinn and Lale Andersen frequented this bar.

Zum Schellfischposten
Carsten-Rehder-Str. 62, 22767 **Tel** *38 34 22*   **Map** *2 E4*

Altona's oldest seaman's pub – an integral part of this area – serves savoury dishes at reasonable prices. Goulash and fish sandwiches figure among the comfort food. This rustic pub has often served as a setting for TV productions like the series *Großstadtrevier*. Ina Müller's programme *Inas Nacht* is also filmed here.

Breitengrad
Gefionstr. 3, 22769 **Tel** *43 18 99 99*   **Map** *2 E1*

A visit to this Sri Lankan restaurant located right behind the Neue Flora is a perfect way to round off the musical experience. Large portions of rice and mixed salads are served with fiery hot dishes (such as chicken curry, chicken Vindaloo and lamb Kashmiri). On Tuesdays and Fridays a vegetarian buffet is featured.

Eisenstein
Friedensallee 9, 22765 **Tel** *390 46 06*   **Map** *1 B2*

The Eisenstein, located in a ships' screw factory, is a trendy restaurant, breakfast place and beer garden all in one. Here business people, filmmakers and visitors enjoy scallops with sweet potatoes or roulades made of saddle of stag with salsify stew – or just a perfect pizza, thin and crisp.

Indochine
Neumühlen 11, 22763 **Tel** *39 80 78 80*   **Map** *1 B5*

This branch of a Singapore restaurant prepares authentic Indochinese cuisine with French additions. Typical dishes are prawns Cambodian style or banana and coconut rice rolls with fruit dips. The spectacular view of passing ships through the panoramic window is yours free of charge.

Shikara
Bahrenfelder Str. 241, 22765 **Tel** *39 90 66 96*   **Map** *1 C2*

Indian specialities coloured by all the world's spices are featured here. Along with Tandoori dishes, there are also lentil dishes with curry, chicken tikka and pakoras (deep-fried vegetables in batter). There are also branches of Shikara in Eppendorf (Eppendorfer Marktplatz 8) and Winterhude (Mühlenkamp 8).

Strandperle
Övelgönne 60, 22605 **Tel** *880 11 12*

Nowhere is Hamburg more romantic on a pleasant summer evening than here, in Strandperle, a popular place to meet. Patrons can sit on the wooden platform, eat fast food and relax, or opt to sit or lie down on the sand – the harbour view is included. Strandperle can be reached by HADAG ferry 62.

Lutter & Wegner
Große Elbstr. 49, 22767 **Tel** *809 00 90 00*   **Map** *2 E4*

This outpost of the famous restaurant on Berlin's Gendarmenmarkt clearly beats its counterpart in the capital in the view department. The rooms are filled with light, the tables are elegantly laid and, on the terrace, the fresh Elbe breeze gently wafts by the guests. No wonder that the establishment's fish dishes taste best here.

Luxor
Max-Brauer-Allee 251, 22769 **Tel** *430 01 24*   **Map** *2 F1*

Viennese *Tafelspitz*, Irish rock oysters or a Provencal fish soup – the fare offered here is international and not Egyptian, despite what the name might lead you to think. Regulars keep coming back just for the fantastic penne with cuttlefish in chilli-garlic oil. ● *Mon.*

Das Seepferdchen
Große Elbstr. 212, 22767 **Tel** *38 61 67 49*   **Map** *2 D4*

This former fish storage hall was turned into a charming restaurant decorated in pleasant sand-coloured tones. Grilled lobster, sautéed haddock, giant prawns or a homemade fish burger – for the variety of delectable fish specialities on offer, the Seepferdchen cannot be beaten. ● *Sun.*

Au Quai
Große Elbstr. 145b–d, 22767 **Tel** *38 03 77 30*   **Map** *2 D4*

Walk inside and look outside – the view of the Elbe river from the tables of Au Quai is absolutely wonderful. Mediterranean cuisine and Asian-influenced decor create a cosmopolitan flair. From the terrace, you can watch the ocean-going giants as they sail away or the sun as it sets over Hamburg. ● *Sun.*

Das Weiße Haus
Neumühlen 50, 22763 **Tel** *390 90 16*   **Map** *1 A5*

While enjoying the view of Museumshafen Övelgönne *(see p135)* from this former pilot station, you can sample the ingenious creations of the chef. At lunch there is a varied menu which changes daily. In the evenings, there is a menu with three or four courses. Reservations are recommended.

Fischereihafen Restaurant
Große Elbstr. 143, 22767 **Tel** *38 18 16*   **Map** *2 D4*

Hamburg's celebrities also love the exquisite fish cuisine served in this gastronomic institution belonging to the Kowalke family. Along with regional fish dishes prepared with turbot, flounder or eel, this restaurant also serves up French oysters and Iranian caviar. This is an ideal place for pampered palates.

Key to Price Guide *see p190* **Key to Symbols** *see back cover flap*

Henssler & Henssler
Große Elbstr. 160, 22767 **Tel** *38 69 90 00*   **Map** *2 D4*

The cuisine here is straightforward and yet rich in contrasts, featuring classic Japanese culinary artistry with modern international influences. From time to time the noise level rises, but this should not detract from the enjoyment of fried tuna sashimi with marinated vegetables, black tiger shrimp or chicken skewers Yakitori. *Sun.*

Landhaus Scherrer
Elbchaussee 130, 22763 **Tel** *883 07 00 30*   **Map** *1 A4*

At the zenith of the Hamburg gastronomic scene, star-chef Heinz Otto Wehmann prepares regional specialities with his very own ideas about what *haute cuisine* is. The menu contains such fine dishes as saddle of Holstein fallow deer and fillet of beef with fava bean puree. The impressive wine menu lists 620 wines. *Sun.*

Rive
Van-der-Smissen-Str. 1, 22767 **Tel** *380 59 19*   **Map** *2 D4*

This restaurant and oyster bar offers everything the ocean provides along with a wonderful view of the Elbe. Delicacies include the seafood platter with oysters, langoustines and mussels, or grilled lemon sole with creamed spinach. The ingredients are purchased fresh at the market. The fish and chips is large enough to satisfy a big appetite.

AROUND THE ALSTER

Alex im Alsterpavillon
Jungfernstieg 54, 20354 **Tel** *350 18 70*   **Map** *10 D2*

This once plush café, a permanent institution on the Jungfernstieg, has been bought up by a restaurant chain. Since then, it is mostly young people who populate the Alex; many come for brunch, some just for a café latte. The view out over the Binnenalster is phenomenal.

Max & Consorten
Spadenteich 1, 20099 **Tel** *280 22 28*   **Map** *6 E2*

This old, traditional pub on the edge of St Georg is a real institution. Simple Hamburg classics on the menu include pickled herring with sour cream, apples and onions, or pan-fried potatoes with a fried egg. Moreover there is a wide selection of pasta dishes.

Casino auf Kampnagel
Jarrestr. 20, 22303 **Tel** *27 87 74 39*

At lunchtime, the Casino is the canteen for everyone working in Kampnagel, a centre for the arts, and the surrounding area. The evening fare is even better, which theatre-goers appreciate. Delicious food with main courses such as duck breast with potato gratin, rice with vegetables and a fillet of fish or Wiener Schnitzel. *Mon.*

Freischwimmer
Fruchtallee 1, 20259 **Tel** *41 45 99 80*

Examples of this restaurant's creative dishes are baby squid with lemon-rosemary risotto and rump steak with Parmesan cheese crust served with homemade tagliatelle. And, for dessert, there is plum tiramisu or chocolate mousse with chillies and pineapple – simply scrumptious. After eating, you can go bowling in the basement.

Kham
Lange Reihe 97, 20099 **Tel** *28 00 48 68*   **Map** *8 E4*

The Asian dishes (primarily from Tibet and India) are especially popular with younger patrons. Chicken soup with coconut milk is a favourite starter, followed by vegetables fried in chickpea batter. A new taste experience is the lamb with spring vegetables, rice, dates and lychees. *Mon.*

Ristorante Galatea
Ballindamm 14, 20095 **Tel** *33 72 27*   **Map** *10 E2*

Here, Hamburg gastronomy shows itself from a different side. This restaurant boat docked at the Binnenalster shore serves Italian food and regional specialities with an emphasis on fish dishes. The tables sway a bit, which is quite natural, but this does not detract from the dining pleasure.

Sâi gón
Martinistr. 14, 20251 **Tel** *46 09 10 09*

Vietnamese fare such as glass noodle soup with chicken and morels, fillet of chicken breast with vegetables, lemon grass and chillies, or a variety of tofu dishes are eaten at very large tables. Anyone who wants to can eat with chopsticks. Try a cocktail with exotic fruits.

Tassajara
Eppendorfer Landstr. 4, 20249 **Tel** *48 38 90*

In Tassajara, one of the most successful vegetarian restaurants in Hamburg, there are many inventive specialities (such as oyster mushrooms on a bed of lentils or gingered spinach with stuffed mushrooms) on the menu. Special wishes such as macrobiotic or Ayurveda diets are accommodated. *Sun.*

Brücke

Innocentiastr. 82, 20144 **Tel** *422 55 25*

This is a small restaurant with few frills. This makes it all the more surprising that it is frequented by Hamburg's in-crowd. Perhaps it is the fabulous Wiener Schnitzel with mashed potatoes and cucumber salad, which is considered unbeatable for its size and taste. The owner Branko Goricki also runs a small wine store next door.

L'Auberge

Rutschbahn 34, 20146 **Tel** *410 25 32*   **Map** *7 B2*

Mediterranean cuisine with a focus on France, created by a *chef de cuisine* from Provence. One of the specialities is *bouillabaisse*, the famous fish soup from Marseille. A light Arab influence can be seen in the use of dates in lamb dishes and in the mint coating for prawns.

La Bruschetta

Dorotheenstr. 35, 22301 **Tel** *27 66 61*

Located in Winterhude, this *ristorante* is also popular with Hamburg celebrities. Whether it is *saltimbocca* or breast of duck, monkfish or turbot – Chef Sandro Convertino (who has his own cooking show on a local TV station) pleases all his guests with his creative variations on "la cucina tipica italiana" (typical Italian cuisine) .

Massimo La Lupa

Sierichstr. 112, 22299 **Tel** *41 42 47 99*

This restaurant is plain, straightforward and unpretentious. The charismatic chef, Massimo, hails from Rome, and is considered by those knowledgeable about Italian cuisine to be one of the best. Whether you order veal carpaccio with porcini, sea bream in foil or vegetarian lasagne – every guest leaves satisfied. *Mon.*

Morellino

Eppendorfer Landstr. 36, 20249 **Tel** *480 22 16*

This Italian restaurant reflects the sophisticated lifestyle on which people in Eppendorf like to pride themselves. Along with classic dishes such as carpaccio, diners swear by the grilled calamari and the octopus salad. You simply must try the *porchetta* (suckling pig) with rosemary roasted potatoes. The cheque is sweetened by ice-cream on a stick. *Mon.*

Jahreszeiten Grill

Jungfernstieg 9–14, 20354 **Tel** *34 94 33 12*   **Map** *10 D2*

This restaurant in the Hotel Vier Jahreszeiten *(see p125)* takes guests right back to the 1920s with its Art Deco lamps, plaster ornamentation and wood panelling. You can choose your own side dishes for some main courses (the *entrecôte*, for example). The wine-list is a vinophile's delight.

Küchenwerkstatt

Hans-Henny-Jahnn-Weg 1, 22085 **Tel** *22 92 75 88*

This is the real Hamburg: authentic Delft tiles and wooden carvings in the high, lofty rooms of an old patrician villa. In summer, the Alster ferry stops directly in front of the door. A popular main course is rack of salt-meadow lamb poached in goat's milk with a purée of onions. Fish dishes include halibut with a curried peanut sauce. *Sun, Mon.*

La Mirabelle

Bundesstr. 15, 20146 **Tel** *410 75 85*   **Map** *7 A3*

"Where wine and cuisine are married" is the motto of this French restaurant. But it is not only wedding parties who appreciate the creations here. One of the top palate pleasers is baby goat – the leg is simmered, and the saddle is roasted. The owner-chef personally helps guests choose just the right wine. *Sun.*

La Scala

Falkenried 54, 20251 **Tel** *420 62 95*

The finest Italian cuisine with all its many facets is served here in one of the best Italian restaurants in the city. The atmosphere is elegant, the courteous service impressive. It is best to order exactly what Chef Mario Zini recommends. In October and November, *tartufo bianco* (white truffles) are an absolute must. *Mon.*

Windows Restaurant

Fontenay 10, 20354 **Tel** *41 42 25 31*   **Map** *7 C3*

Located on the 9th floor of the InterContinental Hamburg Hotel *(see p181),* this restaurant with a maritime theme pampers guests with excellent French cuisine. The wine list offers more than 200 options. The fantastic view over the Außenalster is another treat. *Sun, Mon.*

Goldfisch

Isekai 1, 20249 **Tel** *57 00 96 90*

Here, so close to the water, almost everything has to revolve around fish, though there are also meat dishes (such as poussin with asparagus) and vegetarian fare. The waterside terrace cannot be beaten. A paddling trip is ideal for digestion – the trip starts right on the restaurant's own jetty at the boat rental kiosk.

Haerlin

Neuer Jungfernstieg 9–14, 20354 **Tel** *34 94 33 10*   **Map** *10 D2*

In surveying the majestic restaurant in the Hotel Vier Jahreszeiten *(see p125)*, and studying the princely menu, you get the feeling that the whole world is found here. But one of the primary focuses of the kitchen is on French cuisine; for example, the subtly nuanced *loup de mer* (sea bass) with a purée of fennel and pesto froth. *Sun, Mon.*

Piment
🍷🍴🍸 €€€€€

Lehmweg 29, 20251 **Tel** *42 93 77 88*

Hamburg's gourmets praise Allah that Moroccan chef Wahabi Nouri found his way to the Elbe metropolis. His expert hand with herbs from his native country gives the finishing touch to mouth-watering dishes such as squab in a port *jus* with celery root schnitzel or veal with saffron. The restaurant is decorated in pleasant tones. 🌑 *Sun.*

FURTHER AFIELD

Das Neue Landhaus Walter
V🍴🏃 €€

Hindenburgstr. 2, 22303 **Tel** *27 50 54*

An unusual combination, or proof that beer gardens can also succeed in the North? Here, wicker beach chairs are placed beside picnic tables, and the menu lists fish dishes and pretzels. The Sunday morning live Jazz sessions are very popular. When the weather is inclement, guests get comfortable inside. 🌑 *Winter: Mon.*

Engel
€€€

Fähranleger Teufelsbrück, 22609 **Tel** *82 41 87*

This is a popular excursion destination at the Teufelsbrück ferry stop and is bound to be a hit for a Sunday brunch or a relaxed dinner. Sautéed *loup de mer* (sea bass) with Ligurian-style lentils or *saltimbocca* of corn-fed chicken is pure dining pleasure. The gentle swaying motion of the dock decreases the more wine you drink!

Fischclub Blankenese
€€€

Strandweg, Blankeneser Landungsbrücken, 22587 **Tel** *86 99 62*

As the name suggests, fish – both from the Mediterranean and local waters – is served here. Main courses such as plaice caught in the North Sea, grilled scampis with green asparagus or wild-mushroom risotto with red mullet, taste especially divine when you are sitting near the enormous windows with a premium view of the passing ships.

Witthüs Teestuben
🍷🍴 €€€

Elbchaussee 499a, 22587 **Tel** *86 01 73*

In this splendid thatched-roofed Neo-Classical villa in the middle of Blankenese's Hirschpark, patrons sit at tables covered with flowered table cloths – which is especially popular with ladies in the afternoon. In the evenings, the café and tea-house turn into a restaurant serving dishes such as fish soup or veal with vegetables. 🌑 *Mon.*

Zollenspieker Fährhaus
V🍷🍴🏃 €€€

Zollenspieker Hauptdeich 143, 21037 **Tel** *793 13 30*

Whether the sun is shining or it is miserable outside – a trip to the Fährhaus is worthwhile at any time. After all, egg ribbon noodles tossed with pieces of ocean perch, baked fillet of wolffish, or pan-fried fish taste good whether they are eaten inside or out. Small guests can order dishes such as "Käpt'n Kuddl" – fish-fingers with mashed potatoes.

Dal Fabbro
🍷🍴🍸 €€€€

Blankeneser Bahnhofstr. 10, 22587 **Tel** *86 89 41*

Many consider this to be the best Italian restaurant in Blankenese. Tuna tartar with sour cream and salmon caviar, or turbot in a crust of potato with truffled cream sauce are some of the classic dishes on the menu. And who can say no to *limonensorbet con Prosecco* for dessert?

Stock's Fischrestaurant
🍷🍴 €€€€

An der Alsterschleife 3, 22399 **Tel** *611 36 20*

This country house with terrace is home to one of the finest fish restaurants in the Alstertal. But beware: after a rich starter of *bouillabaisse* made from North Sea fish you might not have enough room for the main course. This would be a shame, since the sautéed red snapper or wild salmon here are excellent. 🌑 *Sat lunch, Mon.*

Jacobs Restaurant
🍷🍴🍸 €€€€€

Elbchaussee 401–403, 22609 **Tel** *82 25 50*

Elegant and classic, Hanseatic to the tips of its napkins, and with hardly an equal for culinary variety. This restaurant, which has a lovely terrace with old linden trees, belongs to the Louis C. Jacob hotel (see p183). It is the darling of all the gourmets, who enjoy the view of the Elbe while dining on red mullet from Brittany or divine lobster cannelloni.

Sagebiels Fährhaus
🍷🍴🍸 €€€€

Blankeneser Hauptstr. 107, 22587 **Tel** *86 15 14*

This half-timbered building appeals to those who set great store in a dignified atmosphere with a touch of the exotic. The latter is provided by several Chinese dishes that complement North German fish cuisine. A typical menu starts pumpkin-orange soup and continues with a Chang Dong seafood platter. 🌑 *Oct–Mar: Mon.*

Seven Seas
🍷🍴 €€€€€

Süllbergsterrasse 12, 22587 **Tel** *866 25 20*

Chef Karlheinz Hauser and his team pull out all the stops in this traditional restaurant to please their demanding guests with the finest food. Their culinary works of art come beautifully plated with every attention to the smallest detail. The cuisine here is French classic with influences from the world's oceans. 🌑 *Mon, Tue.*

Cafés and Snack Bars

When you are under way and suddenly need something to eat, Hamburg offers many choices. Booths selling tasty fish sandwiches or German sausages are plentiful. If you like to linger longer over your food, then try out a snack bar, bistro or sandwich shop. There are also many cosy cafés in Hamburg – there is practically one on every corner of the city. Whether you prefer latte macchiato, café au lait or that German classic – an individual small pot of strong coffee – your coffee will certainly taste good. Tea is also available, and you can take time to relax, people-watch, read the newspaper or leaf through your travel guide.

CAFÉS

The choice of cafés, in which young and old can eat a light snack or just simply drink a cup of coffee, is enormous. Some of these establishments have a terrace, although when the weather is good it might be hard to get a spot. Most cafés open around 9am and close in the mid or late evening. Breakfast is ordered either from a menu or selected from the buffet. At lunch, there is usually a choice of hot dishes and usually one dish or more is still available from the breakfast menu. But in every single café, no matter what time of day it is, the choice of cakes and pastries is extremely tempting.

Cafés with great atmospheres are spread out over the whole city, but none is more centrally located or more opulent than the **Café Paris**. It is not only perfectly located on the Rathausmarkt, but offers an enticing selection of snacks both small and large, as well as many different kinds of French speciality coffees.

Die Rösterei is a Viennese-style coffee house, complete with dark-red velvet curtains. One of the most elegant places for a cosy coffee break is the **Literaturhaus Café**, with its plaster ornamentation. It is worth stopping here for a break during a walk along the Alster. You can come here simply to soak in the atmosphere, or perhaps combine a visit with an event at the Literaturhaus. On a side arm of the Alster lakes you will find the **Café Canale**. This is a really practical establishment for paddlers: you can place your order at the kitchen window and be served promptly. The guests of **Café Prüsse** have a premium seat overlooking the Alster. Here, too, patrons can relish one of the many types of salads, the prawn-skewers, or simply a pot of tea or coffee.

Among the favourites in the Ottensen district west of Altona is **Knuth** (a breakfast joint with many vegetarian spreads to put on your bread, among other fare) and the lovely **König & König** with its changing dishes (partly organic food).

Delicious cakes still warm from the oven can be sampled in the cosy living-room-like atmosphere of the **Petit Café** in Eppendorf. Here, you will also find an especially large selection of teas. At first glance the three branches of **TH²** look a bit plain, but they are always well frequented. While they serve the usual kinds of breakfast foods, what's unique to this chain are the light Belgian snacks on the menu. Sweet temptations come in many forms here, but well worth trying are the Swedish almond tarts and Portuguese vanilla cakes. A wide range of food is offered by **Die Herren Simpel** – café and bar in one. The broad selection ranges from a "Sylt breakfast" to a hearty plate "for men".

Many students and artists are drawn to the **Café Koppel**, which is located in a former machine factory that has been nicely renovated. This café has become well known chiefly because of its scrumptious cakes and its many vegetarian creations. Another example of a successful renovation is **Hadley's**. It is hard to believe that this was once an emergency room. The sterile hospital atmosphere has long been replaced by that of an urbane coffee house.

The **Eisenstein** (café and restaurant in one) pampers with delicious snacks like wood fired oven pizza – or even just simply with a cup of coffee. For a Viennese-style breakfast in the Schanzenviertel, the **Café unter den Linden** is a good choice; it is frequented by students. Many types of breakfast are served in the **Funk-Eck** in the NDR's broadcasting headquarters (Rundfunkhaus).

Most museums also have cafés, and some of these are among the most beautiful in Hamburg. Between the columns and wall reliefs of the **Café Liebermann**, visitors to the Kunsthalle (see pp64–65) can muse about all the wonderful art they have just seen over a cup of coffee. Since history alone does not assuage hunger, **Café Fees** in the hamburgmuseum (see p73) takes care of this need. The elegant lighting (which includes bright chandeliers) creates a very special ambience. Landscape pictures dominate the warm decor of the **Café Destille** in the Museum für Kunst und Gewerbe (see pp130–31).

There is something unique about the **Speicherstadt Kaffeerösterei**. Here, you can watch as coffee is roasted in gas-fired drums several times during the day, and enjoy one of the many freshly roasted coffee specialities.

Due to their pleasant atmosphere and large choice of savoury dishes, cakes and pastries, other cafés worth visiting include **Amphore, Beanie Bee, Bedford, Café Backwahn, Café Johanna, Café Klatsch, Café Smögen, Café Stenzel, Café Stern-Chance, Café Tarifa, Caffèteria, Elbgold, Elia and Max, Hofküche, Kyti Voo, MAY** and **Westwind**.

SOUP BARS

Especially on cold days, soup is an ideal snack if you are strolling about the city or out on a shopping trip. You are guaranteed to find a delicious and filling bowl of soup at branches of the **Soup City** chain. There are usually between eight and ten soups on offer – both classic and exotic, including standards such as potato or tomato soup as well as creations that change every day. Each bowl of soup comes with a bun and an apple.

A bowl of something hot and tasty is also on offer at **Soup & Friends**. Here, you can choose your own toppings which include cheese, herbs, crème fraîche and croutons to spice up minestrone, Indian lentil stew, Argentinian beef soup or carrot and orange soup. **Souperia** in the Schanzenviertel is also a paradise for soup lovers. The soups come with special breads such as ciabatta or moist sourdough bread, and with rice.

SANDWICH BARS

Sourdough, baguettes, panini, bagels and other sandwiches are sold in the many shops that specialize in this quick snack. They are often quite inventive, and many certainly go beyond the snack category and can be considered full meals. Homemade baguettes with every conceivable kind of topping are available at **Prima Pane**. Among their classics are "Baguette Parmigiano" (Parmesan cheese, rocket, sun-dried tomatoes and pesto), and a salmon baguette with pickles and mustard-dill mayonnaise. Or you can opt for a "Piadino Tonno" (pitta bread with tuna, iceberg lettuce and remoulade sauce) or the soup of the day. Naturally, in Hamburg there are also branches of **Subway**, the world's largest sandwich chain. Their gigantic sandwiches, or "subs", are custom made. The choices are huge, from many kinds of meat, sausage and cheese, as well as a good many toppings and your dressing of choice.

From veggie to chicken, from tuna to "Santa Fe" (made with turkey) – branches of the **Bagel Brothers** chain specialize in fresh bagels with many sweet or savoury toppings – among them unusual combinations. Especially popular is the Bagel Burger, a sesame bun with a minced beef patty, salad leaves, tomatoes, pickles and sauce.

The **Jahreszeiten Deli** in the Hotel Vier Jahreszeiten *(see p125)* serves more than 60 different kinds of sandwiches.

GOURMET BARS

Visitors to Hamburg get the opportunity to enjoy an excellent kind of fast food: the quality of dishes offered by some of the city's snack stalls is on a par with restaurant fare. At **Curry Queen**, red deer, buffalo and lamb currywurst is prepared on a lava stone grill, and handed out with a side salad instead of chips. **Döner Queen** has been awarded a quality seal. Here, the choice of dips is impressive – they range from avocado to sweet-and-sour. There are also many vegetarian options. In **Thai-Gourmet-Imbiss,** patrons are pampered with Asian snacks such as shrimp with lemon grass and numerous chillis. Vegetarian meals based on soya or tofu offers **hin & veg.**

CAKE AND CHOCOLATE

Discover the world of chocolate over a cup of coffee at **Stolle Pralinen**, where sweet sins such as marzipan confections, pralines and truffles are handmade by the owner herself. **Confiserie Paulsen** stocks its own truffle-pralines and ginger chocolates, along with tempting products from internationally renowned chocolate-makers.

Lovers of the cacao bean cannot leave empty handed after walking in to **Schokovida**, a combination of café and chocolate shop. **Herr Max** offers many kinds of cakes and muffins. In the dessert salon **Andersen**, the chef's creations include the finest of pralines and a range of tempting layer cakes.

COFFEE BARS

In recent years, the American-style coffee shop has also arrived in Hamburg. Are you in the mood for a speciality coffee, such as espresso con panna, vanilla latte or caramel macchiato? Then the place to go is a branch of Starbucks or **Balzac Coffee**. These chains combine classic coffee-house culture with the modern philosophy of takeaway coffee. There is a huge choice of syrups for flavouring coffees – in fact, they are seemingly limitless. The stores of **Campus Suite** offer a range of coffee specialities. Along with coffee, these coffee shops sell Italian and American baked goods, such as biscotti and cookies.

For a good cup of coffee, the cosy **Carlos Coffee** in Ottensen is a good choice. Speciality coffees and Portuguese snacks is what **Caravela** in St Georg is known for. The Portuguese coffee-bar **Transmontana**, in the Schanzenviertel, serves breakfast from 8am to 6pm.

TEA SALONS

After a stroll along the Elbe, a cup of tea in **Witthüs Teestuben** on the Elbchaussee in Blankenese is just the perfect thing. The atmosphere in this 200-year-old house is extremely cosy. Why not try Russian smoked tea over cherries marinated in rum with a piece of spiced black bread made in the tea house's own bakery? It is definitely "very British" in **Lühmanns Teestube**, which offers a wide selection of teas such as the Cornish Cream Tea, with home-made scones and clotted cream. The **Teeteria** which has a roofed-over tea garden, offers teas and "teemonades" – drinks made of tea with fresh fruit. In the new city district HafenCity **samova Tee-Lounge** is tearoom and shop in one. The range of accessories for a cosy tea ceremony is enormous. **Messmer Momentum** is famous for exceptional teas. The shop in this tea salon offers a great selection of teas.

DIRECTORY

CAFÉS

Amphore
St. Pauli Hafenstraße 140.
Map 4 D4.
Tel 31 79 38 80.
🕐 *10am–1am daily.*

Beanie Bee
Lilienstr. 15.
Map 10 E3.
Tel 32 00 49 79.
🕐 *7am–11pm Mon–Fri,
9am–8pm Sat, 10am–
6pm Sun.*

Bedford
Schulterblatt 72.
Map 3 C1.
Tel 43 18 83 32.
🕐 *11am–11pm daily.*

Café Backwahn
Grindelallee 148.
Map 7 A2.
Tel 410 61 41.
🕐 *10am–7pm daily.*

Café Canale
Poelchaukamp 7.
Tel 270 01 01.
🕐 *10am–7pm daily.*

Café Destille
Steintorplatz 1.
Map 6 E2.
Tel 280 33 54.
🕐 *11am–5pm daily (Thu
until 8pm).*

Café Fees
Holstenwall 24.
Map 9 A3.
Tel 317 47 66.
🕐 *10am–5pm Tue–Sat,
9:30am–6pm Sun.*

Café Johanna
Venusberg 26.
Map 4 F4.
Tel 31 29 53.
🕐 *8am–6pm Mon–Fri,
10am–6pm Sat.*

Café Klatsch
Glashüttenstr. 17.
Map 4 E1.
Tel 439 04 43.
🕐 *10am–7:30pm daily.*

Café Koppel
Lange Reihe 75.
Map 8 E4.
Tel 24 92 35.
🕐 *10am–11pm daily.*

Café Liebermann
Glockengießerwall 1.
Map 10 F3.
Tel 428 54 26 11.
🕐 *10am–8pm Tue–Sun
(Thu to 9pm).*

Café Paris
Rathausstr. 4.
Map 10 D3.
Tel 32 52 77 77.
🕐 *9am–11:30pm
Mon–Fri, 10am–
11:30pm Sat, Sun.*

Café Prüsse
An der Alster 47a.
Map 8 E4.
Tel 24 60 58.
🕐 *11am–9pm daily.*

Café Smögen
Klaus-Groth-Str. 28.
Tel 18 11 24 72.
🕐 *10am–6pm Mon,
10am–10pm Tue–Fri,
9am–2pm Sat.*

Café Stenzel
Schulterblatt 61.
Map 3 C1.
Tel 43 43 64.
🕐 *7am–8pm Mon–Sat,
8am–8pm Sun.*

Café SternChance
Schröderstiftstr. 7.
Tel 430 11 68.
🕐 *11am–midnight
Tue–Fri, 10am–11pm Sat,
Sun.*

Café Tarifa
Große Rainstr. 23.
Map 1 C3.
Tel 39 90 35 29.
🕐 *9am–midnight Mon–
Fri, 10am–midnight Sat,
Sun.*

Café unter
den Linden
Juliusstr. 16.
Map 3 C1.
Tel 43 81 40.
🕐 *9:30am–1am daily.*

Caffèteria
Abendrothsweg 54.
Tel 46 77 75 33.
🕐 *10am–11pm Mon–
Fri, 10am–7pm Sat, Sun.*

Eisenstein
Friedensallee 9.
Map 1 B2.
Tel 390 46 06.
🕐 *11am–1am daily.*

Elbgold
Mühlenkamp 6a.
Tel 27 88 22 23.
🕐 *8am–8pm Mon–Fri,
8am–7pm Sat, 10am–
7pm Sun.*

Elia and Max
Schulterblatt 98.
Map 3 C1.
Tel 43 64 04.
🕐 *8am–11pm Mon–Fri,
9am–10pm Sat,
10am–8pm Sun.*

Funk-Eck
Rothenbaumchaussee 137.
Map 7 B1.
Tel 44 41 74.
🕐 *7:30am–9pm Mon–
Fri, 7:30am–8pm Sat,
Sun.*

Hadley's
Beim Schlump 84a.
Map 7 A2.
Tel 450 50 75.
🕐 *10am–2am Mon–Sat,
11am–2am Sun.*

Die Herren Simpel
Schulterblatt 75.
Map 3 C1.
Tel 38 68 46 00.
🕐 *10am–1am Mon–
Sat, 10am–8pm Sun.*

Hofküche
Schanzenstr. 34–36.
Map 4 D1.
Tel 34 83 65 13.
🕐 *11am–7:30pm
Mon–Sat.*

Knuth
Große Rainstr. 21.
Map 1 C3.
Tel 46 00 87 08.
🕐 *9am–midnight Mon–
Fri, 10am–midnight Sat,
Sun.*

König & König
Ottenser Hauptstr. 28.
Map 1 C3.
Tel 41 35 88 77.
🕐 *8am–9pm Mon–Fri,
9am–9pm Sat.*

Kyti Voo
Lange Reihe 82.
Map 8 E4.
Tel 28 05 55 65.
🕐 *9am–midnight Mon–
Fri, 10am–1am Sat, Sun.*

Literaturhaus Café
Schwanenwik 38.
Map 8 F2.
Tel 220 13 00.
🕐 *9am–midnight
Mon–Fri, 10am–
midnight Sat, Sun.*

MAY
Lappenbergsallee 30.
Tel 32 03 81 62.
🕐 *8am–midnight daily.*

Petit Café
Hegestr. 29.
Tel 460 57 76.
🕐 *9:30am–7pm Mon–
Fri, 10am–7pm Sat, Sun.*

Die Rösterei
Mönckebergstr. 7.
Map 10 F3.
Tel 30 39 37 35.
🕐 *8am–9pm Mon–Fri,
9am–9pm Sat, 10am–
8pm Sun.*

Speicherstadt
Kaffeerösterei
Kehrwieder 5, in Kultur-
und Gewerbespeicher
Block D. **Map** 9 C5.
Tel 31 81 61 61.
🕐 *10am–7pm daily.*

TH²
Klosterallee 67.
Tel 42 10 79 44.
🕐 *9am–7:30pm
Mon–Fri, 9am–6pm Sat,
10am–6pm Sun.*

Mittelweg 146.
Map 7 C2.
Tel 85 10 65 62.
🕐 *9am–8pm Mon–Fri,
9am–6pm Sat, 10am–
6pm Sun.*

Mühlenkamp 59.
Tel 27 88 00 80.
🕐 *8am–8pm Mon–Fri,
9am–6pm Sat, 10am–
6pm Sun.*

Westwind
Spadenteich 1.
Map 8 E5.
Tel 41 92 43 44.
🕐 *11am–midnight Mon–
Fri, 10am–midnight Sat,
Sun.*

DIRECTORY

SOUP BARS

Soup & Friends
Valentinskamp 18.
Map 9 C2.
Tel 34 10 78 10.
🕐 *10am–7pm Mon–Fri, noon–4pm Sat.*

Soup City
Am Sandtorkai 30
(in HafenCity InfoCenter).
Map 10 D5.
Tel 28 41 04 90.
🕐 *10am–6pm Tue–Sun.*

Neuer Wandrahm
(Bei St. Annen).
Map 10 E5.
Tel 28 41 04 90.
🕐 *8am–4pm Mon–Fri.*

Steinhöft 9.
Map 9 B5.
Tel 28 41 04 90.
🕐 *11:30am–3pm Mon–Fri.*

Steinstr. 17.
Map 10 E3.
Tel 32 87 38 87.
🕐 *10am–5pm Mon–Fri.*

St. Pauli Landungsbrücken,
between quays 1 and 2.
Map 4 E5.
Tel 28 41 04 90.
🕐 *10am–8pm daily.*

Souperia
Bartelsstr. 21.
Map 4 D3.
Tel 43 09 95 55.
🕐 *11am–8pm Mon–Fri, noon–5pm Sat.*

SANDWICH BARS

Bagel Brothers
Gänsemarkt 50.
Map 9 C2.
Tel 34 99 43 33.
🕐 *9am–8:30pm Mon–Sat.*

Osterstr. 9.
Map 1 C3.
Tel 21 99 89 97.
🕐 *7:30am–8:30pm Mon–Fri, 8:30am–6:30pm Sat, 9am–7pm Sun.*

Ottenser Hauptstr. 7.
Map 1 C3.
Tel 46 00 87 31.
🕐 *7:30am–8:30pm Mon–Fri, 8:30am–8pm Sat, 9am–6pm Sun.*

Jahreszeiten Deli
Neuer Jungfernstieg 9–14.
Map 10 D2.
Tel 34 94 33 15.
🕐 *8am–6:30pm Mon–Fri, 10am–6pm Sat, Sun.*

Prima Pane
Großer Burstah 53.
Map 9 C4.
Tel 37 50 37 73.
🕐 *7am–7pm Mon–Fri.*

Subway
(Selected branches)
Gänsemarkt 36.
Map 9 C2.
Tel 33 44 19 88.
🕐 *9am–11pm daily.*

Glockengießerwall 8–10.
Map 10 E2.
Tel 46 86 68 85.
🕐 *6am–11pm daily.*

Paul-Nevermann-Platz
15/16 (Bahnhof Altona).
Map 1 C3.
Tel 27 86 20 12.
🕐 *8:30am–10:30pm Mon–Fri, 10:30am–10:30pm Sat, Sun.*

Reeperbahn 102.
Map 3 C4.
Tel 29 82 48 88.
🕐 *10am–1am daily (to 3am Thu, to 6am Fri, Sat).*

GOURMET BARS

Curry Queen
Erikastr. 50.
Tel 52 67 77 62.
🕐 *11:30am–10pm Mon–Fri, 11:30am–8pm Sat.*

Döner Queen
Jarrestr. 57.
Tel 60 00 89 05.
🕐 *10am–11pm daily.*

hin & veg
Schulterblatt 16.
Map 10 E2.
Tel 59 45 34 02.
🕐 *11:30am–10:30pm Mon–Thu, 11:30am–midnight Fri, Sat, 1pm–10pm Sun.*

Thai-Gourmet-Imbiss
Eppendorfer Weg 107.
Tel 40 76 75.
🕐 *12am–3pm, 6pm–9pm Mon–Fri, 5pm–9pm Sun.*

CAKE & CHOCOLATE

Andersen
Wandsbeker Marktstr. 153.
Map 10 D2.
Tel 689 46 04.
🕐 *9am–7pm Mon–Sat, 9am–6:30pm Sun.*

Confiserie Paulsen
Poststr. 5.
Map 9 C3.
Tel 36 77 81.
🕐 *9:30am–7pm Mon–Fri, 10am–6pm Sat.*

Herr Max
Schulterblatt 12.
Map 4 D1.
Tel 69 21 99 51.
🕐 *10am–7pm daily.*

Schokovida
Hegestr. 33.
Tel 87 87 08 08.
🕐 *10am–7pm Mon–Fri, 10am–4pm Sun.*

Stolle Pralinen
Hoheluftchaussee 88.
Tel 50 74 54 88.
🕐 *10am–6pm Thu, Fri, 10am–2pm Sat.*

COFFEE BARS

Balzac Coffee
Tel Main: 80 81 83 00.

(Selected branches)
Gustav-Mahler-Platz 1.
Map 9 C2.
🕐 *7am–8pm Mon–Fri, 7:30am–8pm Sat, 9am–8pm Sun.*

Kurze Mühren 4.
Map 10 F3.
🕐 *6:30am–9pm Mon–Fri, 8am–9pm Sat, 9:30am–8:30pm Sun.*

Lange Reihe/
Danziger Str. 70.
Map 6 E1.
🕐 *7am–8pm Mon–Fri, 8am–8:30pm Sat, 8:30am–8pm Sun.*

Mittelweg 130.
Map 7 C2.
🕐 *7am–7:30pm Mon–Fri, 8am–7pm Sat, 8:30am–7pm Sun.*

Rathausstr. 7.
Map 10 D3.
🕐 *7am–7pm Mon–Fri, 8:30am–7pm Sat, 11am–6pm Sun.*

Steinstr. 25.
Map 10 E3.
🕐 *7:30am–6pm Mon–Fri, 11am–6pm Sat.*

Caravela
Lange Reihe 13.
Map 6 E2. **Tel** 41 29 99.
🕐 *8am–8pm Mon–Fri, 9am–8pm Sat, Sun.*

Campus Suite
Tel Main: 23 85 83 80.

(Selected branches)
Großer Grasbrook 10.
Map 5 C5.
🕐 *7am–7:30pm Mon–Thu, 7am–8:30pm Fri, 9am–8:30pm Sat, 9am–7pm Sun.*

Valentinskamp 91.
Map 9 C2.
🕐 *6am–8:30pm Mon–Fri, 9am–7:30pm Sat, 10am–6:30pm Sun.*

Carlos Coffee
Bahrenfelder Str 169.
Map 1 C2.
Tel 39 90 99 90.
🕐 *6:30am–8pm Mon–Sa, 8:30am–8pm Sun.*

Transmontana
Schulterblatt 86.
Map 3 C1. **Tel** 43 18 40 06. 🕐 *8am–7pm daily.*

TEA SALONS

Lühmanns Teestube
Blankeneser Landstr. 29.
Tel 86 34 42.
🕐 *9am–11pm Mon–Fri, 9am–6pm Sat, 10am–11pm Sun.*

Messmer Momentum
Am Kaiserkai 10.
Map 5 C5.
Tel 73 67 90 00.
🕐 *11am–8pm daily.*

samova Teespeicher
Hongkongstr. 1.
Map 6 D4.
Tel 85 40 36 40.
🕐 *9am–6pm Mon–Fri.*

Teeteria
Hellkamp 11–13.
Map 3 C1. **Tel** 76 99 23 51.
🕐 *9am–6pm Tue–Sun.*

Witthüs Teestuben
Elbchaussee 499a.
Tel 86 01 73.
🕐 *2pm–11pm Tue–Sat, 10am–11pm Sun.*

SHOPPING IN HAMBURG

Hamburg is a true shopper's paradise. From fashion and jewellery to furniture and antiques, from interior design to arts and crafts – the spectrum of goods on offer ranges from the elegant and chic to the unique and unusual to the practical and proven. No one who strolls along Hamburg's streets can fail to be impressed as the city's shops reveal how international and stylish it is, explaining perhaps why it is considered Germany's shopping capital. The magnificent shopping areas in the best downtown locations offer consumers a world of experience. Whether you prefer large shopping centres, the glamorous passages or the countless small boutiques – shopping in Hamburg is an absolute pleasure.

Souvenir with Hamburg motifs

SHOPPING AREAS AND PASSAGES

In the past few years, Jungfernstieg *(see pp124– 5)* has been completely rebuilt and is now considered one of the most impressive boulevards in Europe. One of the main reasons is the glamorously restored **Alsterhaus**. Contributing to the refurbished splendour of this light-filled department store are a large lingerie department and a beauty department. The Neue Wall branches off from the Jungfernstieg. Here, flagship stores of well-known international labels (such as Armani, Joop, Cartier and Louis Vuitton) line this luxury shopping mile. But many Hanseatic stores also have a long tradition of offering luxury wares.

You can find great variety in a small amount of space in the Mönckebergstraße, which Hamburg residents fondly call "Mö". Here, between the Rathaus and the Hauptbahnhof,

large department stores alternate with well-known local shops. In the Spitalerstraße, which branches off from the "Mö", the majority of the stores are branches of larger chains. There is a distinct Mediterranean atmosphere in the Alsterarkaden *(see p58)*, and you can shop without ever getting wet in the passages *(see p76)* between the Rathausmarkt and the Gänsemarkt. Bleichenhof, Galleria, **Gänsemarkt-Passage**, **Hanse-Viertel**, and other covered shopping passages ensure the weather will not spoil your shopping fun. The largest shopping area is the 160-m (525-ft) long **Europa Passage** that runs between Jungfernstieg and Mönckebergstraße. It contains more than 120 shops on five floors.

In the Wandelhalle in the Hauptbahnhof *(see p62)*, the shops are located on two levels. You can shop seven days a week here from 6am to 11pm. Most other stores and boutiques in Hamburg are open Monday to Saturday until 7 or 8pm. Many have extended hours (often until 10pm) on Thursday or Friday to attract more customers.

FASHION

Hamburg is trendy. Luxury labels such as Gucci, Joop, Prada, Louis Vuitton and René Lezard are represented by their own shops on the Jungfernstieg, Neue

Shopping in Alsterhaus, an upmarket department store

Wall or in the passages. Along with haute couture and prêt-à-porter from the fashion design elite, there are also more affordable labels, such as Benetton, H & M, Diesel and Tommy Hilfiger.

But Hamburg is not just a top shopping destination for international designer clothing. Elegant creations are also designed and tailored here, as demonstrated by Jil Sander. And too, the many smaller boutiques stock fashion for every taste. The two proprietors of **Hello** in Eimsbüttel have earned an excellent reputation for their Hello collection. It appeals with timelessly elegant clothes that encourage Hamburgers to be a bit less understated.

Choice clothes for men – and in recent years for women, too – hang in **Herr von Eden**. The philosophy behind **Anna Fuchs** is to provide appealing everyday wear for the sophisticated woman. Clothes with clean lines do not have to be boring, as witnessed by the

A world of pampering lotions and massages awaits patrons of Nivea Haus *(see p204)*

collection designed by **DFM**
near Alsterfleet; their own
creations are supplemented
by carefully selected trendy
labels. **Prayed** has successfully
blended, neatly tailored
clothes with playful details.
Many of the one-off garments
have unusual combinations of
fabrics and colours, and each
is elegant and yet casual at
the same time. Restrained
elegance is the focus of
Garment. In this boutique the
emphasis is on classic lines.

A large choice of furniture and accessories sold at stilwerk *(see p119)*

SECOND-HAND

That second-hand does not
have to mean second-class is
proved by the many shops of
this kind found in Hamburg.
One of the best examples is
Secondella, which sells about
100 designer labels, and
features brand new, elegant
pieces from Armani, Gucci,
Prada, Versace and Chanel's
last collections. In **Classen
Secondhand**, very reasonable
no-name and designer clothes
(such as Prada and Hermès)
are sold. Bags and shoes
complete the assortment.
Vintage & Rags source their
unusual, flashy wares from
the USA – such as crocheted
tops and hippie dresses.

Second-hand clothes of the
finest British sort are found in
the store of **Rudolf Beaufays**.
With examples of the art of
British tailoring and unusual
collections in the classic
British style, Beaufays culti-
vates the art of good taste –
in which other German city
would he be so successful?

**Trendy bags designed by
FREITAG in Hamburger Store**

FURNITURE AND DESIGN

Hamburg is also renowned
for its interior design and
furnishings, and many pieces
of furniture seen in glossy
magazines come from the
Elbe metropolis. Such
seemingly mundane items as
picture-frames or cups have
been turned into design
classics by **Toni Thiel**. It is
not enough that something
is practical; it must also be
strikingly beautiful. There are,
of course, matching carpets
to go with the furniture and
accessories; that wicker chair
absolutely cries out to be
placed on that futuristic
looking 3-D designer carpet.

All those who want to bring
style from the four corners of
the globe into their homes
will find just the
right thing at
Octopus. Furni-
ture from many
countries, from
Swedish sofas to
Italian chests of
drawers, belong
to the assortment
on offer. There is
also Asian-style
furniture. **Die Wäscherei** is an
ideal place for shoppers who
delight in browsing for hours
among furniture, lamps and
fabrics in various styles.

A more suitable place than
stilwerk *(see p119)* could not
be found to house a mecca
for lovers of good taste, an
exclusive centre for furniture,
interior design and lifestyle
accessories. A glass elevator
brings customers from the
spacious lobby to seven floors
filled with stores with names
such as ligne roset, bulthaup
or allmilmö.

**Pottery lighthouses –
a souvenir of the region**

Those who are more budget
minded often find something
in **Yellow Möbel** in Winterhude. Along with practical
shelving systems, the selection also includes accessories.
Flexibility is at the core of
BoConcept. This Danish
company sells modules made
of various fabrics and colours
which customers combine to
create their dream interiors.

JEWELLERY AND WATCHES

Montblanc has been in
business since 1906 and
now has over 360 boutiques
in more than 70 countries –
among them one in Hamburg,
which is also the company's
headquarters. Customers can
choose from watches and
accessories as
well as exquisite
jewellery. The
Montblanc
diamond has
achieved cult
status and can
be seen on cuff-
links, for example. **Goldene Zeiten**
is one of the
oldest and best-known
jewellers and watchmakers in
Hamburg. Collectors can also
purchase the requisite tiny
tools to care for their
horological treasures here.
Precious metals such as
platinum, gold and silver are
turned into unique treasures
by **Ivar Kranz** in his jewellery
store in the Schanzenviertel.

Wempe, headquartered in
Hamburg, produces and vends
deluxe jewellery and watches.
The store's prime location on
the Jungfernstieg suits the
valuable choice of products.

FOOD

There are many shops in Hamburg selling delicious specialities either produced in-house or gathered from around the world that are guaranteed to please the most discerning palates. The number of fine food shops is enormous. The time-honoured **Hummer Pedersen** has been a purveyor of ocean delicacies since 1879. Along with lobsters, there are ocean crabs, crayfish, oysters and many other kinds of bivalves for sale. But there is some very unusual seafood here, too, and parrotfish and scorpionfish also find their takers.

Lovers of fine wines have no trouble indulging in their passion in the North German metropolis. A small shop with a large selection is **La Vigna**, which has a wide-ranging assortment of wines from many different corners of the globe in all price ranges. It has a reputation throughout the city for the regular wine seminars it holds. **Käse, Wein & mehr** not only sells a large selection of cheeses, sausages and antipasti specialities, but also carefully chosen wines, first-class olive oil, various types of pesto they make themselves, sweet and savoury Italian baked goods and much more.

Aficionados of fine coffee must make a pilgrimage to the **Kaffeerösterei Burg**, where a genuine treasure-trove awaits them. Among the specialities from different parts of the world are Ethiopian mocca, Hawai'i Kona and Jamaica Blue Mountain as the most expensive ones. The assortment of teas from Darjeeling, Assam, South Africa and other regions is also extensive.

Chocoholics feel they've died and gone to heaven in **Rob & Stephen's little cake Co**. But buyer beware: the huge choice of exquisite chocolates, pralines, cookies and cakes will throw even the most determined dieter off-track – which is just as the shop's owner likes it. After all, his motto is "A balanced diet is a chocolate in each hand".

BOOKS

In recent years bookshops in Hamburg have started to turn into complete book-buying experiences, with cosy reading nooks and large CD-departments for audio books and music. All large bookshops have a good selection of English books on offer. The **Thalia** group oversees twelve branches in Hamburg, the one in the Spitalerstraße 8 covers 3,200 sq m (35,000 sq ft). It is the largest bookshop in the city. The branch in the Europa Passage on Ballindamm has the largest selection of English books. A further centrally located Thalia branch is on Große Bleichen.

Heymann, with its 16 locations, is one of the leading bookshop chains in the greater Hamburg area. They also organize a series of literary events that include readings and exhibitions.

Opposite the university, the **Heinrich Heine Buchhandlung** offers an excellent selection of literature and all kinds of scientific books.

In Germany's largest bookshop devoted to travel, **Dr. Götze Land & Karte**, there are 70 000 maps, travel guides, globes, navigation systems and all sorts of literature related to travel.

BEAUTY AND LINGERIE

Perfumes and incense, Ayurvedic and Feng-Shui items, natural cosmetics and lines of body-care products, massages and treatments – **Secret Emotion** offers wellness for body and soul. **Lush** has a large assortment of handmade cosmetics, including bath-balls in every conceivable fragrance.

Beiersdorf AG, a company headquartered in Eimsbüttel, a district in Hamburg, opened a lovely oasis for regeneration and relaxation in its home town. Here, in **Nivea Haus**, beauticians pamper their clients from head to toe with massages and cosmetics, and provide advice. Of course, all products used in this huge spa are from the NIVEA label – from body lotion to sunscreen lotion.

In **Palmers**, the clothing ranges from cotton nightgowns to lace body-stockings. This fashion giant sets the latest trends in lingerie.

Braviange offers bespoke lingerie – the perfect fit compensates the dearness.

Many late-night shoppers looking for that extra-special piece of lingerie end up in the **Boutique Bizarre** (open daily to 2am), which is located – where else – on the Reeperbahn.

SPECIALIST SHOPS

Precious woods such as mahogany and rosewood are turned into exquisite writing instruments by **Stefan Fink**. His fountain pens and sketching pencils are small works of art. A few important state documents have been signed by these unique creations. Photo albums and diaries, wrapping paper and postcards can all be found in **Druckwerkstatt Ottensen**.

"There is a hat suited to everyone" insists hat-maker Birke Breckwoldt, owner of the hat shop **Behütet**. From corduroy cap to an artfully made feather hat – even those who are not hat-friendly will find something they like here.

From high heels to ballerina slippers and pumps to boots, **Catwalk** stocks the latest models and fashion trends and is a darling of fashionistas. There are also matching accessories such as handbags and belts.

Local artists present paintings, art prints, tablewear, clothing und many more objects with Hamburg themes in **The art of Hamburg**. **Pappnase & Co**. is a place of wonder for children small and large. The brightly coloured shop astounds and pleases with exciting items from the theatre and circus worlds, among them many masks and equipment for making magic.

In **FREITAG-Taschen**, the popular bags and accessories made of used materials like bicycle inner tubes and airbags come in every colour and design. **Cucinaria** offers exceptional kitchenware like oyster knives.

DIRECTORY

SHOPPING AREAS AND PASSAGES

Alsterhaus
Jungfernstieg 16–20.
Map 10 D2.
Tel 35 90 10.

Europa Passage
Ballindamm 40.
Map 10 D3.
Tel 30 09 26 40.

Gänsemarkt-Passage
Gänsemarkt 50.
Map 9 C2.
Tel 350 16 80.

Hanse-Viertel
Poststr. 33. **Map** 9 C3.
Tel 348 09 30.

FASHION

Anna Fuchs
Karolinenstr. 27. **Map** 9 A2.
Tel 40 18 54 08.
www.annafuchs.de

DFM
Stubbenhuk 38.
Map 9 B4.
Tel 374 27 12.
www.dfm-hamburg.de

Garment
Marktstr. 25. **Map** 4 E1.
Tel 410 84 03.
www.garment-online.de

Hello
Weidenstieg 11.
Tel 40 39 89.
www.hello-mode.de

Herr von Eden
Marktstr. 33. **Map** 4 E1.
Tel 439 00 57.
www.herrvoneden.de

Prayed
Glashüttenstr. 3.
Map 4 E1.
Tel 40 18 78 16.
www.prayed.de

SECOND-HAND

Classen Secondhand
Grillparzerstraße 2b.
Tel 227 32 31.
www.classen-secondhand.de

Rudolf Beaufays
Büschstr. 9. **Map** 9 C2.
Tel 35 71 59 77.
www.rudolf-beaufays.de

Secondella
Hohe Bleichen 5.
Map 9 C3.*Tel* 35 29 31.
www.secondella.de

Vintage & Rags
Kurze Mühren 6.
Map 10 F3.
Tel 33 01 07.
www.vintage-rags.de

FURNITURE AND DESIGN

BoConcept
Große Elbstr. 39.
Map 2 E4. *Tel* 380 87 60.
www.boconcept.com

Octopus
Lehmweg 10b.
Tel 420 11 00.
www.octopus-versand.de

stilwerk
Große Elbstr. 68.
Map 2 E4.
Tel 30 62 11 00.
www.stilwerk.de

Toni Thiel
Hoheluftchaussee 39.
Tel 42 93 87 97.
www.toni-thiel.com

Die Wäscherei
Jarrestr. 58.
Tel 271 50 70.
www.die-waescherei.de

Yellow Möbel
Gertigstr. 24.
Tel 27 07 59 09.
www.yellow-moebel.de

JEWELLERY AND WATCHES

Goldene Zeiten
Gerhofstr. 40.
Tel 35 71 23 30.
www.goldenezeiten.net

Ivar Kranz
Schulterblatt 78.
Map 3 C1.
Tel 43 18 87 49.
www.reingold-schmuck.de

Montblanc
Neuer Wall 18.
Map 10 D3.
Tel 35 11 75.
www.montblanc.de

Wempe
Jungfernstieg 8.
Map 10 D3.
Tel 33 44 88 24.
www.wempe.de

FOOD

Hummer Pedersen
Große Elbstr. 152.
Map 2 D4.
Tel 52 29 93 90.

Kaffeerösterei Burg
Eppendorfer Weg 252.
Tel 422 11 72.

Käse, Wein & mehr
Erikastr. 58.
Tel 46 24 25.

La Vigna
Beim Schlump 10–12.
Map 7 A2. *Tel* 45 20 91.

Rob & Stephen's little cake Co.
Lehmweg 41.
Tel 46 88 10 45.

BOOKS

Dr. Götze Land & Karte
Alstertor 14–18.
Map 10 E3.
Tel 357 46 30.
www.mapshop-hamburg.de

Heinrich Heine Buchhandlung
Grindelallee 26.
Map 7 B3.
Tel 44 11 33 17.
www.heinebuch.de

Heymann
Großer Burstah 50.
Map 9 C4.
Tel 36 70 69. www.heymann-buch.de
One of 16 branches.

Thalia
Europa Passage,
Ballindamm 40.
Map 10 D3.
Tel 30 95 49 80.
www.thalia.de
One of 12 branches.

BEAUTY AND LINGERIE

Boutique Bizarre
Reeperbahn 35.
Map 4 D4.
Tel 31 76 96 93.
www.boutique-bizarre.de

Braviange
Bernstorffstr. 153.
Map 3 C1.
Tel 67 38 28 27.
www.braviange.de

Lush
Spitalerstr. 7–9.
Map 10 F3. *Tel* 40 18 57 84. www.lush.com

Nivea Haus
Jungfernstieg 51.
Map 7 C5.
Tel 82 22 47 40.
www.nivea.de

Palmers
Neuer Wall 17.
Map 10 D3.
Tel 35 71 07 41.
www.palmers.de

Secret Emotion
Bahrenfelder Str. 159.
Map 1 C3.
Tel 390 29 30.
www.secret-emotion.de

SPECIALIST SHOPS

The art of Hamburg
Ditmar-Koel-Str. 19.
Map 9 A5.
Tel 41 42 44 19. www.the-art-of-hamburg.de

Behütet
Weidenstieg 16.
Tel 51 31 02 03.
www.birkebreckwoldt.de

Catwalk
Eppendorfer Baum 34.
Tel 54 80 38 87.
www.catwalkhamburg.de

Cucinaria
Straßenbahnring 12.
Tel 43 29 07 07.
www.cucinaria.de

Druckwerkstatt Ottensen
Ottenser Hauptstr. 44–48.
Map 1 C3.
Tel 398 63 60.
www.druckwerkstatt-ottensen.de

FREITAG-Taschen
Klosterwall 9.
Map 10 F4.
Tel 328 70 20.
www.freitag.ch

Pappnase & Co
Grindelallee 92.
Map 7 A3.
Tel 44 97 39. www.pappnase-hamburg.de

Stefan Fink
Koppel 66.
Map 8 E4.
Tel 24 71 51.
www.stefanfink.de

ENTERTAINMENT IN HAMBURG

Port
musician

The image of Hamburgers as cool and reserved Northerners proves to be just another cliché when you look at the variety of entertainment offered here. Whether you are interested in mainstream culture or looking for something different, there is plenty to do here. You can spend an evening experiencing unforgettable musicals and plays at the many theatres, both large and small, or be amused by vaudeville and cabaret. Without a doubt the district of St Pauli is a melting pot for "alternative" trends. It was here, in the Star-Club, that the Beatles enjoyed their first big breakthrough. And the adjoining Schanzenviertel is also a centre for the alternative scene.

INFORMATION

Hamburg's **Tourist Information** offices are always happy to provide you with an overview of the events taking place in the city. They have several outlets, and all offer extensive information about the city's cultural events. Daily newspapers, as well as smaller local papers like *OXMOX* and *PRINZ,* provide listings for events such as concerts, plays, films and shows.

On the **Hamburg Tourismus GmbH** website (www. hamburg-tourismus. de) you can download the Happy Hamburg Reisen catalogue. It contains great deals for musicals, boat trips and cultural events, as well as attractive package and hotel deals for your trip. The online magazine www. hamburg-magazin.de is also a good source of entertainment information on events ranging from museum exhibitions to film screenings.

Poster for the Rolling Stones Hamburg tour

ADVANCE TICKETS

You can buy tickets at the venues themselves or order them over the telephone. The addresses and telephone numbers of many of the best-known venues are provided on pages 209 and 213. Ticket sales for some events begin several months in advance, and tickets can go quickly. For the big, popular musicals, tickets go quickly, so it is essential to book early; on the evening of the show itself there are usually no tickets available.

However, if you have not been successful in getting a ticket in advance, you can try your luck at the box office an hour or so before the show is scheduled to begin, even if it is officially sold out. Sometimes pre-ordered tickets are not picked up. And you might be in luck and be given a ticket by someone whose "date" has not turned up.

Many tour operators offer tickets for events from culture to sports in combination with package trips to the city. These special deals can be found in newspapers and on the Internet, on the websites of trusted operators.

Kasino Reeperbahn – a magnet for gamblers *(see p102)*

Tickets are also available at branches of the **Tourist Information** office. **Hamburg Tourismus GmbH** also has blocks of tickets for a wide range of events. If it is more convenient, you can also purchase tickets online from one of the many ticket agencies such as www.hamburg-ticket.de

DISABLED TRAVELLERS

Many event venues have special seating places for patrons in wheelchairs and those with other mobility issues, and special equipment for the hearing impaired. Parking spots, entrances and toilets that are wheelchair accessible are clearly marked. Make sure to telephone the box office prior to booking to find out what facilities are available. A download of "Ratgeber Hamburg" can be found at www.behinderten-ratgeber.de, a German-language website with valuable information for disabled visitors. At www. lagh-hamburg.de, the facilities for disabled visitors in each

Colourful and cosy lobby of Schmidts Tivoli *(see p208)*

Shuttle-boat bringing patrons to Theater im Hamburger Hafen for a performance of *The Lion King* **(see p213)**

venue, as well as in cafés and restaurants, are described in detail in the "Hamburger Stadtführer für Rollstuhlfahrer" (wheelchair guide to Hamburg). You can download the guide. It is in German, but the symbols used are easy to understand.

OUTDOOR EVENTS

Hamburg offers many open-air events, especially during spring and summer. In Planten un Blomen *(see pp78–9)*, water-light-concerts are held daily at 10pm from May to the end of August, and at 9pm in September. On the park's lake, coloured lights illuminate spouting jets of water to the beat of classical music, jazz and film soundtracks. From May to September, jazz, pop and other concerts are hosted in the Stadtpark *(see p134)*.

Sign for Hamburg del mar beach club

In early May, Hamburg celebrates the birthday of its port *(see p85)* with a variety of harbour-based events, such as ship parades. "The arts, culture and the culinary arts" are the themes of a ten-day festival on Fleetinsel *(see p76)*. In late summer, a two-day dragon boat festival is held on the Binnenalster, with a fair lasting several days more – the Alstervergnügen *(see p45)*. The Hamburger Dom – fairs lasting several weeks and offering great fun to young and old – are held three times a year on Heiligengeistfeld *(see pp44–6)*. Treats are in store for film buffs at the outdoor summer film festival in Sternschanzenpark *(see p45)* and, in autumn, at Filmfest Hamburg *(see p46)*. The high-point of Pride Week in August is the joyful and celebratory CSD (Christopher Street Day) parade that begins in St Georg.

The shanty choir *De Tampentrekker* **giving a concert in HafenCity**

Music, Theatre and Cinema

Hamburg has much to offer lovers of the performing arts. With its many stages, shows and other events, the city prides itself on a more varied cultural life than that of many other European centres. From serious to modern music, classical to alternative theatre, cabaret to film – the range of performing art offerings in the Hanseatic city is enormous. The names of some of its venues, among them the Staatsoper, resound throughout the world. When it opens in 2013, the Elbphilharmonie will certainly add to Hamburg's illustriousness. Some of the city's approximately 40 theatres look back on a long tradition. Fans of cabaret and comedy find many theatres squeezed into a small area of St Pauli. Clubs with live music are listed on *pages 210–11*; musical theatres are on *pages 212–13*.

OPERA AND CLASSICAL MUSIC

The **Hamburgische Staatsoper** *(see p77)*, founded in 1678, was Germany's first opera house and has long been considered one of the most renowned opera houses in Europe. Under the direction of the Australian conductor Simone Youn since 2005, its repertoire encompasses 400 years of music history – from Baroque opera to modern music theatre. The Staatsoper is also the venue for performances of the Hamburg Ballet under the direction of John Neumeier.

In the **Laeiszhalle** *(see p73)*, concerts by the Hamburg Symphony, the NDR (North German Radio) Symphony Orchestra and the Hamburg Philharmonic are performed. Guest performances by international orchestras and soloists round out the programme. Along with small operas, the **Junges Forum Musik + Theater** of the Hochschule für Musik und Theater Hamburg presents interesting works by and concerts of its students on a regular basis.

THEATRE

The **Deutsches Schauspielhaus** *(see p129)* is not only the largest, but is considered by many professionals to be the most beautiful stage in the country for drama. Its repertory includes the classics as well as contemporary plays. It achieved its great reputation partly under the direction of Gustaf Gründgens (1955–63), a famous German actor. The Junges Schauspielhaus mounts experimental plays and produces matinees in the Malersaal.

Although the **Thalia Theater** *(see p59)* is considered to be Hamburg's "second theatre" after the Schauspielhaus, it is currently presenting exciting productions, and it is no coincidence that it was again voted "Theatre of the Year" in 2007. Typical for the Thalia is demanding drama, including modern classics.

Kampnagel is well-known as a forum for innovative contemporary theatre and dance theatre. Housed in a former machine factory, this cultural institution is a meeting place for first-class ensembles from around the world. Every year, Kampnagel mounts the very famous international summer festival *(see p45)*.

The **Hamburger Kammerspiele**, a renowned private theatre, presents great shows on a small stage – and with a top-notch cast each time. Along with critical dramas, the theatre holds readings and *Lieder* (song) evenings.

With its 744 seats, the **Ernst Deutsch Theater** is the largest private theatre in Germany. It has been a firm presence on the Hamburg theatre scene since 1951. Its programme focuses on the rich offerings between traditional and modern plays. The theatre established a young company called by the name of "Plattform". Productions of plays by British authors performed in the original English are presented by the **English Theatre**, *the* address for Anglophile theatre lovers. The actors are not only professionals, they are also native speakers; for most performances, they are flown in from England. The programme mainly features contemporary plays that are rather conventionally directed.

The **Altonaer Theater** has the character of a municipal theatre; its repertory encompassed comedies and musicals, today classic plays are performed. If you want to really test your German, there is folk theatre performed in Low German (plattdeutsch) in the **Ohnsorg-Theater** *(see p129)*, known to many Germans due to television broadcasts. The **Komödie Winterhuder Fährhaus** stages classic boulevard theatre and comedies from harmless fun to black humour.

In summer, there is also open-air theatre in Hamburg. One classic is *Hamburger Jedermann*, which is performed on eight weekends (Fri–Sun) in July and August in the **Theater in der Speicherstadt**.

CABARET

There has always been alternative theatre in Hamburg, especially in the district of St Pauli, and much of it today is found around the recently renovated Spielbudenplatz. The **St. Pauli Theater**, a theatre steeped in tradition, features well-known actors and cabaret stars. It mounts original shows as well as international musicals, cabaret and comedy. Musical theatre, comedy and vaudeville of the highest quality can be seen in the **Schmidt Theater**. Next door is **Schmidts Tivoli** *(for both see p104)*, a stage for smaller musicals and one of the most beautiful theatres in the city. It is also one of the Reeperbahn's attractions. Both theatres are run by Corny Littmann, a St Pauli celebrity.

The experimental stage **fools garden** has a loyal following. This is the place to watch a variety of artists such as stand-up-comedians and cabaret artists as well as magicians and improvisation artists. Many talented performers have used this supportive theatre as a springboard to larger stages or to television.

The **Alma Hoppes Lustspielhaus** is run by the two members of the Alma Hoppe company – Nils Loenicker and Jan-Peter Petersen. Most of the headliners (such as Jochen Busse and Martin Buchholz) specialize in political cabaret, just like the theatre's two founders.

Since 1975, the first sea-worthy theatre in Europe has been moored at Nikolaifleet: **Das Schiff** presents literary political cabaret, based on texts by popular authors.

CINEMA

Given the wide range of films screened in Hamburg, from art films to the latest Hollywood blockbusters, film buffs do not have to fear missing a classic. Although large companies such as **CinemaxX** (which owns many multiplex cinemas in Hamburg) dominate the film scene, independent cinema is alive and well. Many artistically demanding films premiere in the two art house cinemas: the **Abaton**, Germany's oldest independent cinema, and the **Zeise Kinos**, located in a former ship's screw factory in Altona. They also screen many film series and have a children's programme in the afternoons. **B-Movie** in St Pauli is also known for its curated film series. The speciality of **Metropolis**, which screens films in an historic movie house, are the milestones of movie history. This cinema screens a range of films including silent movies with piano accompaniment. Original versions are presented in **Streit's Filmtheater**.

DIRECTORY

OPERA AND CLASSICAL MUSIC

Junges Forum Musik + Theater
Harvestehuder Weg 12.
Map 8 D2.
Tel 428 48 25 86.
www.hfmt-hamburg.de

Hamburgische Staatsoper
Große Theaterstr. 25.
Map 9 C2.
Tel 35 68 68.
www.hamburgische-staatsoper.de

Laeiszhalle
Johannes-Brahms-Platz.
Map 9 B2.
Tel 357 66 60.
www.elbphilharmonie.de/laeiszhalle

THEATRE

Altonaer Theater
Museumstr. 17.
Map 1 C4.
Tel 39 90 58 70.
www.altonaer-theater.de

Deutsches Schauspielhaus
Kirchenallee 39.
Map 6 E2.
Tel 24 87 13.
www.schauspielhaus.de

English Theatre
Lerchenfeld 14.
Tel 227 70 89.
www.englishtheatre.de

Ernst Deutsch Theater
Friedrich-Schütter-Platz 1.
Tel 22 70 14 20.
www.ernst-deutsch-theater.de

Hamburger Kammerspiele
Hartungstr. 9–11.
Map 7 B2.
Tel 0800 413 34 40.
www.hamburger-kammerspiele.de

Kampnagel
Jarrestr. 20.
Tel 270 94 90.
www.kampnagel.de

Komödie Winterhuder Fährhaus
Hudtwalckerstr. 13.
Tel 48 06 80 80.
www.komoedie-winterhuder-faehrhaus.de

Ohnsorg-Theater
Ernst-Merck-Str. 9.
Map 10 F2.
Tel 350 80 30.
www.ohnsorg.de

Thalia Theater
Alstertor.
Map 10 E3.
Tel 32 81 44 44.
www.thalia-theater.de

Theater in der Speicherstadt
Auf dem Sande 1.
Map 5 C4.
Tel 369 62 37.
www.speicherstadt.net/jedermann.html

CABARET

Alma Hoppes Lustspielhaus
Ludolfstr. 53.
Tel 55 56 55 56.
www.almahoppe.de

fools garden
Lerchenstr. 113.
Map 4 D1.
Tel 43 65 82.
www.foolsgarden-theater.de

Das Schiff
Nikolaifleet/Holzbrücke 2.
Map 9 C4.
Tel 69 65 05 60.
www.theaterschiff.de

Schmidt Theater and Schmidts Tivoli
Spielbudenplatz 24–25 and 27–28.
Map 4 D4.
Tel 31 77 88 99.
www.tivoli.de

St. Pauli Theater
Spielbudenplatz 29–30.
Map 4 D4.
Tel 47 11 06 66.
www.st-pauli-theater.de

CINEMA

Abaton
Allendeplatz 3.
Map 7 A2.
Tel 41 32 03 20.
www.abaton.de

B-Movie
Brigittenstr. 5.
Map 3 C2.
Tel 430 58 67.
www.b-movie.de

CinemaxX Hamburg Dammtor
Dammtordamm 1.
Map 5 C1.
Tel 0180 524 63 62 99.
www.cinemaxx.de

Metropolis
Steindamm 52–54.
Map 6 E2.
Tel 34 23 53.
www.metropolis-hamburg.de

Streit's Filmtheater
Jungfernstieg 38.
Map 10 D2.
Tel 34 60 51.
www.streits.de

Zeise Kinos
Friedensallee 7–9.
Map 1 B2.
Tel 390 87 70.
www.zeise.de

Bars, Clubs and Live Music

The night life in Hamburg is as full of contrasts as the city itself. There is a great deal for night owls to do, from settling into cocktail bars to discuss the day's events with friends, to dancing the night away at trendy clubs. Every kind of taste in music is gratified – there is no scene which is not represented in the city. However, it's hard to pin down the latest places to see and be seen since they change as frequently as the Hamburg weather. And as some older clubs close, new ones are constantly opening. The pulsing heart of Hamburg's night life is St Pauli, where the Reeperbahn is located. The fun really only starts to peak here after midnight. But in the "Schanze", as locals call the Schanzenviertel, a well-established pub and club scene has also arisen. In summer all beach clubs are well-frequented.

BARS

Bar Hamburg in St Georg is stylish down to the last detail. It is divided into various lounges and impresses not only with its large selection of cocktails and whiskies, but also with its exclusive interior design. No less popular is the **Bar Rossi** in the Schanzenviertel. With its excellent cocktails, friendly staff and live DJs, it attracts a chic crowd.

3Freunde is known for mixing the best cocktails; in Smoker's Bar smokers can relax as they imbibe. The **Komet Bar** is located in the most "sinful" corner of the Reeperbahn. This small bar is very cosy although rock music is often played here.

Bar Cabana exudes an enticing caribbean flair. The range of cocktails and cigars is exuberant. Your search for the perfect cocktail might end at **Christiansen's**, where bartender Uwe Christiansen has received awards for his mouth-watering drinks. In the **Alpha Noble Ice Bar** – Germany's first ice bar – the temperature is maintained at a chilly −5 ˚C (23 ˚F), just right for keeping the drinks served there frosty; there are parkas at the ready to keep guests warm. In the Hafen Hamburg hotel *(see p179)*, the **Tower Bar** offers fantastic views over the bustling port from a height of 62 m (203 ft). Guests of **Skybar 20up** enjoy views from a height of even 90 m (295 ft).

CLUBS

A Hamburg institution is the **Astra-Stube**. Cool beer and expensive champagnes are the beverages of choice here. Lovers of indie, reggae and techno music frequent this club. **Café Keese** is a mix of the 1920s, Saturday Night Fever and modern style. Under the glittering disco ball, on the round dance floor, it has been known for feather boas to fly through the air. Still, along with the carefully cultivated nostalgic atmosphere, partying is king here. One of the patrons of Café Keese is German rock star Udo Lindenberg *(see below)*.

Great soul, funk, pop and rock are performed live at **Angie's Nightclub**. Another good venue is **Waagenbau**, where a DJs play drum 'n' bass, techno and hip-hop.

Cult is known for its 1980s parties. This club is decorated with kitsch and plush furnishings; it holds revival parties with music ranging from ABBA to Wham. **Grüner Jäger**, located in a small cottage on a public green space at Neuer Pferdemarkt, is considered one of the best clubs in the Schanzenviertel.

The **Golden Pudel Club** at the Fish Market is a good counter to the increasing chicness of the area. Club-goers happily queue in line for up to two hours to get into **China Lounge**. The DJs spin R'n'B, hip-hop, house and electro.

LIVE MUSIC

Along with large venues such as the open-air theatre in Stadtpark *(see p134)* and the O₂ World Hamburg *(see p215)*, there are also many smaller venues in Hamburg that feature live music. They keep alive the tradition of the legendary Star-Club (which was located at Große Freiheit 39 from 1962–69), in which the Beatles began their international success.

Jazz lovers head to the **Cotton Club**, Hamburg's oldest Jazz cellar, where everything revolves around jazz- and jam-sessions and swing. Other popular jazz venues include **Birdland**, Das Feuerschiff *(see p89)*, Jazzclub Bergedorf and **Jazzclub im Stellwerk**. Blues legends take to the stage at the **Downtown Bluesclub**.

UDO LINDENBERG – GERMAN ROCK STAR

Even though he is from Westphalia, Udo Lindenberg (born on 17 May 1946) is linked with Hamburg's music scene like none other. After arriving in Hamburg in 1968, he played the city clubs with various bands before forming his own, the Panikorchester. He was one of the first German musicians to popularize rock music with German lyrics. Commercial success was achieved by Lindenberg with his album *Andrea Doria*, which he recorded with the Panikorchester in 1973. Trademarks of this musician and songwriter are his ironic lyrics about personal relationships and his characteristic talking-singing style of delivery. Lindenberg, who has always been socially engaged, still goes on tour. When he is in Hamburg, he stays in the Atlantic Kempinski hotel *(see p128)*. On his 50th birthday, Udo Lindenberg was honoured with his own star – modelled on Hollywood's Walk of Fame – which was set into the sidewalk in front of Café Keese on the Reeperbahn *(see pp102–03)*.

Soul, funk, jazz, rock and pop stars perform at the **Stage Club** in the Neue Flora. Many famous interpreters of World Music, as well as rock musicians and jazz players, grace the stage of the **Fabrik**.

"Rock 'n' Roll since 1974" – this is the motto of the club **Logo**. Rock music is also king at **Molotow**. The venue's concert programme encompasses every type of rock there is – The White Stripes and Billy Talent amongst many others. Bands playing indie rock can be seen live on stage in **Knust**. The clubs **Uebel & Gefährlich** and **Prinzenbar** attract music fans with indie pop and other modern music.

BEACH CLUBS

The first beach bar on the Elbe river opened in 2003 and was an instant hit with Hamburgers. Palms, large beach umbrellas, deck chairs, and hammocks create a Mediterranean ambience. None of this is diminished by the view of the bustling port. On the contrary, looking out over the sparkling Elbe river with a cocktail in your hand, it's easy to forget that you are actually in a large city. DJs play chill-out music to enhance the mood. Popular locations are **Hamburg City Beach Club**, **Hamburg del mar** and Strand-Pauli *(see p 109)*.

GAY AND LESBIAN BARS AND CLUBS

Hamburg's gay scene is concentrated in the St Georg district. Some of the most popular meeting spots are located on Lange Reihe. Among them are **Café Gnosa**, which is the best-known gay and lesbian café in Hamburg, and **Generation Bar**, a stylish lit cocktail bar with a fantastic party atmosphere.

Wunderbar – which is located in the district of St Pauli – is a classic gay bar decorated in red plush. The **Frauencafé Endlich**, which is strictly for women only, is in the New Town.

DIRECTORY

BARS

3Freunde
Clemens-Schultz-Str. 66.
Map 3 C3.
Tel 53 26 26 39.

Alpha Noble Ice Bar
Neumühlen 11.
Map 1 B4.
Tel 39 80 78 80.

Bar Cabana
Fischmarkt 6.
Map 3 B5.
Tel 80 00 71 14.

Bar Hamburg
Rautenbergstr. 6–8.
Map 8 D5.
Tel 28 05 48 80.

Bar Rossi
Max-Brauer-Allee 279.
Tel 43 34 21.

Christiansen's
Pinnasberg 60.
Map 2 F4.
Tel 317 28 63.

Komet Bar
Erichstr. 11.
Map 3 C4.
Tel 27 86 86 86.

Skybar 20up
Bernhard-Nocht-Str. 97.
Map 4 D4.
Tel 31 11 97 04 70.

Tower Bar
Seewartenstraße 9
Map 4 E4.
Tel 31 11 37 04 50.

CLUBS

Angie's Nightclub
Spielbudenplatz 27.
Map 4 D4.
Tel 31 77 88 11.

Astra-Stube
Max-Brauer-Allee 200.
Map 2 F1.
Tel 319 75 55 13.

Café Keese
Reeperbahn 19–21.
Map 4 D3.
Tel 390 93 10.

China Lounge
Nobistor 14.
Map 3 C4.
Tel 31 97 66 22.

Cult
Große Freiheit 27.
Map 3 C4.
Tel (0176) 28 60 90 00.

Golden Pudel Club
St. Pauli Fischmarkt 27.
Map 3 B5.
Tel 31 97 99 30.

Grüner Jäger
Neuer Pferdemarkt 36.
Map 4 D2.
Tel 31 81 46 17.

Waagenbau
Max-Brauer-Allee 204.
Map 2 E1.
Tel 41 35 22 45.

LIVE MUSIC

Birdland
Gärtnerstr. 122.
Tel 40 52 77.

Cotton Club
Alter Steinweg 10.
Map 9 B3.
Tel 34 38 78.

Downtown Bluesclub
Hindenburgstr. 2.
Tel 27 50 54.

Fabrik
Barnerstr. 36.
Map 1 C2.
Tel 39 10 70.

Jazzclub im Stellwerk
In Fernbahnhof Harburg over tracks 3 and 4, Hannoversche Str. 85.
Tel 30 09 69 48.

Knust
Neuer Kamp 30.
Map 4 D2.
Tel 87 97 62 30.

Logo
Grindelallee 5.
Map 7 B2.
Tel 410 56 58.

Molotow
Spielbudenplatz 5.
Map 4 D4.
Tel 31 08 45.

Prinzenbar
Spielbudenplatz 19.
Map 4 D4.
Tel 31 78 83 45.

Stage Club
Stresemannstr. 159a.
Map 2 E1.
Tel 43 16 54 60.

Uebel & Gefährlich
Feldstr. 66.
Map 4 E2.
(no tel.).

BEACH CLUBS

Hamburg City Beach Club
Landungsbrücken (at pier 7).

Hamburg del mar
Landungsbrücken (at pier 3).

GAY AND LESBIAN BARS AND CLUBS

Café Gnosa
Lange Reihe 93.
Map 8 E1.
Tel 24 30 34.

Frauencafé Endlich
Dragonerstall 11.
Map 9 B2.
Tel 34 13 45.

Generation Bar
Lange Reihe 81.
Map 8 E1.
Tel 28 00 46 90.

Wunderbar
Talstr. 14–18.
Map 3 C3.
Tel 317 44 44.

Musicals

Without a doubt, Hamburg is Germany's musical theatre capital. In a survey of the most important musical theatre centres in the world it took a respectable third place after New York and London. No other German city stages more musicals. With an amazing 15-year run (1986–2001), the musical *Cats* set the standards. Everyone who loves colourful shows, catchy tunes, exciting entertainment, songs with feeling, perfect choreography and riveting plot-lines is in exactly the right place here in the Elbe metropolis. For many visitors to the city, the chance to see one of these world-famous productions is the sole reason for their trip. Since the shows very often are sold out months in advance, you should make sure to plan your visit to a musical early.

HAMBURG BECOMES A MUSICAL THEATRE CAPITAL

Hamburg's ascent to become a Mecca for musical theatre fans started on 18 April 1986 with the German premiere of *Cats*, an Andrew Lloyd Webber production. This premiere also marked the start of the era of commercial musical theatre in Germany. The project was planned from the very start to run for a long time: the idea was to mount a set piece over a long time-period in the same theatre. It ran without a break, day in day out, and twice a day on weekends! This system had been successfully tested beforehand in the USA, but was greeted with great scepticism in Germany. However, the show was a huge success and its producers proved that they were right. *Cats* ran for about 15 years. When the final curtain fell after about 6,100 performances, more than six million people had seen this success story.

This set free energy and resources: new venues were created to solidify Hamburg's location as Germany's musical theatre capital and to keep the stream of tourists flowing. Two new venues were created solely for the performances of the German versions of *Phantom of the Opera* and *Buddy – The Musical* in 1989/90 and 1995. In recent years, several more hit musicals breathed fresh air into the cultural life of Hamburg. On the heels of the early classics followed musicals such as *Tanz der Vampire (Dance of the Vampires)*, *Mamma Mia*, *Der König der Löwen (The Lion King)*, *Dirty Dancing*, *Ich war noch niemals in New York (I Have Never Been to New York)*, *Tarzan* and, since 2010, *Sister Act*.

THE IMPORTANCE OF MUSICALS FOR THE CITY

Other German cities that also tried to promote musicals enjoyed mixed success. In Hamburg, where the genre had not only become an important part of the entertainment offerings but also a key aspect of its cultural image, the high bar set by *Cats* against which other musicals were measured was met. Thus almost every performance of *Mamma Mia* was sold out, and very few musicals had any empty seats. In this way, the city managed to succeed where others hadn't.

Parallel to the growing enthusiasm for musicals and the rise in the number of tourists and overnight guests, the number of hotels in Hamburg grew: new hotels were built and old ones were thoroughly modernized. Hamburg owes its importance as a travel destination in large part to these spectacular shows – for many visitors to Hamburg, musicals are the reason for (or at least a highlight of) their stay. So-called "musical theatre tourism" is now well-established as a special form of tourism and as an important economic factor. There are many agencies that not only organize a visit to a glamorous stage production but also offer package deals which include a round trip to Hamburg and hotel stay as well as a musical or two.

LARGE VENUES

In the **TUI Operettenhaus** *(see p105)* on Spielbudenplatz, the epoch of the "great" musical theatre hits in Hamburg began in 1986 with *Cats*. Previously, operettas, plays and revues were performed here. After the last performance of that long-running hit in 2001, no one knew whether or not the show that followed – the musical *Mamma Mia* – would be as successful as its predecessor. But after the premiere in November 2002 all doubts were laid to rest. The musical brought the biggest hits of the Swedish group ABBA to the stage – and the very mixed audience danced to the hits of their youth or the hits of their parents' youths. Memories of the golden age of sky-blue eye-shadow and bell-bottoms came alive again.

On stage in the Operettenhaus since December 2007 has been *Ich war noch niemals in New York (I Have Never Been to New York)*, a turbulent yet romantic musical containing 23 of Udo Jürgens' greatest hits – from *Merci Chérie* to *Mit 66 Jahren* to *Griechischer Wein*. The musical's title is also taken from the life and work of its Austrian composer and pop star. His songs have been woven into a story that covers three generations of a family. It tells of unfulfilled dreams, homesickness, joy of living and love. Not uncharacteristically for Hamburg, part of the story takes place on the high seas, and there is an exciting chase on the deck of a cruise ship. It is a story of a life's dream (to travel to America just once!).

Since December 2010 the musical *Sister Act* has been on stage in the TUI Operettenhaus. It tells the story of a lounge singer who is chased by gangsters and goes into hiding at a Roman convent. Her peculiar charm revitalises the nun's chorus. The swinging songs for this musical were composed by oscar-winning Alan Menken.

Due to all the hype about *Cats*, the **Neue Flora** *(see p119)* was built in 1989–90, and is now firmly rooted in the city's cultural life. This theatre, with seating room for 2,000, opened in June 1990 with the musical *Das Phantom der Oper (The Phantom of the Opera)*, which ran until June 2001. This show, too, became a huge hit – it was performed approximately 4,400 times in front of some seven million people.

The following productions in the Neue Flora were shorter-lived: *Mozart!* ran from September 2001 to June 2002, and the production of *Titanic* ran from December 2002 to October 2003. But further successful musicals were mounted: *Tanz der Vampire (Dance of the Vampires)* from December 2003 to January 2006 as well as *Dirty Dancing* from March 2006 to the end of June 2008. This music and dance show was based on the 1987 film of the same name and had its European premiere in Hamburg. Woven into the story were 51 songs from the 1960s to the 1980s.

In October 2008, the fourth Disney musical produced by Stage Entertainment, *Tarzan*, celebrated its premiere in the Neue Flora. It tells the tale of a young man looking for his roots who ends up finding romantic love. Breathtaking acrobatics, ingenious sets and the music of Phil Collins are the key ingredients of this show about friendship, finding one's identity and determination. Some of the performers were chosen on a casting show on SAT.1, a German television broadcaster.

The third and newest of the Hanseatic city's large musical theatre venues is the **Theater im Hamburger Hafen** *(see p92)*. Housed in a permanent yellow tent on the south shore of the Elbe, this theatre

has been attracting attention since 1995. Visitors to *Buddy – Das Musical* took a trip back in time to the 1950s. The musical is dedicated to Buddy Holly, the pioneer of Rock 'n' Roll. In 2001, this show was replaced by *Der König der Löwen (The Lion King)* – an inspiring theatrical experience with a touch of the African exotic. Fabulous costumes, inventive masks and wonderful songs from the pen of Elton John – a mix of African rhythms and western pop – are the framework for the Walt Disney story of the young lion Simba, who fights to take his place as the king.

The experience starts for most audience members with the trip to the show. In just a few minutes, the free shuttle boat takes theatre-goers from the Landungsbrücken to the venue – and back again after the show.

OTHER VENUES

There are several other theatres in Hamburg that mount their own smaller productions. **Schmidts Tivoli** *(see p104)* almost has a cult following. After the audience hit *Fifty-Fifty*, the show *Heiße Ecke – Das St. Pauli Musical (Hot Corner – the St Pauli Musical)* was brought to the stage. In a snack bar called "Heiße Ecke", the St Pauli district is brought alive in song and dance numbers. It is a fast-paced musical revue full of wit and surprises. The production, with its nine actors, singers and dancers playing over 50 roles, is directed by Corny Littmann. St Pauli is portrayed just as it is with all its mavericks, regular people, and failures – everyone is represented.

The **Delphi Showpalast** also produces rousing shows. The pop musical *Westerland* was followed by *Mandy in Love*, an entertaining love story with a range of hits from Elvis Presley to Take That. The ensuing musical *In Dreams* made way for *Starcut* in September 2010. The latest show *Sonne, Strand und Mehr* started in September 2011.

DIRECTORY

LARGE VENUES

Neue Flora
Stresemannstr. 159a.
Map 2 E1.
Tel 43 16 50.
www.neueflora.de

Theater im Hamburger Hafen
Norderelbstr. 6.
Tel 42 10 00.
www.loewenkoenig.de

TUI Operettenhaus
Spielbudenplatz 1.
Map 4 D4.
Tel 31 11 70.
www.tuioperettenhaus.de

OTHER VENUES

Delphi Showpalast
Eimsbütteler Chaussee 5.
Tel 431 86 00.
www.delphi-showpalast-hamburg.de

Schmidts Tivoli
Spielbudenplatz 27–28.
Map 4 D4.
Tel 31 77 88 99.
www.tivoli.de

TICKETS

Since there is great demand for tickets to Hamburg musicals, it is recommended that you book your tickets as far in advance of the shows as possible. Many theatregoers purchase their tickets as part of a package deal, which often includes travel. Tickets for musicals produced by Stage Entertainment *(Sister Act, König der Löwen, Tarzan)* should be booked well ahead of time, ideally by calling the ticket hotline.

Ticket Hotline Stage Entertainment
Tel 0180 544 44 (14 cents a min. from a German landline).
www.stage-entertainment.de

Sports and Outdoor Activities

Whether you play just for fun or are a serious competitive athlete, the range of activities in Hamburg is huge. After all, it is a city of sports lovers, and about 500,000 Hamburgers belong to one of the 800 sport associations. And, since Hamburg lies on the water, there are countless opportunities to take part in water sports. But you can also have fun as a spectator. Hamburg is a venue for many well-known events, from cycling to tennis and equestrian events. Real crowd-pleasers are the Hamburg City Man (a triathlon) and the Hamburg Marathon, in which not only world-class athletes compete but anyone wanting to test their mettle can run, urged on by hundreds of thousands of spectators.

RUNNING

Casual joggers and ambitious marathon runners alike can choose from several routes through varied terrain. One of the most popular is the 7.6-km (4.7-mile) long circuit around the Außenalster. The scenic route takes you along the Alster shore and through expanses of parkland, and there are only a few short sections that are on a city street. Since the route is well lit, it can be used day and night, and in every season. A further magnet for joggers is the Stadtpark, where you can select your preferred route for distance and terrain. The Elbuferweg – a lovely path running along the Elbe between Neumühlen and Blankenese – is well used. For those with stamina, the **Hamburg Marathon** every year in April is an ideal challenge; approximately 20,000 participants run in this marathon each year.

CYCLING

Since there are not too many steep hills in Hamburg, it is an ideal city to explore by bicycle. In Hamburg and its environs, there are some lovely routes, for example along the Elbe and the Alster. Unfortunately, many cycling paths in the city are in bad shape, being either too uneven or too narrow.

Some bicycle shops rent out bicycles by the day or the week. You are allowed to take your bicycle on ferries as well as on the U-Bahn and S-Bahn. The **Allgemeiner Deutscher Fahrradclub (ADFC)** provides suggestions for cycling trips as well as useful tips and information.

The high point of the cycling sport season are the **Vattenfall Cyclassics**. Here, the world's best cyclists are joined by thousands of amateurs at the starting line. The latter can choose between three distances – 55 km (34 miles), 100 km (63 miles) or 155 km (96 miles). The number of participants is limited to 22,000.

SWIMMING

There is bathing fun for everyone in the waters of the Alster at **Naturbad Stadtparksee** in the eastern part of the Stadtpark. The swimming pool is truly gigantic at 124 m (407 ft) long by 107 m (351 ft) wide. There is a separate area for non-swimmers, and numerous pools. The **Alster-Schwimmhalle** offers special attractions such as an outdoor pool that is open all year round, a 10-m (33-ft) high diving platform, a 76-m (250-ft) long slide and the spacious sauna world (800 sq m/8,600 sq ft).

Housed in a protected building, the **Holthusenbad** attracts visitors with an astonishing array of fitness and wellness offerings, such as a stone sauna, a Finnish sauna, massages and a beauty bath. Pure relaxation is on offer at the **Bartholomäus-Therme** with its Ottoman bath. The **MidSommerland** on Außenmühlenteich is considered by many Hamburgers to be the most beautiful baths in the city. Designed in Scandinavian style with a great deal of wood and granite, the complex offers its patrons every kind of facility to promote health and wellness – from a relaxing midnight sauna to an action-packed wild-water canal.

SAILING, ROWING AND PADDLING

It is no secret that Hamburg's citizens consider water their element. When a stiff breeze blows, many Hamburgers can hardly wait to take to their boats. After all, the Elbe flows past the front door, and the Außenalster, a very large inland lake, is located in the heart of the city. But no matter whether you sail the Elbe towards the North Sea or stay on the Alster – hoisting the sails is a wonderful leisure time activity. If you have never sailed, then try it out at least once at one of the many sailing clubs around the Alster and at City-Sporthafen. All are run by professionals.

You can hire boats along the Alster, and take out a boat for a leisurely paddle. To hire a more sporty boat such as a single, double or eight-oared racing shell, you must be a member of a rowing club.

Hamburg's network of canals and narrow channels can be easily explored by canoe or kayak. Boats can be rented from 20 Euros a day from **Gadermann** – a perfect way to get to know the "Venice of the North" from one of its most attractive sides.

TRIATHLON

Over land, by water and on a bicycle – the triathlon event of the **Hamburg Triathlon**, held in July, allows anyone who feels fit enough to participate in the race. There are two competitions: the shorter sprint on Saturday – 0.5 km (0.3 mile) swim, 22 km (14 mile) bike, and 5 km (3 mile) run, and the Olympic challenge on Sunday – 1.5 km (0.9 mile) swim, 40 km (25 mile) bike, and 10 km run.

IN-LINE SKATING

In-line skating has become a very popular sport in Hamburg. In the spring and summer, several events open up routes to recreational rollers exclusively. On several days each year, the streets around the Außenalster are blocked off to traffic for the Alsterrunde. The route is approximately 8 km (5 miles) long. The **Speedlager-Cup Wedel** is held every year. The competition covers a 42.2-km (26.2-mile) long marathon and a 21,1-km (13.1-mile) long half marathon distance, and is open to everyone. You can find out more about in-line skating on the website of the **Hamburg Inline-Skating Club** and on the **CompuSkate** website.

OTHER SPORTS

Along with several golf courses, Hamburg also has a golf centre for beginners and professionals – the **Golf Lounge**. It offers ideal training conditions year-round.

Skiers, too, can indulge in their passion not too far from Hamburg: the **Snow-Dome** in Bispingen (Lüneburger Heide) has a 300-m (984-ft) long ski slope. **Kletterzentrum Hamburg** offers an indoor and outdoor area with routes for all levels.

SPECTATOR SPORTS

Hamburg has two football (soccer) clubs: the **Hamburger SV** (HSV) *(see p134)* and **FC St. Pauli** *(see pp110–11)*. While HSV tries to add to its roster of past successes, FC St. Pauli has often fought valiantly just to stay alive and, in 2010, fans celebrated as it moved up into German Bundesliga for one season.

It feels like a party during ice-hockey games of the **Hamburg Freezers** in the O₂ World Hamburg. The HSV football club also has a successful handball team that, along with the Freezers is *the* long-standing hit in this large venue.

Top tennis players compete annually at the tennis complex **Tennisanlage am Rothenbaum** *(see p45)*. The Deutsches Spring- and Dressurderby at **Derbyplatz Klein Flottbek** is famous. The Deutsches Derby is the crowning end to a week of races at **Galopprennbahn Horn**.

DIRECTORY

RUNNING

Hamburg Marathon
www.marathon-hamburg.de

CYCLING

ADFC Hamburg
Koppel 34–36.
Map 8 E4.
Tel 39 39 33.
www.hamburg.adfc.de

Fahrradladen Altona
Barnerstr. 28.
Map 1 C2.
Tel 390 38 24.

Fahrradladen St. Georg
Schmilinskystr. 6.
Tel 24 39 08.

Vattenfall Cyclassics
www.vattenfall-cyclassics.de

SWIMMING

Alster-Schwimmhalle
Ifflandstr. 21.
Map 8 F4.

Bartholomäus-Therme
Bartholomäusstr. 95.

Holthusenbad
Goernestr. 21.

MidSommerland
Gotthelfweg 2.

Naturbad Stadtparksee
Südring 5b.

SAILING, ROWING AND PADDLING

Bobby Reich
Fernsicht 2.
Tel 48 78 24.
www.bobbyreich.de

Bootshaus Silwar
Eppendorfer Landstr. 148b.
Tel 47 62 07.
www.bootshaus-silwar.com

Bootsverleih Goldfisch
Isekai 1. *Tel* 41 35 75 75.
www.goldfisch.de/bootsverleih

Gadermann
Hummelbütteler Steindamm 70.
Tel 52 98 30 06.
www.gadermann.de

Segelschule Pieper
An der Alster/Atlanticsteg.
Map 8 D4.
Tel 24 75 78.
www.segelschule-pieper.de

TRIATHLON

Hamburg Triathlon
www.hamburg-triathlon.org

IN-LINE SKATING

CompuSkate
www.skateland.de

Hamburg Inline-Skating Club
www.skating-hamburg.de

OTHER SPORTS

Golf Lounge
Billwerder Neuer Deich 40.
Tel 81 97 87 90.
www.golflounge.info

Kletterzentrum Hamburg
Döhrnstr. 4.
Tel 60 08 88 66.
www.kletterzentrum-hamburg.de

Snow-Dome
Horstfeldweg 9, 29646 Bispingen.
Tel 05194 431 10.
www.snow-dome.de

SPECTATOR SPORTS

Derbyplatz Klein Flottbek
Hemmingstedter Weg 2.
Tel 82 81 82.
www.nfr-hamburg.de

FC St. Pauli
Auf dem Heiligengeistfeld.
Map 4 D2.
Tel 31 78 74 21.
www.fcstpauli.de

Galopprennbahn Horn
Rennbahnstr. 96.
Tel 651 82 29.
www.galopp-hamburg.de

Hamburg Freezers
Hellgrundweg 50.
Tel 380 83 50.
www.hamburg-freezers.de

Hamburger SV (football)
Sylvesterallee 7.
Tel 0180 547 84 78.
www.hsv.de

Hamburger SV (handball)
Hellgrundweg 50.
Tel 309 87 60.
www.hsvhandball.com

Tennisanlage am Rothenbaum
Hallerstr. 89. **Map** 7 B1.
Tel 238 80 44 44.
www.german-open-hamburg.de

CHILDREN'S HAMBURG

Hamburg is a good destination for families with children, and given the wealth of activities on offer they certainly will never get bored. Many of the great things to do in the city – such as taking a boat tour of the harbour, visiting the zoo, Tierpark Hagenbeck, or enjoying the water and sand on an Elbe beach –

A pony ride, offered at both Planten un Blomen and Tierpark Hagenbeck

are fun for the entire family. There are also loads of attractions designed specifically to appeal to children. Some renowned museums have created exciting sections for young visitors. The Planetarium has a special children's programme, and the larger parks have well-equipped adventure playgrounds and provide lovely settings for picnics.

A round of mini-golf, always a popular choice with families

PRACTICAL ADVICE

Hamburg's information offices like **Hamburg Tourismus GmbH** can provide you with ideas about how to best plan your stay with children. Organizations such as **Kinder Hamburg** and **Kindernetz Hamburg** will also supply you with information. Many sights and attractions offer child reductions, and there are also discounts on public transit.

PARKS AND ZOOS

Hamburg has a great number of parks that offer more than just lovely walking paths. A visit to the **Stadtpark** *(see p134)* is fun for the entire family. In **Planten un Blomen** *(see pp78–9)*, there are also amusements for children such as mini-golf, pony-rides and much more. Magicians do their best to confound their young audiences, clowns put smiles on their faces and puppets delight the kids at the outdoor children's stage, which is open only during the summer.

Which child does not dream of feeding a giraffe, petting a goat, riding an elephant or admiring colourful parrots? At **Tierpark Hagenbeck** *(see pp136–7)* all this is possible. Among the zoo's attractions are its large outdoor enclosures, in which the animals are kept in their natural habitats. It is easy to spend a whole day here without anyone becoming bored.

PLANTEN un BLOMEN ROLLSCHUHBAHN

Sign for the roller-skating track at Planten un Blomen park

MUSEUMS

It was not too long ago that children dragged their heels on museum visits. Thankfully, this has all changed, and "hands-on" is the new museum mantra. In the **Deichtorhallen** *(see pp62–3)*, children are invited into a painting studio; in the **Museum für Völkerkunde** *(see p128)*, they experience the rituals of other peoples. There are also museums tailored to children: in **Klick Kindermuseum**, the little ones get to explore a construction site; indeed, they are urged to enter it. Another exhibit, "Treffpunkt Körper" (meet your body), lets them play at being dentists. With its copies of famous paintings made by children, a walk through the **KinderKunstMuseum** is a stroll through art history.

Miniatur Wunderland's *(see p84)* claim to fame is the largest computer-controlled model railway in the world, which covers 1,300 sq m (14,500 sq ft). Visitors can have fun switching tracks themselves. Children's hearts also beat faster when they go on board to explore the museum ships **Cap San Diego** *(see pp98–9)* and **Rickmer Rickmers** *(see pp94–5)*.

THEATRE

In Hamburg, there are many theatres for children and youth whose shows generally do not exceed an hour. They

Fun to be had at the Hamburg City Beach Club

Many exciting details to discover in Miniatur Wunderland

are usually suitable for those aged four years and up. One of the best theatres is the **Fundus Theater**, which combines theatre with puppet shows in a spectacular way. The **Theater für Kinder** is the oldest children's theatre in Germany. Along with performances, **Hamburger Puppentheater** offers two-hour workshops on making hand puppets for puppet fans large and small. The **Theater-schiff Batavia** in Wedel offers a rich and varied programme. The **Opernloft** specializes in opera and operetta for both children and adults.

SPORTS

Children get very enthusiastic at the thought of playing beside, in or on the water. A boat trip through Hamburg's canals is a great way to explore the city. Of course, you can also rent a paddle-boat or row boat and tour the Alster under your own steam. Hamburg has many outdoor and indoor pools perfect for bathing fun. **Bäder-land Hamburg** provides information. In summer, the tots can let off steam on the roller-skating track in Planten un Blomen. In the cold saison, ice-skaters head to the **Eis-arena Planten un Blomen**, one of the world's largest outdoor skating rinks.

Hamburg Dungeon in the Speicherstadt

OTHER AMUSEMENTS

Visitors to the **Hamburg Dungeon** *(see p85)* take a trip back in time to the grisliest scenes in Hamburg's history. In the **Planetarium** *(see p134)* every Sunday afternoon it is time for "Sun, Moon and Stars", a show created for children aged five to nine. Great fun for all is to be had at the **Hamburger Dom** *(see pp44–6)* on the Heiligen-geistfeld. This series of folk fairs, fea-turing a giant Ferris wheel, carousels, vendors and much more, is held three times a year. The indoor arena in **SchwarzLICHTviertel** is lit up ultraviolet. Here, you can play a round of mingolf. You soar 150 m (492 ft) up on the **HighFlyer Hamburg** *(see pp62–3)*, a fixed hot-air balloon that rises up into the air in front of the Deichtorhallen.

DIRECTORY

SURVIVAL
GUIDE

PRACTICAL INFORMATION

Hamburg is a city that has always welcomed the world, and there is something to please every visitor among the rich variety of cultural sights and attractions here. A trip to the Elbe metropolis is delightful in all seasons. Its excellent infrastructure and tourism facilities ensure that your stay will go smoothly.

Advertising pillar

Telephones and ATMs are easy to find, and parking is well sign-posted. Going on a bus tour is one of the best ways to gather an initial impression of Hamburg. Try to allow time for a boat tour of the port. Before coming to Hamburg, make sure to check out the events that will be on during your visit and book tickets well in advance.

INFORMATION

You can gather a great deal of information about Hamburg before your trip. Contact **Hamburg Tourismus GmbH** to request that they send you material to help plan your visit. This tourist office also helps visitors find hotel rooms and organizes various package deals. Tickets to various events in the city are also available here.

The Internet gateway **www.gohamburg.de** offers tips for your trip under the heading "Explore Hamburg", as well as suggestions on how to put together a perfect weekend trip that takes in the top sights. Another reliable source of information is the online magazine **www.hamburg-magazin.de**. It provides details about all there is to see and do in the city, as well as lots of useful information about the city itself.

Once you have arrived in Hamburg, you can get information at one of the branches of **Tourist Information** located in the Hauptbahnhof, at Bahnhof Dammtor, at the port or at the airport. Along with maps of the city, there are all kinds of brochures and souvenirs, tickets for tours and plays, musicals and sports events. The Hamburg CARD *(see Hamburg on a Budget, p221)* is also available at tourist offices.

Lifesaving ring on *Rickmer Rickmers*

IMMIGRATION

Citizens of European Union member countries need a valid identity document (a national identity card or a passport). Citizens of non-European Union countries need a valid passport; for a stay of more than 90 days, a visa is also required. Contact the German consulate or German embassy in your country to find out current entry requirements.

CITY TOURS AND SIGHTSEEING FLIGHTS

Visitors to Hamburg can get an ideal overview of the city from land, on the water or in the air. You can enjoy one of the many harbour tours *(see pp240–41)*, take a bus tour, or even a flight over the city. These are all good ways to find your bearings. **Hamburg City Tour** offers tours in a double-decker bus with an open top (when the weather permits). Tours last 2 hours and start at the Landungsbrücken. Your ticket allows you to get off at 15 attractions and continue your tour on a later bus. It is valid for a full day, so you can take your time, stopping

A balloon ride, providing a fantastic bird's-eye view of the city

at the sights that appeal most to you.

On a tour with the **Rote Doppeldecker** visitors also have the advantage of pursuing their exploratory trip according to their particular interests.

Hamburg's oldest bus company **Hansa Rundfahrt GmbH** offers two options – the shorter City-Tour and the longer Gala-Tour, which includes, among other attractions, a drive over the Köhlbrandbrücke *(see p135)*. Visitors might also want to treat themselves to the "Lichter-Tour" – an evening excursion which covers, among other areas, the spectacularly illuminated Speicherstadt as well as the area around the harbour.

Air Hamburg offers flights in four-seater Cessnas. The bird's-eye view of Hamburg is wonderful. Window seats are, of course, guaranteed. Flights last

A double-decker bus for city tours

◁ The east side of the Hamburg Hauptbahnhof *(see p62)*

There are many different harbour tours on offer

either 35 minutes, covering the city centre, or 50 minutes, going further afield. **Hanseballon** or the **aero ballooning company** offer an opportunity to float effortlessly over the roofs and canals of the Hanseatic city.

Segways also provide a convenient way to explore the city. These electric scooters run at a maximum speed of 12 mph (20 km/h). **Mindways Segway Citytour Hamburg** offers tours.

GUIDED TOURS

The history of Hamburg, and stories that illustrate it, are the focus of guided tours, some of which have a specific theme. The "Beatles-Tour Hamburg" takes you on a walk to the place where it all began for the Fab Four from Liverpool, with their moptop haircuts. A stroll past the traditional office buildings of Hanseatic merchants is equally fascinating as a guided tour through HafenCity, Hamburg's newest district. The Rotlichttour (red-light district tour) offers a behind-the-scenes look at prostitution in Hamburg. This tour starts at the Davidwache in St Pauli (see p105).

Tour guide operators are plentiful. **k3 Stadtführungen** counts among the best. Its art tour, which takes visitors to many artistic treasures off the beaten path, is very popular.

As an alternative to a set tour, you can hire a private tour guide and see the things in Hamburg that interest you the most.

MUSEUMS IN HAMBURG

Hamburg has a very lively museum scene with over 80 museums covering a broad range of subjects. In addition to their ongoing displays, many regularly mount temporary exhibitions. New cultural institutions are opening up all the time, such as BallinStadt – Auswandererwelt Hamburg (see p93), which opened in 2007, Prototyp Museum (see p89), which opened in 2008, and the St. Pauli Museum, which opened in 2010. Some museums are being given new homes, including the Maritime Museum, which in June 2008 moved into the renovated Kaispeicher B in the Speicherstadt (see pp86–7).

This travel guide provides information on the city's most interesting museums, as well as on a series of smaller museums that are equally rewarding. More detailed information about specific museums and their current exhibits can be obtained from **Museumsverband Hamburg e.V.** The **Museumsdienst Hamburg** also provides information about additional activities at the museums in Hamburg.

Most Hamburg museums are open from Tuesdays to Sundays between 10am and 5 or 6pm. The museum ships docked at the Landungsbrücken can also be visited on Mondays.

Once a year (usually in April) about 50 Hamburg museums are open until 2am for the "Lange Nacht der Museen" ("Long Night of theMuseums"). You can visit such renowned cultural institutions as the Kunsthalle, the Deichtorhallen or the Altonaer Museum, as well as smaller ones such as the Freie Akademie der Künste on Klosterwall. Hamburg public transit (HVV) provides special buses to help ferry visitors between the various museums. The fare is included in the admission price.

Statue on the harbour promenade

A HADAG ship – a popular way to see the port

THE PORT

It is no surprise that the port is one of Hamburg's top attractions. Most visitors are drawn to the water at least once a day. The port is the heart of the city, whether your destination is HafenCity or Speicherstadt, a museum ship or a tour of the harbour, the Alte Elbtunnel or the Landungsbrücken, the Fisch-markt or the Hamburg City Beach Club. A boat tour of the port is even more special if your boat passes close to one of the big ocean-going ships either when it is on the water or in dry dock. A trip on HADAG-ferry no. 62 *(see p 135)* from the Landungsbrücken to Finkenwerder is also a wonderful thing to do.

Every year in early May, when the port's birthday *(see p85)* is celebrated, the maritime flair of the city is wonderfully accentuated. If you wish to attend the celebrations, make sure to book accommodation well in advance. With a bit of luck, you might get to witness the arrival of a large cruise ship such as the *Queen Mary 2*. Thousands of spectators flock to the shores of the Elbe for an opportunity to see a luxury cruise ship as it sails into the harbour and to watch it dock. Information on cruises starting from Hamburg, departure and arrival times for the large cruise ships, as well as facts and figures on individual ships, can be found at **www. hamburgcruise.de**.

SENIOR CITIZENS

On a visit to Hamburg, senior citizens will find the cosy, relaxed side of the Hanseatic city very enjoyable. The pretty districts, the well-tended parks, and the river banks are ideally suited for undertaking refreshing and inspiring walks. Whether you are strolling through the elegant district of Blankenese *(see p138)*, sauntering through the extensive greenery of Planten un Blomen *(see p78–9)*, or taking a walk along the Elbe river – one of the typical elegant but cosy cafés or characteristic tea salons *(see p199)* is always within easy reach.

Rubbish bin to keep the city clean

Senior citizens are also entitled to various reductions. In many traditional and musical theatres – from the Schmidt Theater to the Neue Flora – senior citizens aged 65 and older are entitled to discounts on a particular day of the week or for particular events.

Reduced fares for the public transport system are only available when purchasing a monthly pass. Even though there is no reduction on the Hamburg CARD *(see p223)*, this ticket generally offers good value.

GREEN TRAVELLING

In Hamburg, environmental awareness is taken very seriously. That is why the city has been nominated European Green Capital (Umwelthauptstadt Europas) of the year 2011 by the European Commission (Hamburg is the second city after Stockholm (2010) to be awarded this title). The accolade emphasizes Hamburg's status as an attractive as well as environmentally friendly city.

The city offers numerous advantages to ecologically minded visitors: The public transport system which includes the harbour ferries is extraordinarily efficient. Hamburg also is a very cycle-friendly city. Bicycles can be hired at many different places throughout the city *(see p235)*. You can take your bicycle with you free of charge on U-Bahns and S-Bahns, as well as on the harbour ferries and in many buses during off-peak hours. In the city centre, Fahrrad-Taxis *(see p237)* are an interesting alternative. Solar-powered boats have been introduced on the Alster, allowing visitors to cruise on the lake noiselessly with zero emission and not a single drop of oil used.

Visitors preferring whole-food nutrition can choose between many restaurants, cafés and shops offering suitable products (also from organic farming). Ottensen in particular offers a broad range of options.

StadtRAD – environmentally friendly transport

HAMBURG ON A BUDGET

If you purchase a **Hamburg CARD** you get a range of discounts. This card entitles you to unlimited public transport in the Greater Hamburg Area and as much as a 40 per cent discount for more than 150 Hamburg museums and other attractions, such as Tierpark Hagenbeck, Hamburg Dungeon, Miniatur Wunderland or the Rathaus. Also included are reduced prices for city and harbour tours, boat tours of the Alster lakes and a number of guided tours. You can also get reductions for performances in numerous theatres and musical theatres (such as Hamburgische Staatsoper, Altonaer Theater, Thalia Theater and Neue Flora), as well as in some restaurants and shops. An overview of the whole range of reductions is published on the website of **Hamburg Tourismus GmbH**.

The Hamburg CARD is available at Tourist Information branches, in many hotels and at ticket vending machines. Passes are valid for either one, three or five days. For a single adult travelling with up to three children 15 years and under, it costs 8.50, 20.50 or 35.90 Euros, respectively. A group ticket for up to five people of any age costs 13.90, 34.50 or 59.90 Euros.

The **Hamburg CARD – plus Region** offers good value to visitors who wish to explore the many attractions in the Greater Hamburg Area. It is valid for the HVV total network. In addition to the discounts offered by the Hamburg CARD, this pass offers further discounts in the Hamburg region, such as for a visit to the Deutsches Salzmuseum (German salt museum) in Lüneburg, an excursion to the bat caves in Bad Segeberg, and the Industriemuseum Elmshorn (museum of industry in Elmshorn) or a trip to the adventure park Erlebnisbahn

Hamburg – »European Green Capital« 2011

Ratzeburg. A one-day pass costs 19.90 Euros for one adult with up to three children 15 years and under. Groups of up to five people of any age can purchase the Hamburg CARD – plus Region for 29.90 Euros.

TIPS FOR STUDENTS

In a city with about 40,000 students, there quite naturally is a huge selection of popular pubs and trendy shops. Much of student life takes place in the university district to the west of the Außenalster; one of the main arteries is the Grindelallee with its down-to-earth cafés and bars. Another alternative area is the Schanzenviertel with its multicultural atmosphere and a large number of witty shops. The Beach Clubs (see p211) on the Elbe river are popular places to unwind.

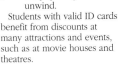

Drinking water dispenser

Students with valid ID cards benefit from discounts at many attractions and events, such as at movie houses and theatres.

There are a number of agencies in Hamburg called Mitwohnbörsen that help students find budget lodgings. These companies arrange flat-sharing in private homes around the city. Some of these accomodation services (such as www.studenten-eg. de) do not charge commission.

INFORMATION FOR NIGHT OWLS

In many Hamburg clubs and discos, it is not unusual for patrons to celebrate the night away, especially on

weekends. For some all-night revellers, a visit to the Fish Market (see p108) on Sunday mornings is the finale of a Saturday night out. The action in the Fish Auction Hall (Fischauktionshalle) continues all morning – it is especially full after the gong has been struck at 9:30am and the market closes. Nothing is better after an all-nighter than a traditional Fish Market buffet. For those who do not feel like fish, a pot of coffee helps to while away the time while waiting for your energy to return.

HAMBURG TIME

Hamburg is one hour ahead of Greenwich Mean Time (GMT). Summer time in Germany is from the end of March to the end of October, as in all European countries.

Personal Security and Health

Hamburg police logo

With its long tradition as a port and trading city, Hamburg is a cosmopolitan metropolis, open and tolerant. In comparison to many other large European cities, it is relatively safe, even though there are sometimes thefts in popular tourist areas. However, if you observe the usual precautions, there is not much to worry about. There are many pharmacies, and it is worth seeking initial advice from a pharmacist for minor health problems. For more serious medical help, you can contact one of the emergency numbers listed on the opposite page for assistance.

The Davidwache, Hamburg's best-known police station

PERSONAL SECURITY

Violent crime is rare in Hamburg, but even so, you should not walk down poorly lit streets at night or frequent large parks or other isolated areas. In the St Pauli district, especially in the Reeperbahn area, the occasional act of violence has been known to occur and tourists have sometimes been hurt, even though this is the district with the highest concentration of police in the city. By taking a few sensible precautions, you can significantly reduce the risks.

As in any large city, pickpockets do operate and will target anyone who looks like a tourist. Be especially vigilant if a stranger tries to distract you by engaging you in a discussion, or spilling food or a beverage on you; pickpockets often work in pairs or groups, with one distracting you while the other lifts your belongings. Places to exercise extra caution are the Fish Market, large fairs such as the Hamburger Dom, the Port's Birthday celebration, and at bus stops, public transit, railway carriages and stations, and department stores. Police regularly patrol the tourist areas, but it is still advisable to prepare the day's itinerary in advance, use common sense and stay alert. Try not to advertise that you are a tourist; study your map before you set off, avoid wearing expensive jewellery, and carry your camera securely. Carry small amounts of cash; credit cards or travellers' cheques are a more secure option. Keep these close to your body in a money wallet or inside pocket.

International pharmacy sign

Make use of the hotel safe for valuable items and important documents. When you are out, keep a close eye on your valuables, especially in crowds, and never leave your luggage unattended at the airport or train station. Just as in many other cities, Hamburg's U-Bahn and S-Bahn stations and platforms are not very inviting, especially late at night. Security patrols are frequent, and they will come to your aid in an emergency. If it is necessary, you can use one of the emergency buttons found on every platform to summon help.

If, despite all your precautions, you are a victim of a crime, go immediately to a police station and report it. In the case of theft, make sure to obtain a copy of the police statement with a list of the stolen items to give to your insurance company.

The Wasserschutzpolizei Hamburg – the police force protecting the city on water and land

LOST PROPERTY

In Hamburg's **Central Lost and Found** (Zentrales Fundbüro der Freien und Hansestadt Hamburg) unclaimed items are stored for up to six months. If you lost something at the Hamburg airport, contact the **Airport Office** for help. But if you have left something behind in the air-plane or your luggage has not turned up, go directly to the counter of whichever airline you travelled on. Items left behind on the S-Bahn are the responsibility of the Deutsche Bahn (German railway); contact their **Lost and Found** (Fund-Service) for assistance in finding your property. If you know where you have misplaced an item there is a good chance of recovering your property.

MEDICAL ASSISTANCE

It is advisable to carry proof of health insurance with you. If you have an EHIC card (Euro-pean Health Insur-ance Card), bring it with you. Doctors can be found in tele-phone books in the Yellow Pages. In the case of serious ill-ness, you will have to call an **Emergency Doctor** (Ärztlicher Notfalldienst). The Hamburg hospitals that have emergency departments are shown on the Street Finder maps *(see pp242–57)*.

There are a large number of pharmacies in Hamburg that keep the same hours as shops. At night and on Sundays, pharmacies hang in their

Old pharmacy sign

doorway the address of the nearest open pharmacy. This information is also published in the daily newspapers. If you take prescription medication, bring an adequate supply with you and carry a prescription in case you need an emergency refill.

Should you need the urgent services of a dentist, you can call the **Emergency Dental Care Service** (Zahnärztlicher Notfalldienst). Hamburg also has a **Drug Hotline** (Drogen-Hotline).

If you live outside Germany, it is a good idea to carry insurance that will pay any expenses you have incurred and the cost of your return to your home country in case of an emergency.

Hamburg police car

Hamburg fire engine

Ambulance

DIRECTORY

EMERGENCY SERVICES

Emergency
(Police, fire and ambulances)
Tel 112.

Emergency Dental Care Service
Tel 0180 505 05 18.

Emergency Doctor
Tel 22 80 22.

Red Cross
Tel 192 22.

Children's and Youth Helpline
Tel 0800 111 03 33.

Drug Hotline
Tel 280 32 04.

Spiritual Advice
Tel 0800 111 01 11.

LOST PROPERTY

Central Lost and Found of Hamburg
Bahrenfelder Str. 254–260.
Tel 428 11 35 01.

Airport Office
Airport Plaza,
Arrivals area.
Tel 50 75 10 10.

Deutsche Bahn Lost and Found
Tel 0900 199 05 99 (59 cents a min. from a German landline).

Banking and Local Currency

Cash machine (ATM)

Hamburg is the second most important banking city in Germany, after Frankfurt am Main. There are about 130 banks here, and over 30 of them have their headquarters in the city. One of these is the Hamburger Sparkasse (Haspa), which is one of Germany's largest banks. Cash machines (ATMs) are located throughout the city centre and beyond in great numbers. Debit and credit cards are widely accepted and a convenient method of paying for accommodation, meals and purchases from shops.

BANKING AND CURRENCY EXCHANGE

If you are coming from a country that has the Euro as its currency, you will not have to exchange any currency. Otherwise, you should use banks to exchange currencies, since they offer a better exchange rate than bureaux de change or hotels. It is a good idea to exchange larger amounts at one time, since you have to pay a fee each time.

Most banks open at 9am and close between 4 and 6pm; only a few (among them, branches of the Postbank) are open on Saturday mornings. Bureaux de change can be found at the Hauptbahnhof, at Bahnhof Dammtor, at the airport and near tourist attractions. They have longer hours of operation, including most Sundays. The convenient ATMs (cash machines) allow you to withdraw cash around the clock – as much as your daily limit permits.

Logo of the Deutsche Bank, one of Germany's largest banks

CREDIT CARDS AND TRAVELLERS' CHEQUES

Since credit cards are widely accepted throughout Hamburg, you do not have to bring large sums of money with you when you travel here. Signs displaying the logos of credit cards that will be accepted are displayed at the entrances to hotels, restaurants and shops. **MasterCard** and **Visa** are the most widely accepted, **American Express** and **Diners Club** less frequently. If you have one, you can also pay with a **Maestro-/EC-Card**.

Traveller's cheques are another secure method of payment. However, not all hotels and restaurants accept them, so they are useful simply as a supplement to cash and credit cards.

2-Euro coin with St Michaelis

The branch of the Hamburger Sparkasse located at the Rathaus

CURRENCY

The common currency Euro (€) is used by 17 members of the European Union: Austria, Belgium, Estonia Finland, France, Germany, Greece, Ireland, Italy, Luxembourg, Malta, Netherlands, Portugal, the Republic of Cyprus, Slovakia, Slovenia and Spain. The Deutschmark, Germany's former currency, is no longer legal tender, but notes and coins can be changed at the Bundesbank (www.bundes bank.de). While Euro notes share a common design, the backs of the coins are minted individually by every country. Every year, member states may issue commemorative 2-Euro coins. A coin showing Hamburg's St Michaelis church was brought into circulation in 2008, a coin showing Bremen Rathaus in 2010.

Euro Bank Notes
Euro bank notes have seven denominations (€5, 10, 20, 50, 100, 200 and 500). Designed by the Austrian Robert Kalina, the notes vary in size, and show architectural elements and styles of different eras, as well as a map of Europe and the flag of the European Union with its twelve stars.

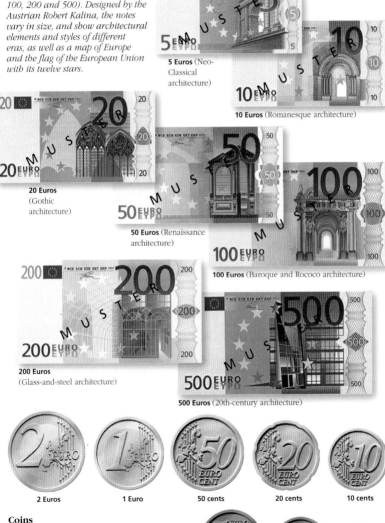

5 Euros (Neo-Classical architecture)

10 Euros (Romanesque architecture)

20 Euros (Gothic architecture)

50 Euros (Renaissance architecture)

100 Euros (Baroque and Rococo architecture)

200 Euros (Glass-and-steel architecture)

500 Euros (20th-century architecture)

2 Euros **1 Euro** **50 cents** **20 cents** **10 cents**

Coins
The Euro has eight coin denominations: €2 €1; 50, 20, 10, 5, 2 cents and 1 cent. Their standardized fronts were designed by the Belgian Luc Luycx. On the reverse side, German coins show the federal eagle, the Brandenburg Gate, and an oak-leaf cluster.

5 cents

2 cents

1 cent

Communications

Deutsche Telekom sign

Germany's telecommunications and postal services function extremely efficiently. Letters and postcards are usually delivered the next working day within the country. The distinctive yellow postboxes are common, and it is usually not far to a post office. There is a telephone booth on practically every corner in Hamburg, and many restaurants and cafés have a coin-operated public telephone. Mobile telephones work well, and there are many shops selling mobile telephones. Most hotels have Internet access, and there are also a number of Internet cafés.

Post-box in Hamburg

LETTERS AND POSTCARDS

Postal rates are based on the weight and size of your letter or parcel. The price of a standard letter up to 20g (0.7 oz) is 55 cents within Germany, 75 cents within Europe and 1.70 Euros to other continents. Postcards cost 45 cents within Germany, and 75 cents internationally. There are fixed rates for special services such as express delivery, registered letters or COD.

DHL delivery van

Postage stamps are available at post offices, from stamp machines and at kiosks selling postcards. Only German-Euro stamps can be used. There are a large number of post-boxes in Hamburg. Collection times are displayed on the post-boxes. You can also use an international courier service such as **DHL** to send letters and parcels to your home country.

POST OFFICES

Post offices are usually open Mondays to Fridays from 8 or 9am to 6 or 6:30pm, and on Saturdays they are open until noon. Airport and railway station branches usually have longer opening hours. Along with general counter service, post offices have public telephones, and at most you can send faxes, make photocopies and buy telephone cards as well as stationery supplies such as letter-writing paper, envelopes and boxes. You can also send post to post offices *(poste restante)*.

USING PUBLIC TELEPHONES

Hamburg has an excellent public telephone network. You will need coins for the coin-operated telephones, which accept 10-cent to 2-Euro coins. If you have overpaid, any unused coins will be returned at the end of

your call. It is far more convenient to use a telephone card, which can be purchased at post offices, T-Punkt shops and many kiosks. An illuminated display beside the telephone receiver shows the amount of credit left on the card. In the past few years, more and more telephone booths in Germany have been turned into starker "base stations". There is no booth and no lighting, just a free-standing column with a telephone that only accepts credit cards or a prepaid calling card (such as a T-card), which are activated after you key in your PIN.

Historic stamp (1973) with Hamburg's towers and churches

T-cards can be purchased in all branches of the Deutsche Post, T-Punkt shops and in the Deutsche Bahn Reisezentrum (travel centre), and most kiosks sell a range of calling cards. T-cards and calling cards can be used in traditional telephone booths as well.

Depending on the time and day, and the distance, different tariffs apply. Usually, the highest rates are charged weekdays between 8am and 6pm. You should avoid calling from your hotel room, since these calls will be much more expensive than those made from public telephone booths.

Ruler for measuring the size of letters

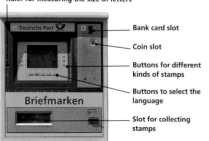

Deutsche Post

Briefmarken

Bank card slot

Coin slot

Buttons for different kinds of stamps

Buttons to select the language

Slot for collecting stamps

A vending machine for postage stamps

MOBILE TELEPHONES

There are no gaps in the mobile telephone network, and all GSM mobile telephones function properly. In 2007, the European Union regulated roaming prices for subscribers travelling within member states. In 2011, a maximum of 35 cents per minute may be charged for outgoing calls and 11 cents for incoming calls. For data transfers prices are limited to 50 cents per megabyte. Note that these prices do not include VAT.

Logo of the television station NDR

INTERNET AND EMAIL

Most hotels offer their guests computers with a WLAN, a local wireless network, often free of charge. Hamburg has many Internet cafés; most of them are open daily between 10am and 10pm. You can access local websites *(see p220)* for the latest information about events in the city.

NEWSPAPERS AND MAGAZINES

Hamburg is Germany's most important media centre – especially for print media. Many of the country's most successful newspapers and magazines are produced in the publishing houses located in the Hanseatic city. The largest subscriber-based newspaper in the Greater Hamburg Area is the *Hamburger Abendblatt*, with a circulation of about 240,000 copies. The *Hamburger Morgenpost* ("Mopo")

Richly decorated and adorned mobile telephone

is seen as a local alternative to *Bild*. Published by Springer, this tabloid sells about three million copies, making it Germany's best-selling daily newspaper. Other national newspapers originating in Hamburg are the *Financial Times Deutschland (FTD)*, *Die Welt* and the Hamburg edition of the *taz*.

DIE ZEIT, Germany's most renowned weekly newspaper, has been published by the Zeitverlag Gerd Bucerius in Hamburg since the first edition appeared on 21 February 1946. Spiegel Verlag's chief publication is *DER SPIEGEL*; it has the largest circulation of any news magazine in Europe. The publishing house Gruner + Jahr, which is the source of such magazines as *stern, GEO, Brigitte, P.M. Magazin* and *Gala*, is the biggest magazine publisher in Europe *(see pp40–41)*.

TELEVISION AND RADIO

The Norddeutsche Rundfunk (NDR) counts among the biggest public television broadcasters in Germany. The *Tagesschau* is one of its most important programmes. The regional broadcasting station NDR Fernsehen is also based in Hamburg. The ZDF also maintains a regional studio in Hamburg. The regional television broadcasting station Hamburg 1 is renowned for its in-house productions.

In addition to public radio stations such as NDR Info (News), NDR Kultur and the station N-JOY which focuses on young listeners private

stations addressing various target groups like Hamburg, Klassik Radio or Oldie 95 also are very popular.

Hamburg daily newspapers

USEFUL TELEPHONE NUMBERS

- German country code: 49.
- Hamburg area code: 040.
- Information: 118 33.
- International enquiries: 118 34.
- **European Emergency** (Police, Fire brigade, Doctor, Ambulance): 112.

- UK country code: 44.
- USA country code: 1.
- Canada country code: 1.
- International calls: first dial 00, followed by the country code, then the area code (leaving off any initial zero), and the number.

GETTING TO HAMBURG

Sign for Hamburg
Airport

Hamburg is one of Europe's central routing points. No matter what mode of transport you choose, Hamburg is easy to reach. Many international airline carriers fly into Hamburg Airport, which lies just outside the city. Four long-distance railway stations serve Hamburg, and they are well-integrated into the ICE and IC train networks that cross Germany and Europe. Since many motorways meet in Hamburg, the city is easy to reach by bus or car. Of course, the most authentic way of arriving in this port city is by ship. Many visitors enjoy sailing into the impressive harbour in style on an equally impressive cruise ship.

Information counter at the
Hamburg Airport

ARRIVING BY AIR

From Hamburg, you can fly non-stop to and from about 13 national and international destinations. Flights into the second-largest German city are offered by more than 70 airlines, among them **Lufthansa**, **British Airways**, **American Airlines**, **Delta Airlines** and **Qantas** as well as Air France, Aer Lingus, KLM, SAS and Emirates. Budget travel airlines are also well represented by carriers such as **easyJet**. Information about flights to Hamburg and destinations that can be reached via Hamburg is available from the respective airlines or directly from the airport. Hamburg Airport maintains an up-to-date website which provides the departure and arrival information for all flights.

If you are planning to fly to Hamburg, then it is a good idea to compare prices before you book. Due to stiff competition between airlines, there are occasionally flights on sale at sensationally low prices. These usually must be reserved and paid for several weeks in advance, there are travel restrictions, and you will pay a penalty if you change your flight. Very often, the ticket prices do not include taxes, such as security taxes and airport taxes. A charter flight or a package tour can be a

Destination boards and check-in
machines in a terminal

reasonable alternative. The latter generally includes airport transfers and accommodation in Hamburg, and sometimes admission to an event or a tour of the city. Before you book, check the location of your hotel to make sure it is not too far outside the city.

HAMBURG AIRPORT

The completion of the second terminal allowed the airport to increase its capacity enormously. The Airport Plaza links the two terminals.

AIRPORT

▪	Administration
▪	Indoor parking
S	S-Bahn station
▪	Police station
▪	Taxi
▪	Bus stop
▪	Information
P	Parking
▪	Restaurant
▪	Café
▪	Shop
▪	Wheelchair access

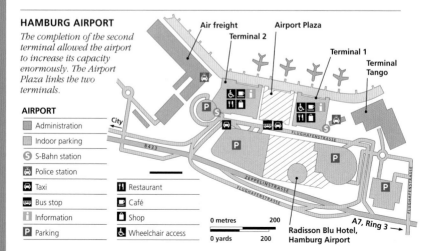

The main hall in Hamburg Airport

HAMBURG AIRPORT

In comparison with numerous other national and international airports, **Hamburg Airport** is relatively close to the city, and travellers find the short trip to the city centre convenient.

From 2001 to 2010 the airport, which opened in 1911, underwent major changes during the ambitious expansion project called HAM 21. Among the key components of this gigantic investment in the airport's future was the construction of a second terminal which was completed in 2005. The Airport Plaza opened in 2008. It hosted many of the festivities celebrating the airport's 100th anniversary in 2011.

The airport offers every convenience that travellers would expect from a modern airport. The duty-free shop alone, the largest retail outlet in Airport Plaza, covers an area of 1,400 sq m (15,000 sq ft). Some of the other amenities are travel agencies, car hire agencies, many kinds of restaurants and snack bars, long-term parking, conference rooms and modern business services, as well as post office and bank services (which include a number of ATMs). There are also medical services on hand.

The **Airport Office** located in the arrivals area is an important source of information for visitors to the city. Here, you can pick up brochures about Hamburg, book a hotel, buy a Hamburg CARD *(see p221)* or tickets to events. From the observation terraces of the restaurants in terminals 1 and 2, there are excellent views of take-offs and landings.

For travellers with limited mobility and those in wheelchairs, the airport offers wide-ranging assistance with transport and luggage. Toilets for the disabled are well sign-posted and easy to find in the terminals.

GETTING FROM THE AIRPORT TO THE CITY

The centre of the city is easy to reach using public transport from Hamburg Airport. Since 2008, the airport is linked to the S-Bahn system, and by taking the S1 line, you can reach the centre of Hamburg in just 25 minutes. The train departs every 10 minutes. Early in the morning and late at night, the train runs only every 25 minutes.

The S-Bahn-station Hamburg Airport is in front of both terminals and is accessible by lifts, escalators and stairs. The line to the city centre runs almost entirely underground.

Taxi ranks can be found at terminal 1 and terminal 2. The journey from the airport to the centre of Hamburg costs about 20 Euros and takes approximately 20 minutes (longer during heavy traffic).

DIRECTORY

HAMBURG AIRPORT

Airport Office
Airport Plaza,
arrivals area.
Tel 50 75 10 10.

Flight Information
Tel 507 50.
www.airport.de

AIRLINES

American Airlines
Tel 069 50 98 50 70.
www.aa.com

British Airways
Tel 01805 26 65 22.
www.britishairways.com

easyJet
Tel 0180 502 92 92.
www.easyjet.com

Delta Airlines
Tel 01803 33 78 80.
www.delta.com

Lufthansa
Tel 01805 83 84 26.
www.lufthansa.de

Qantas
Tel 01805 25 06 20.
www.qantas.com

Europcar – just one of the many car hire agencies at the airport

ARRIVING BY RAIL

Travelling to Hamburg by train makes for a very comfortable trip, but it is often more expensive than flying. The city is well connected by rail to the German and European railway network, with direct connections to many large cities in Germany and throughout Europe.

If you are travelling from Great Britain, a combination of ferries and trains makes for an interesting journey. You can take a ferry from Dover to Calais in France, and travel on to Hamburg by train from there. This route is, naturally, somewhat time-consuming.

Hamburg has four long-distance railway stations: the Hauptbahnhof, Hamburg Dammtor, Hamburg-Altona and Hamburg-Harburg. Most long-distance trains stop at the Hauptbahnhof and then continue to Bahnhof Dammtor before terminating at Bahnhof Altona.

Check the city map before you get off the train to find out which station is best for you. Bahnhof Hamburg Dammtor, where ICE (Inter-City Express trains) stop, is the best station for trade fair attendees. Hamburg-Harburg is the most important railway station for areas of the city south of the Elbe river. Destinations in Hamburg are easily reached on public transport from any of the four railway stations.

Trains run by the **Deutsche Bahn** (German railway) are safe and offer many comforts. Keep in mind that, especially in peak travel times, tickets can sell out quickly, so book well in advance. It pays to book early in more ways than one. The earlier you make your purchase and select the date of travel by reserving a seat, the cheaper the trip will be. Deutsche Bahn offers a range of attractive ticket deals, which change frequently. Their website (www.bahn.de) provides information about prices and special offers. It also contains a large number of attractive package deals for trips to Hamburg, some of which include accommodation and the option of buying tickets for cultural events.

DB

Deutsche Bahn sign

If you are coming from a great distance, a trip on a **City Night Line** is an option. These modern overnight trains offer a number of comforts. You can relax as you stretch out in a sleeping car or couchette car, though regular seats are also available. The advantages are that you do not lose any time and you arrive at your destination wide-awake and ready to see the sights. Wake-up calls are available at your request. For guests in

ZOB – Bus-Port Hamburg in St Georg

sleeping cars, breakfast is included in the price for the overnight train.

ARRIVING BY BUS

Hamburg is not only an important rail hub, but is also the most important motorway hub in Northern Germany. You can travel to Hamburg by bus via several motorways: the A7 (North-South motorway), the A1 (Bremen – Lübeck), the A24 (Berlin – Hamburg) and the A23 (from Schleswig-Holstein). These motorways are so well constructed that usually a bus trip to Hamburg does not take much longer than a trip on the train.

Travelling by bus can be much cheaper than travelling by train. However, there is less freedom of movement on board a bus. Many long-distance coaches entertain passengers with films shown on DVD. Some also offer reclining seats on overnight journeys. Drinks and snacks can generally be purchased on board.

Long-distance buses arrive from many countries at **ZOB – Bus-Port Hamburg**, which is conveniently located just down the street from the Hauptbahnhof. It bustles with travellers practically around the clock. The service area, whose amenities include an Internet café, a fast food restaurant and car hire agencies, is open daily from 5am to 10pm (on Wednesdays and Fridays to midnight). Bus trips can be booked at one of the travel agencies in ZOB

A view over the tracks in the Hamburg Hauptbahnhof

The Hamburg bus station can be seen from quite a distance away due to its striking, huge glass roof, which measures 300 sq m (3,300 sq ft) and curves out in a sickle-shape 11 m (36 ft) over the bus bays.

More than three million passengers arrive at or depart from ZOB every year. The buses travel to all large German cities, and to large cities in almost 30 other European countries.

ARRIVING BY CAR

If you drive into Hamburg from the south, you will end up going through the Elbtunnel to get to the north shore of the Elbe. There are often traffic jams here, especially in rush hour, but attempting to find another route if you are unfamiliar with the city is not recommended.

If you are going to the trade fair, take the Hamburg-Volkspark exit if you are coming from the north, north-west, west or southwest. Take the Hamburg-Centrum exit if you are coming from the south or southeast. Take the Hamburg-Horn exit if you are coming from the east or northeast. No matter which exit you take, once you're off the motorway follow the signs to the trade fair, which read "Messe/CCH".

To drive in Germany, you have to carry a valid driving licence as well as your vehicle's registration document. By law the car must also carry a red triangle in case of a breakdown, and a

Eurolines buses serving Hamburg from many European cities

properly stocked first-aid kit; a safety vest is recommended.

To hire a car in Germany, you need a valid driver's licence, country ID card or passport, and a credit card. In Hamburg, there are many car hire agencies with branches in the city centre, including at the Hauptbahnhof.

ARRIVING BY SHIP

Although the heart of Hamburg is its port, and most visitors spend some time visiting sights on the water, most travellers do not arrive in Hamburg via the water. However, many tourists do go on a boat trip during their visit. The kinds of tours available range from harbour round trips of varying duration, to tours along the Elbe and trips to Helgoland on high-speed catamarans. Information about such excursions on the water is found on pages 240–41.

The most elegant way of arriving in Hamburg is as a passenger on a cruise ship. These huge vessels dock at the **Hamburg Cruise Center (Kreuzfahrtterminal;** see p88). Terminal 1 was expanded in 2006, when a second hall was built. A new terminal in

Motorway sign to Hamburg on the A7

Altona opened in 2010. Thousands of spectators come to the port to watch asone of these giant ocean liners docks or departs.

Hamburg Cruise Center, where the ocean liners dock

DIRECTORY

ARRIVING BY RAIL

Deutsche Bahn (Train Information)
Tel 01805 99 66 33.
(Main service number for the German railway).
Tel 08001 50 70 90
(Recorded announcements. Free call).
www.bahn.de

City Night Line
In Germany:
Tel 0180 514 15 14.
In Switzerland:
Tel 0900 300 300.
www.citynightline.de

ARRIVING BY BUS

ZOB – Bus-Port Hamburg
Adenauerallee 78.
Tel 24 75 76.
www.zob-hamburg.de

ARRIVING BY SHIP

Hamburg Cruise Center (Kreuzfahrtterminal)
Großer Grasbrook/Chicagokai.
Tel 30 05 13 93.
www.hamburgcruisecenter.eu/de

A Deutsche Bahn Inter-City Express – ICE

GETTING AROUND HAMBURG

Although the city is large, the distances between the main sights and attractions of Hamburg are actually quite short. The best way to explore the centre is on foot. The different districts of the city and the surrounding area can be reached easily using public transport. This includes the U-Bahns, S-Bahns and buses as well as a range of boats and ships. Bicycles

Road signs point the way

are another excellent way of getting around Hamburg, especially since the city is rather flat, allowing for easy and relaxed transport. A network of cycling paths extends all the way to the outer city districts. Driving a car gives you flexibility, but in rush hour traffic can move very slowly and parking fees in the city centre are relatively high. Taxis are plentiful and easy to find.

Pedestrian signals with digital displays

WALKING IN HAMBURG

Even though Hamburg is spread out over a large area, the city centre is compact. Distances between the individual sights and attractions are usually short, and there is hardly any destination that requires going a great distance out of your way. With a bit of planning, visitors can get to sights just by

walking to them. One of the favourite walking (and jogging) routes in the city is around the Alster lakes. The route not only follows the water's edge, but it also dips into some of the most elegant districts in the Hanseatic city. There are many inviting cafés with terraces and other lovely places to stop for a break along the way.

Gorgeous views of the Elbe river and the port can be enjoyed from the Hamburger Balkon, which stretches between the Landungsbrücken and the Altonaer Balkon, a lovely park which also offers a fabulous view *(see p117)*. An excellent way of learning about the city, including its many hidden charms, is to take one of the walking tours *(see p222)* led by guides who are knowledgeable about the various areas of the city. The walks are usually organized around a theme, such as history, art, culture or architecture.

DRIVING IN HAMBURG

Germans drive on the right side of the road. A car can come in handy for visiting attractions outside Hamburg. Renowned car hire agencies such as **AVIS**, **Europcar**, **Hertz** and **Sixt** have branches at the airport, at the Hauptbahnhof and in other locations. To hire a car, you will need a valid licence, country ID card or passport, and, usually, a credit card. If your car breaks down, the German automobile club, **ADAC**, offers emergency roadside assistance. Speed traps are often set up at the exits and entrances to motorways, and there are a good number of red-light cameras at intersections in Hamburg. In Germany, the permitted blood alcohol level is 0.5.

Sign showing distances and direction

The three parking divisions in the city centre

A sign showing where parking is available in the city centre

Parking Ticket Vending Machine

Parking ticket vending machines can be found on most city streets. Parking fees usually apply weekdays from 8am to 6 or 8pm. The longest you can park is either 60 minutes or 120 minutes.

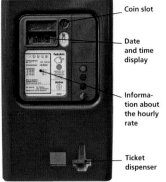

Coin slot

Date and time display

Information about the hourly rate

Ticket dispenser

PARKING

Thanks to an automated guided parking system, finding a parking spot in the centre of Hamburg is fairly easy. The city is divided into three parking areas: red (Mönckebergstraße), yellow (Jungfernstieg) and green (Port/St Michealis). Road signs provide drivers with information about the parking system well before they reach the centre of the city

Indoor parking in the centre of Hamburg accommodates more than 11,000 cars. About 250 digital displays show drivers how many parking spots are left in each of the city's car parks. With the displays changing each minute, the information is always up to date. Fees for using indoor car parks are usually 2 Euros per hour. The maximum amount that can be charged per day is about 10 to 15 Euros. Parking fees can be paid using you mobile phone.

StadtRAD Hamburg – an environmentally friendly alternative

CYCLING

Hamburg is bicycle friendly. Many city streets have a dedicated bike lane, and some go from the city centre all the way to the outer districts. Popular routes follow along the Alster or the Elbe. Hiring a bicycle is easy. You can hire for a single day or for longer periods of time; most hire agencies offer reduced rates for a weekly rental. **Hamburg anders erfahren** delivers your bicycle directly to your hotel. A large selection of bicycles is also offered by **Fahrradverleih Altona**. **Call a Bike** is a subsidiary of DB Rent, which is owned by the German railway. To hire a bicycle, you first need to register with Call a Bike, when you will be assigned a customer number. This serves as a direct withdrawal billing number, but will also allow you to unlock the bike at the train station. Displays show which of the silver and red bicycles are still available at the various DB Rent stations. From **StadtRAD Hamburg**, bicycles can be ordered around the clock via telephone or at one of the 70 stations.

Advertisement for StadtRAD Hamburg

Cyclists will find the Hamburg-Atlas published by **ADFC Hamburg**, Hamburg's cycling association, very useful. As you would in all other big cities, lock up your bicycle when you cannot keep an eye on it.

BOATING

Given the enormous importance of the Elbe and port to Hamburg, and the great number of canals criss-crossing the city, there is a great deal of boat traffic on the waterways in the city centre. Information about taking a boat trip on the harbour, the Elbe, the canals, and the Alster lakes as well as information about longer excursions is provided on pages 240–41.

A special service is offered to those who have purchased a ticket to the Theater im Hamburger Hafen *(see p92)*. The free shuttle boat takes them from the Landungsbrücken across the Elbe.

DIRECTORY

CAR HIRE

AVIS
Tel 0180 521 77 02.
www.avis.de

Europcar
Tel 0180 580 00.
www.europcar.de

Hertz
Tel 0180 533 35 35.
www.hertz.de

Sixt
Tel 0180 525 25 25.
www.sixt.de

ROADSIDE ASSISTANCE

ADAC
Tel 0180 222 22 22.

BICYCLE HIRE

ADFC Hamburg
Koppel 34–36. *Tel* 39 39 33.
www.hamburg.adfc.de

Call a Bike
Tel 0700 05 22 55 22.
www.callabike-interaktiv.de

Fahrradverleih Altona
Thadenstr. 90. *Tel* 439 20 12.
www.fahrradverleih-altona.de

Hamburg anders erfahren
Peutestr. 16–18.
Tel 0178 640 18 00.
www.hamburg-anders-erfahren.de

StadtRAD Hamburg
Scharrenstr. 10. *Tel* 822 18 81 00. www.stadtrad.hamburg.de

Travelling by City Buses and Taxis

Hamburg's well-run public transportation system, HVV, makes it very easy to travel on public transit. You can switch between an HVV bus, an S-Bahn or U-Bahn and ferries, without ever having to purchase a new ticket. One of the cheapest ways to travel on the transit system is to purchase a day pass, which pays for itself after just two trips. The bus network includes many types of buses, from express buses to night buses. Taxis are a much more comfortable and convenient mode of transport, but are considerably more expensive.

HVV

In many large cities, trying to understand how the public transport system works is a seemingly impossible task. But this is not the case in Hamburg, whose transit system, founded in 1965, has yet to find its equal.

The **HVV** (Hamburger Verkehrsverbund) includes more than 30 different transport companies that run various kinds of buses, railways and harbour ferries. One incalculable advantage of the HVV is that its fare system is divided into easy-to-understand zones, and the same ticket can be used on different kinds of city transport.

Hamburg's public transit system covers not only the Free and Hanseatic City of Hamburg, but also extends into the adjacent regions of Schleswig-Holstein and Lower Saxony. The network covers approximately 8,600 sq km (3,320 sq miles). There are more than two-million HVV passengers living in these three German states. Statistics show that about two-thirds of all passenger traffic in the inner-city area is on HVV transportation.

MetroBus – a fast way to travel, often in a dedicated lane

TICKETS

One ticket is valid on all HVV transit, whether you are travelling by bus, rail or on a harbour ferry. Tickets for one-way trips and day-passes (available for either one or three consecutive days) can be purchased from ticket vending machines, as well as from bus drivers. Unlike in many other cities, the tickets do not have to be validated or stamped when you use them. If you are staying in Hamburg for a while, it pays to buy a weekly pass. Anyone with a Hamburg CARD (see p223) can use public transit in the Greater Hamburg area free of charge.

Day passes can be used for unlimited travel on the day of purchase until 6am the following day. The price is determined by the zones. The cheapest day pass (one to two zones) is available for 6.80 Euros. Even cheaper is the day pass that starts after 9am, which costs 5.50 Euros. It is valid from 9am until 6am the following day. Children five years and under travel on the HVV network for free. A day pass is valid for up to three children (13 and under) and two adults.

The tourist group pass (Touristen-Gruppenkarte) is an interesting type of ticket. Each member of the group, which has to have at least five people in it, gets an individual ticket and can use this to

HVV TICKET VENDING MACHINE

Ticket vending machines are found in all U-Bahn and S-Bahn stations, as well as at centrally located bus stops. These machines dispense single-use tickets, day-passes and three-day-passes.

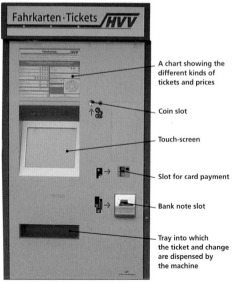

Fahrkarten · Tickets HVV

A chart showing the different kinds of tickets and prices

Coin slot

Touch-screen

Slot for card payment

Bank note slot

Tray into which the ticket and change are dispensed by the machine

travel on the HVV network. It costs 3.60 Euro per person per day. These tourist group passes have to be ordered in writing at least two weeks before you need them from the **HVV Customer Service Centre** (HVV-Kundenzentrum). You will have to know how many people will be in your group and how long you will need the pass before you order.

BUSES

HVV buses include the StadtBus, MetroBus, Schnell-Bus, EilBus and NachtBus. A StadtBus (which usually has a three-digit number) brings passengers to the S-Bahn stations and regional transit stations. A MetroBus links destinations within the central area (lines 1 to 15) and outside the central area (lines 20 to 27). A SchnellBus (lines 31 to 39) travels to the outer districts right from the centre of the city. These buses offer extra comfort, have a large number of seats and cost more. An EilBus (which has an "E" in front of the bus number) links parts of the city that do not have an S-Bahn station with the nearest U-Bahn or S-Bahn station. This type of bus only runs during rush hour. In the mornings, it brings passengers

A typical ivory-coloured German taxi

StadtBus operated by the Hamburger Hochbahn (www.hochbahn.de)

from stops in residential areas to the closest S-Bahn station; in the afternoons, it reverses its journey. A NachtBus (night bus on lines 600 to 688) operates after the U-Bahn and S-Bahn have stopped running every 30 to 60 minutes on Mondays to Fridays all over Hamburg. On weekends, the MetroBus and StadtBus (as well as the U-Bahns and S-Bahns; see pp238–9) run around the clock.

Buses used in the greater Hamburg area are mostly low-floor-buses and do not have steps. People who use wheelchairs get into this type of bus with the help of a short ramp. On the HVV website (www.hvv.de/en), you can find excellent information about barrier-free access in the public transport system, along with route, schedule and ticket information.

TAXIS

For visitors to Hamburg, **taxis** provide a comfortable, if relatively expensive, way to travel. More than 3,500 taxis are licensed to operate in the Hanseatic city. Since taxis are allowed to use dedicated bus lanes, they travel along at a good clip even in rush hour. At night, taxis are often the only option available, especially when a NachtBus has just pulled away right in front of you.

You can hail a taxi on the street, or order one by telephone (for telephone numbers see directory), or pick up one at one of the many taxi ranks

located strategically across the city. The basic fare is 2.70 Euros; the per-kilometer price for the first four km (2.5 miles) is 1.85 Euros, from 5 to 10 km (3 to 6 miles) the cost is 1.75 Euros, for each additional kilometre travelled, there is a 1.28 Euro charge.

Perhaps you would enjoy a trip in a different kind of taxi – a Fahrrad-Taxi (bicycle taxi) of **Trimotion**? These unusual vehicles carry passengers between the most interesting places and sights. In this fun vehicle, the driver not only is transporting you in a way that is environmentally friendly, but will also provide you with interesting bits of information about the sights and attractions you pass en route.

see directory

DIRECTORY

HVV

Information
Tel 194 49.
www.hvv.de/en

HVV Customer Service Centre
Johanniswall 2. *Tel* 32 88 21 03.

TAXIS

Hansa Taxi
Tel 21 12 11 or 31 13 11.

Taxi Hamburg
Tel 66 66 66.

Taxiruf
Tel 44 10 11.

Trimotion
Tel 76 75 57 56.

Bus stop "Auf dem Sande", with signs for MetroBuses and city tours

U-Bahn and S-Bahn

The excellent network of "Schnellbahn" (S-Bahn) lines in the HVV area *(see back inside cover)* gives travellers a fast way to travel, independently of traffic. On weekends, as well as the night before a public holiday, trains on the three U-Bahn lines and the six S-Bahn lines roll through the night every 20 minutes. Tickets for both forms of transport are also valid for other types of transit (buses and some harbour ferries). Lines converge not just at the big railway stations, but at many stops, which makes switching to another line easy. It is also easy to purchase tickets from a vending machine.

S-Bahn sign

U-Bahn sign showing the destination station of the train

S-BAHN

While the U-Bahn runs exclusively in the city, the S-Bahn links Hamburg with the outlying areas. Each day, trains make about 1,000 trips. The network covers 147 km (92 miles), and it transports about 550,000 passengers daily from its 68 stations. With these numbers, it is clear why the S-Bahn is considered the "backbone" of public regional transit in the Hanseatic city.

Trains operate daily between 4:30am and 1am, with service every 10 to 20 minutes. On weekends, the trains run around the clock. Since many lines share the same tracks, waiting times are short in the city centre.

For travellers arriving by air, the Hamburg Airport station *(see p230–31)*, is an important stop. It takes just 25 minutes to get from the airport to the centre of the city on the S-Bahn.

The S-Bahn network will be greatly expanded in the coming years, and more lines are being planned.

BICYCLES

You can take your bicycle with you free of charge on U-Bahns and S-Bahns, as well as on many buses and harbour ferries. There is room for one bike just to the side of each door. There are some restrictions: you cannot take bicycles with you on the

The U-Bahn, which often travels above ground

U-BAHN

Hamburg's U-Bahn (underground train) network consists of three lines, which together travel along about 100 km (62 miles) of tracks. As part of the gigantic HafenCity complex *(see pp90–91)*, a new fourth U-Bahn line is being planned; it is due to begin service in 2012.

Most U-Bahn trains run from 4:30am to midnight every five to ten minutes. During peak times, they run every two to three minutes, and in the slower times (early morning and late evening hours) they operate at 20-minute intervals. The U-Bahn operates all night long on Fridays and Saturdays within the Hamburg area, with trains every 20 minutes.

A feature of Hamburg's U-Bahn network is that it often travels above ground. One of the highlights of a visit to Hamburg, which you should definitely take advantage of if you have the time, is to ride the U3 line on the section where it surfaces

above ground. If you take the U3 line towards Barmbek, the train surfaces shortly after Rathaus station and travels past the Landungsbrücken on a portion of the track known as the Hafen-Hochbahn *(see p92)*. You will have a wonderful panoramic view of the harbour from the train, but make sure to sit on the left-hand side in the direction of travel. This stretch is considered one of the loveliest trips you can take on public transportation in Hamburg. You can also travel this section in the opposite direction.

A platform in an S-Bahn station

S-Bahn and on buses during peak times (6 to 9am and 4 to 6pm) from Mondays to Fridays. On weekends and public holidays, there are no restrictions. You can take your bicycle on harbour ferries at any time, any day.

U-BAHN AND S-BAHN STATIONS

U-Bahn and S-Bahn stations are clearly marked by signs. A square sign with a white "U" on a dark blue background stands for the U-Bahn, a round sign, with a white "S" on a green background stands for the S-Bahn. You can purchase a ticket at any station (see p236). It is a good idea to have small change and small bills with you for the ticket vending machines. Information displayed at the stations will tell you how much your trip will cost. If you are going to take several trips in one day, it pays to buy a day pass. For a longer visit, consider a weekly pass.

Electronic displays suspended over the platforms show the line number, and the final destination for each train that is pulling in. At each stop, and in each U-Bahn and S-Bahn car, there is a map of the HVV-transit network. The lines are marked in different colours, making them easy to

A joint U-Bahn and S-Bahn station, where you can transfer between lines

distinguish. Also helpful are the maps which hang in every S-Bahn and U-Bahn station. These provide information about the area around the station, including exits, entrances and bus stops.

DISABLED TRAVELLERS

Many U-Bahn and S-Bahn stations are barrier free. Either they have wheelchair accessible ramps or a lift wide enough to accommodate a wheelchair. In the newest U-Bahn and S-Bahn trains, the distance between the platform and the car is a maximum of 5 cm (1.9 in), making it easy to get on and off the cars. On older trains, the distance is greater, but this does not usually pose a problem.

On maps depicting the HVV network that hang in every station, it is easy to see those stations that can be used by people in wheelchairs, since they are marked with a symbol. Detailed information about station entrances and exits for S-Bahn and U-Bahn stations, as well as the location of the toilets, is available online at www.hvv.de.

As a special free service for the blind and sight impaired, the HVV will create on demand a schedule and list of the stops tailored to an individual's needs. You can order this specially prepared information by telephoning (040) 194 49.

Tickets for use anywhere on the HVV

SECURITY

On every U-Bahn and S-Bahn platform there are emergency intercoms, which you can use to summon help if needed. As well as making regular patrols, security personnel use cameras to watch over the stations. If there are no inciddents, the recording is erased after 24 hours.

When a passenger has pulled the emergency brake because there has been an accident, the U-Bahn or S-Bahn train will continue on to the next station before stopping. It is easier to provide help (which can also be summoned more quickly) at a station. Every tunnel has clearly marked emergency exits, should passengers be asked to exit the train.

HVV prices and destinations in the local and regional Hamburg area

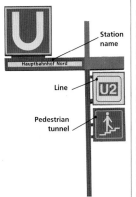

Station name

Line

Pedestrian tunnel

The entrance to a U-Bahn station with various signs

Travelling by Ship

Tickets for a round trip of the port

Hamburg's harbour is as much a part of this Hanseatic city as the Reeperbahn and St Michelis church. A tour by boat will be one of the highlights of your visit – even if your vessel does not pass close to a luxury cruise ship. Taking a boat such as a HADAG ferry is a lovely way to travel the Elbe river. There are many special boat tours offered during the Port's Birthday Bash *(see p85)*. Boat tours of the Binnenalster, Außenalster and the canals are also available. You can get to the Altes Land and Helgoland from Hamburg quite easily by water, but to reach the island of Sylt *(see pp156–7)* it is better to go by rail, car or by plane.

Sign for harbour tours

A large choice of harbour tours are available to visitors

HARBOUR TOURS

Taking a harbour tour is a good way to get to know Hamburg from another perspective *(see pp48–9)*, and sightseeing from the water has its own special charm. If you depart from the city centre to Altona, you will pass by HafenCity, the Speicherstadt and the modern buildings lining the water's edge like pearls in a necklace.

Many tour companies tout their boat trips on the Landungsbrücken. The routes are all very similar. Choose the boat that suits you best.

Tours of the harbour take place all year round. Some have a special theme such as "Treasures and Sacks of Peppercorns", which focuses on Hamburg's importance as a maritime trading centre, or "The Port and Its Whores", concentrating on the history of prostitution. In summer, boat tours of the Speicherstadt at night are highly

Advertisement for boating on the Alster

recommended, when its impressive red-brick buildings are beautifully lit up. Most round trips of the harbour last from 1 to 2 hours. If you are lucky, you will be able to see a large ocean liner up close.

ELBE BOAT TOURS

A fairly inexpensive way of seeing Hamburg from the water is to take one of the **HADAG** ferries. The most interesting ferry routes are plied by No. 61, from the Landungsbrücken to Waltershof; No. 62 *(see p135)*, from Sandtorhöft to Finkenwerder via Neumühlen, with its ship museums in Museumshafen Övelgönne; and No. 64 from Finkenwerder to Teufelsbrück. The cost for a HADAG ferry is the same as for any other form of public transport offered by the HVV. This means you do not have to buy an extra ticket if you have already

been on public transport and are transferring, or if you have a day pass *(see p236)*.

You can travel from the Landungsbrücken to Altes Land *(see p138)* via Blankenese and Willkommhöft *(see p139)* on a HADAG ship run by the **Elbe Erlebnistörns GmbH**. They run on weekends and public holidays from Easter to the beginning of October, and also accept bicycles.

ALSTER BOAT TOURS

Excursions on the Binnenalster and Außenalster are popular with tourists and locals alike. Whoever experiences the metropolis from these lakes quickly discovers that Hamburg does not only have the most bridges of any city in Europe (apparently there are 2653!), but also ranks among the greenest cities. You glide by parks, overgrown shorelines and villas with lovely gardens.

Harbour tours – enjoyed by locals and visitors alike

A boat trip on the Alster – a relaxing way to see the sights

Alster-Touristik GmbH offers mini "cruises" from April to early october. They depart from the Jungfernstieg and cross the Alster to the Winterhuder Fährhaus. You can get on and off at any of the stops as often as you like. This company also offers a tour of the Alster from November to March as a "Punschfahrt" (with mulled red wine and hot chocolate) in a heated cabin. Taking a trip between Jungfernstieg and Harvestehude in the evening could not be more romantic.

But the Alster is at its most idyllic when you cross it on a gondola from **La Gondola**.

Ticket booth for round trips of the harbour, including Speicherstadt

CANAL TOURS

What would Hamburg be without its many canals that course through some of the city's loveliest areas? One of the most popular canal boat tour companies is **Barkassen-Centrale**. On their boats, which are decorated in 1920s style, you glide through narrow waterways and pass under some of the oldest bridges in Hamburg to the impressive Speicherstadt *(see pp82–3)*. Informative historic tours of the canals are also offered by the company **Kapitän Prüsse**.

HELGOLAND AND NEUWERK

Getting to Helgoland *(see p159)*, Germany's largest sea island, is quite simple by water. A high-speed catamaran operated by **FRS Helgoline GmbH** offers a one-day excursion to Helgoland from April to October. The boat leaves daily from the Landungsbrücke 4 *(see p93)*, and reaches the island in just four hours, stopping at Wedel and Cuxhaven along the way. You do not have to make any transfers. Tickets for this trip can be purchased daily from 7:30am at the Landungsbrücken. Prices vary, depending on the season and class you choose. More information is available on the company's website: www.helgoline.de

From Cuxhaven on the coast, you can reach the beautiful island of Neuwerk in the Hamburg Wadden Sea National Park *(see pp140–41)* at low tide on foot or in a horse-drawn wagon. When the tide is high, a ship run by **Reederei Cassen Eils** will transport you there.

DIRECTORY

ELBE BOAT TOURS

Elbe Erlebnistörns GmbH
Tel 219 46 27.
www.elbe-erlebnistoerns.de

HADAG Seetouristik und Fährdienst AG
Tel 311 70 70.
www.hadag.de

ALSTER BOAT TOURS

Alster-Touristik GmbH
Tel 357 42 40.
www.alstertouristik.de

La Gondola
Tel 490 09 34.
www.gondel.de

CANAL TOURS

Barkassen-Centrale
Tel 319 91 61 70.
www.barkassen-centrale.de

Kapitän Prüsse
Tel 31 31 30.
www.kapitaen-pruesse.de

HELGOLAND AND NEUWERK

FRS Helgoline GmbH
Tel 0180 320 20 25.
www.helgoline.de

Reederei Cassen Eils
Tel 0180 522 86 61.
www.helgolandreisen.de

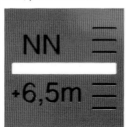

Water-level indicator based on the mean sea level in Amsterdam (NN)

HAMBURG STREET FINDER

The map references given with all sights, hotels, restaurants, shops and entertainment venues described in this book refer to the maps in this section only. A complete index of street names and all the places of interest marked on the maps can be found on the following pages. The key map below shows the areas of Hamburg covered by

Tourists reading a map

the *Street Finder* maps. These are: Altona, 1–2; St Pauli, 3–4; Port and Speicherstadt, 5–6; Around the Alster, 7–8; and New Town and Old Town, 9–10. In addition to the six coloured city areas, other areas are also shown on these maps. The symbols used to represent sights and useful information are listed below in the key.

View of the Elbe with St Michaelis church *(centre)*, Cap San Diego *(right)* and a boat-shuttle *(front)*

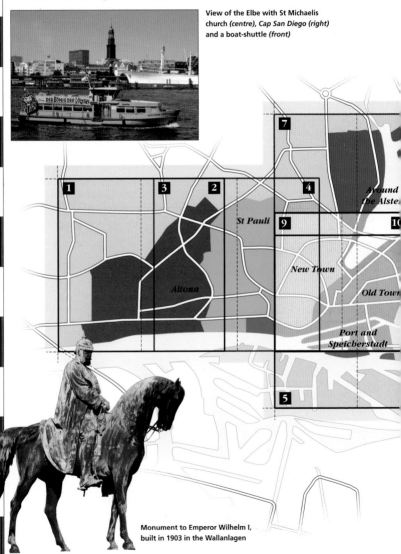

Monument to Emperor Wilhelm I, built in 1903 in the Wallanlagen

HOW THE MAP REFERENCES WORK

The first figure tells you which *Street Finder* map to turn to.

Cap San Diego ⓮

Museum ship *Cap San Diego*,
Überseebrücke. **Map** 9 A5
Tel 36 42 09. ⓤ Baumwall.
Ⓢ Landungsbrücken.
◯ 10am–6pm daily. 🕎
🏠 www.capsandiego.de

The letter and number give the grid reference. Letters go across the map's top and bottom, figures on its sides.

The map continues on map 5 of the *Street Finder*.

KEY

🟥	Major sight
🟦	Other sight
Ⓢ	S-Bahn station
Ⓤ	U-Bahn station
🚆	Railway station
🚌	Bus terminal
⛴	Ferry service
🛳	Boat boarding point
Ⓟ	Parking
ℹ	Information
➕	Hospital with casualty department
🚓	Police station
✝	Church
⊠	Post office
▬▬	Railway
▬▬	Pedestrian street
▭▭	Passage
---	Ferry route

SCALE OF MAPS 1–2 AND 5–6
0 metres   300
0 yards   300   1:14,000

SCALE OF MAPS 3–4 AND 9–10
0 metres   300
0 yards   300   1:10,500

SCALE OF MAPS 7–8
0 metres   300
0 yards   300   1:12,500

Huge container ship docked at Burchardkai

Street Finder Index

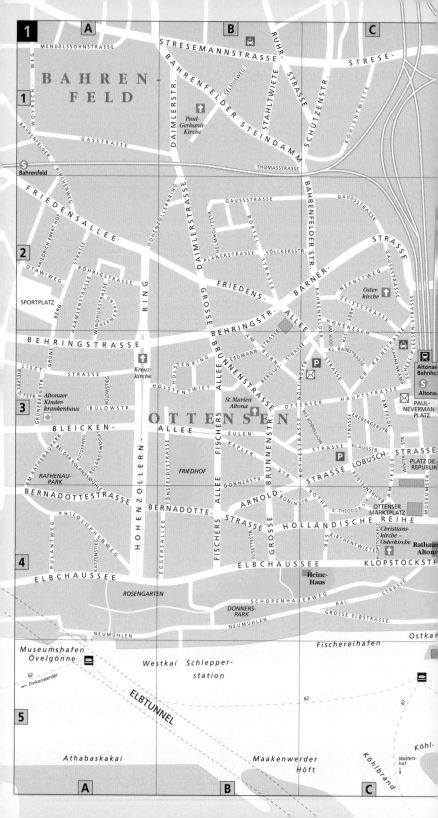

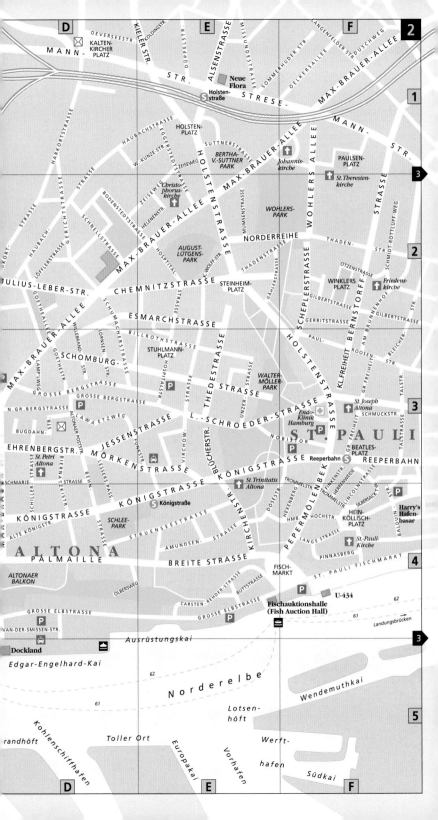

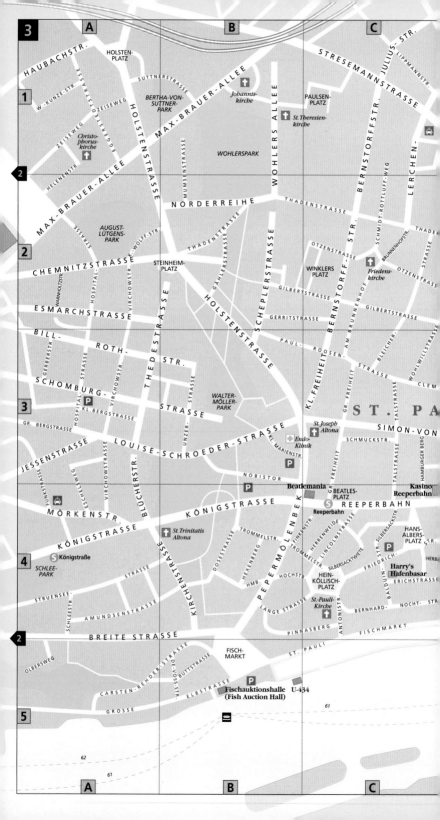

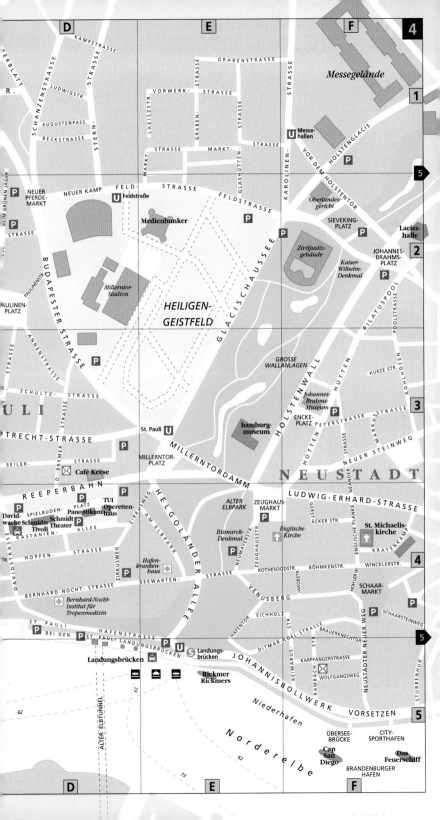

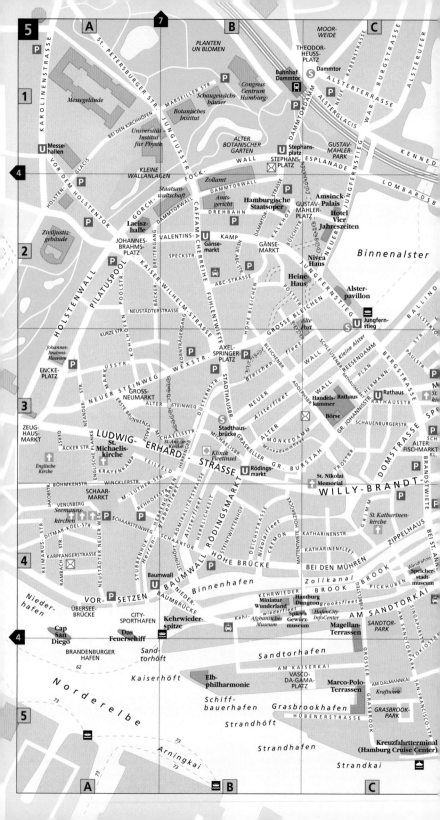

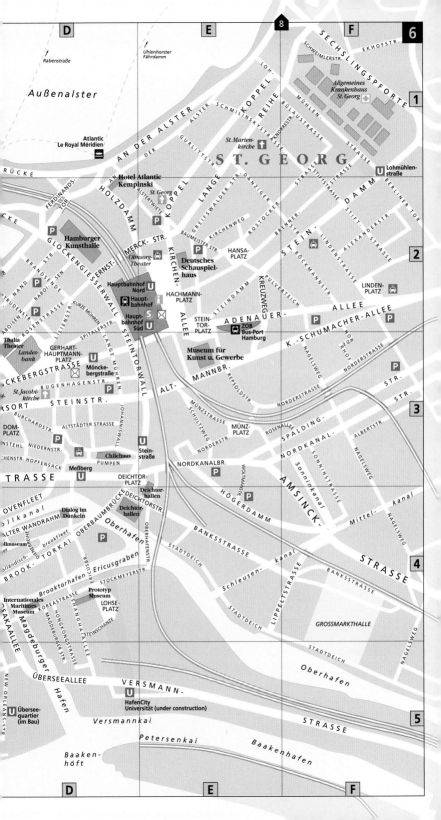

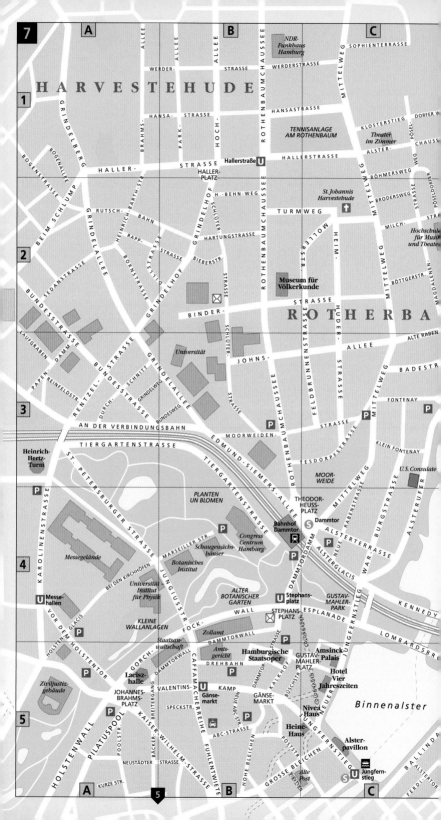

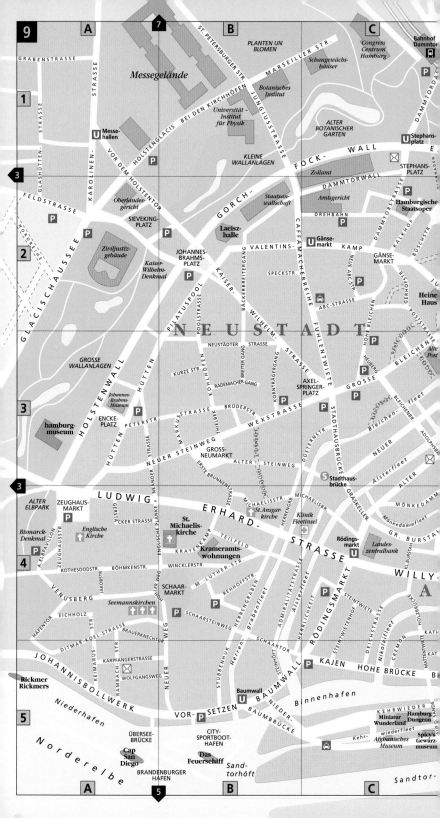

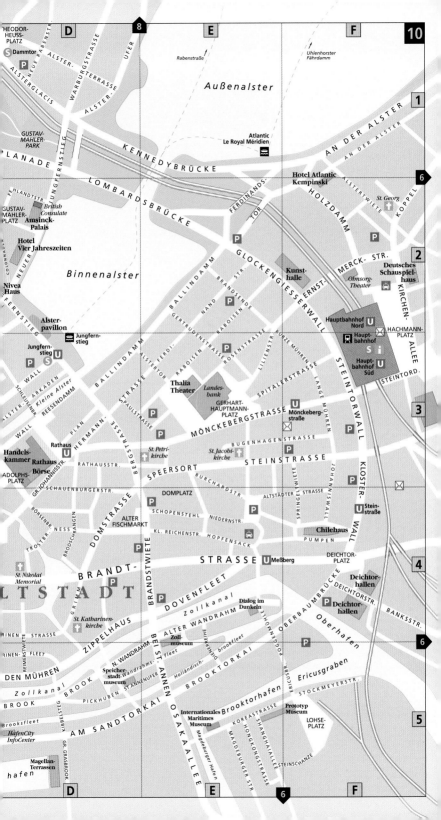

General Index

Acknowledgments

Dorling Kindersley would like thank all the following people whose contributions and assistance have made the preparation of this book possible.

Author
Gerhard Bruschke has a degree in geography and has written Vis-à-Vis travel guide *Dresden*. He also edited the German editions of several Vis-à-Vis travel guides (such as *San Francisco, Moscow, India*) and was the consultant for the English editions of Dorling Kindersley *Eyewitness Guides* to *Germany, Austria, Switzerland* and *Munich & Bavaria*. Moreover Gerhard Bruschke has written for many travel guides, atlases and encyclopedias (print and digital media).

Publisher
Douglas Amrine

Publishing Director
Dr. Jörg Theilacker

Art Director
Anja Richter

Photographers
Felix Fiedler, Susanne Gilges, Olaf Kalugin, Maik Thimm

Illustrators
Branimir Georgiev, Maria-Magdalena Renker, Eva Sixt, Bernhard Springer

Cartography
Anja Richter, Mare e Monte

Editor
Brigitte Maier, Konzept & Text

Picture Researcher, Editor & Co-Cartographer
Stefanie Franz

Consultant
Helen Townsend

Cover
Anja Richter, Kate Everson, Tessa Bindloss

Proofreader, Street Finder Index
Philip Anton

Fact-Checker
Renate Hirschberger

Special Assistance
Special thanks goes to the following individuals, without whose help this book would not have been possible:
Andrew Phillips, Birgit Walter, Dr. Peter Lutz, Jane Ewart, Natasha Lu, Matthias Liesendahl, Barbara Narr, Familie Schiefelbein, Joanna Jordan, Florian Steinert, Susanne Krammer, Andrea Rinck.

Additional Cartography
Casper Morris, DK Cartography

Additional Editorial & Design
Carly Madden, Alison McGill, Susanna Smith

38bl, 39tr, 39cr, 42tr, 42bl, 43tr, 43br, 44tr, 44br, 45tr, 46tl, 48cr, 48bl, 49bl, 50cl, 51cra, 51bl, 53c, 60cla, 60clb, 60bl, 61tl, 61crb, 62bl, 70bl, 74tl, 74cl, 75tl, 75cra, 75crb, 75br, 78tr, 83tl, 84tr, 92br, 93br, 94tr, 94c, 94bl, 95tl, 95cra, 95crb, 95bc, 98tl, 98tr, 98bl, 98br, 98bc, 99tl, 99cra, 99crb, 99bl, 102tl, 111bl, 111crb, 117br, 118br, 119b, 130tl, 130tr, 130ca, 130cb, 131tl, 131cra, 131crb, 132, 133tc, 134tl, 134br, 135tl, 135br, 136tl, 136tr, 136c, 136br, 137tr, 137cra, 137bl, 138tr, 138bc, 139tr, 139b, 142, 143cl, 188crb, 221tl, 222tr, 242tl.

Georgiev, Branimir: 40tl, 90tr, 90br, 102b, 103bl, 122tr.

Gilges, Susanne: 5cl, 10tc, 10br, 16tl, 20br, 29tl, 29c, 31tl, 31cr, 31bl, 33tr, 33cb, 34cla, 35bl, 36tr, 36cl, 36cr, 39tl, 39br, 41cla, 43cl, 44bl, 47tr, 48cl, 50tr, 50bl, 51tl, 51tr, 52–53, 54, 56tl, 56br, 57cr, 57bl, 58tl, 59br, 61cra, 63bl, 66tr, 66bl, 67tr, 67bc, 68, 70tl, 70br, 71tr, 72tc, 72bl, 73tl, 73bl, 73br, 76tl, 76br, 77tl, 77c, 77br, 78tl, 78cl, 78br, 79tl, 79tr, 79cra, 79crb, 79bl, 85tr, 85br, 88tr, 88bl, 89tr, 89bc, 93cr, 100, 101tc, 103cr, 104tr, 104cl, 105tr, 105bc, 108tr, 108c, 110tl, 110tr, 112, 114tl, 114b, 115cr, 116tl, 116bl, 117tl, 117c, 118c, 119tr, 120, 122clb, 122br, 123tc, 123br, 124t, 124b, 125b, 128t, 128c, 129tr, 129c, 144tr, 145cr, 147tl, 148tr, 148cl, 148bc, 149tc, 149bl, 216cr, 217c, 221c, 233cr, 242bl.

Gruner+Jahr: 40bl, 40br, 40crb, 41bl, 41bcl.

Hamburg Airport: 230tc.

Hamburger Verkehrsverbund: 236tr, 238cl, 238br, 239tr.

Hensel, Heike / Pelz, Andreas: 230cl.

Herzog, de Meuron: 25clb, 35br, 37c, 51crb, 90cl.

IMMH: 86tl, 86tr (Michael Zapf), 86cla (Michael Zapf), 86clb (Michael Zapf), 86bc (Michael Zapf), 87tc, 87cra, 87bl (Michael Zapf), 87br (Michael Zapf).

Janke, Dr. Klaus: 140cl, 140bl, 140br, 141tc, 141cr, 141bc, 154cl.

Jung von Matt: 40tr, 40cr.

Kalugin, Olaf: 2–3, 11cr, 16br, 29clb, 46bl, 84bl, 91bl, 93tr, 96–97, 102cl, 103br, 104br, 123tr, 146br, 217tl, 243bl.

KMJ@Wikipedia: 232tr.

Kunstsammlungen Paula Modersohn: 167tl.

Lasdin, Bernd: 164cla.

Moevenpick Hotel Hamburg: 109tr.

NDR: 41tl, 41tr, 41t.

Nogai, Jürgen: 164tr, 165br.

Richter, Anja: 17tl, 23bl, 30tl, 30tr, 30bl, 43cr, 50br, 55tc, 94tl, 111cra, 145cl, 151c, 156tl, 171c, 184tc, 186c, 186c (3 photos), 187bc, 187br, 188tl, 188tr (5 photos), 188c, 188bl, 188bc, 188br, 189tr, 189cla (2 photos), 189clb (2 photos), 189br, 219c, 224cr, 226b, 229cr, 231tl, 231br, 239cl, 239cr, 240tl, 240bl, 240br, 242tc.

Rinck, Andrea: 28, 137bcr.

Scheunemann, Jürgen: 82cla, 82clb, 82br, 83bl, 83br, 147br, 153cl, 164bl, 168tr, 168cl, 169tl, 169cra, 169crb, 169bl, 169br.

DER SPIEGEL: 41cr.

Suhr, Christoffer und Peter (Wikipedia): 21tl.

Theilacker, Dr. Jörg: 4br, 5tl, 10cr, 24cl, 24cr, 26–27, 28, 34br, 45br, 80, 102c, 106–107, 123tl, 143tc, 143cr, 185tr, 185br, 202bl, 203bl, 207bl, 218–219, 224tl, 224cl, 225tr, 225c, 234cl, 234cr, 235tc, 239bl.

Thimc, Maik: 4tr, 19c, 57tl, 91br.

Westerland, Tourismus-Service: 156cl, 156bl, 157cr.

Zefa: 158tr, 167bl.

DIE ZEIT: 41cr, 41c, 144bl.

Front Endpaper:
Left side: Felix Fiedler bc; Susanne Gilges tr, cl; DK Images bl.
Right side: Susanne Gilges tc, tr, cr; Jörg Theilacker br.
Back Endpaper:
Hamburger Verkehrsverbund.

Map Cover:
PHOTOLIBRARY: Thomas Robbin.

Jacket:
Front - PHOTOLIBRARY: Thomas Robbin;
Back - ALAMY IMAGES: blickwinkel tl, imagebroker cla, imagebroker/Justus de Cuveland bl; AWL IMAGES: Jon Arnold clb;
Spine - PHOTOLIBRARY: Thomas Robbin tc.

All other images © Dorling Kindersley.
For further information see
www.dkimages.com

Phrase Book

In an Emergency

Where is the telephone?	Wo ist das Telefon?	voh ist duss tel-e-fone?
Help!	Hilfe!	hilf-uh
Please call a doctor	Bitte rufen Sie einen Arzt	bitt-uh roof'n zee ine-en artst
Please call the police	Bitte rufen Sie die Polizei	bitt-uh roof'n zee dee poli-tsy
Please call the fire brigade	Bitte rufen Sie die Feuerwehr	bitt-uh roof'n zee dee foyer-vayr
Stop!	Halt!	hult

Communication Essentials

Yes	Ja	yah
No	Nein	nine
Please	Bitte	bitt-uh
Thank you	Danke	dunk-uh
Excuse me	Verzeihung	fair-tsy-hoong
Hello (good day)	Guten Tag	goot-en tahk
Goodbye	Auf Wiedersehen	owf-veed-er-zay-ern
Good evening	Guten Abend	goot'n ahb'nt
Good night	Gute Nacht	goot-uh nukht
Until tomorrow	Bis morgen	biss morg'n
See you	Tschüss	chooss
What is that?	Was ist das?	voss ist duss
Why?	Warum?	var-room
Where?	Wo?	voh
When?	Wann?	vunn
today	heute	hoyt-uh
tomorrow	morgen	morg'n
yesterday	gestern	gest'n
morning	Morgen	morg'n
afternoon	Nachmittag	nahkh-mit-tahk
evening	Abend	ahb'nt
night	Nacht	nukht
week	Woche	vokh-uh
month	Monat	mohn-aht
year	Jahr	yar
there	dort	dort
here	hier	hear

Useful Phrases

How are you?	Wie geht's?	vee gayts?
Fine, thanks	Danke, es geht mir gut	dunk-uh, es gayt meer goot
Pleased to meet you	Es freut mich, Sie kennenzulernen	ess froyt mish, zee ken'n-tsoo-lairn'n
Until later	Bis später	biss shpay-ter
Where is/are?	Wo ist/sind?	voh ist/sind
How far is it to…?	Wie weit ist es…?	vee vite ist ess
Which way to…?	Wie komme ich zu …?	vee komma ish tsoo…?
Do you speak English?	Sprechen Sie Englisch?	shpresh'n zee eng-glish
I don't understand	Ich verstehe nicht	ish fair-shtay-uh nisht
Could you speak more slowly?	Könnten Sie langsamer sprechen?	kurnt-en zee lung-zam-er shpresh'n
I'm sorry	Es tut mir leid	es toot meer lyte

Useful Words

big	groß	grohss
small	klein	kline
hot	heiß	hyce
cold	kalt	kult
good	gut	goot
bad	schlecht	shlesht
enough	genug	g'nook
well	gut	goot
open	auf/offen	owf/off'n
closed	zu/geschlossen	tsoo/g'shloss'n
left	links	links
right	rechts	reshts
straight on	geradeaus	g'rah-der-owss
near	in der Nähe	in dair nay-er
far	weit	vyte
up	auf, oben	owf, obe'n
down	ab, unten	up, oont'n
early	früh	froo
late	spät	shpate
entrance	Eingang/Einfahrt	ine-gung/ine-fart
exit	Ausgang/Ausfahrt	ows-gung/ows-fart
toilet	WC/Toilette	vay-say/toy-lett-er
free/unoccupied	frei	fry
free/no charge	frei/gratis	fry/grah-tis

Making a Telephone Call

I'd like to make a phone call	Ich möchte telefonieren	ish mer-shtuh tel-e-fon-eer'n
I'll try again later	Ich versuche es später noch mal	ish fair-zookh-uh es shpay-ter nokh -mull
Can I leave a message?	Kann ich eine Nachricht hinterlassen?	kan ish ine-uh nakh-risht hint-er-lahss'n
answer phone	Anrufbeantworter	an-roof-be-ahnt-vort-er
telephone card	Telefonkarte	tel-e-fohn-kart-uh
receiver	Hörer	hur-er
mobile phone	Handy	han-dee
engaged (busy)	besetzt	b'zetst
wrong number	falsche Verbindung	falsh-uh fair-bin-doong
long-distance call	Ferngespräch	fairn-g'shpresh

Staying in a Hotel

Do you have a vacant room?	Haben Sie ein Zimmer frei?	harb'n zee ine tsimm-er fry?
double room	Doppelzimmer	dopp'l-tsimm-er
with double bed	mit Doppelbett	mitt dopp'l-bet
single room	Einzelzimmer	ine-ts'l-tsimm-er
room with a bath/shower	Zimmer mit Bad/Dusche	tsimm-er mitt bat/doosh-er
porter	Gepäckträger	g'peck-tray-ger
concierge	Concierge	kon-see-airsh
key	Schlüssel	shlooss'l
I have a reservation for a room	Ich habe ein Zimmer reserviert	ish harb-er ine tsimm-er rezz-er-veert

Sightseeing

bus	Bus	booss
tram	Straßenbahn/Tram	stra-sen-barn, tram
train	Zug	tsoog
gallery	Galerie	gall-er-ee
bus station	Busbahnhof	booss-barn-hofe
train station	Bahnhof	barn-hofe
bus (tram) stop	Haltestelle	hal-te-shtel-er
palace/castle	Schloss, Burg	shloss, boorg
post office	Postamt	pohs-taamt
cathedral	Dom	dome
church	Kirche	keersh-er
garden	Garten, Park	gart'n, park
library	Bibliothek	bib-leo-tek
museum	Museum	moo-zay-oom
information	Information	in-for-mut-see-on
closed for public holiday	Feiertags geschlossen	fire-targz g'shloss'n
entrance ticket	Eintrittskarte	ine-tritz-kart-uh
cemetery	Friedhof	freed-hofe
place	Platz	plats
free admission	Eintritt frei	ine-tritt fry

Shopping

Do you have/ Is there…?	Gibt es…?	geept ess
How much does it cost?	Was kostet das?	voss kost't duss?
When do you open? close?	Wann öffnen Sie? schließen Sie?	vunn off'n zee shlees'n zee
Do you take credit cards?	Kann ich mit Kreditkarte bezahlen?	kunn ish mitt kred-it-kar-ter b'tsahl'n
this	das	duss
expensive	teuer	toy-er
cheap	preiswert	price-vurt
size	Größe	gruhs-uh
number	Nummer	noom-er
colour	Farbe	farb-uh
brown	braun	brown
black	schwarz	shvarts
red	rot	roht
blue	blau	blau
green	grün	groon
yellow	gelb	gelp

Types of Shop

antique shop	Antiquitäten-laden	un-tick-vi-tayt'n-lard'n
bakery	Bäckerei	beck-er-eye
bank	Bank	bunk
book shop	Buchladen/ Buchhandlung	bookh-lard'n/ bookh-hant-loong
butcher	Fleischerei	fly-sher-eye

cake shop	Konditorei	kon-ditt-or-**eye**
chemist		
(for prescriptions)	Apotheke	App-o-**tay**-ke
(for cosmetics)	Drogerie	droog-er-**ree**
department store	Kaufhaus	**kauf**-hows
delicatessen	Feinkost(laden)	**fine**-kost(lahd'n)
fishmonger	Fischladen	**fish**-lahd'n
gift shop	Geschenke(laden)	g'shenk-er(lahd'n)
greengrocer	Obst & Gemüse	ohbst & g'**moozer**
grocery	Lebensmittelladen	layb'nz-mitt'l-ladn
hairdresser	Friseur / Frisör	freezz-**er**
market	Markt	markt
travel agent	Reisebüro	rye-zer-boo-**roe**
café	Café	kaff-**ay**
post office	Post	posst
boutique	Boutique	boo-**teek**-uh

Eating Out

Have you got a table for…?	Haben Sie einen Tisch für…?	harb'n zee ine'n tish foor…?
I want to reserve a table	Ich möchte einen Tisch reservieren	ish **mersh**-ter ine'n tish rese-**veer**'n
I am vegetarian	Ich bin Vegetarier	ish bin vegg-er-**tah**-ree-er
waiter	Herr Ober	hair **oh**-bare
The bill please!	Zahlen, bitte!	tsaarl'n **bitt**-er
tip	Trinkgeld	**trink**-gelt
menu	Speisekarte	**shpize**-er-kart-er
(fixed price) menu	Menü	men-**oo**
cover charge	Couvert / Gedeck	**koo**-vair / g'**deck**
wine list	Weinkarte	**vine**-kart-er
glass	Glas	glars
bottle	Flasche	**flush**-er
cup	Tasse	**tass**-uh
knife	Messer	**mess**-er
fork	Gabel	**garb**'l
spoon	Löffel	lerff'l
flatware, cutlery	Besteck	be-**shteck**
breakfast	Frühstück	**froo**-shtook
lunch	Mittagessen	**mit**-targ-ess'n
dinner	Abendessen	**arb**'nt-ess'n
main course	Hauptspeise	**howpt**-shpize-er
starter, first course	Vorspeise	**for**-shpize-er
dish of the day	Tageskarte	**targ**-erz-**kart**-e

Menu Decoder

Aal	arl	eel
Apfel	**upf**'l	apple
Apfelschorle	**upf**'l-shoorl-uh	apple juice with sparkling water
Apfelsine	**upf**'l-seen-uh	orange
Artischocke	arti-**shokh**-uh	artichoke
Aubergine	or-ber-jeen-uh	aubergine, eggplant
Beefsteak	**beef**-stayk	steak
Bier	beer	beer
Bockwurst	**bokh**-voorst	type of sausage
Bohnensuppe	burn-en-zoop-uh	bean soup
Branntwein	brant-vine	spirits
Bratkartoffeln	**brat**-kar-**toff**'ln	fried potatoes
Bratwurst	brat-voorst	fried sausage
Brötchen	**bret**-tchen	bread roll
Brot	brot	bread
Butter	**boot**-ter	butter
Champignon	**shum**-pin-yong	mushroom
Currywurst	**kha**-ree-voorst	sausage with curry
Ei	eye	egg
Eis	ice	ice cream
Ente	ent-uh	duck
Erdbeeren	**ayrt**-beer'n	strawberries
Fisch	fish	fish
Forelle	for-ell-uh	trout
Frikadelle	**Fri**-ka-**dayl**-uh	hamburger, meat ball
Gans	ganns	goose
Garnele	**gar**-nayl-uh	prawn / shrimp
gebraten	g'**braat**'n	fried
gegrillt	g'**grilt**	grilled
gekocht	g'**kokht**	boiled
geräuchert	g'**rowk**-ert	smoked
Geflügel	g'**floog**'l	poultry
Gemüse	g'**mooz**-uh	vegetables
Gulasch	**goo**-lush	goulash
Gurke	**goork**-uh	gherkin
Hähnchen	**haynsh**'n	chicken
Hering	**hair**-ing	herring
Himbeeren	**him**-beer'n	raspberries
Honig	**hoe**-nikh	honey
Kaffee	kaf-**fay**	coffee
Kalbfleisch	kalb-flysh	veal
Kaninchen	ka-**neensh**'n	rabbit
Karpfen	**karpf**'n	carp
Kartoffelpüree	kar-**toff**'l-poor-**ay**	mashed potatoes
Käse	**kayz**-uh	cheese
Knoblauch	k'**nob**-lowkh	garlic
Knödel	k'**nerd**'l	dumpling
Kohl	koal	cabbage
Kopfsalat	**kopf**-zal-aat	lettuce
Krebs	krayps	crab
Kuchen	**kookh**'n	cake
Lachs	lahkhs	salmon
Leber	**lay**-ber	liver
mariniert	mari-neert	marinated
Marmelade	marmer-**lard**-uh	marmalade, jam
Meerrettich	may-re-tish	horseradish
Milch	milsh	milk
Mineralwasser	min-er-**arl**-vuss-er	mineral water
Möhre	**mer**-uh	carrot
Nuss	nooss	nut
Öl	erl	oil
Petersilie	payt-er-**zee**-li-uh	parsley
Pfeffer	**pfeff**-er	pepper
Pommes frites	pomm-**fritt**	French fries
Radieschen	ra-**deesh**'n	radish
Rindfleisch	**rint**-flysh	beef
Rippchen	**rip**-sh'n	cured pork rib
Rotkohl	roht-koal	red cabbage
Rührei	**rhoo**-er-eye	scrambled eggs
Saft	zuft	juice
Salat	zal-**aat**	salad
Salz	zults	salt
Salzkartoffeln	zults-kar-toff'l	boiled potatoes
Sauerkraut	**zow**-er-**krowt**	sauerkraut
Sekt	zekt	sparkling wine
Senf	zenf	mustard
scharf	sharf	spicy
Schaschlik	shash-lik	kebab
Schlagsahne	**shlahgg**-zarn-uh	whipped cream
Schnittlauch	shnit-lowhkh	chives
Schnitzel	**shnitz**'l	veal or pork cutlet
Schweinefleisch	**shvine**-flysh	pork
Spargel	**shparg**'l	asparagus
Spiegelei	**shpeeg**'l-eye	fried egg
Spinat	shpin-art	spinach
Tee	tay	tea
Tomate	tom-art-uh	tomato
Wein	vine	wine
Weintrauben	vine-trowb'n	grapes
Zander	**tsan**-der	pikeperch
Zitrone	tsi-trohn-uh	lemon
Zucker	**tsook**-er	sugar
Zwieback	**tsvee**-bak	rusk
Zwiebel	**tsveeb**'l	onion

Numbers

Number	German	Pronunciation
0	null	nool
1	eins	eye'ns
2	zwei	tsvy
3	drei	dry
4	vier	feer
5	fünf	foonf
6	sechs	zex
7	sieben	**zeeb**'n
8	acht	uhkht
9	neun	noyn
10	zehn	tsayn
11	elf	elf
12	zwölf	tsverlf
13	dreizehn	**dry**-tsayn
20	zwanzig	**tsvunn**-tsig
21	einundzwanzig	ine-oont-**tsvunn**-tsig
30	dreißig	**dry**-sig
40	vierzig	**feer**-tsig
50	fünfzig	**foonf**-tsig
100	(ein)hundert	(ine) hoond't
1,000	(ein)tausend	(ine) towz'nt
1,000,000	eine Million	ine-er mill-yohn
1,000,000,000	eine Milliarde	ine-er milli-arde

Time

one minute	eine Minute	ine-er min-**oot**-er
one hour	eine Stunde	ine-er **shtoond**-er
half an hour	halbe Stunde	**hull**-ber **shtoond**-er
Monday	Montag	**mone**-targ
Tuesday	Dienstag	**deens**-targ
Wednesday	Mittwoch	**mitt**-vokh
Thursday	Donnerstag	**donn**-ers-targ
Friday	Freitag	**fry**-targ
Saturday	Samstag	**zums**-targ
Sunday	Sonntag	**zon**-targ

Hamburg Public Transport Map

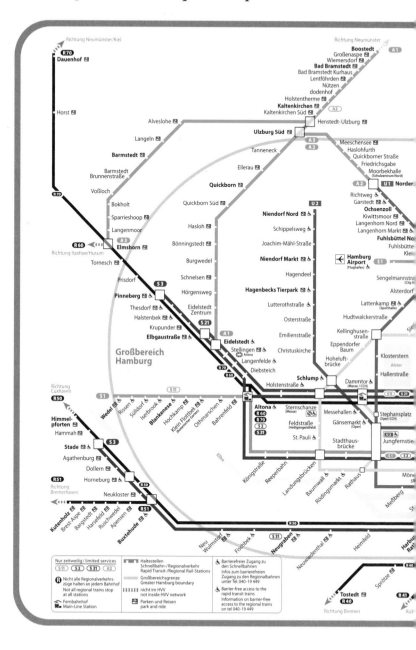